Sacred Treasure

Joseph P. Swain

Sacred Treasure

Understanding Catholic Liturgical Music

A PUEBLO BOOK

Liturgical Press   Collegeville, Minnesota
www.litpress.org

A Pueblo Book published by Liturgical Press

Cover design by David Manahan, OSB. Illustration: *Cantoria* by Luca della Robbia, courtesy of Wikimedia Commons.

Excerpts from the English translation of *The General Instruction of the Roman Missal* © 2010, International Commission on English in the Liturgy Corporation. All rights reserved.

Excerpts from documents of the Second Vatican Council are from *Vatican Council II: The Basic Sixteen Documents*, by Austin Flannery, OP © 1996 (Costello Publishing Company, Inc.). Used with permission.

Scripture texts, prefaces, introductions, footnotes and cross references used in this work are taken from the *New American Bible, revised edition* © 2010, 1991, 1986, 1970 Confraternity of Christian Doctrine, Inc., Washington, DC. All Rights Reserved. No part of this work may be reproduced or transmitted in any form or by any means, electronic or mechanical, including photocopying, recording, or by any information storage and retrieval system, without permission in writing from the copyright owner.

© 2012 by Order of Saint Benedict, Collegeville, Minnesota. All rights reserved. No part of this book may be reproduced in any form, by print, microfilm, microfiche, mechanical recording, photocopying, translation, or by any other means, known or yet unknown, for any purpose except brief quotations in reviews, without the previous written permission of Liturgical Press, Saint John's Abbey, PO Box 7500, Collegeville, Minnesota 56321-7500. Printed in the United States of America.

Library of Congress Cataloging-in-Publication Data

Swain, Joseph Peter.
    Sacred treasure : understanding Catholic liturgical music / Joseph P. Swain.
      p. cm.
    "A Pueblo book."
    Includes bibliographical references (p.) and index.
    ISBN 978-0-8146-6255-7
      1. Church music—Catholic Church. I. Title.

ML3002.S93 2011
782.32'22—dc23

2011042914

It is good to give thanks to the L ORD,
> to sing praise to your name, Most High.
>
> Psalm 92:2

The musical tradition of the universal church is a treasure of inestimable value, greater even than that of any other art.
> *Sacrosanctum Concilium*, article 112 (The Constitution on the Sacred Liturgy, Second Vatican Council, 1963)

Contents

List of Examples and Figures   ix

Acknowledgments   xi

Preface   xiii

Part I: The State of the Art   1

   Chapter 1: Liturgical Music Theory   3

   Chapter 2: The Second Vatican Council and Liturgical Music   23

   Chapter 3: Aftermath of the Council: Rushing to Fill the Void   39

   Chapter 4: Aftermath of the Council: Democratization of the Liturgy   61

   Chapter 5: The Diversity of Catholic Liturgical Music   75

   Chapter 6: The State of the Art   83

Part II: The Sacred Treasure   89

   Chapter 7: Plainchant   95

   Chapter 8: Classical Polyphony   119

   Chapter 9: Operatic and Symphonic Liturgical Music   135

   Chapter 10: Traditions of Popular Liturgical Music   145

Part III: Building Traditions of Liturgical Music   161

   Chapter 11: Primary Considerations   163

   Chapter 12: Understanding Musical Symbols: The Semantics of Sacred Music   175

   Chapter 13: Understanding Musical Symbols: The Infallible Judge   199

   Chapter 14: Understanding Musical Symbols: The Seasons of Liturgical Music   223

   Chapter 15: Understanding Musical Symbols: The Languages of Liturgy   237

Chapter 16: An Eternal Conflict: Creativity and Tradition   261

Chapter 17: An Eternal Conflict: Inculturating Liturgical Music   275

Chapter 18: An Eternal Conflict:
    Participatio Actuosa and Congregational Singing   297

Chapter 19: Foundations   313

Bibliography   351

Index   363

Examples and Figures

Example 3-1	Example 3-1. Robert J. Dufford, "Be Not Afraid," verse 1 (mm. 4–19). © 1975, 1978, Robert J. Dufford, SJ, and OCP Publications, 5536 NE Hassalo, Portland, OR 97213. All rights reserved. Used by permission.
Example 3-2	Fintan O'Carroll and Christopher Walker, "Celtic Alleluia" (mm. 1–8). © 1985, Fintan O'Carroll and Christopher Walker. Published by OCP Publications, 5536 NE Hassalo, Portland, OR 97213. All rights reserved. Used by permission.
Example 3-3	Fintan O'Carroll and Christopher Walker, "Celtic Alleluia" (mm. 9–15). © 1985, Fintan O'Carroll and Christopher Walker. Published by OCP Publications, 5536 NE Hassalo, Portland, OR 97213. All rights reserved. Used by permission.
Figure 7-1	Schematic of music with regular beats. "Celtic Alleluia." © 1985, Fintan O'Carroll and Christopher Walker. Published by OCP Publications, 5536 NE Hassalo, Portland, OR 97213. All rights reserved. Used by permission.
Figure 7-2	Schematic of music with stressed beats. "Celtic Alleluia." © 1985, Fintan O'Carroll and Christopher Walker. Published by OCP Publications, 5536 NE Hassalo, Portland, OR 97213. All rights reserved. Used by permission.
Example 7-1	Gloria "De Angelis" (*Graduale Romanum*, 739).
Example 7-2	*Crucem tuam*, chant for the veneration of the cross, Good Friday; *Alleluia*, chant for the Easter Vigil (*Graduale Romanum*, 175, 191).
Figure 7-3	Gloria "De Angelis" showing centonic aspects.
Example 7-3	Litany from the Easter Vigil (*Graduale Simplex*, 148–49).
Example 7-4	*Kyrie eleison* (*Graduale Romanum*, 763) with Greek and English.
Example 7-5	"Gregorian" Alleluia.
Example 7-6	Harmonized version of "Gregorian" Alleluia.

Example 7-7	Alleluia from Tempus Adventus, Missa I, *Graduale Simplex*, and Advent Alleluia No. 85 from *Hymns, Psalms, and Spiritual Canticles*. © 1972, Boston Boys Choir, Cambridge, Massachusetts. All rights reserved. Used by permission.
Example 8-1	Josquin Desprez, *Missa de Beata Virgine*, Gloria, mm. 80–85. The melody in the third voice from the top is the traditional melody from the so-called Gloria IX. The other three melodies were invented by Josquin to create the polyphonic texture.
Example 8-2	Giovanna da Palestrina, motet *Sicut cervus*, mm. 1–12.
Figure 8-1	Schematic showing the theoretical difference in metric strength between a march and Palestrina's motet.
Example 8-3	Six-voice from Gloria, *Missa Papae Marcelli*.
Example 10-1	Litany from the Easter Vigil (*Graduale Simplex*, 148–49).
Example 10-2	The opening phrases of "O Sacred Head Surrounded."
Example 10-3	Soprano, alto, tenor, and bass melodies from one of J. S. Bach's arrangements of the choral tune "O Sacred Head Surrounded" (German original: *O Haupt voll Blut und Wunden*), opening phrases.
Example 15-1	Latin plainchant *Crucem tuam* with translation below.
Example 16-1	Late eleventh-century polyphony on a traditional *Kyrie* melody.
Figure 17-1	Order of the Gospel Mass at Saint Brigid's Church, Los Angeles.

Acknowledgments

"Alleluia" for Advent. No. 85 from *Hymns, Psalms, and Spiritual Canticles.*
© 1972, Boston Boy Choir, Inc., Cambridge, Massachusetts. All rights reserved. Used by permission.

"Be Not Afraid." © 1975, 1978, Robert J. Dufford, SJ and OCP Publications, 5536 NE Hassalo, Portland, OR 97213. All rights reserved. Used by permission.

"Bread of Life." © 1987, OCP Publications, 5536 NE Hassalo, Portland, OR 97213. All rights reserved. Used by permission.

"Celtic Alleluia." © 1985, Fintan O'Carroll and Christopher Walker. Published by OCP Publications, 5536 NE Hassalo, Portland, OR 97213. All rights reserved. Used by permission.

Joseph P. Swain. "Creativity and Tradition." © 2001, *Pastoral Music.* All rights reserved. Used by permission.

Joseph P. Swain. "Inculturating Liturgical Music." © 2004, *America Magazine.* All rights reserved. Used by permission.

Joseph P. Swain. "Liturgical Latin Reconsidered." © 2003, *Adoremus Bulletin.* All rights reserved. Used by permission.

Joseph P. Swain. "Music is an Uncompromising Meritocracy." © 2007, *Catholic World Report.* All rights reserved. Used by permission.

Joseph P. Swain. "St. Mark in Venice: a Liturgy without Hymns." © 2006, *Pastoral Music.* All rights reserved. Used by permission.

Preface

Sacred Treasure attempts a theory for building authentic traditions of liturgical music for Roman Catholic parishes. It is an exercise in pragmatic music criticism. It explains the continuing turmoil and disappointment in the practice of liturgical music, both within the parish and throughout the world, that has obtained since the Second Vatican Council reformed the liturgy in 1963, and then, by providing a rational basis for evaluating the essential issues, it seeks to show how a spiritually wholesome stability might supplant the confusion.

And so the end is practical, with the modest hope of affecting the lives of real worshipers for the better, but the means are theoretical and abstract. *Sacred Treasure* is not a handbook. There is nothing about how to start and maintain a church choir, no prescription for what is best for a congregation to sing, but rather thinking about their respective liturgical roles and what each body might sing at Mass. There is no categorical ruling about whether it is good to use indigenous folk music in the parishes of New Orleans or Chile, but this book is rather about liturgical and musical principles that govern such decisions. There is no detailed history of Gregorian chant, classical polyphony, symphonic Masses, or popular styles, and no exhaustive survey of those repertories, but instead analyses of their essences and reasoning about whether those essences may build liturgical traditions in the modern world or not. To be sure, many experiences from real life illustrate the abstractions, and certain arguments lead naturally to concrete applications, but primarily this book is a critique of liturgical and musical principles.

Of these, liturgical principles have had by far the greater say in the conversation since the council. The liturgical sources easily outnumber the musical in the bibliography at the end of this book. Music theorists, critics, and historians have contributed little, and their counsel has not been very much sought.[1] Whenever the matter of liturgical music arises, most often in parishes, but sometimes in episcopal

---

[1] As an example of the state of affairs, see M. Francis Mannion, "Forum: The Need for and Adequate Liturgical Musicology," *Worship* 64, no. 1 (January 1990): 78–81.

conferences or in the academy or in Vatican documents, the nature of the music, as music, almost never affects the discussion. Even a matter as fundamental as whether a type of music has meter or not and how that aspect may affect the setting of liturgical text is not touched. Now few would argue that liturgical considerations should not have priority in general, but it is quite another thing to behave as if the nature of music imposed no conditions whatsoever on what could be done in the liturgy. If *Sacred Treasure* has one original contribution to make, this is it: to show how the hard facts of music must be taken into account in any holistic conception and any lasting form of liturgical music.

Since understanding a problem's causes often leads to solutions, Part I of *Sacred Treasure* reviews the sources of liturgical reform regarding music and then the cultural pressures and circumstances after 1965 that allowed key aspects of those reforms to be either ignored or replaced by others less authentic. Part II analyzes the musical essences of the four principal traditions for Catholic liturgical music through history: plainchant, classical polyphony, the operatic or symphonic Mass, and popular styles. Of what use is any of these repertories for modern liturgy? Finally, Part III treats the core issues running beneath the controversies of the last four decades—the sacredness of liturgical music, its beauty, the role of creativity within a tradition, liturgical seasons and language, inculturation, and *participatio actuosa*—in order to separate the wheat from the chaff, that is, to know the principles of liturgical music that are truly essential from those that are ephemeral, superficial, or simply false.

Sacred Treasure is written for anyone who cares about the music at Mass: bishops, pastors, liturgical ministers both lay and clerical, other parish leaders, and of course musicians, both those intimately involved with the church and those more distant scholars interested in Catholic liturgical music as an anthropological artifact. Because of the broad readership, I have tried hard to minimize jargon and to explain the basics of Catholic liturgy to nonliturgists and the elements of music to nonmusicians. Because bringing the hard facts of music into the discussion is a primary goal, some arguments are necessarily technical, but on the other hand, it is a sign of the infancy of this approach that the musical facts in question are so basic that no advanced musical training or theory is required to follow the arguments. Readers unfamiliar with musical notation may not appreciate every piece of evidence from the few printed scores, but the substance of the arguments and their conclusions I hope will remain clear. In such an interdisciplinary subject, the writer cannot take what is known by the reader for granted as with a specialized monograph. I ask the patience of the musician readers while I outline the premises of Western harmony, and of the liturgical theologians if I reiterate too often what happens at a Catholic Mass. Finally, while I hope that all the arguments are supported with evidence and reason in rigorous form, *Sacred Treasure* is not a disinterested anthropological study; the point of view from the beginning is unapologetically Catholic, and I care very much not only about the questions raised but about getting the right answers, even if I may never be certain of them.

All biblical citations, unless otherwise noted, are taken from the New American Bible, Revised Edition.

Some of these observations various journals have published previously, and I acknowledge with gratitude the kind permissions of the editors to reprint some paragraphs here. The sources are given in the chapter footnotes. The Colgate University Research Council advanced the completion of *Sacred Treasure* with a Senior Faculty Research Leave which allowed time off from teaching to write. For this I am very grateful. I also express my deep appreciation to Prof. Katherine Bergeron, Prof. Robert Kraynak, Prof. William Mahrt, Prof. Michael T. McLaughlin, Ms. Julie Saiki, Deacon Mark Shiner, Dr. Bernard F. Swain, Fr. Jerome F. Weber, Prof. James Wetzel, and others who helped me to write this book in ways large and small, including the good offices of the Liturgical Press. Finally, I acknowledge with inexpressible thanks the support of my wife and family.

Joseph P. Swain
Hamilton, New York

Part I

The State of the Art

Chapter 1

Liturgical Music Theory

> Music is likewise given by God's generosity to mortals having rational souls in order to lead them to higher things.
> St. Augustine, Epis. 161: *De origine animae hominis*

> It was the best of times, it was the worst of times, it was the age of wisdom, it was the age of foolishness, it was the epoch of belief, it was the epoch of incredulity, it was the season of Light, it was the season of Darkness, it was the spring of hope, it was the winter of despair, we had everything before us, we had nothing before us, we were all going direct to Heaven, we were all going direct the other way—in short, the period was so far like the present period.
> Charles Dickens, *A Tale of Two Cities*

How surprisingly apt it seems, when contemplating, or better yet, experiencing, the state of Roman Catholic liturgical music today, to recall this epigrammatic opening to *A Tale of Two Cities*. Neither liturgist nor musician, a contemporary of John Henry Newman and the Anglican revival known as the Oxford Movement but not particularly religious, how succinctly Charles Dickens has captured the paradoxes of the state of the art "so far like the present period."

"It was the best of times . . ." At no time in the two-thousand-year history of Christianity have so many Catholics taken such an active interest in the liturgy. Liturgical societies, multitudes of animated clerics and lay ministers of the Word, music, and Eucharist, liturgical documents and instructions, books, conferences, and controversies abound. Less than two centuries ago, the prospect would have been utterly unimaginable. Liturgy then was a rote execution, a tired automaton, a spiritual brushing of the teeth in most places. Only a few odd clerical scholars thought much about it. But those few prepared an intellectual wave eventually known as the liturgical movement that restored liturgy's ancient fascination and culminated in *Sacrosanctum Concilium* (also known as the Constitution on the Sacred Liturgy), the first solemn document promulgated by the Second Vatican Council in 1963.

The movement made sense and was long overdue. For most practicing Catholics, the most concrete, real, and active aspect of their religion in their own lives is the liturgy. This is how they most often meet God and fellow Catholics in a spiritual encounter. *Sacrosanctum Concilium* goes further: "For the Liturgy . . . is supremely effective in enabling the faithful to express in their lives and portray to others the mystery of Christ and the real nature of the true church."[1] And further: "every liturgical celebration, because it is an action of Christ the priest and of his body, which is the church, is a preeminently sacred action" (SC 7).[2] And because the church is composed most fundamentally of its people in union with God, the vitality of the liturgy determines the vitality of the institutional church, as is also freely admitted by *Sacrosanctum Concilium* in perhaps its most frequently cited passage: "The liturgy is the summit toward which the activity of the church is directed; it is also the source from which all its power flows" (SC 10). In this case, perhaps rare, the high-minded theory of the council is ratified by the actions of contemporary Catholics everywhere. "How was the liturgy there?" "How do they do it in . . ." are commonly asked of travelers. The conduct of the liturgy is no longer a routine affair to be taken for granted, as it was in most parishes as little as a half century ago. Rather it is something to lift one's spirit incomparably or to dismay profoundly, to respond to and have opinions about. Feelings may indeed run high because liturgy is central to the Catholic experience.

"How is the music?" There is no more significant shaper of contemporary liturgical experience than its music. No other liturgical aspect occasions more divisive controversy, feelings of inspiration, publications, spilled ink, appreciation, and outrage than does the music at Sunday Mass. Even the musically untutored react to liturgical music because it is natural for human beings to want to praise God. It is part of our design, how God made us.[3] Liturgical music fulfills that natural

---

[1] *Sacrosanctum Concilium*, Dogmatic Constitution on the Sacred Liturgy, in *Vatican Council II: The Basic Sixteen Documents*, trans. and ed. Austin Flannery, OP (Northport, NY: Costello Publishing Company, 1996), art. 2.

[2] The Latin *est actio sacra praecellenter* might be translated as "*the* preeminent sacred action."

[3] *Catechism of the Catholic Church*, pars. 27–28.

desire in a way like no other. Strictly speaking, a valid Eucharist needs no music, only an ordained priest, the proper elements, and the proper words, but Catholicism, traditional and modern, has always regarded the "Low Mass," entirely spoken, as liturgy's poor cousin.[4] After all, why did God give us the ability to sing? Singing does not produce the next generation, grows no food, defends against no enemies, offers no shelter, and yet is found in every culture, every human society in the world. One answer, as attractive as it is unprovable, is that in song God gave humanity a miraculous kind of speech suitable for praising him as we were meant to do.[5] Certainly the religions of the world have concluded with virtual unanimity that the right way to talk to God is to chant. For Catholics, such unanimity becomes sacramental, as theologian Mary Collins describes: "Augustine in his treatise on the Gospel of John penned a line that would become the basis for later Scholastic sacramental theology: *accedit verbum ad elementum, et fit Sacramentum, etiam ipsum tanquam visibile verbum*. When the word of faith is joined with the Church's gesture, the sacrament happens—a 'visible word,' as it were."[6] Because it unites with sacred words, music, the sublimely invisible gesture, is the supreme liturgical art.[7]

---

[4] Jim Castelli and Joseph Gremillion, *The Emerging Parish: The Notre Dame Study of Catholic Life since Vatican II*, 129, report that "A major postconciliar change is the increased use of music in the Mass: 90 percent of Sunday Masses and 70 percent of Saturday Masses had some singing." The sung Mass seems to have been the norm in the early church, too. Edward Foley reports that for many centuries there was no distinction between lector and cantor, which suggests that the readings were always chanted. See *Ritual Music: Studies in Liturgical Musicology* (Beltsville, MD: The Pastoral Press, 1995), 65–87. And Edward Schaefer contends that one of the most significant misrepresentations of postconciliar reform was the promotion of the "Low Mass," without any music, to normative status. See *Catholic Music through the Ages: Balancing the Needs of a Worshipping Church* (Chicago: Hillenbrand, 2008), 147, 168.

[5] See also Joseph Gelineau, SJ, "The Role of Sacred Music," in *The Church and the Liturgy*, trans. Theodore L. Westow (Glen Rock, NJ: Paulist Press, 1965), 59–60; and Foley, *Ritual Music*, 113–16, where he claims five affinities between the nature of music and the nature of God: historical, elusive presence, dynamic, relational, personal.

[6] Mary Collins, OSB, *Contemplative Participation:* Sacrosanctum Concilium; *Twenty-five Years Later* (Collegeville, MN: Liturgical Press, 1990), 44.

[7] See also Philipp Harnoncourt, "Neue Aufgaben der katholischen Kirchenmusik (I)," in *Die Kirchenmusik und das II. Vatikanische Konzil*, ed. Philipp Harnoncourt (Graz, Austria: Verlag Styria, 1965), 54–55. "Die Kirchenmusik ist nicht ein schöner Rahmen, der irgenwie zum Gottesdienst passen muß, also ein Element des bloßen

And the omens for the health and surpassing beauty of music in the divine liturgy have never been better. The training of musicians in the Western world, both in number and in quality, is at its historical zenith. The production and distribution of both printed music and recordings to learn from have never been as economical, within the reach of the most modest parishes. And what music they make available! For centuries now the church has owned a repertory of masterworks that is by far the greatest of any institution, nation, people, or religion in the world. In the last two centuries scholars of music history have stripped off the accretions of dubious performance traditions and edited critical editions of these great works while gifted performers have committed them to recordings that should make their creators weep for joy. To this inexhaustible store have been added musical languages from other parts of the world to make the rich even richer.

"It was the worst of times . . ." On the other hand, this treasure may as well be locked up in heaven's chest, as precious little of it is ever heard on earth. Much of what takes its place "does not bear too much thinking about" by seasoned professionals, an opinion hotly contested by the purveyors and composers of the latest.[8] Amidst the plenty of secular musicians, a famine of trained church organists has broken out in the land; liturgists argue about whether the piano or electronic keyboard can replace this once glorious instrument. In some sad places recorded music apes the department store. The voices of liturgical authority, the Catholic bishops, have not spoken with much practicality, certainly not unanimity, either within their national conferences or within their dioceses. Since they are not, with a few notable exceptions, trained musicians, they seek advice and that advice has conflicted. Musicians of questionable competencies bringing all kinds of music with them, liturgical experts, and other well-meaning people

---

Schmuckes, das von außen zur in sich selbst schon vollkommenen Liturgie hinzutritt, sondern sie ist selbst *integrierendes Element* der Liturgie. Sie ist nicht nur Musik *zum* Gottesdienst, sondern *gottesdienstliche Musik*. Die Musik gehört so wesentlich zum Kult der Kirche, daß ein Gottesdienst ohne Gesang grundsätzlich als eine Schrumpfform beziechnet werden muß." (Church music is no pretty covering that somehow is made to fit the church service, a purely decorative element, which from outside impinges upon a liturgy already complete in itself, but rather it is in itself an *integrating element* of the liturgy. It is not music for worship but worship music. Music belongs so essentially to the religion of the church that a Mass without singing must basically be termed a dwarf.)

[8] Aidan Nichols, *Looking at the Liturgy: A Critical View of Its Contemporary Form* (San Francisco: Ignatius Press, 1996), 9.

have rushed in to fill the vacuum of episcopal guidance, while the professional church musician, the once proud *maestro di cappella*, has by and large been shown the door. The results of this paradoxical situation are in. At no time in the two-thousand-year history of the church has its liturgical music, taken in the aggregate, been so derided as it is today by those who know and love music best.

"It was the spring of hope . . . we had everything before us . . ." There was no derision in the mid-1960s, after *Sacrosanctum Concilium* unleashed waves of reform. Instead there was excitement and great anticipation over the prospects of a revitalized liturgical music, of the new options opened by the introduction of vernacular languages into the Roman Rite, of the resources of local musical styles, and above all of *participatio actuosa*, the insistence of the council on active lay participation in all aspects of the liturgy, in its music above all. And within a very few years, most of these in some form had been accomplished in most first-world parishes. For anyone familiar with the historically normal pace of any kind of change in the Catholic world, never mind in something as staid and hallowed as the Roman Rite, those years must have seemed a whirlwind. Things were happening very fast indeed.

"It was the winter of despair . . . we had nothing before us . . ." The euphoria did not last long. A rancorous fight broke out at the Fifth International Church Music Congress held in Chicago and Milwaukee in summer 1966 over issues of the nature of liturgy and liturgical freedom, elitism, and liturgical propriety and musical style. This event reflected similar controversies over other aspects of liturgy, in particular its texts, translations, and proper ministers.[9] It became painfully clear, especially in competing organizations and societies for liturgical music, that there was no common understanding of it.[10] Now for forty years and more bishops, pastors, musicians, and parishioners have groped and grappled with it, adopted and abandoned songs and styles with unprecedented frequency, embraced the musics of Africa,

---

[9] *Sacred Music and Liturgy Reform: Proceedings of the Fifth International Church Music Congress, Chicago-Milwaukee, August 21–28, 1966*, ed. Johannes Overath (Rome: Consociatio Internationalis Musicae Sacrae, 1969), 89–108. See accounts in Thomas Day, *Why Catholics Can't Sing* (New York: Crossroad, 1992), 95–97; Anthony Ruff, OSB, *Sacred Music and Liturgical Reform: Treasures and Transformations* (Chicago: Hillenbrand, 2007), 363–64; and Schaefer, *Catholic Music through the Ages*, 149–50.

[10] Ruff, *Sacred Music and Liturgical Reform*, 361.

Asia, and Latin America, spurned plainchant and then reconsidered, abolished venerable institutions of traditional music only to establish similar ones elsewhere, and conferred, argued, and experimented. Much time and effort have been wasted chasing false musical and liturgical values. It is true that after a reform as significant as that of the Second Vatican Council, a certain number of failed experiments and dead ends is only to be expected, but there seems to be no end in sight, and certainly no greater understanding of the essentials of liturgical music that could begin to form a consensus about where all the reforms should be heading. And this ignorance is no mere academic matter: it debilitates the liturgy and its spiritual benefits, fragments and divides the church, and offers no clear way out of the morass.

"It was the epoch of belief, it was the epoch of incredulity . . ." It was not for lack of ideas and principles such conflicts arose; rather, a surfeit of them, hopelessly unintegrated, existing in isolation from one another, or worse, in direct conflict and contradiction. Liturgical music should inspire people to holiness. Liturgical music should inspire people to sing. Liturgical music must evoke the presence of the Holy Spirit. Liturgical music is an exalted prayer to God. Liturgical music is a celebration of the community. Liturgical music must be simple. Liturgical music must be beautiful. Liturgical music should be the best we can create. Liturgical music should be an honest expression of the people. Liturgical music should not sound like music in the theater. Liturgical music should sound just like the music people hear in everyday life, so that the lessons of the liturgy play out during the week. Liturgical music should transcend this world altogether and put parishioners in mind of the infinite. Just consider:

> Pastor: Two verses of the opening hymn should be enough for the procession.
>
> Organist: But the third verse praises the Holy Spirit. Shouldn't we include the whole Trinity?
>
> Liturgist: Actually, the choir should simply sing the entrance antiphon proper for the day.

Here are three principles, passing like ships in the night. The pastor assumes that the function of the music is to accompany a liturgical action, in this case, a procession. When the action stops, so does the music. The organist hears the hymn as amplified congregational prayer, and one does not stop mid-thought. The liturgist believes that the music must carry the symbols and tradition of the liturgical season in a fashion solemn enough to prepare the congregation spiritually for the Eucharistic celebration to come. The situation today: almost any piece, any decision about liturgical music can be justified—or condemned—by some principle found somewhere.

"It was the age of wisdom, it was the age of foolishness . . ." Visitors from mainline Protestant churches are bemused when they see the results of these many principles in the conduct of a Catholic liturgy. "Please sing number . . .," "The readings today concern . . .," "Please kneel . . .," "We will now bless . . ." Clearly, Catholics do not know what they are doing; they must be coached like schoolchildren at every juncture. In short, there is a great confusion about Catholic liturgical music.

That is why we need a theory of Catholic liturgical music: to replace ignorance with knowledge; to make sense of, to order, and to justify the vast variety in practice; to form rational criteria for judging the liturgical propriety of musics both new and old, including those beyond the Western experience; to provide standards for music and musical performance; to show how to develop lasting parochial traditions of liturgical music for future generations of worshiping Catholics; to lead from crisis to peace.

If these reasons are so compelling, why doesn't the church, after two millennia, already have some kind of theory or theology of music? First, the circumstances are now more urgent and more complex than they have ever been in times past. Abuses of liturgical music and arguments about them indeed parade through history almost from the beginning, but dealing with one dominant European musical language is vastly simpler than dealing with the multiplicity within Catholicism today. Second, for most of European history, except in the philosophical abstractions of St. Augustine, Boethius, and their medieval colleagues in the liberal arts, music in the real world did not attract the attention of theologians or church leaders, except when it got into trouble with the liturgy. Third, then as now the authorities who did from time to time pronounce upon the practicalities of liturgical music, chiefly popes and bishops, were not themselves trained musicians.[11] Their admonitions, encouragements, and guidelines were

---

[11] A rare exception was Phillippe de Vitry, Bishop of Meaux, France, and one of the leading lights in the compositional practice known as the *Ars Nova*, which, among other things, developed the system of rhythmic notation based on note shapes that has come down to us today.

expressed in terms they knew, necessarily quite general in tone, almost never with technical recommendations regarding composition or execution. Moreover, these documents address particular problems at discrete moments in history and make no attempt to coordinate musical ideals into a comprehensive theory. Again, there never seemed to be much of a need for one, until now.

How to Begin?

The first job of a theory of liturgical music is to discern which principles are valid and central to the tradition, that is, among other things, those which have lasting value, are essentially true, and are not merely an idea that happens to resonate with the prevailing culture at a particular time and place.

The second job is to integrate those principles that are essential. Integration in theory means a kind of coordination, so that the values expressed in the principles support rather than compete with one another as much as possible. Often this means finding which principles take precedence, for not all can have the same value or weight. Just as civil rights of speech, assembly, and the practice of religion are not absolute but have priority one over another according to circumstance, so in liturgical music some principles will outrank others in analogous fashion. Ideally, a theory of liturgical music should coordinate all the various principles into a coherent structure, like a building made of ideas, or better, like the proverbial tree that grows and bends to changing winds without yielding its roots or essential integrity.

A theory should help to ensure that the musical events of a Roman Catholic liturgy are as good as they can be, or at least help to measure how good they are. This goodness has a number of dimensions: the quality of the compositions themselves, especially important at a time when so much new liturgical music appears every year; the judicious use of the historical repertory; performance; and the place of the music within the great sacred drama that is the liturgy. All these are essential. The greatest Mass movement of Palestrina will not make up for poor intonation in singing, nor for singing it in an inappropriate situation. But neither will the finest choir rescue a piece of schlock written by an earnest, amateur composer. We insist on all the excellences of liturgical music. A theory should help us to know where to look and to recognize them when we find them.

In the Western tradition of reasoning, theories grow chiefly from two sources: first principles, from which more specific principles and detailed applications are logically derived, and empirical data, from which they are inferred.

The Data

The best empirical source for a theory of liturgical music is its history and historical traditions. "Those who cannot remember the past are condemned to repeat it." George Santayana's aphorism has not been much heeded of late.[12] Some of the most widespread initiatives in congregational singing in the twentieth century, to take one example, repeated radical Protestant innovations made in the sixteenth, innovations which were quietly put aside in favor of more traditional practices by that century's end. We might have avoided many of the fights over the right character and role of congregational singing had we only looked back.

Here the first postconciliar executors of reform made a mistake. Music in liturgy since the Second Vatican Council has by and large neglected or simply abandoned the historical repertory, the music called by the *Sacrosanctum Concilium* the "treasure of inestimable value" (SC 112).[13] It is true, as Thomas Day has documented, that music older than 1960, indeed almost anything Catholic older than 1960, was regarded with extreme suspicion in the years immediately following the council.[14] A very common kind of musical semantic of association was at work. Traditional kinds of Catholic liturgical music sounded, and still sound for the most part, "churchy," because that is exactly where they were heard. All the talk of liturgical renewal seemed to rule out anything associated with the preconciliar church almost by definition. Therefore the hallowed musical traditions were worse than useless; they were weeds that choked the renewal of faith. A more mature conception of renewal in more recent years has calmed

---

[12] George Santayana, *The Life of Reason; or, The Phases of Human Progress*, vol. 1 (New York: Charles Scribner's Sons, 1905), 284.

[13] There are exceptional places of course, such as the Boston Archdiocesan Choir School founded by Theodore Marier, that made significant recourse to the traditional repertory, adapting it to the reformed liturgy. We have much to learn from them.

[14] Day, *Why Catholics Can't Sing*, chap. 5.

those suspicions somewhat, which is all to the good. We need our music history.

Indeed, the history of our liturgical traditions is like a great laboratory, a fund of empirical data from innumerable experiments. To this we can add the experiences of other religious traditions, for it so happens that the various religions have approached common problems, such as congregational singing, in similar ways. Roman Catholicism has deep roots in the Western tradition and European cultural history, and it would be foolish to pretend that its music is easily compared to other traditions, but it would be equally foolish to ignore what other religions from other parts of the world have experienced in their own sacred musics. Just as knowing a foreign language deepens the knowledge and appreciation of one's own, so might an honest appraisal of some of the world's ancient practices help us recover some of our own.

And recover them we must. Our history offers us the inestimable gift of the repertory, the greatest musical collection—as measured by its quality and by its diversity of genre, provenance, and complexity—in all the world. The church treats this repertory like the fearful steward treated his master's treasure: it is buried, doing no good for anyone. But if, once dug up, it is badly used by way of poor performances or liturgical practices, it may quickly reacquire the same reputation that buried it. The liturgical values of today are not the same as in 1950, as any revival of repertory must recognize. Like archeologists, we must brush away the detritus slowly and carefully, but unlike them, we must imagine contemporary settings for the artifacts, how and whether they are useful today.

Such cooler thinking has become more common in recent years than it was in the hothouse atmosphere of the 1960s and 1970s. Of the many researches both liturgical and musical, three stand out. In his witty and incisive *Why Catholics Can't Sing: The Culture of Catholicism and the Triumph of Bad Taste*, Thomas Day has described the cultural influences active in America mostly in the last half century that seem to have prevented Catholic congregational singing from taking off in the way it was dreamed of in 1965. It is significant that, although Day is an accomplished organist and holder of a doctorate in musicology from Columbia University, his most telling criticism is not about the music per se, but rather liturgical values and attitudes, in particular the rampant egoism that has infected so many liturgical ministers. And there is no mistaking his view that most recent liturgical music is of very poor quality, but how so? To cure this state of the art, we must know objectively the nature of the disease.

The second major contribution is Fr. Anthony Ruff's *Sacred Music and Liturgical Reform: Treasures and Transformations*, a truly compendious summary of the historical tradition of Roman Catholic sacred music. Ruff wants to answer two fundamental questions: what is the meaning of the term "treasury of sacred music" of *Sacrosanctum Concilium*, and what place can this "treasury" hold in the reformed liturgy? (SC 112, 114, 121). To answer, he marshals intellectual, liturgical, and musical histories. These include brief statements on the nature of liturgy and musicological summaries of a few highpoints of the Catholic traditions in Europe, but also rather detailed surveys of essential developments: the musical interests of the liturgical movement, the Cecilian movement, the conflicts in the nineteenth-century revival of Gregorian chant, and the twentieth-century Lutheran revival. Then there is a survey of the most significant twentieth-century church documents, both official and unofficial, that treat liturgical music, beginning with Pope Pius X's *motu proprio* of 1903 (*Tra le Sollecitudini*) through the Snowbird Statement (1996). Ruff's answers to his questions are, in brief, that the treasury is not a repertory of musical works but is rather to be "understood as a dynamic tradition," a view that will find resonance here, and that masterworks of the past will be treasured "not for their own sake, but precisely because they correspond to the nature of the reformed liturgy in exemplary fashion."[15]

More recent is Edward Schaefer's *Catholic Music through the Ages*, another empirical study of the historical tradition of Catholic liturgical music. He infers from history three common principles of musical reform in liturgy, which may be encapsulated thus: liturgical music of the highest quality must own "long-established core values," which are best embodied in Gregorian chant.[16] But why? Without understanding the causes of this historical preference, without articulating the core values more abstractly, the ruthless logic of this principle would disown the musical riches of Gregorian chant's successors and of the non-Western world.[17]

---

[15] Ruff, *Sacred Music and Liturgical Reform*, 357, 609.

[16] Schaefer, *Catholic Music through the Ages*, 160–64.

[17] To be fair, Schaefer does cite certain musical characteristics as a reason for the special affinity of plainchant in the liturgy: "It is also precisely this distinctiveness that reinforces chant's position as the preeminent music for the liturgy. In as much as the liturgy is a most uncommon event, chant, that is, the music that is uniquely bound to the liturgy both musically and historically, is also the only music that can accentuate the exceptional place that the liturgy holds in the life of every Catholic by means of the exceptional commingling of musical characteristics that it enjoys."

So data there are in abundance, but they are nevertheless insufficient. Those theorists of theory known as philosophers of science have shown quite convincingly that even the most rigorously objective of disciplines never regard data uncritically, never observe phenomena without some background assumptions conditioning those observations.[18] In any empirical study there are significant data and irrelevant data. How are they distinguished? Here is where first principles come in.

First Principle?

It would appear that a first principle, or guiding criterion, of any theory of liturgical music would be the liturgy itself. Citing a fragment of article 112 of *Sacrosanctum Concilium*—"Therefore sacred music is to be considered the more holy, the more closely connected it is with the liturgical action . . ."—Anthony Ruff declares on the first page of his long study that "this strong statement reminds us that worship music is, above all, a part of the liturgy, and that the place of music in the liturgy can only be determined from the nature of the liturgy, not from the nature of the musical repertories."[19] And so have thought virtually all liturgists who write about its music. This is a cardinal error.

To begin to see why, let us ask a simple question. How should psalm verses be sung at Mass? The traditional Roman Rite is full of psalm verses: at the very beginning, the introit (entrance) antiphon frames a psalm verse, as often do the offertory and communion antiphons; sometimes one appears as the versicle of the Gospel acclamation; and of course there is the responsorial psalm between the first and second readings, or its older forms of gradual and tract. The Greek word *psallein* is usually translated "to sing accompanied." There is no question that these texts should be sung.

See *Catholic Music through the Ages*, 36. Nevertheless, without a stronger theoretical grounding, it is too much of a leap to claim that these musical characteristics make plainchant "the only music" that can do this. Why should distinctiveness in general, or even plainchant's particular distinctiveness, guarantee liturgical propriety?

[18] This train of thought was touched off by Thomas S. Kuhn, *The Structure of Scientific Revolutions*, 1st ed. 1962 (Chicago: University of Chicago Press, 1970), but many others have followed, especially concerned to save his approach from relativism. See also Mary Hesse, *The Structure of Scientific Inference* (Berkeley, CA: University of California Press, 1974); Clark Glymour, *Theory and Evidence* (Princeton, NJ: Princeton University Press, 1980); and Anthony Ortony, ed., *Metaphor and Thought* (Cambridge: Cambridge University Press, 1979).

[19] Ruff, *Sacred Music and Liturgical Reform*, 1.

But there are many methods, sanctioned by both official instructions and historical practice. Psalm verses may be chanted to psalm tone formulas, that method alone accomplished in several ways, or chanted to elaborate, rhythmically subtle Gregorian melodies, chanted for minutes on end to energetic Gospel rhythms, sung like an opera aria, transformed into a congregational hymn paraphrasing the original text, or replaced entirely by a "another liturgical chant that is suited to the sacred action, the day, or the time of year" whose text has nothing to do with the psalm.[20] Each of these methods—and there are many more—has particular technical musical qualities that differentiate it from the others. If "the nature of the liturgy" is adequate as a first principle, then it should be capable of judging these differences "*only . . . from the nature of the liturgy,*" without recourse to the "nature of the musical repertories," and justifying the various psalm methods as to their relative propriety. For it is improbable in the extreme, with the musical differences so great, that all are "equally" suitable for the liturgy.

I have never read any synopsis of "the nature of the liturgy" that could begin to make this kind of judgment on its own terms. The fundamental purpose of liturgy according to the most fundamental document, *Sacrosanctum Concilium*, is "to celebrate the paschal mystery, reading those things 'which were in all the scriptures concerning him,' celebrating the Eucharist in which 'the victory and triumph of his death are again made present,' and at the same time 'giving thanks to God for His unspeakable gift' in Christ Jesus, 'in praise of His glory' through the power of the Holy Spirit" (SC 6). Anthony Ruff's own formula, repeated several times in his book, is "the purpose of the liturgy itself is to enable the Christian community to respond to and participate in the saving work of God in Christ."[21] Either of these pronouncements could be cited to justify, or even to disqualify, any of the methods for singing psalm verses at Mass.

A true first principle permits of wide application. And in fact, we can imagine "the nature of the liturgy" providing guiding criteria for the architecture of church buildings as many have claimed it should, in a manner analogous to Ruff's contention for music, but not as a first principle. Were church buildings designed by liturgical principles *alone*, no one would dare enter them. Building materials, bricks and

---

[20] This last is the so-called "option four" of the General Instruction of the Roman Missal, art. 48. See also chap. 6.
[21] Ruff, *Sacred Music and Liturgical Reform*, 10.

mortar, have their own natures to be reckoned with, and the notes and harmonies of music no less. The disappointing quality of liturgical music in most places these forty years largely comes from an inflexible top-down approach.

The "nature of the liturgy" fails as a classic first principle. We might have guessed this from the outset. The physicist's "force," the geometer's "point," and the ethicist's "the good" are intrinsically simple, even called by some logicians "primitives." Liturgy is intrinsically complex, a compound of many elements, including the music declared by the council to be "an integral part," and far greater than the sum of all of them. But it is this very summation that resists the easy encapsulation, the fundamental, taken-for-granted essence of a first principle. This explains the widely divergent views of "the nature of the liturgy" that one finds in the recent scholarship,[22] and perhaps why Ruff chose to omit the important qualifying phrase from Article 112 as he began: "whether making prayer more pleasing, promoting unity of minds, or conferring greater solemnity upon the sacred rites." Delight in prayer, unity of minds, and above all solemnity, after all, complicate a first principle quite a lot. The essential contribution of liturgy to the understanding of liturgical music is self-evident, but not as a first principle operating from the top down. A subtler conception of the relation between "the nature of the liturgy" and the building materials of music is in order.

Feedback Relations

The relation between the Scriptures and Catholic dogmatic tradition offers a better model.[23] The Scriptures, as the revealed Word of God,

---

[22] Just compare, for example, Joseph Ratzinger's concept—"The foundation of the liturgy, its source and support, is the historical Pasch of Jesus—his Cross and Resurrection"—in *The Spirit of the Liturgy*, trans. John Saward (San Francisco: Ignatius Press, 2000), 60, with Mark Francis's—"Liturgy, as the public worship of the church, celebrates who we are and who we are called to be because of God's love for us in Jesus Christ"—in *Shape the Circle Ever Wider* (Chicago: Liturgy Training Publications, 2000), 20.

[23] Kevin W. Irwin proposes that this model be the foundation for understanding the entire liturgy and its history: "We understand there to be an *ongoing dialectical relationship* between *text* and *context* where the ecclesial and cultural settings in which the liturgy takes place—*context*—influence the way we experience and interpret the liturgy—*text*. But just as *context* influences how the *text* of liturgy is

are the foundation and source for Catholic belief. But "the church does not draw its certainty about all revealed truths from the holy scriptures alone." Instead, "tradition transmits in its entirety the word of God which has been entrusted to the apostles by Christ the Lord and the holy Spirit; it transmits it to the successors of the apostles." Perhaps the most famous illustration of this relation is the doctrine of the Trinity. "Trinity" never appears in the Bible, but Catholics hold it to be an essential article of faith abstracted from the Bible. Then, as an essential article of faith, the traditional Trinity doctrine informs the rereading of the Bible, which in turn may give birth to new doctrinal abstractions, and so on. That "sacred tradition and sacred scripture . . . bound closely together . . . communicate one with the other"[24] is an example of what cognitive scientists often call a feedback relation, and it characterizes some of the most fundamental perceptions and cognitive behaviors of humanity.[25]

Such a conception of the relation between "the nature of the liturgy" and its music provides what has been missing from the discussion: the facts of music. For, like the building materials of the architect, the facts of music exist in the real world and can be very stubborn things. Reconciliation occurs when principles of liturgical music condition the selection of actual works, which in turn by their own natures reform the understanding of those principles.

A theory of liturgical music must be grounded in "musical truths," or the perceptions of music shared by the members of a musical community. B-flat sounds higher than A; plainchant has no meter; a pair of four-bar phrases make an easily perceived structure; dissonances in traditional harmony are unstable and imply some kind of resolution. For musicians these statements are just as true as "a team's inning has

---

interpreted, the other side of the equation concerns how that data we call *text* necessarily influences the church's theology, spirituality and life—*context*." One might wonder whether, unlike the fixed Scriptures, this model is free of any absolute criterion of evaluations. See the entire second chapter of *Context and Text: Method in Liturgical Theology* (Collegeville, MN: Liturgical Press, 1994).

[24] All citations in this paragraph come from *Dei Verbum*, Dogmatic Constitution on Divine Revelation, in *Vatican Council II: The Basic Sixteen Documents*, trans. and ed. Austin Flannery, OP (Northport, NY: Costello Publishing Company, 1996), art. 9.

[25] The most striking real-time mechanisms occur in music perception and speech perception, where dozens of decisions about function and meaning occur each second. See Stephen Handel, *Listening: An Introduction to the Perception of Auditory Events* (Cambridge, MA: MIT Press, 1989).

three outs" and, like the latter statement, are susceptible to implication, inference, and deduction, just as in any rational discourse. Very little criticism of liturgical music, both recent and historical, has informed itself with this kind of discourse, which is the principal reason why discussions of what is good, bad, appropriate, and unsuitable degenerate so quickly into battles of taste. You like this, I like that, and there is nothing more to be said. Even as important an idea as Edward Schaefer's, that the proper balance between the expressive and formative powers of liturgical music has been lost in most contemporary compositions, is a matter of personal opinion until it can be justified in the musical facts of those compositions. A good theory does not try to eliminate the elements of personal preference or good judgment, but it can show how to rise above the battle and get beyond the idiosyncratic to reach for a common good. To be that persuasive, it has to begin with evident truths, the technical facts of music.

Bringing in the hard truths of musical reality can begin to formulate, in dialogue with "the nature of the liturgy," a synthesis of music in liturgy. How should psalm verses be sung at Mass? There are many methods, but when we begin with the liturgical proposition that it should be sung and then consider the musical exigencies for congregational performance—as in the modern responsorial psalm—and then the musical semantics that connote "prayer more pleasing" and "greater solemnity," we see those many methods as more and less appropriate, better and worse, for the sacred liturgy. An informed music criticism, made in musical terms, is no enemy of "the nature of the liturgy," but neither is it always subservient to it.

Anthony Ruff and his many colleagues may actually agree, despite his dictum on his opening page. Shortly thereafter he allows that "there are good theological reasons for embracing artistic beauty in worship music as part of its purpose of fostering artistic and cultural goods."[26] This is precisely what is meant by a reality of music—its intrinsic and independent aesthetic value—impinging upon liturgy through theological reflection so that the understanding of "the nature of the liturgy" is changed, just as our understanding of Scripture may be changed through the reading glasses of tradition. The Catholic understanding of what a psalm is must be more than the words in the Scripture; it must embody music as well and may eventually include

---

[26] Ruff, *Sacred Music and Liturgical Reform*, 17.

texts outside the Psalter, antiphons and the concluding lesser doxology. The only way to maintain the absolute priority of "the nature of the liturgy" in the face of musical aesthetics is to claim that musical beauty is actually a liturgical value, but the incorporation of musical categories into the liturgical merely erases the distinction between the two realms, and in practical terms ends up with a feedback relation anyway.

The Natures of Liturgy

This critique hardly implies that the concept of "the nature of the liturgy" is fictitious, irrelevant to our musical problems, or useless in theorizing. No, Ruff is most correct in his view that the liturgy provides fundamental criteria for judging its own music. It is only the strict top-down application of such criteria, and the exclusion of musical realities thereby, that has maintained the present confusion.

Confusion comes, in part, from the breadth of opinion among liturgical experts themselves, in their interpretations of what the Second Vatican Council meant. *Sacrosanctum Concilium*'s image of liturgy (quoted above) is a christocentric action. At the same time, the presence and assent of God's people forms an essential part of this christocentric action. "The faithful indeed, by virtue of their royal priesthood, share in the offering of the Eucharist. . . . Taking part in the Eucharistic sacrifice, the source and summit of the Christian life, they offer the divine victim to God and themselves along with him."[27] Yves Congar, one of the most prominent theological minds behind the council, wrote shortly afterward in agreement that the liturgy is "the expression of a Church actively living, praising God and bringing about a holy communion with him."[28] This image of the people of God bound up in Christ is the source of the renewal of their participation in the liturgy.

---

[27] *Lumen Gentium*, Dogmatic Constitution on the Church, in *Vatican Council II: The Basic Sixteen Documents*, trans. and ed. Austin Flannery, OP (Northport, NY: Costello Publishing Company, 1996), arts. 10–11.

[28] Yves Congar, *Tradition and Traditions*, trans. by Michael Naseby and Thomas Rainborough (New York: Macmillan, 1966), 428–29. Shortly before the council, Congar wrote, "Liturgy is first and foremost the means through which one penetrates into, and thus experiences, the paschal mystery." *La foi et la théologie* (Paris: Desclée, 1962), 145–46, quoted in Irwin, *Context and Text*, 24.

In overreaction to the near exclusion of the laity from the liturgy in centuries past, liturgists in the decades following the council often seem to have missed this delicate balance and overshifted the weight of the liturgy's significance to the community's presence in the here and now.[29] To the nuts-and-bolts practicing musician this may seem to be rather an abstract, even arcane, issue, but the shift signifies a substantial and audible reorientation of the very purpose of music in the liturgy.[30] Cardinal Joseph Ratzinger, perhaps the most significant contributor to liturgical music theory in the twentieth century,[31] explains why in his critique of this shift:

> The primary subject of the liturgy is neither God nor Christ, but the "we" of the ones celebrating. And liturgy cannot of course have adoration as its primary content since according to the deistic understanding of God, there is no reason for it. There is just as little reason for it to be concerned with atonement, sacrifice, or the forgiveness of sin. Instead, the point for those celebrating is to secure community with each other and thereby escape the isolation into which modern existence forces them. The point is to communicate experiences of liberation, joy, and reconciliation; denounce what is harmful; and provide impulses for action. For this reason the community has to create its own liturgy and not just receive it from traditions that have become unintelligible; it portrays itself and celebrates itself.[32]

There is no question that the exclusive focus on the community of the moment and the concomitant rejection of liturgical traditions, indeed of the very notion of tradition itself, has depressed the state of liturgical music since the council up to the present. To have even a hope for liturgical integrity, a theory of Catholic liturgical music must assume the liturgy's multivalent nature as the council has written of it. It is a synthesis of great subtlety.

---

[29] See a review in M. Francis Mannion, "Liturgy and the Present Crisis of Culture," *Worship* 62, no. 2 (March 1988): 98–123.

[30] This is essentially the critique offered by Jonathan Gaspar and Romanus Cessario: contemporary musical styles "all conspire to push man toward the center of the liturgy." See "Worthy of the Temple," *Nova et Vetera* (English Edition) 3, no. 4 (2005): 679.

[31] In the opinion of M. Francis Mannion, *Masterworks of God: Essays in Liturgical Theory and Practice* (Chicago: Liturgy Training Publications, 2004), 177.

[32] Joseph Ratzinger, *A New Song for the Lord: Faith in Christ and Liturgy Today*, trans. Martha M. Matesich (New York: Crossroad, 1997), 32.

Regardless of how one stands on such questions, the reference point of all students of liturgy and liturgical music is the Second Vatican Council and its foundational liturgical constitution, *Sacrosanctum Concilium*. A theory of liturgical music begins there.

Chapter 2

The Second Vatican Council and Liturgical Music

> No, I will not come, because I understand these things, I know that all of the Councils give rise to nothing but confusion and fighting, so I will not come.
> St. Gregory Nazianzen (ca. 325)

The Second Vatican Council (1962–65) is now the reference point for the liturgical reforms in the twentieth century. Since then, liturgical matters are classified as preconciliar or postconciliar.

In popular understanding, the council is admired or blamed for three radical changes in the music of the liturgy. First, it banned the singing of liturgical Latin and instead mandated the use of local vernacular languages. Second, in parallel, it promoted the composition of new liturgical works in popular styles to replace the outmoded Gregorian chants and high Renaissance polyphony. Third, and above all, it championed the active participation of the congregation in liturgical music and discouraged any liturgical music that could not accommodate congregational singing.

The three reforms seem almost symbiotic, all of a piece. If active participation is the chief concern of pastors, then naturally Latin, a dead classical language spoken by no one outside the Vatican and read only by scholars and priests, must give way to languages that lay Catholics can understand, that is, their own local vernacular languages. If they are to sing, then complex polyphonies and even most plainchants are out of the question not only because of their Latin texts but because their music is far beyond the competence of the typical parochial congregation. Liturgical music must be simple, easy to learn, and composed in a familiar style. The logic is persuasive. Perhaps that is why these ideas have sounded time and again in scholarly journals, the *New York Times*, and from the lips of contemporary Catholics, for they are part of the common parlance of modern Catholicism. This is unfortunate, because all these readings of the council, at least in part, are false.

Sacrosanctum Concilium (the commonly cited incipit of the Constitution on the Sacred Liturgy, the first of the sixteen conciliar documents of the Second Vatican Council) was promulgated on December 4, 1963, exactly four hundred years after the promulgation of the last pronouncement of the Council of Trent on sacred music.[1] As the only comprehensive statement on the divine liturgy from a worldwide ecumenical council of the Roman Catholic Church in the twentieth century, the constitution deserves its status as the point of reference for liturgical matters. Nevertheless, history reveals the document not as a lone beacon of enlightenment but as the brightest among a constellation, nor as a revolution, for a number of significant papal encyclicals preceded and prepared its coming, beginning most emphatically with the *motu proprio* of Pope St. Pius X in 1903. And a series of instructions and clarifications followed *Sacrosanctum Concilium*, up to and including the centenary chirograph on sacred music issued by Pope John Paul II on November 22, 2003, and the discussions of the General Synod on the Eucharist in October 2005.[2]

The council fathers devoted an entire chapter of *Sacrosanctum Concilium*, the sixth, to liturgical music, which attests to the preeminence of music among the fine arts in liturgy, the only one that does not merely adorn but actively constructs the liturgy by animating its words. Its ten articles, 112 to 121, articulate the inestimable value of the "treasury," the roles of plainchant and polyphony, and the activity of the congregation, among other matters. Still other articles touching on liturgical music fall under other headings (see especially articles 30, 36, 54).

Regarding the proper liturgical language, which affects materially the range of liturgical music that may be used, *Sacrosanctum Concilium* says this:

---

[1] See *Concilium Tridentiunum Diariorum*, ed. J. Massarelli, 9 vols (Freiburg, Germany: 1901–24), 754. The Council of Trent's musical reforms appear at various points between September 10, 1562, and December 3, 1563.

[2] For a survey of these and other relevant documents through 1975 and their historical contexts, see Richard J. Schuler, "A Chronicle of the Reform: Catholic Music in the Twentieth Century," http://www.musicasacra.com/pdf/chron.pdf, (last consulted May 2011); repr. from Robert A. Skeris, ed., *Cum Angelis Canere: Essays on Sacred Music and Pastoral Liturgy in Honour of Richard J. Schuler* (St. Paul, MN: Church Music Association, 1990).

> The use of the Latin language, except when a particular law prescribes otherwise, is to be preserved in the Latin rites. (SC 36.1) But since the use of the vernacular, whether in the Mass, the administration of the sacraments, or in other parts of the liturgy, may frequently be of great advantage to the people, a wider use may be made of it, especially in readings, directives and in some prayers and chants. (SC 36.2)
>
> A suitable place may be allotted to the vernacular in Masses which are celebrated with the people, especially in the readings and "the common prayer," and also, as local conditions may warrant, in those parts which pertain to the people, according to the norm laid down in article 36 of this constitution.
>
> Nevertheless care must be taken to ensure that the faithful may also be able to say or sing together in Latin those parts of the ordinary of the Mass which pertain to them. (SC 54)[3]

"Latin rites" in article 36 here means not rites conducted in the Latin language, which would be tautological, but rites of the Roman tradition, as distinct from Ukrainian, Byzantine, or one of the other twenty-two rites of the universal church. The articles provide, to be sure, for the use of vernacular languages, but in the form of exceptions to the normal use of Latin: "suitable place," "as local conditions may warrant," "wider use." In no sense does the constitution banish Latin from the liturgy.

On the priorities of Gregorian chant, polyphony, and popular styles of music in liturgy:

> The church recognizes Gregorian chant as specially native to the Roman Liturgy. Therefore, other things being equal, it should be given pride of place in liturgical services.
>   Other kinds of sacred music, especially polyphony, are by no means excluded from liturgical celebrations, so long as they accord with the spirit of the liturgical action, as laid down in article 30. (SC 116)
>
> In some places, in mission lands especially, there are peoples who have their own musical tradition, and this plays an important part in their religious and social life. For this reason their music should be held in due esteem and should be given a suitable role, not only in forming their religious sense but also in adapting worship to their native genius, as indicated in articles 39 and 40. (SC 119)

---

[3] Article 113, on music for the liturgy, refers back to articles 36 and 54 regarding the language to be sung.

> Composers, animated by the Christian spirit, should accept that it is part of their vocation to cultivate sacred music and increase its store of treasures.
>
> Let them produce compositions which have the qualities proper to genuine sacred music, and which can be sung not only by large choirs but also by smaller choirs, and which make possible the active participation of the whole congregation.
>
> The texts intended to be sung must always be in conformity with Catholic doctrine; indeed they should be drawn chiefly from sacred scripture and from liturgical sources. (SC 121)

Sacrosanctum Concilium does not sweep away the traditional repertories of plainchant and polyphony into the dustbin of history.[4] Rather, it grants them a singular recognition, to plainchant in particular, as the music to be sung in liturgy if at all possible. Yes, musical styles of other cultures are permitted and one might even say encouraged, but note the qualifications: again the "suitable role," with "qualities proper to genuine sacred music" and texts "sung in conformity with Catholic doctrine."

There is no doubt that promoting the active participation of the congregation in the liturgy is a major theme of the *Sacrosanctum Concilium*. The phrase *participatio actuosa* or some close variant of it appears in twelve of the articles.[5] Besides the one mention relevant to composition just noted, the others most important for music are:

> To develop active participation, the people should be encouraged to take part by means of acclamations, responses, psalms, antiphons, hymns, as well as by actions, gestures, and bodily attitudes. And at the proper time a reverent silence should be observed. (SC 30)

> The treasure of sacred music is to be preserved and cultivated with great care. Choirs must be diligently developed, especially in cathedral churches. Bishops and other pastors of souls must do their best to ensure that whenever a liturgical service is to be accompanied by chant, the whole body of the faithful may be able to take that active part which is rightly theirs, as laid down in articles 28 and 30. (SC 114)

---

[4] Schuler, "A Chronicle of the Reform," 23, records that some dioceses actually did prohibit any use of Latin and Gregorian chant, and thereby contributed to the mistaken interpretation of the constitution.

[5] The precise meaning of the expression is controverted. See chap. 18.

> Religious singing by the faithful is to be skilfully encouraged so that in devotional exercises as well as in liturgical services the voices of the faithful may be heard, in conformity with the norms and requirements of the rubrics. (SC 118)

Yes, the fervor of the council fathers for a singing congregation is unmistakable. But the articles, taken together as they must be in interpreting a document of such depth, hardly require the congregation to sing the entire liturgy or call for the dissolution of church choirs. Again there is a balance of legitimate and traditional interests, an enthusiastic desire that "the voices of the faithful may be heard" on the one hand, but only "in conformity with the norms and requirements of the rubrics" on the other. Article 30 names particular moments when this might happen most fruitfully, and then there is Article 28, which one critic calls "the most important liturgical principle to have been recalled by the Second Vatican Council's Constitution on the Sacred Liturgy, a principle that is still to this day honored more in the breach than in the observance":[6]

> All taking part in liturgical celebrations, whether ministers or members of the congregation, should do all that pertains to them, and no more, taking into account the rite and the liturgical norms. (SC 28)

In short, the congregation has an essential role in the sacred liturgy that music should accommodate, but it is one role among several and not necessarily the predominant one, and what precisely constitutes *participatio actuosa* of the congregation is left without explicit definition.

The Antecedents

Is, then, *Sacrosanctum Concilium* as revolutionary a document as its reputation would have it? At least in regard to liturgical music, no. Every one of these principal reforms—vernacular liturgical language, indigenous musical styles, and active participation of the congregation—had been anticipated by three papal encyclicals stretching back

---

[6] Denis Crouan, *The Liturgy Betrayed*, trans. Marc Sebanc (San Francisco: Ignatius, 2000), 53.

to the beginning of the twentieth century.[7] The famous *motu proprio* ("by our own initiative") of Pope St. Pius X, *Tra le Sollecitudini* (Among the Concerns), of November 22, 1903, the first major pronouncement on music from the Vatican in over 150 years and the most comprehensive ever, tried to restore a firm footing to liturgical music on the plainchant tradition. Promulgated on November 20, 1947, Pope Pius XII's encyclical on the entire sacred liturgy, *Mediator Dei* (The Mediator of God), glossed a number of his predecessor's concerns, and his more particular *Musicae Sacrae Ministerium* (The Ministry of Sacred Music, December 1955) precedes *Sacrosanctum Concilium* by only eight years.

It is true that the prospects for a liturgical vernacular language appear grim at first:

> The language proper to the Roman Church is Latin. Hence it is forbidden to sing anything whatever in the vernacular in solemn liturgical functions—much more to sing in the vernacular the variable or common parts of the Mass and Office. (*Tra le Sollecitudini* 7)

Even here, though, the door is left open a tiny crack. "Solemn liturgical functions" is a limiting circumstance, an implicit recognition of the significant amount of vernacular singing that occurred in previous centuries, particularly in Germany. In the later encyclicals of Pope Pius XII, the crack widens considerably:

> The use of the Latin language, customary in a considerable portion of the Church, is a manifest and beautiful sign of unity, as well as an effective antidote for any corruption of doctrinal truth. In spite of this, the use of the mother tongue in connection with several of the rites may be of much advantage to the people. (*Mediator Dei* 60)

> Where, according to old or immemorial custom, some popular hymns are sung in the language of the people after the sacred words of the liturgy have been sung in Latin during the solemn Eucharistic sacrifice, local Ordinaries can allow this to be done "if, in the light of the circumstances of the locality and the people, they believe that (custom)

---

[7] Schuler, "A Chronicle of the Reform," 42. Anthony Ruff, OSB, "Part IV: The Treasure of Sacred Music in the Roman Documents on Worship Music of the Twentieth Century," in *Sacred Music and Liturgical Reform: Treasures and Transformations* (Chicago: Hillenbrand, 2007), 271–357. Fr. Ruff organizes his survey by document rather than by topic as here, but he supplies much useful detail about the historical background and context of each one.

cannot prudently be removed." (*Musicae Sacrae* 47; citation from canon 5.22, Code of Canon Law, Council of Trent)

The first citation admirably summarizes the crux of a principal argument about liturgical language, the tradeoff made between Latin as a sign of worldwide catholicity and a vernacular as a means of particular custom and understanding. Nevertheless, both documents concede both the existence and rightness of a limited vernacular use. *Sacrosanctum Concilium* merely opens the door a little wider.

The provisions for indigenous musics, grudging perhaps but nonetheless real, occur in precisely the same context as in the constitution, chiefly the missions.

> But it [sacred music] must, at the same time, be universal in the sense that while every nation is permitted to admit into its ecclesiastical compositions those special forms which may be said to constitute its native music, still these forms must be subordinated in such a manner to the general characteristics of sacred music that nobody of any nation may receive an impression other than good on hearing them. (*Tra le Sollecitudini* 2)

> In this way these people can have, in contrast to their own religious music which is frequently admired even in cultivated countries, sacred Christian hymns in which the truths of the faith, the life of Christ the Lord and the praises of the Blessed Virgin Mary and the Saints can be sung in a language and in melodies familiar to them. (*Musicae Sacrae* 70)

> Despite the fact that they [popular hymns] are short and easy, they should manifest a religious dignity and seriousness. When they are fashioned in this way these sacred canticles, born as they are from the most profound depths of the people's soul, deeply move the emotions and spirit and stir up pious sentiments. When they are sung at religious rites by a great crowd of people singing as with one voice, they are powerful in raising the minds of the faithful to higher things. (*Musicae Sacrae* 63)

This leads naturally to the matter of congregational participation. On this point, the precedent encyclicals at times signal an enthusiasm every bit as warm as that in *Sacrosanctum Concilium*:

> The faithful assemble for no other object than that of acquiring this spirit from its foremost and indispensable font, which is the active

participation in the most holy mysteries and in the public and solemn prayer of the Church. (*Tra le Sollecitudini* preamble)

Special efforts are to be made to restore the use of the Gregorian Chant by the people, so that the faithful may again take a more active part in the ecclesiastical offices, as was the case in ancient times. (*Tra le Sollecitudini* 3)

We also exhort you, Venerable Brethren, to promote with care congregational singing, and to see to its accurate execution with all due dignity, since it easily stirs up and arouses the faith and piety of large gatherings of the faithful. Let the full harmonious singing of our people rise to heaven like the bursting of a thunderous sea and let them testify by the melody of their song to the unity of their hearts and minds, as becomes brothers and the children of the same Father. (*Mediator Dei* 194)

Nevertheless at Masses that are not sung solemnly these hymns can be a powerful aid in keeping the faithful from attending the Holy Sacrifice like dumb and idle spectators. They can help to make the faithful accompany the sacred services both mentally and vocally and to join their own piety to the prayers of the priest. This happens when these hymns are properly adapted to the individual parts of the Mass, as We rejoice to know is being done in many parts of the Catholic world. (*Musicae Sacrae* 64).

On the evidence of the documents then, taken at face value, the Second Vatican Council represents much less a revolution in liturgy and liturgical music and much more a culmination of the thinking, writing, and discussion about liturgy that had developed throughout the preceding century and more.[8] Indeed, some researchers had already found their practical applications in, for example, the experimental usages of vernacular languages in the "dialogue" Masses, the restoration of the Easter Vigil liturgy in 1951, and the reform of the entire Holy Week cycle in 1955, nearly seven years before the council opened.[9] In theoretical terms, the council provided no new categories,

---

[8] For more details about this essential continuity, see Franz Bischof Zauner, "Die liturgische Konstitution und ihre Grundtendenzen," in *Die Kirchenmusik und das II. Vatikanische Konzil*, ed. Philipp Harnoncourt (Graz, Austria: Verlag Styria, 1965), 13–32.

[9] Aidan Kavanagh, "The Concilar Documents: Liturgy (*Sacrosanctum Concilium*)," in *Modern Catholicism: Vatican II and After*, ed. Adrian Hastings (New York: Oxford University Press, 1991), 69.

nothing that contradicted any Vatican stance. The sense of the articles on music, taken as a whole, is close to their precedents. "To interpret the [Second Vatican] Council on the supposition that it marks a break with the past, *when in reality it stands in continuity with the faith of all times,* is a definite mistake," stated Pope John Paul II.[10]

The all-important work of the Consilium, the body charged with the writing of the "instructions" that put flesh and bones on the general language of *Sacrosanctum Concilium* after the close of the council, confirms this reading at least on the musical points. Fr. Annibale Bugnini, one of the chief proponents and architects of liturgical reform in the church, describes in his rather defensive account *The Reform of the Liturgy 1948–1975* three collections of liturgical music published by "Group 25," the subcommittee of the Consilium given the responsibility of adapting plainchants for the revised Missal. They are the *Kyriale simplex* (1964), "a little anthology of very simple Gregorian chants;" *Chants of the Missal* (1964), "a collection of chants regarded as useful or necessary in a sung Mass, in compliance with the new norms for Mass;" and a more comprehensive *Graduale Simplex* (1967), "a final attempt to lend solemnity to the Latin liturgy and prevent a complete loss of the priceless patrimony of traditional Latin chant," but one that included "innovations very useful for participation."[11] These facts

---

[10] Speech of February 27, 2000, Vatican City, par. 4. See http://www.vatican.va/holy_father/john_paul_ii/speeches/2000/jan-mar/documents/hf_jp-ii_spe_20000227_vatican-council-ii_en.html. Last consulted May 2011. Emphasis in the original.

[11] *The Reform of the Liturgy 1948–1975*, trans. Matthew J. O'Connell (Collegeville, MN: Liturgical Press, 1990), 119–21. An anonymous reviewer of this book comments on this history: "The author is simply wrong in stating . . . that Group 25, in producing the *Graduale Simplex*, felt they were fulfilling the council's wishes for *actuosa participatio* of the people or congregational singing. There was another *coetus* (Group 14) that was to deal with songs for the Mass. I was appointed by Pope Paul VI to be a member of that group. It disbanded after three meetings because it had become evident that such music would be in the vernacular and no single group could deal with such a phenomenon from all over the world." This contradicts Bugnini's view: "The manner of singing, in which one or more cantors alternate with the congregation, which sings a refrain verse, is the oldest and most traditional in the Church. . . . If we want to lead the congregations and small choirs to the regular practice of the sung Mass, no other way is feasible" (894, 895). But even if it did not, the fate of Group 14 has no bearing on the argument at hand because the reviewer confounds what the council intended with what actually happened, a distinction that is precisely the subject of this chapter.

speak for themselves. When the council fathers confirmed the preeminence of plainchant for sacred liturgy in articles 116–17 of *Sacrosanctum Concilium*, they were in earnest. When they affirmed the laity's right to active participation, it was plainchant that they wanted the congregations to sing.

The entire postconciliar instruction *Musicam Sacram* of March 5, 1967, confirms the reading again. It elaborates in greater detail and practical application the musical norms of the constitution, but maintains the same priorities. Notable are the six articles devoted to the necessity, formation, and liturgical role of the choir (19–25). Far from being made obsolete by the new emphasis on active participation, the choir becomes its chief agent.

Unintended Consequences

Well, then, what happened?

Obviously, the state of liturgical music today, and even within a decade following *Sacrosanctum Concilium*, bears little resemblance to the image provided in the document. With lightning speed, vernacular languages replaced liturgical Latin throughout the world.[12] Nearly at the same pace, popular musical styles, including all manner of world folk musics, replaced other types commonly associated with liturgy. Plainchant, as a practical music for liturgy, declined to the verge of extinction.

This last apparent consequence of the Second Vatican Council is one of its great historical ironies. The great surge of intellectual energy dedicated to reviving the spirit of the Roman liturgy known as the liturgical movement carried as one of its highest banners the singing of plainchant by the congregation. Pius X went so far as to say in his *motu proprio* that congregational singing was the whole point of recovering the plainchant tradition. Later on, it is true, this happy marriage soured. Fr. Anthony Ruff has detailed how more progressive voices, notably Pius Parsch, riled the musical wing of the liturgical movement in the three decades preceding the Second Vatican Council

---

[12] Symbolic of the frenzy was the decision of the American Benedictines, who were certainly familiar with ecclesiastical Latin and needed to accommodate few lay people, to sing all the Divine Offices in English as early as 1964. See Anthony Milner, "Music in a Vernacular Catholic Liturgy," *Proceedings of the Royal Musical Association* 91 (1964–65): 21–32.

by interpreting active participation as chiefly congregational singing, and thereby threatened to eliminate at a stroke virtually the entire official Catholic repertory of liturgical music.[13] But these same years saw the minor miracles of Justine Ward, whose method of plainchant instruction penetrated deeply into the American Catholic schools; of Gregor Schwake, who with his "liturgical weeks" could teach parishes four or five plainchant ordinaries; and of reports of plain, working-class folk singing chant from Italy to Africa.[14] In the 1950s, "the average Roman Catholic thinks of the [liturgical] movement, as does the average priest, as an interest in the singing of Gregorian chant."[15] Perhaps this was one of those rare historical moments prized by John Henry Newman when the vox populi spoke with their actions a greater wisdom than the wise. In any case, the catastrophic demise of the plainchant program was most certainly never imagined by the architects of the liturgical movement, the fruit of which was the Second Vatican Council.

It is a great and unfortunate error to bind the music of plainchant (Gregorian chant or any other type) with the "old church," the horrible bogeyman of the preconciliar liturgy. Before the council, local parishioners almost never heard plainchant at Mass. It was rare even in most cathedrals. Thomas Day describes the saccharine song, if any there was, heard instead, chiefly the products of an Irish Tin Pan Alley.[16] Ernest Koenker, writing on the scene in 1954, reported that "the quality of the music generally heard in her churches is poor. In some cases it borders on the vulgar; the tunes of some hymns are just as sugary and frivolous, the words are just as platitudinous, as those one hears in a fundamentalist church. . . . Here are hymns that induce the same emotional 'jag' as popular love songs, which they closely resemble: 'Panis Angelicus' by César Franck . . . Schubert's operatic 'Ave Maria' . . . ."[17] Historian Aidan Kavanaugh reports simply that most parishes heard no liturgical music at all.[18]

---

[13] Ruff, *Sacred Music and Liturgical Reform*, 243–50.

[14] Ibid., 220–28.

[15] Koenker, *The Liturgical Renaissance in the Roman Catholic Church* (Chicago: The University of Chicago Press, 1954), 18.

[16] Thomas Day, *Why Catholics Can't Sing* (New York: Crossroad, 1992), chap. 3.

[17] Koenker, *The Liturgical Renaissance*, 153–54.

[18] Kavanaugh, "The Conciliar Documents: Liturgy (*Sacrosanctum Concilium*)," in *Modern Catholicism: Vatican II and After*, ed. Adrian Hastings (New York: Oxford University Press, 1991), 69.

Mutatis mutandis, this was the sad situation in nineteenth-century Europe that Dom Prosper Guéranger (1805–75) set out to rectify. He established the Benedictine Abbey of St. Pierre at Solesmes in 1833, and his great study *The Liturgical Year* is considered one of the founding documents of the liturgical movement.[19] His concept of a restored and invigorated liturgy embraced music wholeheartedly. He sent his monks to all parts of Europe to collect the ancient manuscripts containing the oldest recorded music of the Western world, then proceeded to supervise the construction of an authoritative edition of plainchant in the Gregorian tradition. Meanwhile, Fr. Franz Xaver Witt (1834–88) in 1869 founded the *Allgemeiner Deutscher Cäcilien-Verein* (General German Cecilian Society) for the purpose of providing practical publications of chant and church polyphony to parishes large and small. The Cecilians and the Benedictines of Solesmes entered into a strange political competition to provide the standard of "Gregorian" chant restoration, not resolved until the turn of the twentieth century when the Vatican adopted the Solesmes versions for its *editio typica*.[20]

The details of such decisions, while fascinating to lovers of plainchant, need not distract us from the main point: the primary music of most factions and interests of the liturgical movement through most of its history was plainchant. Plainchant was the music that would inspire the laity to song and revive the listless liturgies of the post-Enlightenment period. Standards of notation were adopted, pedagogical methods devised, and plainchant found its way into parochial schools in Europe and America. "In Father Hellrigel's remarkable Holy Cross Parish the children, from the second grade on, learned three Masses and *Credo* I between September, 1940, and Easter, 1941."[21]

But such efforts—and there were many—did not move quite fast enough.[22] When the council promulgated *Sacrosanctum Concilium* in December 1963, the practical recovery of plainchant in the Catholic world had not progressed anywhere near the point where articles

---

[19] Prosper Guéranger, *L'Année Liturgique*, 15 vols (Paris: H. Oudin et Cie, beginning in 1841 [unfinished]); Translated by Dom Laurence Shepherd, OSB, as *The Liturgical Year*, 15 vols. (Wesminster, MD: Newman Press, 1948–50). 1833 was the first year of occupation. In 1837, Guèranger was officially recognized as the abbot of St. Pierre de Solesmes. I thank Fr. Jerome F. Weber for this information.

[20] For historical details, see Ruff, *Sacred Music and Liturgical Reform*, 108–29.

[21] Koenker, *The Liturgical Renaissance*, 159. Holy Cross Parish is in St. Louis, Missouri.

[22] Kavanaugh, "The Conciliar Documents: Liturgy (*Sacrosanctum Concilium*)," 69.

116–17 would have represented a mere affirmation of a status quo. Instead they seemed to express wishful thinking. There was in most places a musical vacuum, which the tremendous impetus and drive for active participation by the laity filled all too rapidly. This is the cruel irony of the council and music. It fostered, by historical accident, a near extinction of plainchant through renewal: the progressive movement to reform the liturgy destroyed its own spearhead. And therein is the puzzle. If the documents mean what they say, why the explosion of wildly uncoordinated reform when *Sacrosanctum Concilium* proclaimed nothing really new? Why has the practice of Catholic liturgical music after 1965 strayed so far from the council's intentions?

Remember the nuanced and heavily qualified language of the documents:

> The church recognizes Gregorian chant as specially native to the Roman Liturgy. Therefore, other things being equal, it should be given pride of place in liturgical services. (SC 116)

Phrases such as "other things being equal" represent in part the Vatican diplomatic habit of never drawing the line too firmly, never burning the last bridge if it can be avoided, but in the context of the Second Vatican Council they also betray a certain factionalism. Council fathers coming from Asian and African lands, in particular, wished for more latitude to introduce aspects of their native cultures, especially their musics, into the sacred liturgy and found allies among the leaders of the liturgical movement. They debated, at times passionately, about the use of the vernacular and other musical traditions with those who saw immense value in the received liturgical traditions. Article 116 represents the kind of compromise that in some sense could offer each side a consolation, if not a victory. In cases such as this, these exception clauses can provide a very wide range of interpretation. They would provide the tinder for the wildfire of practical reforms.

But the earlier documents also had such exception clauses, although, to be sure, not as many and not as prominent as the ones in *Sacrosanctum Concilium*. There had to be something else that ignited the explosion.

The new element was the tremendous event of the ecumenical council itself, a body of over two thousand voting fathers drawn from the whole world, convoked by Pope John XXIII himself, and therefore to be taken most seriously by centralized authority invested in Vatican

City. This automatically gave its *Sacrosanctum Concilium* and other documents an authority considerably above anything that had preceded them. "The documents of the Second Vatican Council have provided the Catholic Church with what is undoubtedly the weightiest body of official teaching in the twentieth century . . . the authority of an ecumenical council, more representative of the whole world than any previous council, working responsibly and prayerfully across four years with all the support it could get from the ablest theologians, is clearly in human and ecclesial terms as considerable as can be."[23]

The council fathers clearly sensed the excitement and power of the moment. In liturgical music this meant not so much the discovery of new principles but the authority to interpret according to local circumstance those already part of the Church's musical tradition. This explains the political and practical significance of what first appears to be bureaucratic housekeeping:

> Regulation of the sacred liturgy depends solely on the authority of the church, that is, on the apostolic see and, in accordance with law, on the bishop. (SC 22.1)
>
> In virtue of power conferred on them by the law, the regulation of the liturgy within certain defined limits belongs also to various kinds of groupings of bishops, legitimately established, with competence in given territories. (SC 22.2)
>
> Therefore no other person whatsoever, not even a priest, may add, remove, or change anything in the liturgy on their own authority. (SC 22.3)
>
> In order that sound tradition be retained, and yet the way remain open to legitimate progress, a careful investigation—theological, historical, and pastoral—should always, first of all, be made into each section of the liturgy which is to be revised. (SC 23)

Again we hear, particularly in article 22.3, the voice of centralized authority, but again with crucial qualifications, such as the opening of article 23, which presumes a continuing development of the liturgy. The key phrase for the future of liturgical music, however, is article 22.2 because it makes local bishops working within the approved norms, not the Vatican, the principal authority of liturgy within their dioceses.

---

[23] Adrian Hastings, "The Key Texts," in *Modern Catholicism: Vatican II and After*, ed. Adrian Hastings (New York: Oxford University Press, 1991), 56.

Fr. Bugnini points out that this decision was clarified and defined even more clearly by Pope Paul VI in his *Sacram Liturgiam* issued January 25, 1964, little more than a month following the promulgation of *Sacrosanctum Concilium* itself. And Vatican II historian Joseph A. Komonchak notes that the council fathers revised the original schema for the constitution to eliminate the words "with the approval of the holy see" in regard to episcopal government of liturgy.[24]

Add to these new episcopal powers the enormous prestige of the council and the expectations of the outside world. The modern world could follow the progress of this ecumenical council as no other in history, and great things were awaited. *Sacrosanctum Concilium* was in many respects the least contested of the planning schemata forwarded in advance to the council fathers, and finally approved by majorities of well over ninety-nine percent.[25] *Lumen Gentium*, *Gaudium et Spes*, and other documents have since perhaps garnered the lion's share of theologians' and church historians' attention, but nothing has affected the everyday lives of Catholics as has *Sacrosanctum Concilium*. In retrospect, John Paul II was surely right in saying that "for many people the message of the Second Vatican Council has been experienced principally through liturgical reform."[26]

Add to this imperative for bishops to act, once the constitution had been approved, the clearest of all imperatives that it presented: *participatio actuosa*, or "active participation," as it is usually translated, by the laity. This is by far the strongest note of change and renewal sounded in the document. Add to that, alas, a general ignorance of the musical tradition. Few bishops knew plainchant. It was considered a remarkable innovation symbolic of *Sacrosanctum Concilium*'s reform when a Fr. Franquesa requested of the pope that the concluding Mass of the council's first session be sung entirely in plainchant.[27]

The combination of an emboldened episcopacy, euphoric after its unique and intensely collegial experience, a document capable of

---

[24] Joseph A. Komonchak, "The Struggle for the Council during the Preparation of Vatican II (1960–1962)," in *History of Vatican II*, vol. 1, ed. Giuseppe Alberigo, English version ed. Joseph A. Komonchak, (Maryknoll, NY: Orbis, 1995), 209.

[25] Michael J. Walsh reports only four negative votes against, out of over two thousand cast. See "The History of the Council," in *Modern Catholicism: Vatican II and After*, ed. Adrian Hastings (New York: Oxford University Press, 1991), 42.

[26] John Paul II, *Vicesimus Quintus Annus*, art. 12.

[27] Komonchak, "The Struggle for the Council," 185.

broad interpretation on key points concerning liturgical music, a common *cause célébré* in the active participation in the laity, and an urgency to fulfill worldwide expectations proved explosive. The rapid introduction of new kinds of liturgical music was largely uncontrolled, certainly uncoordinated despite the constitution's advice to the contrary,[28] and for the most part unpredictable. Few foresaw the virtual disappearance of liturgical Latin within two or three years among the secular and even much of the regular clergy. Few predicted the near total demise of plainchant. No one imagined how some experiments with folk music in the sacred liturgy in the 1960s would grow into a cultural and economic force that determined most of the liturgical music in the United States at the end of the twentieth century.

These were the consequences, surely unintended, of a right-minded and well-meaning liturgical reform carried out with undue haste. The contrast with the liturgical reforms of the Council of Trent, Vatican II's great predecessor, is instructive. That council opened in 1545 and deliberated for 18 years, promulgating its liturgical documents on December 4, 1563, precisely four centuries in anticipation of *Sacrosanctum Concilium*. Not until 1614, nearly seventy years after the council's opening invocation, were the last chant books released. But all that work of preparation was centralized in Rome, and the world expected nothing much. No need to hurry. The pace of liturgical change after 1963 seems almost born of a crisis atmosphere by comparison.[29] The sheer worldwide scope of the task of suddenly involving the laity, something that should have required decades of reflection and training, required many of the crucial initial judgments and initiatives to be handed over to amateurs, "lovers" in the root sense, yes, of music and of liturgy, with hearts all in the right places, but in serious ways unqualified for the tasks asked of them.

---

[28] SC 23 reads in part: "As far as possible, notable differences between the rites used in adjacent regions must be carefully avoided."

[29] Kavanaugh, "The Conciliar Documents: Liturgy (*Sacrosanctum Concilium*)," discusses the consequences of haste, 70.

Chapter 3

Aftermath of the Council: Rushing to Fill the Void

> If sustained too long, confusion begets demoralization, self-doubt, and finally resignation, a void. All manner of things rush in to fill this void.
> Aidan Kavanaugh, church historian, 1991

To be sure, the reforms initiated by *Sacrosanctum Concilium*, including the musical reforms, were radical in their urgency and worldwide scope. Their focal point was *participatio actuosa*. The pressure for the participation of congregants in the sacred liturgy and liturgical music had been building for over a century, and the force of its explosive release in 1963 was tremendous. Things changed fast: new languages, new orientations, and certainly new music appeared overnight.

Participatio actuosa was immediately understood as "congregational singing." Given the hasty temper of the times, the error is understandable, for congregational singing is certainly the most visible sign of *participatio actuosa* of the entire laity present at a liturgy, and reformers wanted visible results fast to show the world. But the simplistic translation created another problem. The essential difficulty of congregational singing was not really in reforming, in the usual sense of correcting a practice that already existed, but rather in building something almost from nothing. If the fathers of the Second Vatican Council had decided, however improbably, to scrap Gregorian plainchant and substitute Ambrosian instead, that would have meant, in practical terms, church choirs simply exchanging one set of chant books for another. But the fathers asked for no change in the repertory of liturgical music; rather, they asked for a change in its role in the liturgy.

In so doing, they attempted to fill a great void. Yes, there had been various experiments in congregational singing scattered through the world, but no consistent practice that anyone could call a tradition of Catholic congregational singing analogous to, say, the great tradition of Lutheran congregational hymns. Changing the practice, not the repertory, of Catholic liturgical music, even in the most orderly and leisurely of circumstances, meant unseating dispositions, habits, and thinking about church music that had characterized Catholic worship for generations. As Thomas Day has so richly detailed,[1] few Catholic worshipers were ready to transform themselves so suddenly from "dumb and idle spectators" into throaty Welshmen singing "like the bursting of a thunderous sea."[2] Whether this be recalcitrance, inertia, or just plain stubbornness, it is understandable. The liturgy is a complex action, and intelligent participation in it requires years of acculturation, if not explicit training and practice. To ask large groups of musically untutored people accustomed to worshiping in silence to contribute on short notice to the highly specialized and ethereal art that liturgical music should be was a tall order, to say the least.

And yet in the mid-1960s congregational singing quickly became a matter of great urgency, a reform to be initiated as soon as possible. This is also understandable, wrong-headed though it may have been. The euphoric power of the Second Vatican Council could not be wasted, its force deflating slowly over time. Leading Catholics, bishops, and theologians were excited about Catholic renewal. Liturgy was its most visible and visceral sign, and music was the most palpable symbol of the liturgy.

Urgency led to haste, which has proven costly. Rapid instantiation of reforms without sufficient reflection naturally brought about a certain stereotyping and downright misreadings of the documents and intents of the council. We still read them in newspapers today: the banning of Latin and the obsolescence of plainchant are two of the most common leitmotifs. We still feel them in prejudices toward liturgical practice, certainly toward music: plainchant, traditional hymns, and high Renaissance polyphony are "churchy," "old church," and therefore unable to advance renewal, whereas extroverted and emotional popular music embodies the spirit of Vatican II ipso facto. Along with bad stereotypes, the rush to reform brought vernacular translations of traditional prayers with such crude errors that first-year students of Latin could spot them. These effects are all understandable in hindsight, the mistakes one makes when in a hurry.

---

[1] Thomas Day, *Why Catholics Can't Sing* (New York: Crossroad, 1992), chap. 2.
[2] Pius XII, *Mediator Dei*, art. 194.

One ready-made solution to the problem of getting congregations to sing as quickly as possible presented itself in the American church: the sources of Protestant congregational hymns, mostly from the Lutheran and Anglican traditions, were opened so that what had been a trickle of experiments here and there now became a flood. Generally, these hymns replaced the proper antiphons at the entrance of the celebrant, at the offertory, and at Communion, and a recessional hymn was simply added on to the Roman Rite in imitation of Protestant practice.[3] These became "the four hymns" of the Mass (see chap. 10). And in truth, if one had to move quickly on the issue of congregational singing, the importation of Protestant hymnody in some fashion was a reasonable solution. Here was a large repertory of music explicitly designed for congregational singing, winnowed by three or four centuries of practice so that mostly hymns of excellent musical quality remained. But precisely because of such ageing, their sound was redolent of Christian tradition, if not quite the "old church." Within a decade of the council, Catholic musicians who offered their congregations "Praise to the Lord" or "Holy, Holy, Holy," ironically became known to prefer "traditional Catholic church music."

Reformers in the United States wanted a completely new musical symbology, and they turned to a ready-made source: the folk revival. This move begot another historical and musical irony of the council's aftermath. For while they sincerely meant to build new traditions of congregational singing, the proponents of popular folk music in liturgy chose a style that could only guarantee failure and retard any authentic musical renewal for decades.

The Folk Revival Repertory

The coincidence of *Sacrosanctum Concilium* and the early days of the American popular movement known as the folk revival must have seemed a godsend to the proponents of new congregational liturgical musics. Here was a music that, while certainly popular in its origins, was yet a kind of countercultural reaction to the commercial behemoths of both Tin Pan Alley, in its last days, and rock. Its originating

---

[3] Here "antiphon" refers to the texts provided for these liturgical moments by the Roman Missal, regardless of musical setting. The substitution of a congregational hymn meant first of all that the proper texts, almost always biblical, would be eliminated from the liturgy in favor of psalm paraphrases or sacred poetry.

spirit—a kind of "back to basics" aesthetic of acoustic guitars, natural singing, and simple harmonization—seemed kindred to that of the Second Vatican Council itself, whose liturgical constitution *Sacrosanctum Concilium* proclaimed that "the rites should radiate a noble simplicity" (SC 34). There was nothing sacred in the semantics of its musical style. But that was an advantage in many proponents' view, for any sacred semantics were likely to be preconciliar, therefore out-of-bounds. After all, what kind of music could better symbolize liturgical renewal? Having almost nothing in common with any of the "old church" treasures of Catholic musical traditions, the folk revival marked the new liturgical beginning as no other Western music could. And if its connotations were not explicitly religious, they could be still to the good: pacifism, antimaterialism, care for God's earth.

"Be Not Afraid" of Robert J. Dufford, SJ, is as fine an example of this type of liturgical folk music as may be found. Published in 1975, a decade after the close of the council, just after the crest of the first wave of popular liturgical styles, it has all the earmarks of a folk-revival song: a rhythmically subtle, improvisatory melody accompanied by slow chord changes perfectly suited to a guitar, all bound together in consistent four-measure phrases.

Example 3-1. Robert J. Dufford, "Be Not Afraid," verse 1 (mm. 4–19). © 1975, 1978, Robert J. Dufford, SJ, and OCP Publications, 5536 NE Hassalo, Portland, OR 97213. All rights reserved. Used by permission.

Melody: The Complexity of Simplicity

The trademark of the folk revival was an aesthetic simplicity that made its music seem austerely natural by comparison with its commercial rivals. Nothing more than a folksinger and a guitar were required. Artifice was avoided at all costs. The music sounded profound without virtuosity either in composition or performance. When the singers accompanied themselves, it was almost as if the songs were being invented on the spot, inspired improvisations coming directly from the heart.

"Be Not Afraid" has exactly this kind of melody. The first three phrases are nearly monotonic, the first centering on D, the second higher on the tonic G, and the third higher still on B, a design that sounds nothing like a design, and yet creates a gentle rise in tension as the song proceeds. This tension blooms in the fourth phrase, "You shall see . . . ," as it breaks free of monotony while actually pausing in a summary fashion on all three of the structural pitches heard earlier. The second phrase of the refrain, "I go before you always," continues working with this same arch-like melodic contour. The whole is a beautifully coherent idea.

The melody presents at the same time a wondrous variety of rhythmic figures. There are fast pickup notes at the very beginning ("You shall"), single dotted patterns in both the more common long-short form ("speak your words in") and the unusual short-long form ("wander"), *double* dotted patterns in both forms ("cross the" and "desert"), and a few very long notes. The longest note in the song is twenty-eight times as long as the shortest, a remarkable index of the rhythmic range of the piece. The reason for such range, not at all uncommon in this style, is a meticulous setting of the lyric. The composer seems almost to have translated the normal speech rhythms of the text directly into musical notation. This accounts for the writing out of verses two and three, not shown in the example 3-1, which have basically the same tune but slightly different rhythms owing to small changes in word accentuation. The melody stresses important syllables with long notes or by locating them on the strong (first or third) beats of measures. The diction of the melody is as natural as conversation.

The monotonic structure and rhythmic detail of the melody combine to make a paradoxical impression: the tune sounds almost improvised, as if the singer were inventing it while singing. The impression is paradoxical because its elements are anything but simple, merely confirming what has long been known from the history of Western music: to compose something that sounds easy and made-up on the spot involves a great deal of learning, work, calculation, planning, and ingenuity. It does seem the epitome of naturalness that someone with a guitar improvising on this lyric would borrow the rhythms of speech and at least begin with a simple melodic form such as a monotone. To retain this character in a permanent, well-formed piece is no small feat.

But the tune cannot survive congregational singing. This is the sad fact. It has been tried in thousands of American liturgies, and I have never once heard it sung correctly, as notated. The melodic contour and range offer no problems, but no human congregation can possibly execute all those various rhythms with any accuracy or ensemble. Indeed, a congregation cannot even sing together the beginning. Even for a trained choir, the first two short notes in moderate tempo are very hard to sing together. They take just one half of a beat![4]

The irony of this situation is that Bob Dylan or Joni Mitchell would not sing the song "correctly" either. Play any of Dylan's published

---

[4] What usually happens in an actual liturgy is that, after a ragged entrance by the congregation, the various dotted rhythms so meticulously matched to the lyric are all regularized, with the sixteenths doubled in length to make easier eighth notes. This rhythmic alternation creates not only an uncertainty about what to sing, but another problem altogether having to do with simple rhythms, as will be discussed shortly.

songs on the piano in strict rhythm; they are almost completely enervated of their original force. The folk-revival style depends on subtle jazzlike departures from the "real," idealized rhythms expressed in notation. Musical notation captures but an outline, a line drawing of what really happens when Dylan sings. Much of the natural and improvisatory character of folk-revival singing comes from just that, improvising on a tiny rhythmic scale, never to be repeated, too small to be notated but plenty big enough to be heard and appreciated.

This is why "Be Not Afraid" cannot succeed even with an ideal congregation. Imagine one as angelic as you wish. It will indeed sing the song note perfect, but in its perfection and rhythmic precision, sung by a large group rather than an individual singer, it must have unanimity, and it will lose all of the improvisatory character essential to the folk-revival style and come out as a stilted and stuffy exercise, as if the Rockettes all together danced the part of the prima ballerina. Dufford has done a remarkable thing in translating this character into rhythm and melody, but he cannot divorce the style from what it essentially is: a solo style.

Translating the Harmony

Listening to other artists cover Bob Dylan's songs throws into relief an important aspect of his original arrangements: they are harmonically ascetic, often surviving with just two or three chords from the key of the song and a minimal number of changes.[5] This seems to be conscious refusal on his part to exploit the harmonic richness latent in his conceptions, which covering artists in many cases have mined with apparent joy. But harmonic asceticism, again, is typical of the early folk-revival style, and we hear vestiges of it in "Be Not Afraid."

The first phrase is carried entirely by one essential harmony, the tonic harmony of G major. One can read this fact easily in the guitar chord symbols written above Theophane Hytrek's keyboard arrangement (which, incidentally, probably enriches Fr. Dufford's original guitar harmonization considerably). Every symbol, if not a simple G chord, is a variant based on G. In the keyboard part, the left hand is

---

[5] A "cover" is a new arrangement of a popular song by an artist other than the composer or originating artist. Dylan's early songs, spartan in their original simplicity, have been covered by many artists who typically dress up the music with more varied harmonies and fuller instrumentation.

dominated by the low G sustained over all four measures of the phrase. Scanning further on, the symbols change at a somewhat faster pace, but the rate of harmonic change, what is called the harmonic rhythm, is in general much slower than that of, say, a traditional Anglican hymn such as "O God Our Help in Ages Past."[6] Another fact to note: the harmonic changes, without exception, are aligned with strong beats, that is, the first or third beats of the four-beat measure.

The leisurely harmonic progressions are all of a piece with the naturalistic aesthetic of the folk revival. Whenever one harmony progresses to another in any Western style, the change requires a kind of coordination of the harmony with the melody, a momentary interdependence which constrains both elements. Fast harmonic rhythm, as in "O God Our Help" and other hymns, limits the freedom of the melody a great deal and produces a song that sounds learned, accomplished, and by comparison to the folk song, artificial in one sense, because in fact it takes a great deal of musical training to be able to control this melodic and harmonic coordination that is the very soul of Western music.[7] On the other hand, very slow harmonic rhythm, as in the beginning of "Be Not Afraid," allows the tune to move as freely as a bird, naturally abetting the illusion of simplicity and extemporary invention direct from the common man's inspiration.

This musical texture—a prominent, strong melody with a simple and fairly slow harmonic background—is known as homophony, and is typical of all kinds of harmonized folk music.[8] It is no accident that the acoustic guitar was the principal instrument of the folk revival, for it is the natural instrument for this homophonic texture. A decent picking technique, or even an energetic strum, can enliven a single

---

[6] This is the technical reason why, with this kind of music, one often hears singers, both in the choir and congregation, improvising a vocal harmony with the main tune. With the harmonies lasting so long, it is easy for anyone with a reasonable musical ear to find a third over the tune or a sixth below. *Why* singers should feel compelled to do so points to the liturgical poverty of the style.

[7] The popular images of Bach and Mozart as inspired geniuses who naturally composed great counterpoint without any learning is not correct. Geniuses they were, but they and Handel, Beethoven, Palestrina, and all the other big names took lessons from their older predecessors in precisely this art of coordinating melody and harmonic changes.

[8] It should be noted that most of the world's indigenous folk musics, in their traditional forms, are not harmonized. Harmony, or the presence of simultaneous melodies, is what sets Western music apart from that of other cultures.

chord lasting four measures enough to hold our interest, without getting in the way of the singer's melody. When we bring "Be Not Afraid" into church, however, and replace the guitar with an organ, the slow harmony becomes a deadweight. The organ is built for sustaining tones; it is just possible to mimic the rhythmic articulations of an acoustic guitar, but the effect is ridiculous because that is not the organ's idiom.[9] On the organ, the sustained harmony that opens "Be Not Afraid" just sits there, inert. The obvious and easy solution of simply restoring the guitar or using the piano, which has some power of rhythmic articulation, brings its own semantic problems.[10] Simply put for now, the guitar or the piano (or the jazz combo or kazoo band) in liturgy do not carry the same connotations as does the organ. Instruments are not semantically neutral.[11]

The Tyranny of the Phrase

Western music of the last four centuries has a certain grammar, expected sequences that govern its harmonic changes. The chords have functions to perform in the music, such as beginning, ending, creating and resolving tension, carrying motion forward, and so on. When harmonic rhythm is slow, as in "Be Not Afraid," the amount of time required to accomplish these functions stretches over a significant period that extends beyond listeners' capacities to hold all the musical information in working memory.[12] There must be a formal unit shorter

---

[9] This explains the presence of many notes in Hytrek's keyboard arrangement that do not belong to the prevailing chord: they attempt to enliven a static harmony.

[10] See chap. 12.

[11] As evidence, witness the recordings of "new age" church favorites, where traditional melodies, such as the Latin hymn *Pange lingua*, are clothed with a warm blanket of strings, and the plainchant melody is played by an alto saxophone. Virtually none of the original sacred semantic remains, even though the tune is identical to the one chanted a cappella during the Eurcharistic procession that ends the Mass of the Lord's Supper on Holy Thursday. Indeed, it is difficult even to recognize it.

[12] The limitations on human memory constrain traditions of composition in all cultures. Most musical structures, especially hierarchical ones, owe some part of their explanation to the limits of human capacity to process rich incoming information in real time. The psychological literature on this topic is quite large. For an introduction particularly germane to music, see Bob Snyder, *Music and Memory* (Cambridge, MA: MIT Press, 2000), 47–58.

than the harmonic sentence to organize this information for the listener, and in the style of the folk revival, as well as in most other kinds of popular music of the last century, that unit is a periodically articulated phrase. The phrase itself is constructed of even shorter units of time called measures, almost always an even number of them, such as two, four, or eight, because these numbers subdivide evenly into symmetrical halves or even quarters which make the music easy to process and understand.[13] This is why so many popular song forms are twelve, sixteen, or thirty-two measures in length, all exponential expressions of the basic two-measure unit. "Be Not Afraid" is no exception. Each of its four phrases in the first verse is exactly four measures long.

One fundamental rule of all songwriting is to coordinate these melodic phrases with the textual. The musical phrase must contain a group of words that is syntactically coherent. No songwriter worth his salt would ever end a beautiful melodic curve with the word "the" or "and," except in very extraordinary, usually comic circumstances, such as in some Broadway satire. Therefore an articulated periodic song form such as the verse of "Be Not Afraid," composed of four four-measure phrases, must set a quatrain, four lines of similar length and accent pattern, each of which makes a complete grammatical unit of some kind. And in fact, the lyrics here are quite conservative: three lines of hexameter, one of pentameter, each a complete sentence.

One liturgically unfortunate consequence of this matching is the frequent need to sustain words or even single syllables for far longer than they would otherwise warrant, just to maintain the symmetry of phrasing. The last line of the opening verse in "Be Not Afraid"—"You shall see the face of God and live"—has only five accents (poetic feet) rather than the hexameter of the previous three lines. But the melodic structure cannot tolerate amputating a portion of its length to match the fewer syllables. Symmetry requires a phrase of four measures just like all the rest preceding. Therefore the word "live" is sustained for nearly two full measures, twice as long as any previous phrase ending.

---

[13] This is because the mind more easily apprehends like structures to combine them into higher-order structures in a hierarchical arrangement, the basis for most complex information processing. A four-bar phrase splits into two two-bar half phrases, similar to each other in terms of their time length, so important in music, which in turn can split into two similar measures each. See David Butler, *The Musician's Guide to Perception and Cognition* (New York: Schirmer, 1992), 103–14.

Well, why didn't Dufford stick in two more syllables to make the text match up? Probably because he needed a long D harmony, an important tension function called the dominant in the key of G major, in order to set up the refrain. Because the general harmonic pace of the song is so slow, a shorter D harmony would not carry sufficient weight for the verse's half cadence.

The periodic melodic phrasing limits the folk revival and most any other popular style to texts of traditional, conservative poetic form: strong meters, frequently articulated with rhyme, and lines of commensurate length as measured by accents. The form and diction of the text are ruled by the form of the melody.

What can this mean, then, when we consider the Ordinary prayers of the Mass, the five traditional texts set to music by hundreds of composers for thousands of years—the *Kyrie* (Lord, Have Mercy), the *Gloria* (Glory to God), the *Credo* (I Believe in One God), the *Sanctus* (Holy, Holy, Holy), and the *Agnus Dei* (Lamb of God)—the prayers that should enjoy a liturgical precedence over songs that replace the traditional entrance, offertory, and communion antiphons?[14] It means, first of all, that the longer prayers of *Gloria* and *Credo* are nearly impossible to render in this musical style. They have prose texts without the slightest regularity of form. Imagine the extension of the word "live" just noted in "Be Not Afraid" applied at every turn in these long prayers and one can understand immediately why they have rarely been turned into folk songs.

One such "Glory to God" from the *St. Louis Jesuits Mass* was composed by John B. Foley, SJ, and first published in 1978.[15] It shows the same features as "Be Not Afraid." Every musical phrase is two or four measures, the relentless symmetry requiring the extension of the single, unaccented syllables "-ry" from "glory" and "-cy" from "mercy" to one and one-half bars. Even then, the setting cannot survive without deforming the traditional text. To give some kind of comprehensible song form to the piece, the opening, "Glory to God in the highest and peace to his people on earth," must be composed into a refrain of two

---

[14] Regarding the liturgical precedence, see *Musicam Sacram* (Instruction on Music in the Liturgy), given March 5, 1967, art. 30. From this point, I refer to these by their traditional Latin incipits, more traditional and more economical.

[15] Oregon Catholic Press. It may be found in several publications, such as *Heritage Missal 2007* (Portland, OR: Oregon Catholic Press, 2006), 47.

balanced four-measure phrases.[16] This is typical. Such rare examples of the *Gloria* and the *Credo* as do exist can only have employed un-canonical texts, versified, often with refrains, stretched and shrunk to fit the procrustean bed of the periodic phrasing.

There are numerous popular settings of the shorter Ordinaries, and they suffer from the same tyrannical periodic phrasing, surviving only by virtue of their brevity. We hear syllables unnaturally extended to fill out the musical phrase. We hear troped texts—"Jesus, Lamb of God" is a current favorite—to provide extra syllables to take up the musical slack. And we hear entire texts such as "Christ has died, Christ has risen, Christ will come again" needlessly repeated; needlessly, that is, from the liturgical point of view. From the musical point of view, the necessity is all too apparent, since a single musical phrase for this short text cannot make a balanced, symmetrical melodic form, can it? There must be a minimum of two phrases, whether the liturgy warrants them or not.

The Facts of the Case

Without even touching on the divisive semantic issue of whether it is a good thing to introduce the folk-revival style into the sacred liturgy, the lesson of "Be Not Afraid" is clear: the technical aspects of the folk-revival style—its building blocks, its elements—are such that it can never be the foundation of any enduring renewal of liturgical music. In several ways, "Be Not Afraid" is an admirable composition: it has a logically constructed yet freely varied melody, a good traditional form, subtly varied rhythm, and sturdy harmonic construction. It would do very well in a coffee house or in a retreat setting. Our appreciation of it actually teaches a good lesson: good music never guarantees good *liturgical* music. The uncomfortable facts speak the truth. The song's leisurely harmonic rhythm and lockstep melodic phrasing are incompatible with the dynamic action that is the liturgy. But most ruinous of all is the piece's lovely tune, for it cannot be sung by a congregation.

But how composers have tried to save it!

---

[16] This translation of the *Gloria* is now obsolete, replaced by the revised Missal, which in the United States has been used since Advent 2011. However, the newer translation poses the same problems for the folk-revival style.

An alternative wave of popular liturgy song gathered headway in the 1970s, represented by pieces such as "Hosea (Come Back To Me)" by Gregory Norbet, OSB (1972), "Sing A New Song" by Daniel L. Schutte (1972), Foley's "Glory to God," and the famous "Celtic Alleluia" by Fintan O'Carroll and Christopher Walker (1985).[17] These songs and their like deal with the melodic problems of "Be Not Afraid" with surgery: all the rhythmic difficulty is simply cut away.

Example 3-2. Fintan O'Carroll and Christopher Walker, "Celtic Alleluia" (mm. 1–8). © 1985, Fintan O'Carroll and Christopher Walker. Published by OCP Publications, 5536 NE Hassalo, Portland, OR 97213. All rights reserved. Used by permission.

---

[17] M. Francis Mannion offers a different but very useful typology of the modern repertory in his chapter "Paradigms in American Catholic Liturgical Music," in *Masterworks of God: Essays in Liturgical Theory and Practice* (Chicago: Liturgy Training Publications, 2004), 116–43.

The phrasing of this refrain is exactly as it was in "Be Not Afraid," four phrases of four metrical groups each.[18] Its symmetry is even more rigorous, as the first pair of phrases (mm. 1–4) is matched to the second pair (mm. 5–8) in a traditional mirror structure known in classical music for three centuries as the antecedent-consequent period, a kind of question and answer form, with the cadences making the essential difference. The harmonic rhythm is basically two changes per measure, or better, one change for each three-beat group, the real meter here. The only exceptions are occasional brief D chords occurring at the end of groups.

The departure from the founding style of the folk revival is in the tune, vastly simpler and much easier for a large group to sing than that of "Be Not Afraid." Each of the four phrases has a nearly identical rhythmic pattern. The longest note is only six times as long as the shortest, not twenty-eight times, a much more manageable range, and there are only three different rhythmic patterns to learn: the long-short, the three even notes, and the dotted pattern, each occupying precisely one easily digestible metric group. There are no difficult pickups to negotiate; the tune starts right on the beginning of the measure, the easiest point for congregations to enter. There can be no doubt about parishes' experiences with the popular "Celtic Alleluia": it is as easy for congregations to learn and to sing as a child's nursery rhyme.

And that is about the level of musical sophistication that it attains. In the classic folk-revival style of the 1960s, all the song's musical interest and rhythmic complexity, which can truly be formidable, is

---

[18] Here the musical notation obscures somewhat a structural identity. The meter of the refrain is undeniably triple, but rather than notate the music in 3/8 measures, the composers use the more common 6/8, which is easier for musicians to read. One measure of 6/8 is equal to two of 3/8, which is why I claim the structural identity with "Be Not Afraid," since the 3/8 represents the perceptually real group of triple. The 6/8 is technically known as a compound meter, a combination of triple on the low level and duple on the high level, but in this work the combination of tempo and harmonic change are such that the duple level is negligible, and the whole song could be renotated into 3/8 with no noticeable change in effect.

Measure 7 is notated in 9/8, but again, this hides a perceptual identity. Every phrase to that point has placed the phrase ending on the second half of the 6/8 bar, and listeners will not change their habits at the end. They will hear the "-ia" in the same metrical position as in the other three phrases, with the last tone in measure 8 merely extended, as if under a fermata. Bar lines and time signatures do not determine listeners' perceptions. See Joseph P. Swain, *Harmonic Rhythm: Analysis and Interpretation* (New York: Oxford University Press, 2002), 91–97.

concentrated in the singer's melody. The soloist creates and controls the artistry, chiefly through the subtlest rhythmic inflections in performance. The second wave of pop liturgical music has cut away all that subtlety, without the least compensation in the other musical elements, the harmony or the phrasing, which remain the same as before. The result is a style not merely simplified; it is impoverished. No wonder that so many singers of this kind of music improvise a vocal harmony over the top melody. There is a nakedness that needs covering.

This radical melodic simplification in many of these songs offends against good taste with an overbearing sense of beat that increases the impression of a nursery rhyme that much more. To understand how this comes about, we must know a bit about musical meter.

Singsong Syndrome

The perception of meter arises when the beats of the music seem grouped together in a consistent number, most often in twos or threes, which produce duple and triple meters, the most common types in the Western tradition.[19] They distinguish marches, foxtrots, and "Be Not Afraid" (all duple) from waltzes, Irish slip jigs, and the "Celtic Alleluia" (triple). Meter is expressed in musical notation by the bar lines, which explicitly show the beat groups. Between each pair is notated a consistent and precise number of beats. The first beat of a group or measure is called the downbeat, from the conductor's traditional downward motion of the hand, and is always metrically strong, or stressed, defining the beginning of each group.

Notation, by itself, cannot produce a sense of duple or triple; it only reflects what the composer believes the meter to be.[20] The composer must write into the music regular stresses—longer notes, very high or

---

[19] In musical notation, the two basic meters have various expressions: 2/4, 4/4, and 2/2 are all duple meters, while 3/8, 3/4, 3/2 are all triples. Compound time signatures such as 6/8 explicitly indicate what is always true, that meter has different levels of experience. The salience of duple or triple in pieces written with a compound time signature depends upon many local factors, including tempo, harmonic rhythm, and other phenomena. For more on the psychology of meter, see Justin London, *Hearing in Time: Psychological Aspects of Musical Meter* (New York: Oxford University Press, 2004).

[20] Notation usually expresses the prevailing meter of a piece in the top numeral of the time signature located at the very beginning. The numeral "2" or one of its multiples indicates duple meter; "3" or one of its multiples, triple; the lower

very low notes, phrase beginnings, loud notes, chord changes, etc.—which mark the beginnings of groups, from which the listener abstracts a meter. This is much easier to do than to describe. Children making up songs create meter quite naturally and unconsciously.

The artistry of meter is not so much in its categorical distinction between duple and triple, a straightforward affair, but rather in controlling its salience or strength of presence in the music. Meter is not simply duple or triple, on or off, but can have degree within: strongly duple, mildly duple, weakly triple, even changing as the piece goes on. The key is how the composer handles all those aforementioned methods of stressing the beats.

In "Be Not Afraid," for example, duple meter arises chiefly from the harmonic changes, one of the most powerful of musical stresses, occurring every two beats. But the duple meter of the song is not the driving beat of a disco dance or rock song. Rather it is a very gentle duple, because the composer keeps other kinds of stress away from those all-important chord changes. The melody starts ahead of the bar line, not on the strong beat of the measure. Many long notes of the tune, naturally stressed, sound in the middle of the measure, not at the beginning.[21] Then again, the first phrase has no really important chord changes at all, so the perception of meter at the song's opening is winsomely inchoate. Generally, the rhythmic complexity that puts the melody beyond the reach of a congregation creates a variable metric quality that suits a solo singer very well.

The "Celtic Alleluia," by contrast, is a singsong, with its relentless triple meter pounding with the subtlety of a sledge hammer. Here the harmonic changes, defining the strong beats, are aligned with the other stress factors: the longer notes, the higher notes, the beginnings and endings of phrases. One may wonder whether those D harmonies on weak eighth notes in measures 1, 3, and 7 might mitigate this effect. In fact they exacerbate it, because D harmony in a G major tune such as this represents the most powerful harmonic function of the dominant, a musical tension point that is metrically weak and leads naturally to the downbeat. They act like extra drivers for the sledge, not distracting restraints. If the song has a childish character, it is because the

---

numeral indicates which kind of written note is assigned the duration value of one beat.

[21] The refrain does this to an even greater degree. The second phrase, "I go before . . . ," begins on the weak beat.

composer has written into its metric patterns exactly what children do naturally when they invent their nursery songs. The "Celtic Alleluia," "Sing a New Song," "Hosea," and all the other simplified folk songs solve the problem of rhythmic complexity for the congregation but only at the enormous cost of a presentation that is inevitably trite.

Harmonic Betrayal

The rapid demise of most of these creations perhaps convinced some composers of liturgical pop that something had to take the place of the rhythmic interest lost in the effort to accommodate congregational singing. Their solution, glimpsed in the versicle of the "Celtic Alleluia," is chromatic harmonization.[22]

Example 3-3. Fintan O'Carroll and Christopher Walker, "Celtic Alleluia" (mm. 9–15). © 1985, Fintan O'Carroll and Christopher Walker. Published by OCP Publications, 5536 NE Hassalo, Portland, OR 97213. All rights reserved. Used by permission.

[22] Chromaticism in music is the use of pitches not in the key or scale in force.

The singsong effect is less here, owing to some harmonic changes that depart from the steady diatonic diet of strong chords in G major heard in the refrain: the F major on the words "servant is . . ." and then the C minor and B-flat harmony just before the last suspenseful half cadence. It is difficult to say whether the F major harmony, the lowered seventh of the key of G, is an allusion to the ancient church modes of hallowed tradition or simply a borrowing of the same kind of altered dominant that crops up in much popular music of the 1980s and 90s.[23] But there is no doubt that the shift into the minor mode of G at the words "speak are everlasting . . ." is a typically romantic ploy of creating chromatic disturbance just before the cadence, building into a Hollywood climax leading to the triumphant return of the refrain. Remarkably, the last phrase is only two perceptual measures long, a welcome if temporary escape from the four-measure straitjacket that binds the rest of the song; but in actual practice the straitjacket is so strong that most performers add two more measures (one printed measure) of D major harmony to make the song "come out right" before refrain resumes.

The composers of this third wave have abandoned all pretense to the natural aesthetic of the folk-revival style, for which such chromatic devices were anathema, the commercial trappings of the establishment songs of Henry Mancini and his Tin Pan Alley dance band crowd. Such chromaticism has been enjoined to save the musical poverty of the singsong, and the strategy is technically sound, but the rescue has merely exchanged the trite for the secular. The associations of an easy-listening romanticism emanating from family restaurants and department stores of the late twentieth century are much too strong to ignore. Now we touch on the issues of semantic propriety in liturgical music, which are complex indeed.[24]

One disturbance lingers in the face of all this reasoning: if the music of the folk-revival style and its mutants is as bad as the facts would tell and so unsuited to liturgy, why does it still hang on? "Be Not Afraid" is over thirty years old and is still heard, although with de-

---

[23] "Church modes" refer to a system of scales as old as our earliest musical sources. The modes differ in their technical makeup—their internal patterns of half steps and whole steps—from the major and minor scales that modern Westerners are familiar with. They are the basis of Gregorian and other plainchants as well as most polyphony composed before 1700.

[24] See chap. 12 for a full treatment of the semantics of liturgical music.

clining frequency, in liturgies of respectable parishes. The "Celtic Alleluia" seems ubiquitous. The empirical argument of widespread success—"it works, so it must be all right"—would seem to overpower all theoretical argument. The data supporting such an argument are not what they seem.

First, evidence of great singing is almost always overstated. If fifty worshipers in a congregation of two hundred sing—the usual proportion I have observed—yes, one will hear some sound, but that hardly counts as a ringing success for congregational singing. "The folk music which became a symbol of the post-Vatican II Mass leads to very mixed results: it is often associated with very enthusiastic participation, but the participation is usually by a limited part of the congregation. Just as often, a congregation is quite unresponsive to folk music," baldly states The Notre Dame Study, a major sociological survey of the mid-1980s.[25] In most cases it is impossible to say how enthusiastic and spirited the singing is, because the congregation is dominated by a song leader armed with weapons of mass destruction, the microphone and amplifier. Originally imagined as the perfect modern device to encourage singing, the microphone has the opposite effect, much as when amateur golfers suddenly become shy about their playing with the arrival of a pro. But the microphone will indeed cover a multitude of sins of omission with a glitzy blanket of artificial sound.

Second, our perspective is necessarily myopic. Thirty years for us who live through them seem long, but for the history of the music of the Catholic Church, they are no more than a watch in the night. Other periods of musical waywardness have lasted far longer.[26] In short, the success story, if such it be, of the folk revival music is too short to trust. Third, the confusion in the current state of the art amplifies the promise of mediocrity. When there are so many solutions that are offered and so little promise of stability, even a lightweight and temporary anchor seems better than none.

Fourth, to observe that the music works well means little as long as no comparisons have been made; it judges the best of one or two

---

[25] See Jim Castelli and Joseph Gremillion, *The Emerging Parish: The Notre Dame Study of Catholic Life since Vatican II*, (San Francisco: Harper & Row, 1987), 130.

[26] One could point to the entire eighteenth century. Then the situation of liturgical music was so poor that it spawned two renewal and recovery movements (see chap. 2).

candidates. The musical slate of American congregations for forty years has been folk-revival repertory and its descendants, a large dose of Protestant hymnody, and a few Catholic chestnuts such as "Immaculate Mary." Most American and European Catholics have never heard a *novus ordo* (reformed Roman Rite) Mass sung without most of the propers replaced by songs.[27] The preference of *Sacrosanctum Concilium* —plainchant—remains almost completely untried, owing to prejudice, that is, judgment without knowledge. It is as reasonable to conclude that folk-revival music must be good for liturgy because it is everywhere as to say that a one-candidate election in a dictatorship produces the most popular and best president.

Finally, the argument assumes that the fact of singing is the only virtue to be sought. That is, as long as all two hundred worshipers did sing "Be Not Afraid," the poor quality of the musical offering to God need not concern us, even if the congregation could not start that fussy rhythm without being ragged, could not end the first verse without flagging on the long, long "live," and could not keep up with the varying rhythmic inflections meticulously matched to each new verse. Even if by a minor miracle they could do all these, the result would be an emasculated folk-revival song, like the Mormon Tabernacle Choir singing "Blowin' in the Wind," sadly laughable. The assumption is false. The simple fact of congregational singing is not good enough for liturgy; what comes forth should be something worthy of it. To argue otherwise is to admit that what happens at liturgy is less important than what happens at the local high-school concert, where everyone strives to provide the best music their talents allow. That worshipers do sing is indeed a liturgical value, but only one among many.[28]

The discomfort of postconciliar liturgical music derives not necessarily from a lack of artistry, although that is certainly common enough, but from a gross mismatch of the musical style, the liturgy, and the character and competence of the congregation. The rhythmic ingenuity of the folk revival is essentially soloistic. There is no saving

---

[27] The replacement is canonical. For more details, see chap. 6.

[28] The same point was made back in the mid-1960s by Robert I. Blanchard, no opponent of liturgical reform: "Participation of the people (congregation as opposed to choir) at any cost is one extreme. As long as the people are singing, it matters not *what* they are singing. We have heard the results of this thinking . . ." See "Church Music Today—the Center Position," in *Crisis in Church Music?* (Washington, DC: The Liturgical Conference, 1967), 67.

this technical contradiction of style and liturgy. Even if a congregation were trained to the point of perfect rhythmic precision, that very precision would ruin the free play of the sung rhythm that the style is supposed to embody.

Mediocrity has another cause too. This music has support from outside the world of music, in contravention of the musical facts. The culture at large wishes it to succeed, even when, in the long run, it cannot. Now we must face the politics of this music.

Chapter 4

Aftermath of the Council: Democratization of the Liturgy[*]

> Liturgy can only be liturgy to the extent that it is beyond the manipulation of those who celebrate it.
>
> Joseph Cardinal Ratzinger (1986)

Ecumenical councils, being human enterprises, albeit carried out with divine assistance, are subject to political and cultural forces of their times. As others have judged, the Second Vatican Council's views on liturgy were influenced mightily by many decades of historical research, both in liturgy and Scripture, that recorded the many incremental changes occurring over the centuries and saw many of them as so much tarnish to be scrubbed off to reveal the pure Grail of the liturgy.[1] Aidan Nichols, in *Looking at the Liturgy* (1996), has criticized this view as informed by an immature sociology that fails especially to take into account what had been learned about the accrual of symbols and rituals in communities. But another cultural force, too obvious to be analyzed by scholars, perhaps affected actual practice of liturgy and liturgical music even more. The Cold War made it seem particularly virtuous, and even since 1989 the rise to power of autocracies in Africa and in the Islamic world has only increased its allure: democratization.

This term and its verbal parent, "democratize," imply the making or reform of something into a democracy—or at least into having a democratic character—of something that formerly was not. To say

---

[*] A version of this chapter appeared as "Music is an Uncompromising Meritocracy," *Catholic World Report* 17, no. 5 (May 2007): 41–47. Used by permission.

[1] The attitude is curiously reminiscent of the early Protestant, especially Anglican, view of Catholic theology, that it had to be purified of "developments" incorporated through the centuries in order to recover the "primitive" doctrines of the apostolic traditions.

that democratization is an important agent for change in the modern church is an understatement, and in liturgy in particular it can explain many of the reforms, both lauded and lamented, of the past four decades. Since in the popular conception democratization means distributing power among the members of the body politic, the perceived value of the individual rises in comparison to any central authority, indeed even in comparison to God. Everyone has a right, yes, even a responsibility, to some role in liturgy. "All the faithful should be led to take that full, conscious, and active part in liturgical celebrations which is demanded by the very nature of the liturgy, and to which the Christian people . . . have a right and to which they are bound by reason of their Baptism" (SC 14). Every individual is potentially important and deserving of attention, which means that everyone has access almost regardless of qualification, in the same way that most everyone in a democracy can vote.

The value of democratization is unquestioned, and it is true that some of its effects on the institutional church have been most salutary, most of all in its reinforcement of *participatio actuosa*, the Second Vatican Council's insistence that congregants actually pray and sing together in a corporate spirit and body that transforms them from spectators to contributors to the liturgical action. Nevertheless, as Robert P. Kraynak argues in *Christian Faith and Modern Democracy*, the reconciliation of democratic principles with Roman Catholicism, whose theology makes the kingdom of God a central image and yet recognizes a freedom of conscience, is problematic to say the least. No less problematic is the democratization of liturgical music.

Music and democracy do not get along very well. Music is the most communal of the fine arts, so this seems a paradox, but is nonetheless the fact. When music aspires to anything greater than the pub song, democracy proves to be highly impractical, and the greater the number of people involved (usually a sign of a successful democracy) the greater the impracticality.

Symphony orchestras and large choruses, the two proud flagships of Western music, are among the least democratic of human institutions. Here, highly skilled and artistically gifted men and women surrender precisely what democracy prizes most—individual opinions, interpretations, decision-making, improvisation, physical autonomy, and, to a great extent, freedom of speech—to the absolute rule of the philosopher-king who is the conductor. Individualism of any kind is the enemy of such music. The last thing orchestra violinists or singers want is to be heard as individuals, to have audible character. Rather, their goal is to blend into the group as much as possible, to become an anonymous supernumerary.

And why do these intelligent people cede their rights so cheerfully? In order to create a work of high art, unique in all creation, whose becoming depends upon their total dedication and surrender to the communal action that is the orchestra or chorus. But the point of it all is not communal action itself, communal spirit, togetherness, or any such thing, but the music itself, to make it as great as its potential allows. It is not a bad analogue for liturgy.

Because democracy and sophisticated music making are not compatible, liturgical reforms that democratize its music have serious effects.

Folk and Popular Music

One effect is an open and uncritical engagement of popular musics the world over. The commonly accepted notions of democracy naturally prize the arts of the commoners, so indigenous songs that liturgical authorities would never have admitted to liturgy before Vatican II are now the liturgical music of choice.[2] "Therefore, in the musical training of missionaries, special care should be taken to ensure that they will be capable of encouraging the traditional music of those peoples both in the schools and in sacred services, as far as may be practicable" (SC 119). Despite the particular context of the missions for article 119, there is more than a hint of encouragement for a massive importation of native musics in *Sacrosanctum Concilium*.

The liturgical music of the American folk revival beginning in the mid-1960s, despite its intrinsic obstacles to congregational singing, began the flood.[3] By the late 1980s if not sooner, the guitar idiom crossed the Atlantic to European parishes, and American pop styles could be heard in the great Gothic and baroque churches of Italy. But even if American culture had not been as chic as it was, cultivated

---

[2] This is not to say that indigenous popular songs never found their way into Catholic liturgy before 1963. On the contrary, the history of Catholic liturgical music reform is largely one of how to incorporate popular inventions appropriately into the liturgy while preserving the proper semantics and liturgical functions. See chap. 10.

[3] See chap. 3.

among the European youth even if disdained by their elders, something similar would have happened anyway. In Latin America and Africa, too, local idioms became the basis of liturgical music. It is an easy and attractive solution to the problem of what to sing in the liturgy, of filling the Catholic musical void, at least at first, and not without certain virtues, one of which is certainly that the music is not imposed from outside by a foreign tradition but arises naturally from the people and therefore seems as democratic as music can be.

In most cases, the acceptance of folk idioms has been entirely uncritical. That is, whether a composition, as music, is excellent or not, whether it is appropriate for liturgy or used properly within liturgy, seem rarely considered. In many places, to suggest that a popular idiom would not do for the divine presence was to brand oneself as a reactionary who rejected the spirit of the council, no longer to be taken seriously. This refusal to judge the music has proved in many places to be a costly mistake, for in place of a robust tradition of liturgical music, parishioners, at least in America, have a revolving door.

Anyone alive today who remembers the liturgical folk music of the 1960s knows the revolving door very well. The first wave brought Dylanesque melodies in symmetrical phrases, enlivened with syncopated rhythms, and pedestrian harmony that could accommodate both the expert guitarist and the master of three chords. The 1970s brought the rhythmically impoverished songs from the Weston Priory, located in wholesome Vermont, and from the St. Louis Jesuits; in the 1980s *Glory and Praise* became the latest bestseller; in the 1990s a less centralized set of composers turned to modal and chromatic harmonies to compensate for melodies shorn of their rhythmic interest and difficulty. The new music in each decade ushered out the old stuff of the previous. And that is only the big picture. At the parochial level, music directors introduced local favorites and even new Mass Ordinaries regularly, while those learned the previous year were forgotten, perhaps no longer printed in the latest issue of the disposable missalettes.[4]

---

[4] The Notre Dame Study found that in the mid-1980s "Parishes which used missalettes were more likely to show a lack of community awareness during Mass. They were also more likely to have a celebrant who dominated the liturgy but had little rapport with the congregation and who gave dull homilies emphasizing traditional teachings with little relevance to daily life." See Jim Castelli and Joseph Gremillion, *The Emerging Parish: The Notre Dame Study of Catholic Life since Vatican II* (San Francisco: Harper & Row, 1987), 129.

The revolving door of parochial repertory is a chief reason why people are unhappy with current liturgical music: it never acquires, for most of the year, the status of Christmas carols, the familiar comfort of a favorite aunt, songs that we have known from the cradle that provide a distinct and warm sense of return every time the year rolls around again. The parish that has carols like that for every liturgical season, as all should have, is a rare parish. Instead, worshipers feel a subliminal tension each week: "What will they throw at us now?" The most embarrassing symptom of this discomfort is the common practice of interrupting the sacred liturgy with airport-like announcements of the next song or thing to do. Visitors from mainline Protestant or Orthodox churches cannot help but wonder why Catholics with forty years of experience with the reformed rite cannot get through their own liturgy without being directed like schoolchildren.

Why is the turnover so high? One cause is the musician's desire to create. Ordinarily, creativity in a musician is a most natural and laudable attribute, and historically it has been exercised by all responsible musicians according to their talents and role in the musical enterprise, from those who created by executing their notes as faithfully as possible all the way up to supremely talented composers who created by enriching the repertory. But democratization has leveled creativity. Mere execution within a tradition no longer counts. One must make one's visible and individualized mark, even if that creativity consists of no more than choosing a new song for the parish. In the current politic, this creativity gives free rein to anyone wishing to volunteer and supports a fundamentally uncritical attitude, a reluctance to judge music in a popular idiom, that lends the music an aura of democracy. And so we spend a lot of time on music of poor quality. The reason why the door revolves so easily, why the song a congregation worked hard to learn last year is forgotten this year, is that it can no longer stand to hear or sing it. The piece has failed, abysmally, the test of time. Once fresh and exciting, it has now become an embarrassment, ridiculed by the youth it was supposed to attract. And so our Sisyphean labor continues.

Fall from Grace

The popular conception of democracy is thoroughly egalitarian. Everyone's vote is equal in weight; therefore, by extension, everyone's voice is equal in influence. This is an ideal, of course, seldom realized except perhaps in the voting booth, but nonetheless taken seriously, if not consciously, by most Westerners, especially Americans. Authority and expertise are suspect; the majority rules.

It is worth saying again: this conception is alien to the real world of music making, which, except where it is corrupt, is an uncompromising meritocracy. All musicians are definitely not created equal. Some play better in tune than others. Some play more wrong notes than others. Some can play very fast. Some can sing so as to fill a large hall with beautiful tone. Some can improvise and some cannot. There are better musicians and worse musicians and, when things are going well, the best ones are in charge.

A second and logical effect, then, of the democratization of liturgical music is that the professionally trained parish musician has been chased from the scene. In August 1988, Father M. Francis Mannion, an American authority on liturgy and liturgical music, wrote in the journal *Liturgy*: "There is a whole generation of mostly young Catholic musicians who are severely disillusioned with the state of church music in the United States and who feel thoroughly unrepresented by the nation's liturgical music establishments. . . . They experience incredible frustration because their training is not taken seriously. . . . They worry, with good cause, that the ministerial conception of liturgical music often involves a bias against professional excellence."[5] The city of Rochester, New York, epitomizes Mannion's assessment. Rochester is home to the Eastman School of Music and one of the best graduate programs in pipe organ in the world. Graduate students there earn money every weekend by taking local jobs in most every kind of church except Catholic ones, where they refuse to play, because they cannot stomach what they are asked to sing, play, and direct. Their counsel about repertory is ignored. Meanwhile, Catholic parishes are dying for musical direction, starving in the midst of plenty.

If a parish were to install a new heating system, or to replace the roof or a crumbling foundation, can anyone imagine that notices would be placed in the Sunday bulletin asking for volunteers? Of course not; the parish would hire an expert to consult and then execute the plan. But in the business of music, which is many times more complex than any heating system, the typical American parish shuns the professional and his advice. This is quite unprecedented in the history of Catholic

---

[5] M. Francis Mannion, "Concert Masses: A Reply," *Liturgy 80* 19, no. 6 (August–September 1988): 10–11.

music. Josquin Desprez and Palestrina were widely admired both within and without professional circles and commanded high salaries. For centuries, in city cathedrals or well-endowed establishments, choristers were paid. All of this signaled the esteem for liturgical music, an excellence that was considered essential. Now the very topic elicits derision. Among the professional community, Roman Catholic liturgical music has become a laughingstock. Then again, why should their view matter? Professional musicians are a minority, their collective wisdom outvoted.

This perversity only makes sense in the context of democratization. "Excellence" evokes absolute standards of good and bad, judges of those standards, opinions and prerogatives of unequal weight, and other enemies of the democratic spirit. The fact is that professional musicians are an elite. Most of them train for twenty years and more to do their jobs, much more than in most any other profession. They have instincts and skills that set them apart. And that distinction is unwelcome.

Three Chords

A Catholic priest I once knew, who also happened to be a concert pianist and a highly skilled composer, remarked that all it took to compose liturgical music today (then, 1988) was someone who could play "three chords on a guitar," presumably the I, IV, and V of a key that taken together can harmonize any traditional melody.[6] A hyperbole, no doubt, but nonetheless indicative of the decline in standards of composition. In the Western musical tradition of the last four centuries, to compose with such a limited harmonic vocabulary, without compensations from rhythm or improvisation such as we have in jazz, is like writing a novel without relative clauses, a technique that severely limits what may be achieved.

This third effect of democratization in liturgical music—the collapse of standards in composition of the music itself—has two causes. One is the antipathy against musical professionalism already described; this is just a specific case of it. The other cause is a body of underqualified church musicians creating a market for music within their reach.

---

[6] This is the harmonic diet of most of the folk-revival repertory. Occasionally a lowered VII will replace the V.

The compositions that satisfy them in turn only propagate the low standards which increases the demand for more such pieces—a vicious cycle of amateurism. The problem of composing so that a congregation can sing along without sacrificing the integrity of the composition is as old as church music itself, but at least in times past composers could count on certain professional resources, a trained director and choir at least. That foundation for composition is now gone. The new standards are imposed from below.

Local Color

Democratization naturally favors local traditions and autonomy over catholicity, the ideal of universality in the church. If the parishioners of St. Mary's in Hamilton, New York, prefer popular music and the good people of St. Malachy's, twelve miles south, prefer plainchant, then so be it. The votes for each parish are in and the majority rules. When every parish takes this attitude, a voluptuous variety of liturgical practices and music is the natural result (Chapter 5). In its extreme forms, democratization, once again, makes no attempt to evaluate the choices of music according to some standard of quality, because any such evaluation would make authorities out of those qualified to evaluate it, and their opinions would thus count more. But in a democratic election, the vote by someone who has carefully analyzed a candidate's platform counts no more than the vote by another who likes how the candidate dresses. In democratized liturgy, the parish chooses its music in quite the same way.

Democratization, by elevating the individual worshiper's personal identity, at the same time encourages a simplistic notion of creativity, the idea that personal contributions to liturgy are more valuable than following any kind of standard practice, even if universal. Local creativity has innumerable expressions, some very good, and some very poor. When uncontrolled, it leads to liturgical egoism: the cantor who ensures predominance by blaring into a microphone, the celebrant whose informal chatting from the altar takes up more time than the Eucharistic prayer, the lector who attracts more attention to his elocution than to the Word of God. How ironic is it that the impulse to make worshipers more equal in their participation has produced perhaps the most self-centered liturgies in history.

Perhaps the most common complaint about the reformed liturgy, which indicts not the form of the liturgy but its performance, is the lack of solemnity. Like music itself, solemnity is not quite comfortable with democratic ideals. We are solemn in the face of awesome, infinite power, something far greater than ourselves. Solemnity restrains our behavior and makes us speak quietly, if at all, and sing otherworldly music. Solemnity implies attention to something other than ourselves, even other than our own families or community. All such attitudes are dismissed in a democratized liturgy, which, in case we forget, is of, by, and for the people. Formality implies a social rank (witness the decline of the formal verb forms in French, Italian, German, and other European languages in the last thirty years and the ubiquitous use of first names in the United States). Natural, conversational speech, on the other hand, is for normal folks, and that is why a democratized liturgy prefers uninhibited informality, improvised prayer, and all manner of expression emphasizing the importance of individual participants and of the egalitarian community they constitute. No less is true of the liturgy's music with its household instruments, casual beginnings and fade-outs that mimic the radio, and cheery invitations to sing from the microphone, the very picture of studied informality.

Relevance

The ideology of relevance had its heyday in the 1960s, once again coincident with the hothouse days of liturgical reform. It was most frequently heard on college campuses: traditional curriculum, particularly the classics, had to be either reformed or scrapped to make room for more relevant studies that would have direct political impact on students' lives. Traditional requirements of the educated person, such as familiarity with literary classics and competence in a foreign language and mathematics, died in the 1970s. Fortunately, many were revived thereafter (to the vindication of some universities that never abandoned them) when it was discovered that history was not a dead letter and that Homer could say quite a lot about modern warfare after all.

Insofar as it must please the greatest number, relevance is an artifact of democratization, and in liturgy it appears mostly as a sincere but misguided interest in encouraging *participatio actuosa*. In the extreme, relevance aims to connect worshipers with the concrete world here and now, and it is in spirit completely opposed to liturgy, which through divine inspiration is the bridge leading worshipers to the transcendent, eternal world to come. Nevertheless, relevance made its impact. Language, rituals, and above all the music had to be updated in order to make Catholicism relevant to Catholics. A musician in the late 1960s asking "what good does it do for a minister to show a good film and speak about the relevance of the Church in our daily life if we are going to follow the sermon with a hymn from another century?" gives a fair image of the thinking.[7] Relevance would transform, inspire, and energize the church.

In some respects, this prediction came true, particularly when relevance came to mean putting into practice the social teachings of the Gospel. In this respect, contact with the real, modern world is all to the good. But because symbols acquire their richness of allusion over time, often centuries, the attempt to make over all liturgical symbols into images and reflections of today's world robs them of almost all their symbolic properties, their capacity to communicate ineffable things.[8] Thus the banality of so many banners, invented rites, and much recent liturgical music.

It is a curious thing that of all liturgical artifacts, music is chosen to bear the greatest burden of relevance by far. Celebrants still wear garments reminiscent of ancient Rome. The host is still the simplest unleavened bread. Despite an architectural blight in the 1950s and 1960s and a lot of self-indulgence since then, churches still do not look like the homes or banks or offices of everyday life. But music had to be relevant, particularly to "today's youth," who would certainly desert the church if anything other than their own brand of popular music were heard inside it.

It is hard to imagine a worse argument. For one thing, it assumes that contemporary church music in popular style is really a youthful idiom. Perhaps in the 1960s it was close to some of the music that some young people enjoyed, but it certainly has not been since. A soldier of those times, Francis Schmitt, director of music at Nebraska Boys Town,

---

[7] Robert W. Hovda and Gabe Huck, "Music: We Must Learn to Celebrate," *Liturgical Arts* 38, no. 2 (February 1970): 43. A thorough critique of the relevance ideology for liturgy may be found in James Hitchcock, *Recovery of the Sacred* (New York: Seabury Press, 1974; repr., San Francisco: Ignatius Press, 1995).

[8] This is why the empirical argument made by pointing to the evangelical megachurches fails. Those services are certainly worship, but not the liturgical action of the Eucharist articulated by a rich palette of symbols. Being of the moment, not of history, their music changes with every generation, following the evolution of popular styles from the secular world, appropriately sanitizing each upon arrival. Even some evangelical spokesmen are uncomfortable with the explicit consumer strategy—relevance—of such musical programming. See Sally Morgenthaler, *Worship Evangelism: Inviting Unbelievers into the Presence of God* (Grand Rapids, MI: Zondervan, 1995).

recognized immediately how ridiculous the proposition was: "I have been dealing with the outcasts of the inner core all my life and they are quite capable of and content to sing everything from Gregorian to de Monte to Hindemith for three or four months of Sundays without ever repeating a musical setting of the text. I wouldn't ask them if they wanted to do a hootenanny [folk] mass because they would laugh me off the campus."[9] Is there a commercial radio station out there that plays music anything like Marty Haugen's? If there were, would any self-respecting teenager listen to it? The notion that today's popular liturgical music appeals to youth is laughable on its face. Young people at the century's turn ridicule it mercilessly as much of it deserves. Of course the Catholics on college campuses do play it, but only because they have had no choice. They belong to a lost generation born after 1965 and know nothing better.

Secondly, the premise that relevant music, whatever that might mean in practical terms, attracts converts and keeps our own faithful is a false premise. It has no historical basis, and makes no sense even on its own terms. If everything about liturgy sounds like, feels like, looks like, and talks like the world we know every day, why would anyone bother with it? They do such things much better on television. Superior pop music is to be heard in the stadium or in the night club. Worshipers do not come to Mass to find the everyday world, but to have some experience, however fleeting and subliminal, of the next world, of the divine. This is why our priests do garb themselves like no other people in the world, why our churches do stand apart from other buildings. This is why a bizarre fashion for Gregorian chant begun by the Santo Domingo monks arose in the early 1990s and why small Catholic colleges that provide, or even require, participation in traditional sacred music, such as Palestrina's, now thrive. These musics are highly irrelevant, after all, except perhaps to the basic human need for transcendent experience.

The Irony of It All

So we come at last to the irony of the democratization of liturgical music: it has alienated almost all of the people it was intended to save. Anyone who can still believe that the new "relevant" liturgical music

---

[9] Francis Schmitt, "Leaning Right?," in *Crisis in Church Music?* (Washington, DC: The Liturgical Conference, 1967), 60.

inspires the vast Catholic flocks needs only be shown the revolving door. If it is so inspirational, why do we replace it so quickly? They need only hear the typical performance. Why can we only hear those in the band with the microphone, while the congregants, for the most part, stand mute?

An article in the March 1999 issue of *The American Organist* celebrated the establishment of a choir school at the Cathedral of the Madeleine in Salt Lake City, Utah, in August 1996. Author James E. Frazier, former director of music for the Archdiocese of St. Paul and Minneapolis, describes how the school "draws on the church's rich legacy of choral music while remaining rigorously faithful to the conciliar reforms,"[10] with a broad repertory of Renaissance polyphony, twentieth-century French and American works, and several Gregorian Mass Ordinaries, among other things. The congregation, in harmony with conciliar exhortations, "is at once active and attentive, with acclamations, hymnody, and antiphons, a duty they exercise enthusiastically."[11] But then a single sentence blots this bright picture: "It will come as no surprise to readers of this journal that a significant and vocal outcry, with charges of elitism, came early on from employees of other Catholic schools and from pastors throughout the diocese who opposed the choir school."[12]

This response, perhaps it should be emphasized, is hardly typical of common parishioners, who appreciate fine church music quite openly and honestly. And why shouldn't they? Professional athletes are not disdained as elitist, though they obviously are a very, very small and privileged group of people, as are test pilots, Hollywood actors, and any number of other kinds of highly trained and talented professionals. No, the charges of elitism, unfortunately, come from those in charge, another irony of democratization. The authorities, schooled neither in musical professionalism nor in Catholic musical traditions, but merely in a liturgical democracy of their own invention, impose their prescriptions for proper liturgical music from the top down upon the masses.

The last and saddest irony is how unnecessary it all has been. The aesthetics of a fine piece of sacred music and the ideals of *participatio*

---

[10] James E. Frazier, "A New Choir School of the Roman Catholic Cathedral of the Madeleine in Salt Lake City," *The American Organist* 33, no. 3 (March 1999): 57.
[11] Ibid.
[12] Ibid.

actuosa are in no way incompatible. Take a simple plainchant. For the typical congregant who is not a musician, it is easy enough to learn.[13] For the music lover, still not a musician, it has a timeless sacred semantic that drives the growing revival of plainchant in so many places.[14] For the church musician, it poses more than enough challenges in performance and subtleties in appreciation. And it doesn't even matter that everyone does not belt it out, for plainchant often sounds better understated, rising mystically and anonymously from the people of God. Or take a good hymn, such as "O Sacred Head." Again, the tune is easy to learn. But the accomplished choir singer knows more: there are actually four melodies (soprano, alto, tenor, bass), each beautiful in itself and yet made to sound together in glorious harmony. The professional organist finds it most satisfying to play them.

Most masterworks of liturgical music, indeed most masterworks in any art, have the power to appeal to nearly everyone on some level, for that is one of the things that makes them masterworks. In this regard, they are true democratic art, far more so than the banalities that can satisfy, at best, the lowest common denominators of taste. If this is true, the rediscovery of the treasure of the Catholic musical tradition is perhaps inevitable. For after forty years of mediocrity, the people will demand it.

---

[13] A recent example: On Sunday, December 9, 2007, at St. Malachy's parish, I taught schoolchildren aged eight to fourteen the proper offertory antiphon for the Fourth Sunday of Advent from the *Graduale Simplex*. It took 20 minutes.

[14] William Mahrt writes, "The most recent issue of *Pastoral Music* (January, 2011), the journal of the National Pastoral Musicians, traditionally no particular friend of chant, has devoted an entire issue to the theme 'Chant and Her Children in Today's Liturgy,' with articles on chant, polyphony, and organ music. An introductory essay by J. Michael McMahon, the president of the organization . . . encourages the membership to make 'chant an integral part of the repertoire of your worshipping community.'" "Practical Sacrality," *Sacred Music* 137, no. 4 (Winter 2010): 5.

Chapter 5

The Diversity of Catholic Liturgical Music

> What a grand bond of unity becomes clearly evident when a multitude of diverse peoples sing in unison! Like a harp with many strings sounding a single melody!
>   St. Ambrose (fourth century)

Here are a few images of what is happening in Roman Catholic music early in the twenty-first century. In the Church of San Simeon Piccolo in Venice, every Sunday at 11:30, a fine organist and small choir sing the entire Mass in Latin plainchant, using the so-called Tridentine rite of the 1962 Missal. Five minutes to the south, at the Basilica di Santa Maria dei Frari, organ music from a beautifully restored Italian instrument accompanies the opening procession, the offertory procession, and the procession after the final blessing. No singing. The Mass is said in vernacular Italian. The timeless Byzantine mosaics of the Basilica of St. Mark in the same city reflect mostly a saccharine popular music derivative of American precedents, except at the *Messa solenne* mid-morning on Sundays. Then a full choir and brilliant organ provide music, mostly in Latin, from a repertory ranging from the seventeenth to twentieth centuries.[1] At other Venetian churches not a note of music is heard, and the pipe organ lies in disrepair.

The small parish of St. Malachy's in rural Sherburne, New York, in the diocese of Syracuse, sings Latin plainchant for the shorter Mass Ordinaries (*Kyrie, Sanctus, Agnus Dei*) and the *Gloria* during Christmastide and Eastertide; it sings English-language settings of these in Ordinary Time, a variety of acclamations, responsorial psalms in harmonized Gregorian tones, and two to three hymns of Catholic and Protestant origin composed mostly before 1950. A small but

---

[1] For a detailed program, see chap. 18.

adequate pipe organ accompanies everything except plainchant. St. Mary's in Hamilton, twelve miles to the north, uses a digital piano for much of its music, little of which is older than twenty years.

At the funeral of Pope John Paul II on April 8, 2005, televised to billions, the papal choir sang plainchant harmonized by the organist and a kind of revisionist nineteenth-century polyphony, not always in the best of tune. In Utah, at the Cathedral of the Madeleine, a choir school founded in 1996 provides authentic chant and polyphony.[2] In Cambridge, Massachusetts, the Boston Archdiocesan Choir School sings psalms in Gregorian formulas updated with modal harmonizations and antiphons composed by the late Theodore Marier, founder of the school, as well as a variety of Mass Ordinaries in English and Latin, either chanted or in settings by famous twentieth-century composers, as well as organ hymns of many styles. In Minneapolis, the pastor of St. Agnes, the late Monsignor Richard J. Schuler, frequently commanded a professional orchestra and chorus singing a symphonic Mass of Haydn, Mozart, or Schubert (as happens also in the Stefansdom and St. Augustin in Vienna). Down the street at St. Peter Claver, a historically African-American congregation sings Mass almost entirely with Gospel music.

In Ghana, congregations sway and dance in place as they sing processional songs of local origin. The sparse Catholics of India might sing *bhajan*, inspirational Hindu songs whose words have been subtly generalized for Christian use.[3] In Taiwan, churches mostly use Western music, and organists from that country, Japan, and Korea are now fixtures on the recital circuit.

Publishers of Catholic liturgical music feed this bewildering diversity and in fact have come under some scrutiny because of the power they wield. The old Desclée editions of Latin plainchant are long out of print, but Desclée has brought out new ones, approved by Rome, with the traditional music adapted for the *novus ordo*, the new Roman Rite established in 1969.[4] G. I. A. Publications of Chicago, once known as the Gregorian Institute of America, publishes hymnals ranging from

---

[2] James E. Frazier, "A New Choir School of the Roman Catholic Cathedral of the Madeleine in Salt Lake City," *The American Organist* 33, no. 3 (March 1999): 56–68.

[3] For more details, see Stephen F. Duncan, *A Genre of Hindustani Music (Bhajans) as Used in the Roman Catholic Church*, Lewiston, NY: E. Mellen Press, 1999.

[4] The principal ones for Mass would be the *Graduale Romanum* and the *Graduale Simplex*.

the compendious *Worship*—containing Mass Ordinaries, including chanted ones, a fine selection of hymns, and an adequate if pedestrian Psalter—to *Gather*, a collection dominated by popular-style liturgical music of the last three decades. Every liturgical magazine lists dozens of new works and collections. And then there is the missalette, printed on newsprint because of its short lifespan ending in the trash bin, the temporary measure created in the aftermath of liturgical reforms forty years ago that became the painless permanent solution in many dioceses.

Now, to have a range of liturgical practices all presenting themselves as Catholic is nothing new. Since the first Pentecost, music in the church has never been uniform. To be sure, certain experimental periods in history have produced a greater diversity of liturgical music, while other periods of reform and retrenchment reduced it. But if the current situation per se is not at all unprecedented in church history, its magnitude at the present moment certainly is.

The difference in degree—that is, that the practice and repertory of liturgical music calling itself Roman Catholic is greater than ever before—has a number of sources. One was the impetus provided by the liturgical movement beginning in the late eighteenth century, coming to fruition in the Second Vatican Council, and spawning numberless experiments in congregational singing.

Another powerful source, more recent, is the ever-growing reach of the faith in the world. When the Council of Trent reformed the liturgy in the early 1560s, Catholicism was a European religion. Yes, different places in Europe had different music, but those differences lay within the confines of a common musical language. Most worshipers today would be hard put to hear much difference in a sixteenth-century antiphon sung in Rome and one in Milan, although the rites were officially distinct. The melodies are certainly not identical, but the concepts behind the melodies are: the grammar, the ordering of notes, the available pitches. In the early twenty-first century, Roman Catholicism is a world religion, growing fastest in non-European cultures, whose musical languages may not even share the same pitch collections, never mind the grammar, of European music. Every new mission enriches the store of liturgical music available to the church.

This enrichment, which seems to follow directly from Christ's command to "Go, therefore, and make disciples of all nations, baptizing them in the name of the Father, and of the Son, and of the holy Spirit" (Matt 28:18) would seem to be an unequivocal good. The treasure house of Catholic music may be the greatest in the world, but who could object to a worthy increase by means of new and different kinds of music? Indeed, *Sacrosanctum Concilium* explicitly states that "Composers, animated by the christian spirit, should accept that it is part of their vocation to cultivate sacred music and increase its store of treasures" (SC 121). Cultural diversification of liturgical music certainly chimes well with the current esteem of ethnicity, and the democratization of liturgical music favors local practices at the expense of universal ones, since, as the maxim goes, "all politics is local."

But another provides that "there is no free lunch," and the art of music rarely gives without taking something in return. Liturgical traditions, performance interpretations, and composition itself seldom experience absolute improvements. Rather, it is a matter of tradeoffs. Every compositional choice denies alternatives. Larger orchestras mean a louder sound and more varied timbre but a less intimate experience for the listener and less individual creativity for the player. A faster tempo may favor the perception of harmonic progression in one passage while obscuring it in another. What have we traded for this unparalleled richness of diversity in liturgical music?

The essential effect of liturgical diversity is simple and logical: what is different cannot be the same. The liturgy is an action. If the action diverges according to place, parish, diocese, nation, then in some sense we do not enact the same liturgy. The catholicity of the act comes into question.

But the essence of the Eucharist is always the same regardless of the language of the anaphora and the kind of liturgical music settings by which the people offer it up to God. *Sacrosanctum Concilium* presumes this in stating that "the Liturgy is made up of unchangeable elements divinely instituted, and of elements subject to change. These latter not only may be changed but ought to be changed with the passage of time, if they have suffered from the intrusion of anything out of harmony with the inner nature of the liturgy or have become less suitable" (SC 21). In some sense, the particularities of any liturgical celebration are superficial; that is, embellishments vary the surface of an essential identity within.

The problem with the argument is that the essence of the immutable Eucharist is abstract, while most of us of weak faith depend on sensible phenomena to symbolize the action and bring us into the right spirit of communion and awe of the real presence that the liturgy asks of us. If this were not so, there would never have been a liturgical history at all, since it reflects nothing if not a deep and constant concern about the forms and practices of these superficialities. No one would ever need to get excited about liturgical music. Why would it matter?

It matters because these external elements, the clothing of the liturgy, musical and otherwise, profoundly affect the spirits of those in attendance and their relations with the Lord whom they meet there, even if the worst music never nullifies the awesome truth of the central event. *Sacrosanctum Concilium* assumes as much, and perhaps more, in its opening premise: "as a combination of sacred music and words, it [sacred music] forms a necessary or integral part of the solemn liturgy" (SC 112). A diversity of liturgical music must therefore have diverse effects.

Attending a solemn Mass at St. Peter's Basilica in Rome on Trinity Sunday, 2002, I stood surrounded by people of every race and nation from across the world, or so it seemed, a moving experience sure to become ever more common in the twenty-first century. Their singing was heartfelt—whenever it could be. For many that was not often. The principal language was Italian. An effort at some accommodation was made in the opening hymn, a *Te Deum* to the tune *Hursley* (or *Grosser Gott*) that Americans may know as "Holy God, We Praise Thy Name," with one verse in Latin, the next in Italian, the next in French, and the last in German. The music that encouraged the best singing, although still of a minority, were the settings of the shorter Ordinaries, the *Kyrie, Sanctus,* and *Agnus Dei.* Yes, we shared a common faith, reverence, and spiritual hunger for what was happening, but had grown up with diverse liturgical practices and music, so that even as we acted together in the essential celebration of the Eucharist, there was no practical sign for us acting together in its accompanying music.

One tradeoff of a rich diversity of liturgical music would then certainly appear to be a practical liturgical unity among Catholics. When we visit neighboring parishes, dioceses, and nations, and even when we gather in the world's most Catholic city, there is no guarantee, indeed little reason to think, that we will find a liturgy clothed with familiar and congenial elements, that we will sing with our Catholic brothers and sisters. The loss of practical unity entails a loss of symbolic unity for the worldwide church too. The secular world outside may find it hard to imagine why we call ourselves "catholic" (universal) if our most solemn and devout celebrations appear to differ so greatly one from another. Of course we are essentially united in faith, but faith is bound to liturgy in the famous principle *lex orandi, lex credendi*, that how we pray reflects what we believe.[5]

In the United States and in some other places, divergent liturgical practices have spawned a kind of parochial comparison shopping, where Catholics fortunate enough to live within traveling distance of more than one parish church can choose the liturgy to their liking. Naturally, one of the most attractive items on offer is the kind and quality of liturgical music. If widespread, this consumerist attitude radically transforms the demographic structure of the church. The parochial community is no longer geographical, neighbors in a certain place bound by faith. Rather, it is a group bound by faith and similar tastes and, very likely, other social aspects. What is the Christian nature of a community where members gather by choosing their liturgy from an open market rather than sacrificing something of themselves for the common action that is the liturgy? Is it not ironic that an extreme diversification of liturgy actually may produce socially segregated congregations?

The flowering of diversity in liturgy is part of a much broader idealization of ethnicity that has characterized American society for some decades now. Its main premise resists assimilation into any social mainstream and rather proclaims that it is good to cultivate and celebrate cultural differences among us. This resonates with the practical truth that no two of us are exactly alike and with the moral truth that we must therefore live in charity with our differences. Liturgies that orient their music and ancillary practices to a particular ethnic group —or better yet, single liturgies that yet reflect a variety of cultures— would embody this moral imperative.

But where are we to draw the line around the group that defines the music we are to sing? The extreme application of the theory of celebrating differences extends right down to the individual worshiper, but it is obvious that such an accommodation is ridiculously impractical and in fact contradicts essentially the nature of Catholic liturgy as a communal, corporate action, which was central to the thrust of the entire liturgical movement that engineered the reforms of the council.[6] In a liturgy, the community of faith performs the action that God has

---

[5] Edward Schaefer cites this principle to found his persuasive argument about the formative power of liturgical music. See *Catholic Music through the Ages: Balancing the Needs of a Worshipping Church* (Chicago: Hillenbrand, 2008), 27–29.

[6] Dom Gregory Dix, *The Shape of the Liturgy* (London: Dacre Press, 1945), 1.

given it with God himself both as its center and its co-actor; that is of the essence. Does the boundary of the community, then, stop at the parish church's door? At the diocese? At the nation? It would seem most difficult to justify any definition of Catholic community, and therefore of liturgical community, short of the whole world, which of course is what the word "catholic" entails and why a liturgy such as that of Trinity Sunday in Rome could ever occur.

Perhaps this is why the passages of *Sacrosanctum Concilium* concerning the liturgical use of native musics, including explication in a more recent instruction *Varietates Legitimae*, always place this matter in the context of missions, the first efforts to bring the Gospel message to people who have never heard it.[7] And a key clause in the distinction just cited in the constitution on the eternal and changeable elements of liturgy is "with the passage of time," which presents the injunction to change things mainly in response to historical developments, not geographic or cultural differences. In other words, the practicalities of evangelization and the inevitable changes of circumstance through time that affect the divine liturgy are yet informed by a vision of a time when the liturgy throughout the world will be unified in particulars as well as in essence, a reflection of the traditional Christian hope that "they may all be one" (John 17:21).

But in every particular? A rigid liturgical conformity in specifics has never been the aim of even the most stringent reform movements in the church. Surely the Council of Trent must be counted one of these, and its unifying liturgical books still exercise influence today, but its fathers specifically exempted from them those local traditions that could show two centuries of continuity such as the Dominican Rite in England and the Ambrosian Rite in Milan. "The intricate pattern of local variety overlaid on the unchanging apostolic core of the rite is the product of history. It is the proof that the Christian liturgy is not a museum specimen of religiosity, but the expression of an immense living process made up of the real lives of hosts of men and women in all sorts of ages and circumstances. Yet the underlying structure is always the same because the essential action is always the same . . ."[8] Catholic liturgies have always been local in the veneration of local saints. Indeed, the nature of the liturgical year itself offers a supreme

---

[7] In *Sacrosanctum Concilium*, see art. 119. In *Varietates Legitimae*, see arts. 6 and 28.
[8] Dix, *The Shape of the Liturgy*, xii.

exemplar of a liturgy that changes its colors, its tones, its theological emphasis, its very aesthetics, without ever losing its essential center in the Eucharist. The liturgical year and its proper expressions are what, in great measure, have given us the vast and varied treasure of liturgical music that we call Catholic.[9]

Sacrosanctum Concilium would not have spoken of the sacred treasure of music so often and so highly had the fathers not intended that it be used, and using it entails a variety of practices because the music itself is far from uniform in what it may require. A rural parish, by and large, will not be capable of Palestrina, but should that fact rule out polyphony for the cathedral choirs that are capable? Music, of all the arts, responds to the immediate context, which in fact determines a great deal of its meaning.[10] Even in the most practical terms, then, to mine the treasure must mean to form the practice to the needs of the celebration at hand. This is not only practical but charitable.

We have then, as so often in liturgical matters, a situation of competing yet legitimate values. Some diversity in liturgy and liturgical music is to be expected, indeed prized, but an extreme diversity produces an unholy fragmentation of worldwide Catholics and an unwholesome homogeneity in individual congregations. At the same time, a rigid uniformity is infeasible and cannot respond to local and temporary circumstances in charity. But somehow the pilgrims from every land attending Mass at St. Peter's on the Feast of the Holy Trinity should be able to sing the parts of the liturgy that pertain to them while never losing the feeling that they indeed are in Rome. Surely there must be a via media.

---

[9] See chap. 14.
[10] See chap. 12.

Chapter 6

The State of the Art

> Is Liturgy primarily latreutic, concerned with the adoration of God, or is it first and foremost didactic or edificatory, the conscious vehicle of instruction of individuals and the upbuilding of a community?
> Aidan Nichols, OP (1996)

The facts of postconciliar liturgical music and practice lead to a hard, sad, and inescapable truth: the landscape of Roman Catholic liturgical music in the Western world today is a desert of mediocrity, dotted with oases of sublimity for those thirsty enough to look for them, richly diverse, and peopled by good-hearted souls with the best of intentions gone awry.

The mediocrity both in liturgical music and in the liturgical practice to which it is so intimately bound seems well entrenched. Happy exceptions exist to be sure—the oases of St. Mark's in Venice, St. Paul's in Cambridge, Massachusetts, the Abbey of the Genesee in rural upstate New York among many others—but the reigning powers in liturgical music sustain the lowest common denominator of musical and liturgical standards.

This is a sad thing. Once, Roman Catholic liturgical music was a crown jewel of Western civilization, and its fundamental discoveries underlie every significant achievement of European and American musical art to the present day. Now music lovers laugh at its contemporary efforts, or perhaps cringe if they must attend the funeral or christening Mass of a friend. While no one in our affluent society would consider for a moment using cinderblock garages or convenience stores as houses of worship, pouring wine and water out of plastic soda bottles, or decorating the altar with plastic flowers, we tolerate and indeed applaud the musical equivalents of these in too many places every week. This is an injurious thing. Mediocrity can harm the spirit. It deprives worshipers of a foretaste of the heavenly banquet which is rightfully theirs, and teaches Catholic children that the music of the true faith is no different and no better than what is blared out in shopping malls. Why should they believe that what actually happens at Mass is any more valuable and real?

The historical causes of this mediocrity are many, but may be summarized as three principal ones. The first was as simple as "haste makes waste." The hurry to get Catholic congregations singing as quickly as possible after 1963, without due reflection on the practicalities entailed, without any coordination among local bishops (never mind episcopal conferences), and without any time at all to develop an appropriate repertory, was an error of historic magnitude.[1]

Haste led to the second cause, the choice of the folk-revival style as the symbol of choice for liturgical renewal in the Western world, a style that cannot possibly accommodate congregational singing of good quality. We still live with the consequences of this rashness. This style, with its rhythmically impoverished or chromaticized descendants, survives owing to a mistaken notion of musical creativity, which in turn is born of a mistaken ideal of democratized liturgy. The individual is prized at the expense of the congregation; amateurism and egoism become good, if not in word, then certainly in deed. It survives because the Second Vatican Council has become a myth, a symbolic shibboleth to be wielded rather than a historical event to be studied. The myth spawned the popular misunderstandings that banished Latin and plainchant, and turned a supple and subtle principle of *participatio actuosa* into a simplistic ironclad rule: the more the congregation sings, the better, no matter what and no matter how. And nowadays the popular style survives mostly out of ignorance, not only of what *Sacrosanctum Concilium* really says, but ignorance of what that document calls the sacred treasure, the Catholic musical tradition and the repertory that embodies it. A starving man fed only cotton candy cannot help but think that cotton candy is the greatest food on earth.

---

[1] This was typical of the urgency of the whole council for liturgical reform. "Left unmentioned were problems caused by the quantity and rapidity in the reforms themselves, problems that reflect perhaps the greatest of all the reform's weaknesses, namely, the almost total absence of any anthropological dimension in the approach to revision of so massive and long-standing a ritual system. For ritual patterns, which have much to do with sustaining identity and the social bond, are for these reasons essentially conservative and normally need to change slowly." Aidan Kavanagh, "The Conciliar Documents: Liturgy (*Sacrosanctum Concilium*)," in *Modern Catholicism: Vatican II and After*, ed. Adrian Hastings (New York: Oxford University Press, 1991), 71.

The third cause of mediocrity has been low standards of composition. Johann Sebastian Bach once took umbrage because a contemporary referred to him as a *Musikant*, a fiddler, a street musician, rather than the more professional *compositeur* or *Kapellmeister*.[2] Lately the *Musikant* has been preferred; modern-day Bachs, if any there be, are too often shown the door.

For those who have been unwilling or unable to recognize the mediocrity of the music itself, two objective symptoms of it stand out. One is the revolving door, the constant exchange of new songs for old, that is, as old as a few years or perhaps a decade. We acquire new liturgical songs for the same reason we get new clothes: the old ones are worn out, out of fashion, we can no longer stand to look at them, and we feel silly wearing them.

The second symptom is the total abandonment of the sung propers of every Sunday Mass, those prayers which specify and bring to life a moment in the liturgical year, the introit (entrance antiphon), offertory, and communion being among the most important. The current General Instruction of the Roman Missal provides four options for these moments:

> In the Dioceses of the United States of America there are four options for the Entrance Chant: (1) the antiphon from the Missal or the antiphon with its Psalm from the *Graduale Romanum* as set to music there or in another setting; (2) the antiphon and Psalm of the *Graduale Simplex* for the liturgical time; (3) a chant from another collection of Psalms and antiphons, approved by the Conference of Bishops or the Diocesan Bishop, including Psalms arranged in responsorial or metrical forms; (4) another liturgical chant that is suited to the sacred action, the day, or the time of year, similarly approved by the Conference of Bishops or the Diocesan Bishop.[3]

It is "option four" that justifies the replacement of these propers by the "processional song," "offertory song," and "communion song."[4] Virtually all Americans would think these songs to be the actual

---

[2] May 4, 1737, J. A. Scheibe, in his journal *Critische Musikus*. See the discussion in Christoph Wolff, *Johann Sebastian Bach: The Learned Musician* (New York: Norton, 2000), 1–3.

[3] General Instruction of the Roman Missal (Collegeville, MN: Liturgical Press, 2011), art. 48.

[4] There is no official liturgical analogue for the "recessional hymn."

requirement of a canonical liturgy, not a fourth-ranked substitute, and would think quite strange a liturgy where the proper antiphons for the day were sung instead. This universal practice of "option four" provides for, if it does not assure, mediocre compositions. The first option is superb music; so is the second, although simpler in character. The third option at least will have psalmody, the best of sung texts.

But the "suitable liturgical song" of the fourth option has become a free-for-all. It has become the first priority of all liturgical planning, at the expense of sung Ordinaries (*Kyrie*, *Gloria*, etc.), acclamations, and of course the propers. "The four hymns" are the referent for virtually all discussion of "liturgical music," even though this new norm is a gross distortion of the liturgy and its priorities. Ironically, "option four" completely frustrates one of the most important priorities of the Second Vatican Council, to make more of the Bible familiar and accessible in liturgy. The reformed three-year cycle of Scripture readings does this in great measure of course, but so does the cycle of sung propers, almost all of which are biblical and reinforce key passages read during the Liturgy of the Word. Quotations traditionally allied with particular moments of the liturgical year are forgotten, replaced by poems which, at best, must be at some remove from Scripture, and at worst get no closer than a self-esteem pamphlet.

The diversity of Roman Catholic liturgical music available today is historically unprecedented, but its breadth is primarily geographical. If it is true that most American and European Catholics only hear and sing music composed since the Second Vatican Council, then the historical reach of this experience is also unprecedentedly narrow. Thus we live in a paradoxical moment. The many cultures of the world have enriched the Catholic repertory with their musics, while their warm reception is curiously blinkered, blind to the historical riches that remain buried like an undiscovered archeological trove.

The speed of this growth in multicultural repertory has left unexpected results in its wake that bear some thinking about. Does diversity threaten a permanent fragmentation within the Church by liturgical means? As liturgies become ever more specific to a culture, and ever more entrenched with differing languages, rituals, symbols, and music, will the various Catholic communities throughout the world lose the ability to celebrate in common, as has happened to the Orthodox churches and other rites that have insisted throughout history on their local prerogatives? "Unity, not uniformity" is the cry often heard among the apologists for inculturation, but unity must be signified in order to be verified and experienced. Who has asked what signs of unity in liturgy can there possibly be if not uniform practices and prayers? Finally, if cultures may insist on their own ways, what constitutes a charitable invitation to those visiting strangers? "I was a stranger and you welcomed me," read the cheerful gold shirts of the Roman youths who guided the pilgrims in the great jubilee year of 2000.[5] Does liturgical music bound to culture cease to welcome Catholics beyond the parish boundary, Catholics of the world?

There should be no doubt that many aspects of the current state of the art in Catholic liturgical music are good. The liturgical reform of the Second Vatican Council has awakened all over the world what might be called a liturgical conscience, an awareness of liturgical virtues. The innate desire of every person to sing in praise of God is a good thing. The consequent desire of the laity to be actively involved in liturgy and therefore to sing liturgical music is a good thing. The enrichment of the liturgy by a wide variety of cultural resources is an inevitability and a good thing. And musical creativity, as a gift from God, is of course a good thing. All these virtues are recognized explicitly in the sixth chapter, concerning liturgical music of *Sacrosanctum Concilium*.

But liturgical virtues all together are good only insofar as they are practiced in concert with one another so that the whole liturgy is vastly greater than the sum of its parts. Within the liturgy, liturgical virtues become subordinate to the liturgy itself. This synthesis becomes a form of Christian self-sacrifice: not everyone can perform every aspect of the liturgical action in the same way. All gifts of God, like all gifts, must be rightly used to honor and properly thank their giver, and the practice and right use of liturgical virtue is contingent upon the whole. This is where reform of liturgical music has often gone awry. Virtues of creativity, congregational singing, and cultural expression, as real but extreme virtues tending toward the absolute, have driven the liturgy, rather than the liturgy governing the right use of those virtues.

On balance then, the situation is still essentially good—sad at the moment, far short of its ideal, but far from hopeless. Intentions are good, errors are slowly coming to light by honest appraisal of forty

---

[5] See Matt 25:35. The inscription on the shirts was in Italian: "Ero forestiero e mi avete ospitato."

years' experience, and the enormous potential realized by the council remains. Certainly the idea of *participatio actuosa*, the single, strongest, uncontested reform of the council, has taken hold despite misunderstandings of it in the current state of the art. Very few would wish to restore the typical preconciliar congregation, described by Pius XII as "dumb and idle spectators."[6] But to harness this potential and exercise our liturgical virtues rightly, we have to understand their true nature and right use in the context of the liturgy and its musical traditions. The cost of ignorance has been very high indeed.

---

[6] *Musicae Sacrae* 64. Some might take exception to this, pointing to the revival of the "Tridentine" Mass by Pope Benedict XVI in his encyclical *Summorum Pontificorum* of 2007. But it is unlikely that any enthusiasm for this "extraordinary Roman Rite" comes from a desire to sit back and get lost in one's personal devotions at the liturgy. Rather, it comes from a deep dissatisfaction with the *novus ordo* Masses, as they are known, with egocentric leaders, trite music, and loss of transcendence. Were *novus ordo* Masses celebrated as the council intended and according to the official liturgical books, with due gravity and solemnity, most proponents of the Tridentine Mass would have little to prefer.

Part II

The Sacred Treasure

The Roman Catholic tradition owns the richest repertory of music of any nation or religion in the world. Two historical events account for this legacy.

The first has no specifiable time, place, or author, but is rather a change of attitude that goes back at least to the fourth-century Western Roman empire. The eternal question of all religions—what kind of music can qualify for divine worship—somehow took a critical turn that set Western practice apart from Eastern practice among Christians, and from that of other religions. The criterion for sounding sacred enough to be included in the liturgy became one of sufficient distinction from secular music rather than strict adherence to what had been handed down from ancient tradition. In other words, a Christian setting of a sacred text, say a psalm, need not remain unaltered as long as its music could not be confounded with that of the pagan Romans. As in many religions, music was considered to be an almost supernatural mode of speech given by God to render worthily back to him his own words of Scripture, but in Roman Catholicism the music—its tones and melodic patterns—was not itself the Word of God. In the great Eastern religions, including some Christian sects such as the Copts, the music was indissoluble from the Word, and therefore inalterable. The only means of creating new music in the Byzantine tradition, for example, was to compose new texts, which, while not of biblical status, could still be sung in the Divine Office. Since a vital musical tradition almost always requires some creative outlet in composition, tens of thousands of Greek hymns were composed and compiled since the sixth century. Hymns were also composed in the West, of course, but before the Reformation they never attained very high liturgical status because there was little need for them. Composers could satisfy their creative drives by setting and resetting the most sacred biblical and liturgical texts, as long as those settings remained essentially distinct from the music of the secular world. In the West, the musical composition of Masses did not die with the canonization of its texts.

But all the creative efforts of sacred musicians would have counted as so much irrecoverable water over the dam were it not for the second crucial event somewhere around the turn of the ninth century: the invention of a musical notation that could preserve the music for posterity.[1] It does not matter that the motives for this preservation—a political integration of Charlemagne's empire partly effected through liturgical uniformity—were not the holiest, nor that perfect uniformity of chanting was never achieved. It only matters that from that time grew an ever-greater stockpile of recorded chant that could serve as a model and foundation for the new compositions that continued to flow from creative minds, which in turn, as long as they retained their sacred distinction, could generate future developments. All these were preserved by an increasingly sophisticated notation.

It is these two characteristics of Western sacred music—a limited freedom to compose new works upon traditional texts and a means to record them—that gave the Western tradition its music history and a repertory equaled by none other.

Nearly all of this music remains completely unknown to modern Catholics, stowed away out of sight like long-forgotten attic treasures. This is nothing new. For most of the last thousand years, the church has presented only a fraction of the music it owns in actual liturgy. The sacred repertory is like the art collection at the Louvre Museum, so vast that most of it must be stored out of sight. Often, when works are brought back to light, they require a kind of restoration, a purgation of cultural accretions or in some cases an entire reconstruction, according to our own lights, of some lost tradition.

The fraction on view depends greatly on the cultural priorities of the moment, with new works usually enjoying a priority owing to their freshness and a culture's natural chauvinism. The same is true today. What is different today is the intensity of the controversy about the propriety of musical styles for the liturgy and a concomitant, sometimes romantic, interest in some quarters for a restoration of traditional music. It does seem a shame that most of the church's musical heritage lies unheard in the attic, but history would show that it has not all been equally useful at all times. Some reflection and wisdom

---

[1] It is curious that other major religions around the world developed notations within three centuries of the Western invention: Byzantine chant books in the tenth century, *samāvedic* chant in India in the eleventh century, Jewish *piyyutim* in the eleventh century, Chinese *ya-yüeh* in the twelfth century. But these notation systems did not act as a foundation for an increasingly varied repertory built on preserved compositions as they did in the West, owing to the indissoluble Eastern relation of word and music. These systems seem to have been introduced to prevent the inevitable subliminal changes that always occur with oral traditions.

are in order here. Different kinds of music have different musical and liturgical strengths. What in the church's Western repertory is of any use for modern Catholics scattered over the world?

Another question perhaps even more central to an understanding of Catholic liturgical music is whether this repertory somehow constitutes a standard for liturgical propriety, whether it is actually heard or not. If it does, it acts as an unseen disputant in so many battles over modern liturgical composition and use, and therefore to be ignorant of it is to fight blind.

We need our music history very much. Part II of this book analyzes four broad categories of sacred music of the Roman Catholic tradition: plainchant, classical polyphony, operatic or symphonic music, and popular music. The intention is not to survey the repertories, which would require several books for each one, but to outline the essential musical characteristics that define them in order to delimit their advantages and disadvantages for liturgy, and to speculate about what role, if any, they might play in modern liturgy around the world. How does music of times past function in a living tradition?

Chapter 7

Plainchant

> For Gregory . . . had the glory of being the great organizer of the office of the clerics. From the time of St. Benedict, the order of psalmody had never been fixed with the precision in the Psalter and the Antiphonary; it was the incomparable Pope Gregory of happy memory, himself a zealous observer of the Rule of St. Benedict and imitator of monastic perfection, who organized it under the direction of the Holy Spirit.
>
> Amalarius, Bishop of Metz (ca. 825)

The expression "Catholic music" brings to mind plainchant first and foremost. When producers of television documentaries and advertisements want to summon instantly the Catholic ethos for purposes good or ill, the choice of background music is easy: they use Gregorian chant. Even though most Catholics have never heard a chanted liturgy in their lives, this is the musical icon of Roman Catholicism.

The term "Gregorian chant" has in recent years attained a certain status in popular culture, owing somewhat to a less than felicitous association with "new age" spiritual movements, which in turn made a bestseller out of a recording by Spanish monks at the monastery of Santo Domingo de Silos, released in 1994.[1] It is an evocative, efficient, but problematic term. "Gregorian" comes from an eighth-century Carolingian (early French) attribution to Pope St. Gregory the Great

---

[1] The Benedictine Monks of Santo Domingo de Silos, *Chant*, Angel Records CDC 7243 5 55138 2 3, 1994. The music on the disc was recorded in the 1970s and 1980s, but it was the 1994 compilation that sold so widely. It had sold in Spain as part of a Christmas package. At that point, EMI records promoted it heavily in other countries, eventually selling seven million CDs of plainchant.

In 2008 this minor miracle was repeated by the Cistercian Monks of Stift Heiligenkreuz with their recordings called *Chant: Music for the Soul*, Decca B0011489-02, Decca B0012322-02. I thank Fr. Jerome F. Weber for all this discographical information.

(c.540–604), who is sometimes depicted in medieval iconography writing down the melodies dictated to him by the Holy Spirit. Modern scholars no longer take seriously this lovely image, although they do credit St. Gregory with important influences on liturgical music: the importation of certain Byzantine practices and perhaps the foundation of the papal choir, the Schola Cantorum. The severest scholars restrict the term "Gregorian chant" to about 600 pieces dating as far back as the late seventh century that set Mass propers, that is, those prayers such as the introit (entrance antiphon) or offertory belonging to particular celebrations, such as Christmas or the first Sunday of Lent. Other scholars would add the propers for the Divine Office, the shorter prayer services sung by monastics at particular times throughout the day, such as Lauds and Vespers. Then, even though they were composed later, sometimes many centuries later, more casual parlance would call "Gregorian" the chanted Mass Ordinaries, that is, those prayers sung at every solemn Mass: *Kyrie* (Lord, Have Mercy), *Gloria* (Glory to God in the Highest), *Credo* (I Believe in One God), *Sanctus* (Holy, Holy, Holy), *Agnus Dei* (Lamb of God), and in some cases *Ite, missa est* (Go, the Mass is ended).[2] And finally, for most Catholics, any plainchant used by the church is "Gregorian" as far as they are concerned.

The fact is that Christianity has known a great number of chant traditions—Byzantine, Coptic, the *znamenñiy raspev* of Russian Orthodoxy, and Anglican, to name just a few—and even the Roman Catholic Latin Rite has through its history recognized several traditions within itself, including the Ambrosian in the diocese of Milan, the Mozarabic around Toledo, and the Sarum chant of Salisbury, England. The prestige of Gregorian chant comes chiefly from the political ambitions of Charlemagne, the early Frankish monarch who wished to unify his growing empire with a uniform liturgical practice. From the ninth century on, Gregorian chant dominated the liturgies of Europe, but it is just one chant repertory of many. "Plainchant" is a more comprehensive term.

The interesting thing about plainchant in modern culture is that, despite their extremely limited experience with this music in actual liturgy, most Catholics and most other people too will recognize it as

---

[2] This is the general case. The *Gloria* was traditionally omitted during the solemn seasons of Advent and Lent.

sacred music without hesitation. It appears to be the most fundamental kind of religious music.

The empirical argument for this assertion is straightforward: virtually every religious tradition of the world has a kind of chant for its important acts of worship. Even those traditions such as the Islamic that officially legitimize no other kind of music have a chant for their sacred writings. Only the hymn approaches the universality of plainchant.

Theoretical arguments for the assertion that plainchant is fundamental to all sacred music are more complicated. They begin with the technical features of the music itself.

What Makes Plainchant Sound like Plainchant

In its purest forms, Catholic plainchant has three essential characteristics operating in mutual interdependence to define its unique sound: it is sung in unison, it has free rhythm, and it is unaccompanied.

The most peculiar of these three for modern ears is the free rhythm. More precisely, the rhythm of plainchant is without meter, or nonmetric.

We have already heard in the samples of the folk-revival style how the presence and strength of musical meter can affect the character of a piece, how it can be overpowering, as in disco music and the "Celtic Alleluia," or so weak as to practically disappear, as in passages of Debussy and other twentieth-century masters.[3] Another aspect more germane at the moment is meter as a sign of modernity and the secular world. Virtually all the music modern Westerners hear has meter and has it in spades. In the music that most people grow up with, popular music and dance music above all, a driving, metrically organized beat is indispensible.

To understand the free rhythm of plainchant, a somewhat more sophisticated account of the perception of meter is in order. If listeners are to perceive a meter, the music must provide two things. The first is a stream of phenomenal events from which the listener can abstract a standard measure of duration: a regular beat.

[3] See chap. 3.

Al - le - lu - ia.   Al   le - lu - ia.

Figure 7-1. Schematic of music with regular beats. "Celtic Alleluia." © 1985, Fintan O'Carroll and Christopher Walker. Published by OCP Publications, 5536 NE Hassalo, Portland, OR 97213. All rights reserved. Used by permission.

Beats are typically established by the beginnings (onsets or attacks) of musical notes, since notes are usually the most perceptually salient phenomena, but not every note need be as long as one beat, especially once the music is underway and the unit of time is established. The human mind easily abstracts some basic time unit—the beat, what we tap our feet to—from the notes it hears, when they are all some whole number multiple or fraction of the basic beat, that is, twice, three, or four times as long, or half or one quarter as long, etc. In the "Celtic Alleluia," notes may last one beat (eighths), two (quarters), three (dotted quarters), three quarters of a beat (dotted eighths), and one half of a beat (sixteenths). The essential thing is that all the note durations have simple proportional relations with the basic beat (eighths). Simple proportionality allows the listening mind to abstract the beat.

But having regular beats is not enough to give music a meter. The second thing the music must provide for the listener is a regular pattern of emphasizing some of the beats at the expense of other beats: periodicity.[4]

Al - le - lu - ia.   Al   le - lu - ia.

Figure 7-2. Schematic of music with stressed beats. "Celtic Alleluia." © 1985, Fintan O'Carroll and Christopher Walker. Published by OCP Publications, 5536 NE Hassalo, Portland, OR 97213. All rights reserved. Used by permission.

---

[4] An alternative way used by music theorists to express this principle: music has meter when there are two hierarchical (nested) levels of regular beats; what I call a stressed beat here in this formulation becomes a beat on the next higher structural level.

Composers have at their disposal many means of stressing beats: by using long notes rather than short notes, loud notes rather than soft notes, having instruments or singers enter or exit, sounding deep bass notes, and by changing the harmony, among other things. Composers can manipulate these factors more or less independently to produce meters of subtly varying flavors and strengths, from the gentle duple of a Lutheran hymn such as "O Sacred Head Surrounded" to the swinging triple of a "Celtic Alleluia." They need only take care, particularly at the beginning of a piece when there is no metric pattern yet perceived, to make the stressed beats perceptually distinct from their neighbors, and above all to make the stresses periodic, that is, separated by a consistent number of beats: every second or third beat is typical of the Western tradition.

Plainchant has neither of the basic requirements for meter. In most performances, its note lengths are not in simple geometric proportions, such as in the "Celtic Alleluia," but they are rather of infinitely variable quantities.[5] Therefore there is no basic unit, no regular beat that jazz, rock, and other modern popular styles must have. Furthermore, because plainchant is unharmonized and sung a cappella, no harmonic changes or instruments create stresses. What stresses remain, weak as they are, come at irregular time intervals. The description here is made in somewhat negative terms—what plainchant is missing—but that is simply for the purpose of comparing it with music that is more familiar. The result is most positive indeed: the mystical, apparently effortless flow that we know as plainchant.

Effortlessness comes from plainchant well sung, and to get to that point may actually require a great deal of effort. The simplicity of the musical texture belies the difficulty of many chants. Without standard beats there is nothing for singers to count, so even a small group

---

[5] Some would dispute this. Owing to the ambiguities in both the medieval musical notations and medieval theoretical accounts of chant performance, a variety of rhythmic interpretations have been assigned since the revival of the Gregorian repertory in the nineteenth century. See the fine overview in Richard L. Crocker, *An Introduction to Gregorian Chant* (New Haven, CT: Yale University Press, 2000), 163–72. If a scheme assigns a regular alternation of single and double durations of a consistent time unit, for example, then a strong triple meter will result. Proponents of such proportional plainchant are in the tiny minority of scholars and performers, however. David Hiley dismisses the possibility of the music aligning regularly with poetic accents as "moot" in *Western Plainchant: A Handbook* (Oxford: Clarendon Press; New York: Oxford University Press, 1993), 284.

singing plainchant must learn from one another the subtlest of rhythmic patterns and nuances just to stay together. It is a misconception to think that plainchant has "no rhythm"; rather, its rhythm is all too real, with a refinement and touch quite unknown to the iron metric grid of more familiar Western music.

The second of the three defining characteristics of plainchant is that it is sung in unison, one pitch at a time. There is no harmony, because harmony needs two or more different pitch classes sounding at once to make chords. The technical expressions for this effect are monophonic texture, or monophony. For Westerners weaned on music that is always harmonized, except for nearly extinct informal folksinging and an occasional "Happy Birthday," the monophonic aspect of chant can be quite alien, which of course contributes to its distinctive mark. In fact, in its monophony, Catholic plainchant has more in common with the non-Western musics of the world, most of which have no harmony and instead prize their intricacies of melody.[6]

The monophonic and nonmetric features of plainchant reinforce one another. That there are no regular beats to count discourages harmonization, at least in the sense of simultaneous and independent melodies in the Western aesthetic, because singers would have no easy means of coordinating their different melodies in time. For its part, monophony helps to preserve the mystical flow of plainchant without meter, since harmonic change is one of the most powerful means of stressing a beat. The absence of chord changes means that single notes of the plainchant are unlikely to be unduly accented.

The third defining characteristic, again expressed in somewhat negative terms for the sake of comparison, is unaccompanied singing. In its pure forms, plainchant is sung a cappella (Italian for "in the chapel style"), which has come to mean "without any instrumental accompaniment" at all. The sound of human voices all singing the same thing together in a kind of hushed undertone, reverberating through the arcades of a large church, is like no other music in the Western tradition.

To be sure, plainchant through history has very often not been sung in the pure, textbook form described here. For centuries the pipe organ has accompanied plainchant in some places; it is not always clear

---

[6] Later Byzantine chants are often accompanied by a drone, a sustained and unchanging tonic pitch called the *ison*. Also, any plainchant, when sung at the same time by men and women, will have simultaneous pitches an octave apart. These exceptions do not seriously qualify the monophonic aspect of plainchant.

whether it simply doubled the melodies sung by the choir or whether the organist added improvised harmonies, once such idioms became commonplace in the West. The same happens today. The Benedictines at Sant' Anselmo in Rome and at the mecca of Gregorian chant, St. Pierre de Solesmes in France, use organ harmonizations from time to time. The character of plainchant remains.

Why Plainchant Is Essentially Sacred

These three essential qualities of plainchant ground at least five arguments as to why it is the fundamental form of sacred music and therefore explain why it is common to all religions.

Once again, it is wrong to think that plainchant has no rhythm. On the contrary, its rhythm can be the subtlest in the world. But what is this rhythm? Generally, the rhythm of chant is the rhythm of speech, or, more specifically, the rhythm of prayer. That plainchant has no meter to impose itself on the language being sung means that it may freely follow the rhythms of ecclesiastical Latin, regardless of the particular form of the prayer. A strophic text, such as that of a hymn, can even create a kind of large-scale pattern arising from the lengths of its lines, if they are regular. In short, the overriding rhythm of plainchant is that of its chanted language.

But that language, of course, is sung, so that while the rhythmic patterns of the language are preserved, plainchant often elongates them and amplifies the entire utterance into a kind of exalted speech, a language appropriate for God.

In some religions, notably Islam, plainchant and prayer are virtually synonymous. To pray means to chant and to chant means to pray. Juridical Islam, in fact, does not consider the chants that invite the faithful to prayer (ʿadhān) and the ritual chanting of the Qurʾān (tajwīd) to be music at all. Music belongs to the secular world, to be avoided; the tones heard in the mosque are prayer.

The first argument, then, for the precedence given to plainchant is that it is considered in its nature to be an exalted form of speech proper for praising the divine. The second argument follows directly on: it is the best form of music for holy writings.

Whether we speak of the Bible, the Qurʾān, the Hindu Vedas, or the Buddhist sutras, the sacred scriptures are by and large not written in poetic forms suitable for strophic songs and other folk types. Their languages are usually not poetic at all, and when they are, they lack the strong poetic meters and rhyme schemes that can match up with a musical phrase pattern. The Psalms and other canticles, from both the Old and New Testaments, have been sung since they were composed, but all the evidence suggests that in ancient times they were chanted, never sung as songs with strong metric and strophic profiles. To sing them that way would have done extreme violence to the texts. The only way to make a song out of a psalm is to paraphrase it, to box it into the confines of a strophe. Psalm paraphrase was indeed an essential feature of early Protestant music and it still occurs with great frequency in new compositions today, but historically, in most religions, paraphrasing a sacred text was anathema.

The rhythmic freedom of plainchant ensures that it can mold itself to any text. After all, it is prophetic, elevated speech. "One of the chief reasons why chant is so prized is that the antiphons, psalms, *Kyrie, Gloria, Sanctus, Agnus Dei*, and other chants *of* the Eucharistic liturgy, not texts *added to* it . . . are supported by singing this comparatively simple style of music in order to underscore the liturgy itself."[7] Moreover, plainchant is rhetorical. Because it is sung, because it has high, middle, and low pitches, because it can repeat pitches at length or suddenly leap to a melodic peak, plainchant can emphasize key words and expressions in a mystical flourish. The name of the Lord is so underscored in the well-known Gloria "De Angelis":

Tu so - lus Al - ti - si mus,— Je - su— Chri - ste.

Example 7-1. Gloria "De Angelis" (*Graduale Romanum*, 739).

The last syllable of a Latin Alleluia, traditionally heard before the gospel reading, often extends itself in such a rhapsody that this part of the chant acquired a technical name, the *jubilus*, from the Latin for "rejoice."

On the other hand, plainchant is almost completely without "expression" in the modern sense of communicating or imitating an emotional state.[8]

---

[7] Kevin Irwin, *Context and Text: Method in Liturgical Theology* (Collegeville, MN: Liturgical Press, 1994), 236. Emphasis in original.

[8] That music does this even in modern sensibilities is not to be taken for granted. Indeed, the aesthetic position that music is a "language of the emotions" or sym-

Cru-cem tu - am a-do-ra-mus Do - mi-ne: et sanc-tam re-sur-rec-ti-o-nem tu - am.

Al - le - - lu - ia.

Example 7-2. *Crucem tuam*, chant for the veneration of the cross, Good Friday; *Alleluia*, chant for the Easter Vigil (*Graduale Romanum*, 175, 191).

The liturgical roles of these two plainchants could hardly contrast more starkly. The first is sung moments after the dramatic reading of the passion according to St. John, the gospel reading for the Good Friday liturgy ending with the death of the Lord. The second is sung some thirty hours later, moments before the reading of one of the gospel resurrection accounts for the Easter Vigil, indeed the first "alleluia" heard since before the beginning of Lent. The first is a moment of awe and penitence in the face of the magnitude of the sacrifice, the second one of inexpressible joy at the victory won in the face of defeat. Yet the modes and melodic shapes of the two chants are quite similar. Absent the words, many listeners might be hard put to distinguish them. One will listen in vain for the typical distinctions in musical semantics that we find in modern songs, operas, film scores, musical plays, and any music whose job it is to express the dynamics of human relations. That is because human relations are not the center of liturgy. It is surely not that plainchant tells worshipers to be cool in the presence of awesome mysteries, not that it would be wrong to experience the sorrow of guilt on Good Friday or the joy of redemption on Holy Saturday. Far from it. Rather, plainchant points to the deeper mysteries causing those human reactions. Mysteries are not to be comprehended fully, and plainchant does not attempt to capture them, only to allow God's

---

bolic of human emotions is highly contested. For some prominent surveys of the problem, see Peter Kivy, *The Corded Shell: Reflections of Musical Perception* (Princeton: Princeton University Press, 1980); Suzanne Langer, *Philosophy in a New Key: A Study in the Symbolism of Reason, Rite, and Art*, 3rd ed. (Cambridge, MA: Harvard University Press, 1956); and Roger Scruton, *The Aesthetics of Music* (Oxford: Clarendon Press, 1997).

people to sense their holiness through the elevation of their sacred words.

Such melismas (melodic extensions on a single syllable) are exceptional in Catholic plainchant. They are mostly heard in prayers with short texts, such as the *Kyrie* (Lord, Have Mercy) of the Mass or the *Benedicamus Domino* (Let us bless the Lord) of the Divine Office. More generally, notes and syllables move smoothly along in something close to a one-to-one relationship, as in all psalms and canticles, the longer Mass Ordinaries, chanted readings, and hymns. The tempo is more or less the tempo of normal speech, occasionally a bit slower. Compositions require no introduction and, of course, no instruments; they begin from silence, and when they are done, they melt back into silence, no small part of their effect. Plainchant is liturgically efficient, a third reason why it is found in all major religions.

Plainchant is therefore the obvious solution to the problem of singing longer liturgical texts: the *Gloria*, the *Credo*, and the psalms. In many parishes, often quite musical otherwise, these are the prayers that are not sung, despite their liturgical priority over recessional hymns, reflections, and other *periphera*. This is particularly sad in the case of the psalms, which were composed to be sung and always have been in most every Jewish and Christian denomination. Because it can be sung in a rapid-fire rhythm of one note per syllable on a single pitch, more or less, a psalm tone formula guarantees that chanting the psalm will take little more time than reciting it. Any extra time comes from the more florid antiphon. The Gregorian tradition matches the particular psalm tone to the mode or key of the antiphon of the day, which smoothes the transition between psalm and antiphon beautifully. The responsorial psalm of a modern Latin Rite liturgy can do the same, even if the psalm is abbreviated and the congregation interpolates the antiphon between each pair of psalm verses.[9]

---

[9] When the responsorial psalm is sung in the reformed Latin rite today, it should work this way:

(1) The cantor sings the antiphon proper to the feast; the congregation repeats it.

(2) The cantor chants a pair of psalm verses, with or without harmonic accompaniment from the organ or other instrument, to a melodic formula called a psalm tone, which adapts itself to any length of verse; then the congregation repeats the antiphon.

(3) The cantor sings the next pair of psalm verses to the same psalm tone, the congregation responds with the antiphon, the cycle repeats until the last antiphon.

Because they are prose, the *Gloria* and *Credo* are seldom chanted to formulaic tones but are instead completely through-composed. Traditional plainchants again are almost completely syllabic, with one note for one syllable, except for the concluding Amen and a few other key words as noted above (Ex. 7-1). The melodies, while not formulaic, typically reuse the same melodic ideas in a flexible way known as centonicism. Figure 7-3 shows how only three brief motives, slightly varied to fit the words, comprise the opening third of a plainchant *Gloria*.

Figure 7-3. Gloria "De Angelis" showing centonic aspects.

So, while the prayers are indeed long, a congregation can pick up the melodies faster than one might otherwise think. At two churches in Venice, St. Mark's and St. Simeon's, these prayers are chanted in Latin with great success to traditional melodies using a traditional technique

---

This is quite close to traditional Gregorian psalmody, the only differences being that in the Gregorian, the antiphon, sung to a much more elaborate melody than the psalm tone, is chanted only at the beginning and end of the psalm, and the last psalm verse is always followed by singing the lesser doxology ("Glory be to the Father," etc.). Some scholars believe that in the early centuries of the church, the antiphon was indeed sung between groups of verses as well as at the beginning and end, which, if true, would make the ancient practice even closer to the current one. Other scholars believe that there is insufficient evidence to support this claim.

This practice evolved into the traditional Gregorian one with its framing antiphon, presumably because in ancient practice psalms were sung in their entirety, not excerpted as in modern liturgies. Singing the antiphon between each pair of psalm verses would have made for a sumptuously long chant indeed.

called *alternatim*, whereby the choir sings one phrase and then the congregation (with the choir supporting) respond with the next phrase. This means that the congregation need learn only half the melody, yet the whole is sung without loss of time. The *Gloria* and *Credo* are easier to learn than psalmody in one respect, of course, in that the words never change, allowing important verbal-melodic associations to reinforce the memory. The Venetian congregations actually sing without the benefit of printed music.

A Mass sung in plainchant throughout, then, takes but a fraction more than one that is spoken throughout, perhaps ten or fifteen minutes longer, while the difference in spiritual effect between the two is, let us say, as the heavens are above the earth.

Some plainchants, especially common in Eastern religious traditions, are repetitive in the extreme. Litanies are a good example common in the Western tradition:

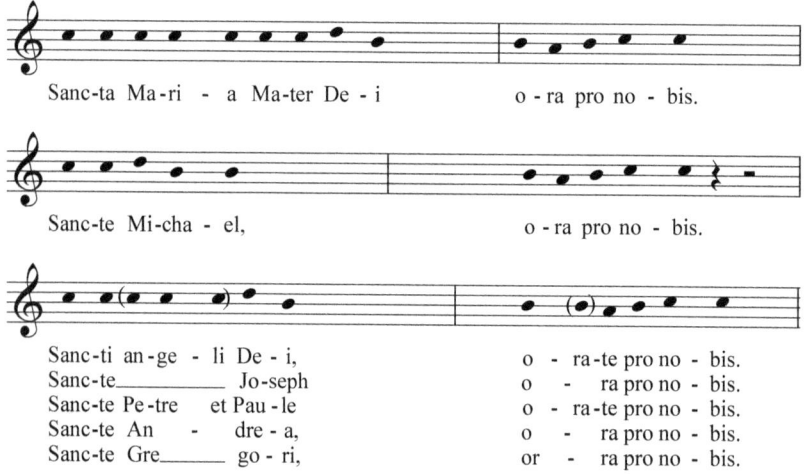

Example 7-3. Litany from the Easter Vigil (*Graduale Simplex*, 148–49).

Such repetition means that the mind need not concentrate on the business of singing, need not attend to the music as music, and can instead give itself over to spiritual contemplation, the fourth argument. The music is merely the means of clearing the mind, and the tones, particularly when arising from a large group, are credited with inducing a spiritual state.

The fifth argument harks back to the hallmark of sacred music in the Western tradition: the mark of distinction. The rhythm of the music that Westerners hear through the media, that they sing, that they grow up with, is strongly metric; the rhythm of plainchant is free. Western music is harmonized, and indeed that is what sets it apart from the world's other cultural traditions; plainchant is monophonic. And Western music is heavily accompanied by instruments, mostly electronic nowadays; plainchant is sung a cappella, without the slightest hint of technological artifice. No Western music is stranger to the Western ear than plainchant, and this very strangeness affords it power.[10]

That power comes from its musical semantic, its symbolic properties, which in turn derive from plainchant's exclusive association with Catholic ritual and liturgy. Plainchant seems sacred in the same way that gold chalices, the priest's Roman chasuble, the *orans* posture, and cruciform architecture seem sacred: they are never experienced anywhere else but in churches.

Plainchant Today: The Obstacles

The virtues of plainchant—as a mystically elevated prayer, as the music best suited to singing Scripture, liturgically efficient, conducive to meditation, and utterly distinct from the secular world—would seem to justify completely the Second Vatican Council's nomination of "Gregorian chant as specially native to the Roman Liturgy," to be "given pride of place in liturgical services" (SC 116).[11] Why is it then so seldom heard?

Two prejudices have prevented the revival of plainchant for common parochial use. One is that the entire tradition smacks of "old church," the state of liturgy and of Roman Catholicism in general, before the Second Vatican Council. As such, plainchant embodies reactionary attitudes to liturgical reform, ignorant and sentimental desires to "turn back the clock" to the days when priests presented their backs to

---

[10] Using a different argument, Edward Schaefer arrives at the same conclusion: "It is also precisely this distinctiveness that reinforces chant's position as the preeminent music for the liturgy." *Catholic Music through the Ages: Balancing the Needs of a Worshipping Church* (Chicago: Hillenbrand, 2008), 36.

[11] Professor William Mahrt remarks in a personal communication that the Latin *principem locum* is more accurately translated as "first place" rather than "pride of place." In addition, the Latin *proprium*, here translated as "native," might be rendered "suitable" or "proper."

a dumb congregation. The second belief holds that plainchant would severely limit congregational singing.

The "old church" associations with plainchant are quite simply irrational, which is not to say that they are not powerful, only without reason. The historical irony could hardly be more bitter. In preconciliar parishes, plainchant was even rarer than it is now. The great dearth of any good liturgical music in the experience of preconciliar Catholics was what the liturgical movement and most of its high-minded reformers wished to remedy more than just about anything, so much so that plainchant was their very standard, the first thing Catholic intellectuals thought of when they heard the phrase "liturgical movement."[12] When those Catholics who came of age in the 1960s and 1970s recoil at the mention of plainchant, they can only do so because they assume that anything with a preconciliar existence must be spiritually insalubrious, and therefore plainchant must frustrate the "spirit of reform," an assumption both preposterous and contrary to history. But it is extremely difficult to reason with these deeply learned prejudices; they are fading slowly, and in turn plainchant is reviving, but the generation will likely have to pass away before the church is completely free of them.

No small part of plainchant's bad taste for these people is its language. Latin chants set Latin texts and the issue of Latin versus the vernacular in the liturgy was one of the most emotional of liturgical matters debated at the council, and it remains emotional today. Liturgical language is a complex matter, with musical ramifications to be discussed in due course.[13] Here the technical question on the table is the stringency of the union between the Latin language and the notes of plainchant.

The historical repertory of Catholic plainchant sets Latin texts (Greek for *Kyrie eleison*) from the old Vulgate Bible of St. Jerome and many other sources. Most scholars and lovers of chant agree that the union between the music and the Latin language is most felicitous,

---

[12] Ernest Koenker, *The Liturgical Renaissance in the Roman Catholic Church* (Chicago: The University of Chicago Press, 1954), 18. Anthony Ruff details a number of dissenting voices within the leadership of the last decades of the liturgical movement, but it remains unclear whether this dislodged the movement's centrality of plainchant in the wider view. See *Sacred Music and Liturgical Reform: Treasures and Transformations* (Chicago: Hillenbrand, 2007), 243–50.

[13] See chap. 16.

some going so far as to claim that Latin, owing to its many vocalic endings, is the best language for singing. Advocates for liturgy completely in the vernacular then have two choices if they want to chant: fit vernacular translations or adaptations to the original plainchant melodies or compose entirely original chant melodies to vernacular texts already approved for the liturgy.[14]

Here is a possible adaptation of the simple *Kyrie* melody found in the Roman Gradual, the standard collection of plainchant for the Roman Rite.

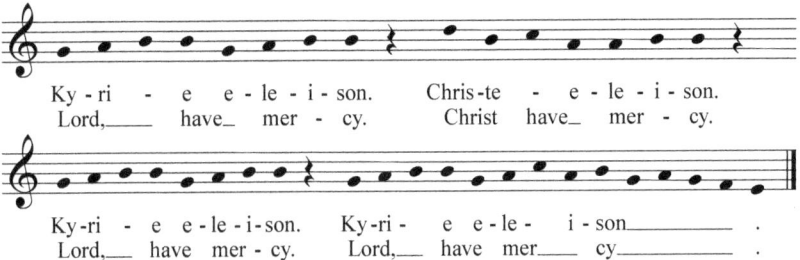

Example 7-4. *Kyrie eleison* (*Graduale Romanum*, 763) with Greek and English.

Compromises are inevitable. The Greek invocations have seven and six syllables respectively, the English ones four. This makes it practically impossible to change the syllables when pitches repeat, as one always wants to do to have sufficient articulation of the repeated note. There seems no remedy in "Christ, have mercy," except to omit the second A. The melisma setting the very last syllable sings better in Greek because the back vowel /on/ allows a more fully rounded mouth than the frontal /y/ in English. Still, the translation does work, even if it is a trifle awkward. The *Kyrie* is a better candidate than many plainchants because the original syllable-to-note ratio is not consistently one-to-one, allowing a little flexibility when moving to English. Psalm tones have even more flexibility, owing to their recitation tone whose length is determined by the number of syllables in the verse

---

[14] Edward Schaefer lists "few quick attempts to adapt the Proper to English" shortly after the close of the Second Vatican Council in *Catholic Music through the Ages*, 53.

being sung.[15] In the long, syllabic *Gloria* (see Ex. 7-1), however, retaining the integrity of the original melody would be more difficult.

So instead one can compose an original chant to the English text, as Theodore Marier did for his *English Chant Mass*.[16] This solution brings its own set of problems, not least of which is composing a worthy melody. Putting one's new creation up against chants that have survived a thousand years of cultural testing would seem, to say the least, daunting. As a hedge against such invidious comparisons, some composers change the game by adding a harmonization to their plainchants. Lucien Deiss' "Keep in Mind" is a well-known example of modern chant, but one not very highly esteemed among musicians precisely because of that harmony's sentimental effect. Harmonizing chant has its own set of technical and semantic problems.

Congregations and Plainchant

Sacrosanctum Concilium promoted both Gregorian chant and *participatio actuosa* (active participation) in the liturgy. It seems that the council fathers saw no contradiction in this, and yet the fear that plainchant would inhibit congregational singing has probably discouraged its parochial revival more than anything else. To be sure, the revival effort has been stunted for decades by the relevance argument, and since ready sources of plainchant arrived only after folk music had taken the field in the late 1960s, it has had to battle simple inertia as well. But there are some substantial issues to resolve when considering whether congregations are ready for plainchant: its difficulty, its origins in Christian Europe, and its very strangeness.

Plainchant has a certain reputation, particularly among those who know and study it, of sublimity of such refinement that it may be sung well only by a professional liturgical choir. Certain works indeed demand that level of competence, and the apparently effortless unanimity of sound, such as a *schola* produces, is well worth the effort of maintaining one. But plainchant is a repertory larger and with more variety than most. Like any significant repertory, it comprises works of great difficulty, particularly the elaborate Mass propers, such as the

---

[15] Paul R. Ford has translated many of the chants of the *Graduale Simplex* into English. These are almost entirely short antiphons combined with psalm tones. See *By Flowing Waters: Chant for the Liturgy* (Collegeville, MN: Liturgical Press, 1999).

[16] Theodore Marier, *English Chant Mass*, in *The Adoremus Hymnal*, 250–54. San Francisco: Ignatius Press, 1997.

graduals and offertories that are sung but a few times in the course of an entire liturgical cycle. The repertory also has much simpler compositions.

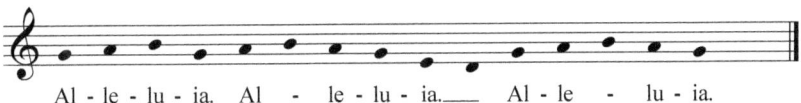

Example 7-5. "Gregorian" Alleluia.

This Alleluia is sung easily by congregations in many parishes throughout the world, and it has as much right to be called plainchant as the most serpentine of the many other Alleluia settings.[17] Latin hymns such as *Pange lingua*, with their more regular phrase structure, are well within the competence of an average congregation. The *Kyrie* of example 7-4 resounds heartily every week from the church of St. Malachy's in little Sherburne, New York, as does a plainchant *Sanctus*, *Agnus Dei*, Our Father, and many short responses. Some are sung in Latin in antiphony, with the cantor or choir intoning each phrase, the congregation responding. The famous basilica of St. Mark's in Venice sings plainchant in similar fashion.[18] A good choir increases the range of possibilities greatly, no doubt, but the fact is that plainchant is not at all the natural enemy of congregational singing.

Harmonizing Plainchant

Congregations singing plainchant touches on the matter of harmonizing chant with a pipe organ and other instrumental accompaniment.[19] It keeps everyone on pitch, which can slip steadily downward in choral chanting. It also keeps everyone together; the organ can gently push the congregation with enough volume. Finally, it gives the

---

[17] Some chant specialists will argue that because this setting of Alleluia is actually a psalm antiphon from the Divine Office, it therefore had a different liturgical function. I thank Professor William Mahrt for pointing this out. But this fact does not in any way prevent its liturgical semantics from being redefined by a different usage in a different community, just in the way that semantics of natural language also constantly change with their contextual use. As chap. 12 shows, musical semantics are flexible and heavily dependent upon the context of use.

[18] For a detailed description of this liturgy, see chap. 18.

[19] Instrumental accompaniment other than the organ brings semantic problems; see chap. 12.

congregation an extra measure of security. To modern Westerners particularly, unused to public singing anymore and very much used to loud instruments, unaccompanied chanting can seem exposed, almost a kind of musical nakedness. A warm harmonization from the organ offers a more comfortable blanket of sound. To harmonize, then, or not to harmonize, and if so, how?

The history of Catholic plainchant does not decide the issue clearly. The pipe organ does not appear in church before the tenth century, and the overwhelming documentary evidence of chant books indicates, although without absolute certainty, that plainchant was just that—plain singing, unharmonized and unaccompanied—in most places in Europe, especially in smaller parishes and monasteries. This would seem to be the pure, unadulterated, *Urform* of Gregorian and other plainchants. On the other hand, there is also a great body of evidence indicating that plainchant in later centuries was both accompanied and harmonized in various ways, depending on the time and place. The Catholic tradition offers both possibilities.

Harmonizing a plainchant introduces a radical change of idiom. Converting from a monophonic to a polyphonic (many-voiced, i.e., harmonized) texture can affect other aspects of the music, and whether the harmony helps or hurts depends very much on the kind used and even on specific chord choices.

One possible effect of harmonization is that the plainchant acquires a meter alien to its pure form.

Example 7-6. Harmonized version of "Gregorian" Alleluia.

If the harmony is anything more than a drone, the chords must change, and there is no surer way of accenting a note than changing a chord along with it. The arrangement given in example 7-6 gives the familiar Alleluia a clear triple meter through such chord changes. First, the melody's original durations, variable and indeterminate, are given definite durations in whole number ratios all related to the eighth note. There is now a uniform beat, symbolized by that eighth note. The changes of harmony occur precisely on every third of these beats. Both conditions for meter are fulfilled, and a mild little dance results.

The threefold iteration of the word "alleluia" and the seven measures of the harmonization are both asymmetrical and afford some vestige of the plainchant's original suppleness, despite the clarity of the meter. But symmetrical phrasing and relentlessly regular chord changes, the kind heard in the "Celtic Alleluia," can make an utter triviality of a chant once simple and noble.[20]

Functional and Nonfunctional Harmony

Harmonization may injure not only by its timing, its rhythmic patterning, however, but also by its type.

Harmony simply means sounding more than one pitch at a time, which in the Western tradition produces simultaneous melodies, the distinguishing aspect of Western music. The ways of doing this are virtually infinite, but we can classify the harmonic practices of the West into two broad groups, the functional and the nonfunctional. Nonfunctional harmony was the only kind available from the beginning of polyphony in the tenth century until sometime in the sixteenth, when the harmonic syntax of secular music changed. From the seventeenth century through the present, functional harmony has dominated, although nonfunctional idioms were either revived or invented throughout the twentieth century in certain kinds of art music and intentionally anachronistic sacred music.

The difference? In functional harmony, the kind Westerners have grown accustomed to for four hundred years and more, the chords have a syntax in and of themselves. We expect certain harmonic patterns (progressions) as we expect the verb to follow a noun in a sentence. It need not always happen, just as verbs do not always immediately follow the noun, but that is the reigning pattern. In the harmonized Alleluia above, for example, the G chords and the D chords have a kind of polarity: the D is suspenseful and tense, the G is resolved and conclusive. Notice how the second phrase concludes on a D chord. This produces harmonic tension, and so we expect and wait for the last phrase. The last harmony of the piece must be the tonic

[20] See chap. 3.

chord G. Ending with any other harmony would be akin to finishing a sentence with "and then . . ."

In music with nonfunctional harmony, the harmony of Palestrina and Debussy, the chords have no such fixed relations or "functions." Chords result almost purely from coincident notes of simultaneous melodies. There is a syntax of consonance and dissonance within the chords, to be sure, so that the combinations of pitches are not at all random, but the chords, as chords, do not lead from one to another in predictable patterns.

When plainchant is arranged with functional harmony, like the Alleluia in example 7-6, two things generally happen. First, the idiom automatically begins to resemble popular music, because that is the way almost all Western pop for the last two centuries has been harmonized. Second, the metric aspect of the rhythm is amplified, because chord functions have metric associations. The tense, dominant function of the D chord in the Alleluia has an upbeat, or weak (unstressed) beat, association, while the tonic function of the G chord has a downbeat, or strong (stressed) beat, association. We heard how these associations turn the important measures of the "Celtic Alleluia" into great big "beats" themselves, so that the meter of the song is strong not only within the bar, but beyond the bar. Each bar, as a big beat, is stressed or not in an alternating pattern that produces the singsong sensation of a big duple imposed on a small triple.

When a plainchant is arranged with nonfunctional harmony, none of these metric effects need occur.

Example 7-7. Alleluia from Tempus Adventus, Missa I, *Graduale Simplex*, and Advent Alleluia No. 85 from *Hymns, Psalms, and Spiritual Canticles*. © 1972, Boston Boys Choir, Cambridge, Massachusetts. All rights reserved. Used by permission.

Example 7-7 compares a traditional plainchant Alleluia with its adaptation for organ accompaniment by Theodore Marier. Notice that there are no bar lines in the notation, implying that there is no meter. But notation guarantees nothing about the perception of meter. That arises from the stresses in the music itself.

There are two duration values in the melody, eighth notes and quarter notes, ratio 1:2. However, the second G, on the second "-ia" syllable, has a long mark over it, asking the singers to elongate this note by some little but indeterminate time. This is Marier's way of discouraging the perception of regular beats, the first requirement of meter. And in fact the melody sounds better, as does all plainchant, without a rigid, metronomic attention to note lengths. This is easy to do as long as the harmonization remains in the hands of the organist who can follow the vicissitudes of the unison chant. After all, a free rhythm is the point.

What about those harmonic changes from the organ? The first F-sharp minor chord lasts four eighth notes before giving way to D major, two eighth notes, followed by an inversion of D major for three eighth notes. Then come E minor for six and B minor for two before ending on F-sharp minor again. No periodicity. Each change creates a musical accent, but without periodicity the second requirement for the perception of meter is completely absent. This is also true of the phrases: the first Alleluia takes six eighths, the second five, and the last seven. The arranger, omitting bar lines, was as good as his word: the music has no meter.

Neither has it any sentiment or other secular connotation that could threaten its propriety for liturgy. When we sing Deiss' "Keep in Mind" and arrive at the climactic phrase "He is our saving Lord," it is easy to imagine in the mind's ear a hundred Hollywood strings rising to meet the descending melody, because that is precisely the syrupy associations that his brand of functional harmony brings. Marier's harmony, by contrast, is a specific nonfunctional type called modal, because it derives from the ancient church modes, the system that classifies almost all traditional Roman Catholic plainchant. Marier wrote his Alleluia in the Phrygian mode, also known as Mode III or the E mode (here transposed to F-sharp), and his harmonies accord with it. Despite their mild occasional dissonances that betray their twentieth-century origin, they imbue the music with a semantic redolent of the mystery, antiquity, and venerable tradition of plainchant itself.

There is no doubt that, especially for modern Westerners, pieces with strong metric structures are easier to learn than nonmetric plainchants because both the harmony and the metric patterns themselves, interlocking the measures with phrase lengths and chord functions, provide many more cognitive markers for the memory, just as a rhyming jingle in an advertisement will grip even the unwilling mind much more than any free prose explanation of the product's virtues.[21] This is why congregational psalm responses (antiphons) published in missalettes are invariably arranged with an easy functional harmony in a pithy four- or eight-measure phrase. Lots of cues and lots of symmetry make a catchy tune. That these sound trite arises from a gross overuse of musical structure, rather like foisting massive flying buttresses onto a one-story country church because the builder once admired them in Paris. Meter organizes longer musical forms, at the level of the strophic song at least, and a one-phrase antiphon has no need of its structural undergirding. Furthermore, that metric phrase almost always requires completion by a long note at the end, an inefficiency made more ponderous by contrast with the chanted verses of the psalm. An Alleluia sung week after week in this way can wear in the same way and for precisely the same reasons as does the advertising jingle.

The Value of Strangeness

But jingles are familiar stuff, enticing, immediate and cloying in their attraction, which is precisely why advertisers use them to bring their products to our attention. One perhaps can understand the evangelicals' embrace of such idioms for their megachurches: they want prospective believers to buy in. The first great purpose of Catholic liturgy, however, is not to attract but to praise and give thanks to the Most High through the sacrifice that Christ gave us to re-present in each Mass. In the end, a worthy liturgy will indeed attract believers because that fundamental purpose is built into everyone, but that is a deep attraction, requiring the time of acculturation and reflection, not the instant, superficial appeal and lure of the jingle.

It is also understandable how, in the first years after the Second Vatican Council, when the urgency of inventing a Catholic congregational music seemed great, bishops and pastors opted for the strategy of relevance, of choosing musical idioms most familiar to the widest body in order to get them to sing. That strategy has failed aestheti-

---

[21] Bob Snyder, *Music and Memory* (Cambridge, MA: MIT Press, 2000), 170–80.

cally, liturgically, and even in its main goal of spirited congregational singing. Now plainchant, once rejected for its strangeness and irrelevance to modernism, is getting a second look.

For plainchant is indeed very strange at first acquaintance, alien in all its earmarks to most any kind of music that modern Westerners hear for enjoyment, rock, jazz, film music, office music, Broadway and opera and symphonic music, whatever is encountered in the secular world. That music forms itself around strong, sometimes pounding, beats producing a clear and steady meter. Chant is rhythmically free. Secular music dresses itself in all manner of instrumental colors, rainbows of sound color. Chant arises from voices alone. When sung, secular music depends on an aggressive vocal projection, amplified to inhuman scales by the inevitable microphone. Chant is sung almost to oneself, an interior singing that need never be loud. Secular music has harmony, many melodies going on all at once. Chant is one note at a time, melody in solitude. It is an image of Franciscan poverty turned into music.

Its strangeness is its saving grace. For it is the very strangeness of liturgy that most often inspires and helps us somehow to transcend the familiar, secular world, though momentarily. The everyday is not what spiritual pilgrims look for in a church, not in its architecture, not in its vessels and vestments, and certainly not in its liturgy. Plainchant, like Catholicism, is in the world and does not reject its means, but attempts to place it at some remove and to draw our focus elsewhere. Its reliance on voices alone is a musical asceticism reflecting our spiritual ideals about the material world as something to rejoice in when used in simplicity and for right purposes, the foremost of which is the Eucharist, giving thanks and praise to God. Its unison singing reflects our unity of faith. Above all, its free rhythm, a rhythm unmeasured, is a kind of time out of time, a temporality offering a glimpse of that end time when it shall cease altogether.

In its very defining characteristics, then, plainchant embodies a Catholic worldview, sufficiently distinct and so powerful that television producers gladly use it as a ready symbol of the sacred. One wonders when the church will reclaim this treasure to do the same.

Chapter 8

Classical Polyphony

> The type of music in divine services . . . should be sung so that the words are more intelligible than the modulations of the music.
> Council of Trent (1562)

If plainchant is the music most iconic of Roman Catholicism, the classical polyphony of the high Renaissance is a close second. Whenever a solemn liturgy such as the funeral of Pope John Paul II is broadcast to the world from St. Peter's Basilica at the Vatican, it is polyphony that dominates the liturgy's music. In one sense, polyphony signifies Roman Catholicism much more specifically than plainchant. Plainchant, after all, in some form is sung by all the world's major religions, which affords it an unrivalled sacred semantic to be sure, but not a specifically Catholic semantic. But harmony in the West owed its origin and development to the polyphonic embellishment of Gregorian chant, and since the eleventh century it was Catholic liturgy that provided the main venue for the great evolution of this idea of simultaneous melodies. The more radical of the Protestant reformers of the sixteenth century—Zwingli, Calvin, and later the dissidents in England, among others—in fact viewed polyphony as a Roman diabolical excrescence and banned it entirely from their liturgical programs. The Lutherans and Anglicans retained and developed it in their own distinct fashions, namely the Lutheran hymn and the English anthem, but their repertories changed with the times and thus grew to be indistinguishable from secular choral music. The Roman Catholic polyphonic tradition also knew corruption and neglect, but in ways that did not change the basic character of the genuine article from the sixteenth century. In the general sense, then, Catholics were left alone holding the field as the champions of this great repertory of sacred music.

The sound of polyphony is certainly distinct. Imagine a small group singing a Gregorian chant. Then imagine another, separate from the first, singing a different Gregorian chant. Imagine a third, fourth, fifth,

119

and perhaps a sixth, all singing their own chants, which, while clearly different from one another in melody, have certain things in common: mode, general speed, type, and the words. Finally, imagine hearing all six different chants at once, and, rather than competing and clashing horribly with one another as randomly chosen melodies should do, by some miracle they coordinate and harmonize with one another in a breathtakingly beautiful fusion of tone. This is the essence of polyphony.

The repertory referred to in Catholic documents as "classical polyphony" is a subset of a larger repertory known merely as "polyphony." The first is a misnomer on at least two counts. "Polyphony" simply means more than one melody sounding at once; that is, it identifies the hallmark of Western music and therefore legitimately refers to any harmonized music of the last 1,000 years. Music historians generally reserve "classical" for Western art music composed roughly from 1775 through 1825. Catholic documents, by contrast, refer to a repertory of liturgical music composed from the late fifteenth to early seventeenth centuries and associated above all with Giovanni da Palestrina, but also Josquin Desprez, Orlandus Lassus, Tomas Luis de Victoria, William Byrd, and many other colleagues in all parts of western Europe. By tradition, if not authenticated historical practice, the music is sung by choirs of roughly twelve to thirty voices without instrumental accompaniment, that is, a cappella. Polyphony it certainly is; it is "classical" only in the sense that this particular repertory has come to symbolize an ideal of composition.

Two kinds of liturgical composition dominate this repertory: Ordinary Mass movements and motets.

Because they could be sung at any Mass, rather than only at Masses for a particular feast day, polyphonic settings of the Mass Ordinaries —*Kyrie, Gloria, Credo, Sanctus,* and *Agnus Dei*[1]—far outnumber settings of proper prayers. A Mass by Palestrina or one of his colleagues therefore consists of five separate compositions, each setting one of the Ordinary prayers. The Latin title for the set is *Missa,* almost always followed by a subtitle that identifies a circumstance of composition— for example, *Missa Papae Marcelli* (Mass for Pope Marcellus)—or an existing composition from which the composer borrows for both semantic and constructive purposes—for example, *Missa Dum Sunt*

---

[1] The dismissal *Ite, missa est* could also be included in this group, but by the fifteenth century this text was rarely set polyphonically.

Dies Pentecostes (Mass using the motet "When the days of Pentecost were completed").

Motets are polyphonic settings of Latin texts from the Old and New Testaments, especially psalms, prayers such as the Our Father, and devotional poetry. Their sixteenth-century uses in worship are obscure; officially, they could have had but a peripheral liturgical role in the Mass, but, as with congregational hymns today, this principle was probably honored more in the breach than in the observance.

Creativity and Tradition Combined: The *Cantus Firmus*

Some scholars believe that polyphony began sometime around the turn of the millennium as a way of solemnizing a Gregorian chant for an important feast. A second singer or group of singers would shadow the original melody at some fixed interval, most often the perfect fifth. This was nothing more than a kind of sonic decoration that occurs in a number of cultures. The crucial step that distinguished the Western from all other musical traditions of the world came when that added melody no longer merely shadowed, note for note, the original plainchant but became rhythmically and melodically independent of it, yet harmonizing with it, probably in early twelfth-century France. That gave the West not only a music of an entirely original constructive principle that would prove fertile beyond all imagining, but also, by the fourteenth century, a sophisticated rhythmic notation, which allowed the coordination of truly independent melodies, so that their simultaneous tones bring out a succession of harmonic splendor.

Example 8-1. Josquin Desprez, *Missa de Beata Virgine*, Gloria, mm. 80–85. The melody in the third voice from the top is the traditional melody from the so-called Gloria IX. The other three melodies were invented by Josquin to create the polyphonic texture.

So polyphony is a shoot sprung from the stem of plainchant. For centuries almost no polyphony was composed without choosing a *cantus firmus*, a traditional plainchant or fragment of one on top of which were added newly composed melodies. The process of polyphonic composition might be compared to glossing a sacred text, or building a new church around a much older one.

Polyphony caught on and spread throughout western Europe in part because it solved one of the pernicious problems of all sacred music, the conflict of creativity and tradition.[2] The *cantus firmus* method of construction allowed an outlet for outstanding composers' natural urge to create new music, while at the same time binding that new creation indissolubly to the archetypical Catholic musical tradition, Gregorian chant. The notes of the plainchant never changed;[3] its polyphonic adornment was ever new.

Cantus firmus—or, more generally, the use of traditional music in a new composition—provides a modus operandi for well-educated

---

[2] See chap. 16.

[3] Or so it was believed; as in any ancient musical tradition with an oral history, there are variants of the same melody in different places, even after the development of notation.

composers of all kinds of Christian sacred music, both vocal and instrumental, right up to the present.

The Golden Age

The name of Palestrina epitomizes "classical polyphony" like no other, for reasons mythological, historical, and, in the end, musical. The legend was born hardly a decade after his death in 1594 when a contemporary credited a hearing of Palestrina's *Mass for Pope Marcellus* with persuading the fathers at the Council of Trent in their last session (1563) to forbear banning all polyphony in their liturgical reforms. The doubts about the historical veracity of this story surfaced far too late to prevent Palestrina's music from being cited time and again in seventeenth-, eighteenth-, and nineteenth-century textbooks as the model for the pure style of ecclesiastical polyphony. Giuseppe Baini published a major biography of Palestrina in 1828, later used as the source of an opera; by 1903 a complete set of his works was available.

Naturally, Palestrina became the adopted patron saint of the Cecilians, a musical branch of the liturgical movement that began in the late eighteenth century and dedicated itself to the restoration of plainchant and classical polyphony in opposition to the operatic styles that dominated the large churches then.[4] To prove the vitality of his music, the Cecilians promoted and published new works that tried to imitate his style. Unfortunately, as is the case with most consciously anachronistic music, these works could not avoid entirely their nineteenth-century harmonic idioms, cloying and trite in their a cappella guise, nor the stiffness that comes of a familiarity with the musical language that is academic rather than native. They were sung right into the present century at the Vatican, to the exclusion, unfortunately, of the actual music of Palestrina and his friends.

But Palestrina's preeminence over his contemporaries, while exaggerated, is hardly without musical merit. He composed 104 polyphonic Masses, a record among major figures of his time, and it is clear that he was the most famous composer of his century, perhaps with competition only from Orlandus Lassus, another unbelievably

---

[4] See chap. 9. For a fine summary of the Cecelian movement, see Anthony Ruff, OSB, *Sacred Music and Liturgical Reform: Treasures and Transformations* (Chicago: Hillenbrand, 2007), 88–104.

fecund master of the highest art. Palestrina probably taught Tomas Luis de Victoria, the great Spanish composer. It is unfair that the Palestrina myth once eclipsed the status of Lassus, Victoria, William Byrd, and many other excellent composers from the golden age of classical polyphony, but the sharpened appreciation of music composed before 1700 as well as hard historical research has redressed the balance for the most part. So to understand the essence of this classical polyphony, we need make no apology for taking as our exemplar one of Palestrina's most beloved motets.

The Essence of Classical Polyphony

The compositional problem that has driven the history of polyphony from about 1000 AD until the present is how to coordinate, both in time and in pitch space, all the melodies which sound at the same time. Paramount is the control of harmonic dissonance: what musical intervals—combinations of tones—would sound good and when. Beginnings and endings (cadences) of things naturally seemed appropriate for consonant intervals, at first the perfect octave and fifth, later also the thirds, both major and minor, because of these intervals' intrinsically low tension. Other intervals deemed dissonant—seconds, sevenths, and the famous tritone, principally—had to offer just the right amount of harmonic spice without offending the ear unduly.[5] At the same time, the progress of the individual melodies from one note to the next—the aspect known as voice-leading—had to ensure the most effortless kind of singing, with generally small intervals and a small range of durations from shortest to longest note. In short, the melodies were to have all possible integrity as melodies, as if they had no awareness of the other melodies sounding with them. Ideally, the melodic-harmonic union is a paradox: composed within a highly restrictive syntax, it creates a stream of mystical sound that seems effortless. It is indeed for exactly this *trompe l'oreille* that Palestrina's music was justly prized.

---

[5] The perfect fourth is consonant except when it involves the lowest sounding voice. These are the basic consonances and dissonances according to sixteenth-century harmonic syntax; earlier harmonic languages differed considerably in their harmonic grammars.

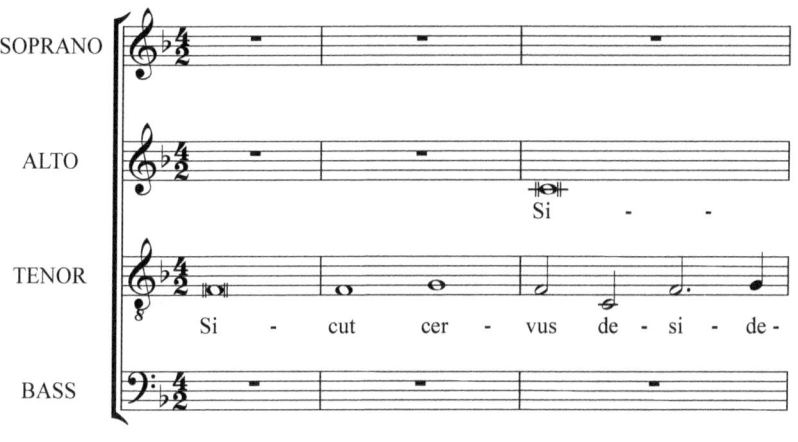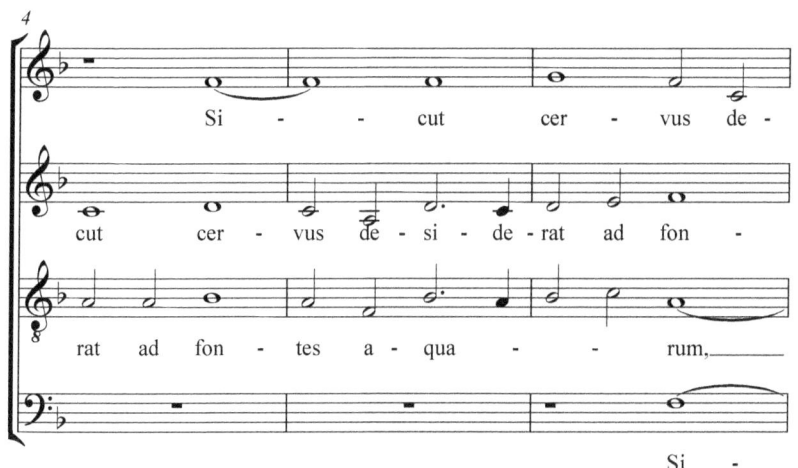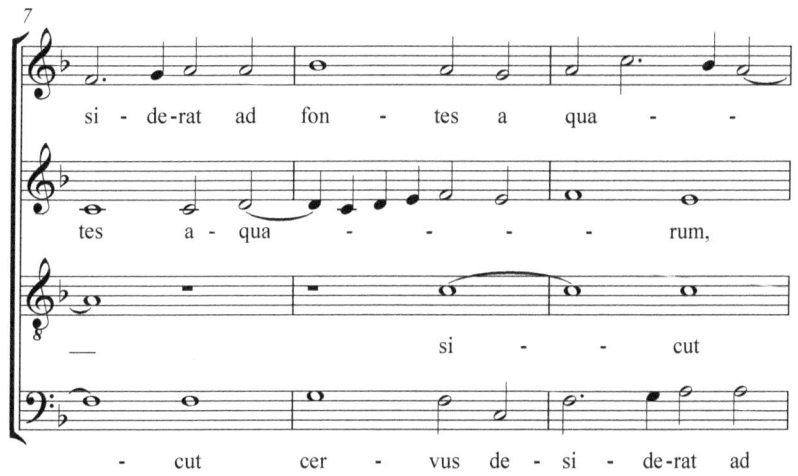

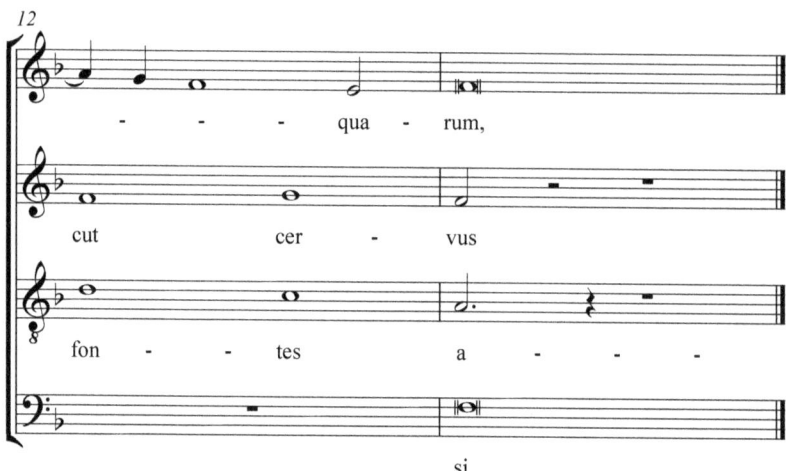

Example 8-2. Giovanna da Palestrina, motet *Sicut cervus*, mm. 1–12.

The opening of his motet *Sicut cervus*, a setting of the first verses of Psalm 42, is a textbook case of this marvelous control. The melodies seem to grow from the smallest premise, a move from the tonic F up to G and back again. Occasional fourths and fifths, nearly always involving the secure tonic F, are the most audacious intervals to be sung; everything else is smooth step motion. At first, harmonic dissonance is virtually absent: a single passing note in the third measure, another in the seventh. Gradually and gently, the composer increases their number to create a subliminal momentum before they subside once again around the cadence at the end of the quotation.

This is but half of Palestrina's magic. Traditional theory of Palestrina's counterpoint has concentrated so much on the technique of melodic-harmonic coordination that another aspect, equally essential to the style, has gone almost unnoticed: the rhythm. For classical polyphony is cousin to plainchant not only in its heritage and *cantus firmus* technique but also in a mystical flow that seems utterly unconstrained. This is another illusion. The hallmark rhythm of Palestrina and his colleagues depends on a technique and control of at least three different rhythmic aspects that is every bit as fine as the control of intervals.

The first and most obvious is the pattern of note durations. Just as the density of harmonic dissonances rises without our noticing, so does the speed of the notes. The strategy is quite the same: begin with long notes, a state of absolute calm, apply the most subtle of accelerations toward the peak of the melody, and then slow again at the cadence. The pattern is as natural as getting up, walking across a room, and sitting down again.[6]

The second aspect is the meter of classical polyphony. Of course, unlike plainchant, there is a meter, because a polyphony of this complexity would be impossible without a uniform beat to measure the time and coordinate the harmonies. In *Sicut cervus* the meter is duple throughout. But as we have seen the sense of meter may be strong, as in a march or "Celtic Alleluia," or so weak as to nearly disappear, as happens sometimes in this motet.[7] The perception of the duple meter itself depends on every second beat being made perceptually salient, or stressed, at the expense of its neighbor. But the strength of that perception depends upon the difference between stressed and unstressed beats.

---

[6] One might justly comment that Palestrina's principal motive owes something to the accentuation of the words *sicut cervus* as pronounced by an Italian, but diction cannot account for the weak-beat placements of the subject in the soprano and bass voices.

[7] See chaps. 3 and 7 for basic explanations of meter.

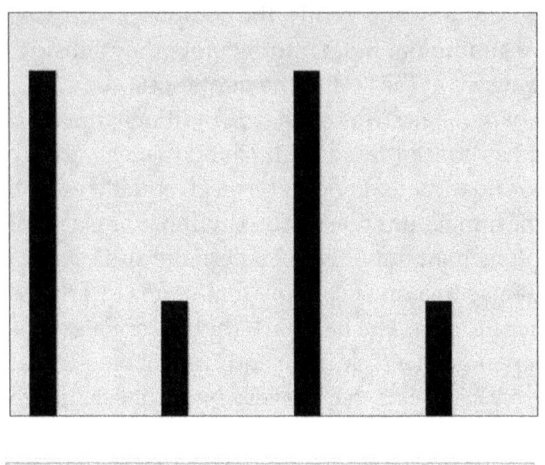

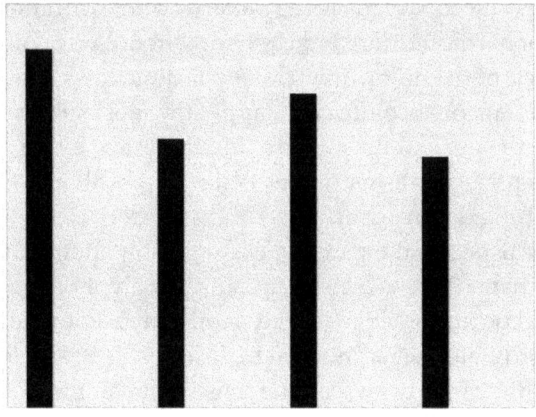

Figure 8-1. Schematic showing the theoretical difference in metric strength between a march and Palestrina's motet.

Someone hearing *Sicut cervus* cannot begin to abstract the duple meter until the third measure, when the entrance of the alto voice confirms an accent on the fifth beat of the composition. The accent on the seventh beat owes something to the A in the tenor, the highest pitch in that voice so far, but because the F-A-C harmony has not changed, it is a weak accent. With the entrances of the soprano and bass voices on what should be offbeats, the meter is practically reversed, surviving only by the listener's faith in consistency until the alto rescues the matter in measure ten by reentering with a long tonic.

This is not an extraordinary passage, except perhaps in its beauty; metrically, it is quite typical. Meter in high Renaissance polyphony is never the foot-stomping variety ensuring that dancers step together; rather, it is a gentle and sometimes ephemeral pulse, like a slow, rolling ocean wave.[8] This contributes to the illusion of freedom, of course, and it makes polyphony seem close to plainchant.

One more rhythmic aspect strengthens that illusion: the rhythm of imitation. In *Sicut cervus*, one can hardly fail to notice that the four voices making up the choir—soprano, alto, tenor, and bass—all sing the same tune, with a few very minor variants, like some angelic round. Imitation—the overlapping of a melody with itself in time—became the preferred technique for composing church music in the late fifteenth century and has remained with us, in some form or other, until the present. The entrance of each voice creates an easily perceived musical event, and yet because it is always the same melody, the texture is always completely unified no matter the number of voices. Imitation combines in a single technique the two basic perceptual requirements for musical composition: creating events and organizing them.

When a composer writes a melody to be imitated, the normal case is that it will be overlapped at the same time interval with each entrance. Here Palestrina performs another bit of magic, because his subject is overlapped at time intervals of two measures, one and one half measures, and two and one half measures. The imagination required to create a melody that can do this so euphoniously is little short of miraculous, but this music is far from the sort of technical showpiece that we often associate with imitation. On the contrary, the variance in Palestrina's entrances builds the illusion of a polyphonic plainchant. A predictable, regular entrance at, say, every two measures imposes a predictable, regular sort of phrase rhythm reminiscent of secular music. Palestrina's solution, created within and because of the strictest discipline, gives the motet its sacred freedom. If St. Augustine had composed, this would be his music.

---

[8] The minimal difference between stressed and unstressed beats applies at what is called the *tactus* level of beat, here the whole note, that is, the rather long beat, supposedly close to the human pulse while resting, that a choir director would use to mark the time. But meter is hierarchical, and at the lower level of the half note, the difference between the stressed half and the unstressed half is much greater, insuring the integrity of the half note as a uniform beat.

Classical Polyphony in Liturgy

If Palestrina saved polyphony from the council's anathema, even if only in legend,[9] what were the abuses that aroused opposition to this sublime music, and how was the opposition satisfied?

One complaint concerned the clarity of the text when sung. In a texture such as that of *Sicut cervus*, highly imitative, the various vocal parts of the choir will sing the words of the psalm at different times. In other words, the imitative overlap makes different parts of the text sound simultaneously, and the words are therefore nigh impossible to understand, since we cannot successfully attend to more than one linguistic stream at a time.[10] The council documents, and a number of Vatican pronouncements since 1563, demanded that polyphonic music "should be sung so that the words are more intelligible than the modulations of the music."[11]

Since imitation is the structural linchpin of this music, that demand created a severe compositional problem. One solution kept the imitative texture but laid the text under the melodies so that the words always lined up when more than one voice was involved. *Sicut cervus*, for example, would have the alto enter with the syllable /vus/ to align with the tenor and the soprano with the word *fontes* to align with both tenor and alto, and so forth. The trick does make the text much easier to hear, but destroys the often intimate relation between musical motive and word. In such a revised *Sicut cervus*, the voices still copy the same note patterns, but the unifying effect is somewhat deadened if the words are not copied with identical melodic figures as well. Another solution, more common, abandoned imitation between voices altogether and made do with simple textures that cadenced frequently. A third, Palestrina's typical stratagem, replaced the imitation of individual voices with imitation between subsections of a choir. A six-voiced choir could be broken into four-voice subgroups, each briefly overlapping the other in imitation, while within their own sections words could be aligned.

---

[9] For a history on what really happened concerning music at the Council of Trent, see Lewis H. Lockwood, *The Counter-Reformation and the Masses of Vincenzo Ruffo* (Venice: Fondazione Giorgio Cini, 1970).

[10] See Harold E. Pashler, *The Psychology of Attention* (Cambridge, MA: MIT Press, 1998), chaps. 3, 5, and 6.

[11] Robert F. Hayburn, *Papal Legislation on Sacred Music, 95 A.D. to 1977 A.D.* (Collegeville, MN: Liturgical Press, 1979), 27.

Example 8-3. Gloria, *Missa Papae Marcelli*, mm. 8–12.

In truth, textual clarity was likely a red flag hoisted by those who want only plainchant in the liturgy, for the issue is hardly serious. After all, the music under debate here is the polyphony of Mass Ordinaries. The Council of Trent, responding to the new music of the Reformation, worried about its most public liturgical face, the Mass, and said nothing significant about the music in the Divine Offices. Polyphonic Mass propers were rare because they can be sung only once per year, so composers scarcely wrote any.[12] Settings of *Kyrie eleison*, the *Credo*, and the other three Ordinary prayers could be sung

---

[12] Collections of polyphonic propers were composed: Heinrich Isaac's *Choralis Constantinus* (composed before 1517, published in 1550, 1555) and William Byrd's *Gradualia* (published 1605, 1607) are the most famous examples from the Council of Trent period. These were far outnumbered by polyphonic Ordinaries, and there is

at any Mass, and that is what the polyphonic Masses of Palestrina and his colleagues contain.

So what exactly is the problem of clarity? *Kyrie eleison* has six words, the *Agnus Dei* eleven. The longer *Gloria* and *Credo*? Any serious Catholic could recite them from memory. What is it that needs to be heard?

With psalm settings such as *Sicut cervus*, yes, textual clarity is desirable, but that is not the repertory the Council of Trent wrote about, and in modern times cheap printing and paper obviates the problem.[13]

The second complaint of the council, much more serious, was the inclusion of "lascivious or impure" aspects of secular music in Mass settings.[14] This referred to the common practice of parody, or composing a new polyphonic Mass by using an extant polyphonic composition as a model, a source of imitative ideas and textures, analogous perhaps to a jazz player using a standard tune as a point of departure for improvisation. Thus the title of Palestrina's *Missa Dum Complerentur* means that his settings of the *Kyrie, Gloria, Credo, Sanctus,* and *Agnus Dei* that make up this work all are modeled on his own motet *Dum Complerentur Dies Pentecostes* and in fact sound very much like it at the beginning of each movement.

The council had no complaint with such derived Masses *per se*, but when parody Masses took as their models not sacred motets but rather secular songs or madrigals, as frequently happened, then the council worried about the salacious semantics of the secular music carrying over into the sacred liturgy. The number of such Masses declined significantly in the last third of the sixteenth century. In the seventeenth century, the invention of opera made the issue moot with respect to parody Masses, but the clash of sacred and secular semantics in music remained very much a live issue and in fact lies behind most contemporary controversies over liturgical music today.[15]

Today, virtually no Catholics could recognize even the most explicit erotic references in a sixteenth-century parody Mass, just as they would miss many of the off-color jokes in Shakespeare without coaching, because our distance from the musical language is too great. But

---

no evidence that the council fathers considered any other kind of polyphony than Mass Ordinaries.

[13] That is, if understanding the text is the only problem. The subtler issue of direct versus indirect textual comprehension is treated in chap. 15.

[14] Hayburn, *Papal Legislation on Sacred Music*, 28.

[15] The issue of sacred semantics in music is treated in chap. 12.

the passing of the council's immediate concerns does not remove all the problems of using classical polyphony in modern liturgy.

One difficulty springs from its most cherished feature: its apparent effortlessness, its sublime and meditative wash of sound that arises quietly from silence and echoes back into it upon ending. All this ease and naturalness is illusion. In truth, the music is very difficult to perform well, and the greater the desired effortlessness and grace, the more professional the singers must be. In some kinds of music, part of the point is to show off technique; classical polyphony treasures the reticent anonymity of perfect blend above all, and achieving this requires as much musical skill as the virtuoso. As with any great repertory, of course, there are less difficult works, and one can compromise its a cappella aesthetic with a discreet organ accompaniment to help the singers stay in tune, but the proper blend, the boy-choir sound associated with the style is virtually impossible to develop in aging volunteers. It is not a music that tolerates much imperfection in performance; most who love it would much prefer that the local church choir stick to simple plainchants rather than inflict a ragged polyphonic *Kyrie* on the liturgy.

This means that classical polyphony is confined to professional choirs, or at least choirs composed chiefly of well-trained singers. A parish can always hope to build such a group, a laudable thing to do, but everyone should know that it is a long-term project requiring sustained effort and professional direction.[16] Obviously, there is no question of a congregation singing this music.

Classical polyphony is generally not liturgically efficient, a second difficulty. Plainchant adds little time to the execution of a prayer; a chanted psalm or *Agnus Dei* takes little longer than the spoken versions. A complete Mass of Palestrina—*Kyrie, Gloria, Credo, Sanctus,* and *Agnus Dei*—on the other hand, would add at least twenty minutes to the Mass.[17] (It is not a sin to perform a subset of the five movements.)

---

[16] Richard J. Schuler's detailed account of efforts to establish polyphony in the United States during the 1950s records only major urban churches. See *A Chronicle of the Reform: Catholic Music in the Twentieth Century,* http://www.musicasacra.com/pdf/chron.pdf, repr. from Robert A. Skeris, ed., *Cum Angelis Canere: Essays on Sacred Music and Pastoral Liturgy in Honour of Richard J. Schuler* (St. Paul, MN: Church Music Association, 1990), 11.

[17] In speaking of liturgical "efficiency," the concern is certainly not about making the Mass as short as possible, for if we believe that the sacred liturgy is as important as we say, the length of time required to do it should be of little moment. The

In those rare places where one may be heard, the celebrants and congregation usually sit during the longer prayers. Before the *novus ordo* of 1970, the rubrics permitted the *Sanctus* to be sung while the celebrant recited the eucharistic prayer (Canon) quietly, and that is why polyphonic *Sanctus* settings are sometimes quite florid and luxuriant in proportion to its short text. If the congregation must hear the eucharistic prayer in the new rite, the celebrant must wait for the conclusion of the *Sanctus* before beginning.[18]

If the choir sings motets as entrance, offertory, and communion antiphons, the extra time they require can be used for processions, incensing the altar and congregation, and reflection. "An example of adaptation of inherited repertoire to contemporary ritual in ways unforeseen by the composer would be the use of a polyphonic *Agnus Dei* to accompany the lengthy ritual action of breaking the bread and preparing the chalices for the Communion of the faithful."[19] Such practices indicate that classical polyphony associates best with solemn Masses where every part is prolonged. Those rituals reflect and integrate with the portentous sacred semantic of the music.

And that kind of usage recalls the supposed original use of polyphony as an enhancement of chant for solemn occasions, and as such there is nothing quite like it. Its liturgical costs are high in terms of preparation, training, commitment, and of the liturgy itself, but, given the right occasion, its spiritual benefits for singers and congregants alike can be immense. Impressive and profound without being showy, glorifying without overwhelming the chant aesthetic, there is no other music that offers so much to God in a spirit of humility.

---

concern rather is for the proper balance of the liturgy, keeping the focus on the principal action, with everything else related to it. If a polyphonic *Gloria* lasts ten minutes, the gospel takes but three, and the eucharistic prayer before the consecration five, one might legitimately complain that the *Gloria* is too long, not in absolute terms, but in proportion to the rest of the action.

[18] Joseph Cardinal Ratzinger believed it still possible to sing the *Benedictus* portion of the *Sanctus* after the consecration: "If a filled silence and an interior greeting of the Lord along with the choir take place after the consecration event, it corresponds profoundly to the inner structure of the occasion. The pedantic proscription of such a split, which came about not without reason in the development, should be forgotten as quickly as possible." See *A New Song for the Lord: Faith in Christ and Liturgy Today*, trans. Martha M. Matesich (New York: Crossroad, 1997), 145.

[19] Ruff, *Sacred Music and Liturgical Reform*, 543. His entire chap. 21 on the polyphonic Mass Ordinary has much useful information.

Chapter 9

Operatic and Symphonic Liturgical Music

> At the present day a new kind of chant has crept into the temple which is new, eccentric, broken up with a swing and certainly far from religious. It is more suitable for the theater and dance halls. It interests us and stirs our curiosity, but in reality we neglect devotion.
> Pope Benedict XIV, *Annus Qui* (1749)

The invention of *dramma per musica* in Italy at the close of the sixteenth century is the most pivotal discrete event in the history of Western music of the last five centuries. Like any new genre, opera gave composers an additional creative outlet, in this case a musical texture that glorified the solo voice as never before by supplying just enough harmony and bass line counterpoint to hold the music together while keeping out of the way of the singer. But opera did much more: it converted the musical culture of Europe, one could say, from a largely medieval view of music to the modern. Before opera, music functioned as a means of contemplation, either of God in sacred music, or of human love in secular song. After opera, music became an agent of the theater, a new kind of narrative that eventually learned to tell abstract stories on its own, without the help of words. Here is the origin of our most common metaphors for describing musical experience: a "dramatic" change of harmony, "yearning" melodies, "tragic" symphonies, and the like.

The new operatic sound clarified once and for all a growing split between the styles of music written for church and for the court. The sixteenth-century experiments with intimate text expression and chromaticism in the secular forms, chiefly in the Italian madrigal, inevitably affected the language of church polyphony. This influence is in part what the Council of Trent tried to repel with its reforms of 1563.[1]

---

[1] See chap. 8. For a fine summary of Pope Benedict XIV's attempt at musical reform, see Edward Schaefer, *Catholic Music Through the Ages: Balancing the Needs of a Worshipping Church* (Chicago: Hillenbrand, 2008), 96.

Opera reordered all the musical features of secular humanism so distasteful to the council fathers as well as to their Protestant colleagues in northern Europe into a new style dedicated to music drama. The sound of this music, emphasizing virtuosic singing and simple, if harmonically adventurous accompaniments, was so far from that of high Renaissance polyphony that no further confluence or confounding of the two was possible. After opera, a composer made a discrete choice when he picked up his pen, either to compose in *stile antico* of classical polyphony, whose natural evolution ceased after the council, or the *stile moderno* of opera.[2]

The turn in musical aesthetics was soon ratified by a revolution in musical practicalities. In 1637 the first public opera house opened in Venice; the early 1640s found six in the island city. By the middle of the century, opera had spread to Germany and France, and the rest of western Europe would have it by the century's end. Public opera houses transformed the place of music in society and culture. For the first time, sophisticated compositions (and unsophisticated ones, to be sure) became available to a paying audience in a social context outside the church and the court, close to our modern concept of a concert. Most important, the professional composer with a flair for the dramatic had another means of making a good living, a choice beyond employment by the bishop or local aristocracy. He could work for himself and sell his art to the public.[3]

---

[2] It is true that the *stile antico* continued to inspire many works of later centuries, some of them great ones, such as Claudio Monteverdi's *Vespers of 1610*. But the best of these are syntheses of at least two musical languages, and the very fact that seventeenth-century writers commented on such syntheses reveals already a consciousness of a historical language, as Dante and his contemporaries were conscious of Latin and Latinisms in their more contemporary inventions in vernacular languages. Such syntheses cannot be considered natural evolutions of a language, but deliberate juxtapositions of alternative ones. See Joseph P. Swain, "Evolution of Musical Languages," chap. 7 of *Musical Languages* (New York: Norton, 1997). The Monteverdi *Vespers* is a brilliant conception, but no one would mistake a moment of it for the music of Palestrina or of anyone else of the Roman school of polyphony. If he wished his music to be taken as such, he composed the *Missa da Capella* for six voices, a parody of a work of Nicholas Gombert printed in the very same publication that contained the synthetic *Vespers of 1610*. Had the *stile antico* been evolving naturally, there would have been no need to demonstrate a facility with it, or to treat it as an entirely separate language, as it is in this print.

[3] Reinhard Strohm believes that for two centuries very few composers could live entirely as operatic freelancers, so that court positions and church appointments

Whether opera was a symptom or a partial cause of the increasing secularization of European society, it doomed the métier of the professional church composer, or at least made its own alternative so attractive that it was the inevitable choice of the most talented. Johann Sebastian Bach died in 1750, the last major composer to avoid the operatic infection and work for the church, but even he did so not out of professional preference but out of a deep sense of spiritual vocation. Why otherwise should a Handel or a Mozart take a church appointment, where prestige and pay would both be lower than in the opera house, and where they would either be composing in the musical language of church polyphony—anachronistic, fixed and frozen in the past like Latin—or in an operatic language that seemed in many respects ill-suited to the sacred liturgy?

The choice for the seventeenth-century church composer was just about that stark. To follow the outline of the Council of Trent and therefore to please conservative church authorities meant composing music that sounded as much as possible like that of Palestrina twenty-five, fifty, and one hundred years and more after his death. To please himself and to keep up with the state of the art meant setting sacred texts, including the Ordinaries of the Mass, as one of the many new genres spun off from opera: sacred concerto, sacred symphony, concerted motet, cantata, Neapolitan Mass. Note that nearly all the genre names indicate a hybrid of sacred and secular, except for one more, oratorio, which is little more than a sacred opera without staging. These types all had one thing in common: operatic texture and its emphasis on the expressive solo voice that drew attention not upward in some transcendental action to the divine, but selfward, to the singer as a created character. When the soprano opens the *Gloria* of Joseph Haydn's "Lord Nelson" Mass (1798) with a catchy tune high in her register on *Gloria in excelsis Deo*, immediately echoed by the full chorus, it is hard to say who, God or the soprano, is the more glorified. Opponents had one very good point to make: the music lifted one's spirit not to heaven but across town to the theater, where this kind of music was normally heard. A classic semantic association was at work here: music connotes, in part, the context where it is usually experienced.

---

were still highly prized through the eighteenth century. Nevertheless, the slow emancipation of composers from church and patron surely began with opera's commercialization. See *Essays on Handel and Italian Opera* (Cambridge: Cambridge University Press, 1985), 98.

The situation partially explains why both plainchant and classical polyphony fell into disuse and decrepitude during the seventeenth and eighteenth centuries. Despite all good attempts to quarantine the sacred traditions from infection, the mere existence of the operatic aesthetic made plainchant and polyphony so uninteresting for talented composers that if these styles were not compromised then they simply died of neglect.[4] Ironically, even the Council of Trent indirectly contributed to the decline when the new chant books that were supposed to make universal and solid the great plainchant tradition, the so-called Medicean chant of 1614, offered a plainchant repertory revised according to humanistic principles and accordingly pruned of its medieval extravagances and some of what makes it beautifully mysterious. There was none of that historical consciousness of authenticity taken for granted today. No one had any practice in conserving an anachronistic repertory, for it had never been done before. In another irony, the historical sense of the original had to await the revival efforts, very much like archeological digs, of the scientific nineteenth century.

The one characteristic of the new operatic sacred music that faintly echoed the *stile antico* was the chorus, a luxury that public opera houses could seldom afford.[5] Except for its Latin language, the music of a baroque solo aria from a *Magnificat* of Vivaldi is indistinguishable from an aria from one of his operas.[6] But because it had a least four voice parts, the chorus preserved the kind of imitative counterpoint that had been the engine of polyphonic motets and even when Handel made them all sing together at once in his inimitable hammer strokes, just the sound of such a group recalled the old sacred semantic, however dimly. Handel's *Messiah* was, in fact, almost single-handedly

---

[4] Edward Schaefer notes that some composers who worked with the *stile antico* could not resist dressing up Palestrina in contemporary orchestration and harmonic arrangment. See *Catholic Music Through the Ages*, 98.

[5] French operas had large choruses throughout the seventeenth century and well into the eighteenth, but that was largely because French opera during this time continued to be funded by the state.

[6] Only on the level of form might one tell, because the opera aria would likely be in the traditional ternary *da capo* form demanded by *opera seria* librettos, whereas the sacred aria would be through-composed. But semantic connotations are rarely drawn at the perceptual level of form; they are rather in the phrase-to-phrase operation of the musical language. In Bach arias, of course, even the formal distinction fails.

responsible for a new kind of choral organization, the amateur choral society so familiar today, because the early publication of the work in inexpensive singing editions encouraged such groups in England to sing it regularly. One would like to think that amateurs wished to preserve some of that sacred semantic, but it is more likely that they did it for the sheer joy of singing the work. No matter, the growth of these choral societies throughout England and also Germany made possible any number of works like *A German Requiem* of Johannes Brahms. This turned out to be indeed a saving grace at a period when interest in liturgy in all western Europe was at a low ebb.

Strong choral traditions, whether professional or amateur, preserved some identity of operatic and symphonic Masses as authentic sacred works rather than vocal symphonies or operas with Latin words. The repertory is significant. Mozart's sacred works represent one tenth of his catalog. There are six late symphonic Masses of Joseph Haydn composed at the height of his powers, and another half dozen of Franz Schubert. All these were composed as liturgical works and all have seen authentic liturgical use. Quite a different case is *Missa Solemnis* of Beethoven. The composer had in mind the installation of his friend Archduke Rudolph of Austria as Archbishop of Olmütz at the Cologne Cathedral, but the Mass outgrew all normal proportions and when Beethoven finished it in 1823 the installation was long past. The work lasts seventy-five minutes and did not see a liturgical performance until the celebration of the four hundredth anniversary of the University of Freiburg in Breisgau on August 4, 1857. The first performance, of the *Kyrie, Credo,* and *Agnus Dei* only, was at a concert in Vienna on May 7, 1823.

The *Missa Solemnis* thus precipitates the final stage of secularization begun with the invention of opera.[7] The Ordinary texts are now vehicles for a composer's personal devotion, or indeed personal statements, not always religious,[8] to be expressed not in a Catholic liturgy, which would be inappropriate in any case, but in a concert hall. Even

---

[7] It has, of course, a great predecessor in spirit in the *Mass in B Minor* of Johann Sebastian Bach. The purpose of that work, two hours in length, is still under debate. In any case, since we know of no performance in Bach's lifetime and since it was not published until after Beethoven's, it did not affect the course of symphonic Masses in the latter half of the eighteenth century.

[8] Some of the most remarkable Masses of the twentieth century, such as the *Glagolitic Mass* of Leos Janacek, are composed by agnostics.

if works such as this, as well as the *Messa da Requiem* of Verdi and the *Grande Messe des Morts* of Berlioz and other such grandiose conceptions, once saw a liturgical performance shortly after their composition, the fact is that now they are concert works, enjoyed by believer and unbeliever purely as music. Almost never are they heard in a liturgical setting.

Might they be? There are at least two places where a symphonic Mass by Schubert or Mozart is regularly performed as the Ordinary of the Mass, at the Stefansdom and the Augustinerkirche in Vienna and at St. Agnes in St. Paul, Minnesota. The essential questions are two: first, the sheer practicality of mounting such performances and integrating them into modern liturgy, and second, whether they are really sacred music appropriate for the Roman Rite, that is, whether they own a sacred semantic for the modern world.

Performing a symphonic Mass of Joseph Haydn would require a professional ensemble of at least forty players and singers.[9] Obviously a permanent state subsidy or a large endowment is in order; in most places the expense would make such a thing impossible except perhaps for very special occasions. Spatial logistics present another obstacle. Where in the church can such a group be situated so that their not inconsiderable presence does not overwhelm what should be the center of attention?

Even in the Stefansdom in Vienna, large and rich enough to solve these problems, the essential problem of liturgical integration remains.[10] The Haydn Mass adds forty-five minutes of solid music to the liturgy, and this, it should be noted, represents a compromise of wills. In a well-known letter, Mozart chafes at the time limits imposed on symphonic Masses by his Emperor Joseph II, a great lover of music who also cared deeply for the integrity of Catholic liturgy.[11] Composers

---

[9] The singers, including four soloists and a chorus of at least twenty, need not all be professionals, as long as they are given sufficient rehearsal time; to do such a liturgy on a regular basis, however, would demand all professionals with excellent reading skills.

[10] The chorus and orchestra are located well to the right as one faces the high altar, which means that every congregant very naturally looks away from the altar during the singing of the Ordinary prayers of the liturgy.

[11] "Our church music is very different from that of Italy, since a Mass with the whole *Kyrie*, the *Gloria*, the *Credo*, the Epistle sonata, the Offertory or Motet, the *Sanctus* and the *Agnus Dei* must not last longer than three quarters of an hour. This applies even to the most Solemn Mass said by the Archbishop himself." Emily

wanted and needed more time for the long texts; liturgical reformers, alarmed at the way Masses were turning into concerts, wanted less. Strange compromises were brokered. Sometimes composers, in setting the *Credo* for chorus and orchestra, would compress the text by having different parts of it sung simultaneously by different parts of the choir. One article of faith would be offered by the tenors while another was sung by the sopranos at the same moment, in a most ironic rejoinder to the Council of Trent's quest for clarity. It was also a regular practice, not completely suppressed until after the Second Vatican Council, to sing the *Sanctus/Benedictus* while the celebrant prayed the Canon of the Mass by himself. This allowed composers a breathing space, and indeed these settings are often the most musically luxuriant parts of a symphonic Mass. Beethoven, true to character, paid the rules no attention at all and composed a concert Mass in his *Missa Solemnis*, a supremely great one in those terms to be sure, but not at all practical for liturgy.

Like a Mass of Palestrina, the symphonic Mass admits no possibility of congregational singing of the Ordinary prayers. However, the psychological distance from the execution of the music, the feeling of being a spectator, is quite probably greater with the symphonic Masses even though their harmonic language is more familiar to the modern listener. Polyphony has that illusion of effortlessness, of an easy and natural inspiration welling up from the choir, which can draw a congregation in and make worshipers believe that, yes, they too could sing that if they but had a score in front of them. A symphonic Mass gives no such illusions. On the contrary, the premises of the musical language are theatrical, to be showy and virtuosic. In fact, the choruses of a Haydn Mass are technically easier to sing than those of one by Palestrina, but they do not sound that way and they are not supposed to. After all, the godfather of this great ensemble is opera. The chorus, orchestra, and soloists are on stage; everyone else in the church is audience.[12]

Anderson, ed., *The Letters of Mozart and His Family*, vol. 1 (New York: St. Martin's Press, 1966), 476.

[12] Of course, it is still possible to have congregational singing when a Mass of Haydn is sung in liturgy, just not during the Ordinary prayers. As chap. 18 will describe, congregational singing may be wonderfully integrated into such a liturgy through responses and other prayers.

Haydn's late Masses were criticized in their own day by some as being "too cheerful," and in fact, save certain movements of the "Nelson" Mass, major modes and sprightly tempos prevail in all of them. Do symphonic Masses connote any sense of the sacred for the modern Catholic?

To the large majority of worshipers whose acquaintance of the classics of the Western musical tradition is casual, a symphonic Mass sounds simply "classical." As such, it may enjoy a certain prestige, like the classics of literature, respected even if little known, and certainly it sounds different enough from the more familiar popular music of the current civilization to convey the sense that something extraordinary, even transcendental, is happening on the altar.[13] To the remaining minority who know the tradition well, a symphonic Mass of Haydn, Mozart, or Schubert will sound very much like their favorite symphonies, concertos, and operas of Haydn, Mozart, and Schubert that they hear in the concert hall. Because these sounds have strong associations with secular events—that is, concerts—for these people, it is quite possible that such a liturgy will strike them as an extraordinary kind of concert, a liturgy with entertainment provided. Should certain later nineteenth-century exemplars ever come to a liturgical performance, that impression would be strengthened manyfold. The *Sanctus* of the renowned Verdi *Requiem* ends with a brassy, chromatic flourish that could bring down the curtain anywhere.

But does it matter if only a minority react this way? Alas, musical organizations and influences have never followed the one man, one vote rule.[14] If that same minority exercises authority in cathedral programs of liturgical music, as should be the case if it is a highly qualified minority, then it surely would matter.

On the other hand, the blessed naiveté of those little acquainted with the masters makes an interesting point. What allows the symphonic Masses to sound appropriate in church for them is cultural distance, in this case a simple lack of familiarity with the tradition because of its age. Verdi is old and Schubert is older and Haydn older still. Only

---

[13] It is perhaps for this reason that Monsignor Richard Schuler, who regularly directed performances of symphonic Masses during liturgies at St. Agnes in Minneapolis, sensibly remarked, "I don't think that these Masses should be sung everywhere all the time. But they should be sung somewhere, and we can sing them, so we do." Quoted in Schaefer, *Catholic Music Through the Ages*, 103.

[14] See the discussion of liturgical democratization in chap. 4.

those few who attend the musical museums of symphony concerts know how close the sacred music of those masters is to the secular they composed at the same time. For everyone else, it is simply old music and "different."

But if the small cultural distance between the present and a Verdi can suffice for the unacquainted, perhaps a larger one can do the same for the cognoscenti.

This seems to have happened with the music of Johann Sebastian Bach. No composer fills modern Christian churches of all the Western denominations with as much music as Bach. But it is not, save in unusual circumstances, with the choral movements of church cantatas, the motets, and surely not the Masses. No, the Bach mainly heard in Christian churches today is the much more abstract organ works above all and movements from his secular sonatas and concertos.[15] Occasionally there might be an aria from one of his cantatas, but that hardly affects the balance of sacred and secular here, as his arias on secular texts are musically indistinguishable from his arias on sacred texts, and in fact Bach himself frequently converted the former into the latter whenever he believed it appropriate. All this music composed originally for aristocratic court entertainment, coffee house diversion, civic celebrations, and organ recitals outside the liturgy can work well in modern liturgy when presented as prelude or postlude music, or music that covers a reflective period after Communion.

Some kind of semantic shift has occurred. What was once associated with action outside liturgy is now normatively associated with action within liturgy. All of Bach, in some sense, sounds sacred now.[16] Semantic shifts occur constantly in natural languages of course. Think of what has happened to "chip," "file," and "issue," among countless other words in recent years. If an abstract cultural token, be it a single word or a musical style, is consistently applied to a new context, it takes on a meaning associated with that context, thus a new meaning.[17]

---

[15] The most common Bach heard in churches, of course, are his hymn arrangements. These will be considered in chaps. 10 and 17.

[16] Again, not for Bach specialists perhaps. I, for one, am discomfited when hearing a gigue from one of his suites used in church, but for the vast majority of even attentive and experienced listeners, Bach's counterpoint overcomes the dance character sufficiently.

[17] This process of semantic shifting gets a broader theoretical treatment in chap. 12.

In a similar fashion, certain compositional techniques and textures, such as fugue or passages sung a cappella, have acquired a sacred symbolism, like musical icons, owing to their long associations with high Renaissance polyphony, imitative writing, and the music of Bach. They can give even the most modernist work a patina of the sacred. But in that context, they too often have a rather quaint effect because they are anachronisms. Whether any purely modernist musical language, arising from a secularized culture, can achieve a sacred semantic is very much open to question. Answering it requires some theory of musical semantics.

Chapter 10

Traditions of Popular Liturgical Music

> Shout with joy to the Lord, all the earth;
> break into song; sing praise.
> Sing praises to the LORD with the lyre,
> with the lyre and melodious song.
>
> Psalm 98:4-5

Long before all the talk of *participatio actuosa* and congregational singing had culminated in the Second Vatican Council, there had grown up a significant and diverse repertory of Catholic music among the laity. For centuries preceding the Council of Trent (1545–63), devout lay Catholics would have sung praise to God in their homes, in religious processions, and in devotional meetings, most commonly in their own vernacular languages. Household "devotional music" is a concept strange to the modern Catholic in the Western world, for whom "sacred music" is synonymous with "liturgical music" or "music in church." The ever-advancing technology of phonographic reproduction has virtually exterminated all live performance of music in the home, religious or not, and the picture of the family gathered around the upright piano to sing some favorite hymns on a Sunday evening is now quaint, if not simply ridiculous, to the younger generations at the beginning of the twenty-first century, but in olden times religious music was alive in the homes of believers. The immense popularity of the *Genevan Psalter*, which saw sixty-three editions between 1562 and 1565, and other early Protestant collections attests to the thirst of the laity for this kind of music.

Like popular music in the secular world, religious folk songs would come in and go out of fashion. Before the nineteenth century, they were often *contrafacta*, religious poetry set to well-known folk tunes that originally set lyrics of love, drinking, war, and work. So the repertory turned over regularly with the passage of time, never—with a few exceptions, such as the *Stabat mater*—attaining the official status enjoyed by settings of the liturgical texts of the Mass and Divine Office.

Most familiar to modern experience would be the carols. Now associated exclusively with Christmastide, in the Middle Ages they could also commemorate Passion- and Eastertide. Sung in local tongues, sometimes with familiar Latin phrases such as *Gloria in excelsis Deo* mixed in, carol traditions varied by place and nation: the English carol, the French *noël*, the German *Wechselgesang*, and so on. Italian pilgrims and other migrant penitents sang a particular kind of popular devotional song during the wars and plagues of the thirteenth and fourteenth centuries called the *lauda*, from the Latin word for "praise." By the fifteenth century, some of these came to be arranged polyphonically and could be heard in the peculiar Venetian institutions known as *scuole grandi* (great schools), confraternities of middle-class merchants and craftsmen devoted to a particular saint.

However diverse in language and purpose, all popular sacred songs have two characteristics in common: they are simple in form and character, and they are at some remove from liturgy.

One of the oldest types of popular sacred music, dating from Old Testament times, is the litany.

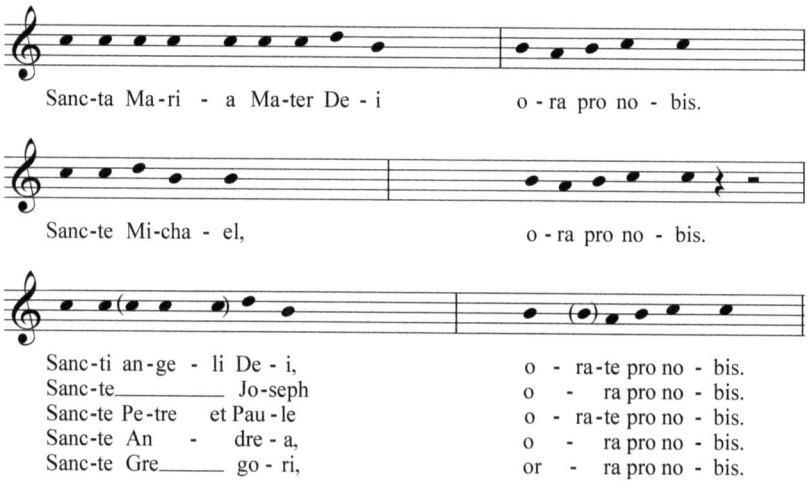

Example 10-1. Litany from the Easter Vigil (*Graduale Simplex*, 148–49).

It is hard to imagine a simpler music, and as such, the litany embodies the essential elements of popular religious song before the twentieth century. A cantor or leader intones the particular invocations and the congregation responds with a short motive with the same words every time, in the manner of a refrain. Anyone with normal hearing and even meager musical gifts can learn the response in a few moments.

Popular hymns, carols, and other religious songs are more involved, of course, but they all use the same basic strategy found in the litany: simplicity of tune and much repetition. The text of a popular hymn is organized into strongly metric stanzas with clear rhymes to aid the memory. This music is likewise strongly metric to reinforce the structure of the poetry and to make it easier to remember, and the tune is almost invariably strophic (the same for each stanza), very often a quatrain of periodic phrases. Refrains are common.

Except for rare liturgical pieces, such as the Litany of the Saints quoted above, the text language of such songs would be the congregation's native language. Sometimes a little Latin might creep in to yield a "macaronic" text with slightly stronger sacred flavor, but these are almost always stock phrases such as *Ave Maria* or *Deo gratias*.

The reason for all this constraint is perfectly clear: in times when the great majority of the laity could not read and had only the native musical training that comes with growing up in a culture, devotional music, like any other, had to be easy to learn and to remember in order to assure the performance of everyone present. Put baldly, any music intended for everyone to sing must aim at the lowest common denominator of musical competence. Anything more ambitious is, in some sense, exclusive. The character of simplicity is by no means a particularly Catholic solution. The same strategy of repetition includes the later Jewish *piyyutim*, the Islamic *qawwali*, and the Japanese (Buddhist) *wasan*. It is a universal necessity for congregational singing.

World religions also seem to enforce a certain distance between popular religious music and their most solemn rites. This varies quite a bit. In strict Islam, popular hymns have never been included in mosque worship. The popular Hindu *bhajan* may be heard in connection with a number of rites, but not in chanting the Vedas. In many Christian Orthodox Divine Liturgies, most of the singing is done by celebrant and choir. Occasionally the congregation may join in on a hymn, but they are not encouraged to do so.[1] The general situation might be summarized this way: there is a great range in most religious traditions, from the simplest popularly oriented music to the most

---

[1] At least this was my experience at San Giorgio dei Greci in Venice and at St. Vladimir's in Utica, New York.

subtle chants for the highly trained, and the most solemn occasions favor the latter.

This is not unreasonable. While popular religious song may indeed arise from a natural human disposition to sing in praise of the Divine, it collides with an equally profound awe for sacred writings—the Bible, the Vedas, the Qurʾān, etc.—which become the principal sources for liturgical prayer. These are complex texts, rarely poetic, and cannot be turned directly into strophic songs. To remain close to its sacred writing, any liturgical tradition will naturally resist the simplification that popular religious song must have.

Second, the chant to which sacred writings are traditionally set is often complex and difficult. Highly trained liturgical musicians naturally regard their art as exalted, as the only proper means of addressing the Divine. Tunes often arising from popular culture might easily be considered unworthy of liturgy, since they bring with them the taint of the corrupt secular world. That such borrowing frequently occurred merely strengthened the hand of those who would safeguard the liturgy from secular corruption. The Sephardic Jews of the Iberian peninsula adapted *piyyutim* texts to popular Arabic melodies, Martin Luther and John Wesley did not stint at making new hymns of folk songs and opera hits, and the issue of whether melody itself embodies sacred meaning is very much with us today.

Such concerns have set up the historical conflict between the professional liturgical musician—priest, cantor, chorister—and the layperson. Both sides have laudable interests at stake. No one can deny the laity's natural desire to praise God in joyful song, for to do so is to deny nothing less than something of God's will for our being. On the other hand, the professionals respond, the laity's contribution to liturgy, while amateur in the best sense of "a lover of art," is nonetheless amateur. Shall we not honor the Most High with the best we have? Shall we offer plastic bottles while reserving the crystal for ourselves? And so, through the ages until quite recently, a certain compromise has endured: the people may sing in praise of God at home, at shrines, at popular devotions such as the rosary, in procession to the church, but not in the divine liturgy itself.[2]

---

[2] Richard J. Schuler notes how the slow spread of congregational singing that took place during the 1940s in the United States occurred especially in novenas. See *A Chronicle of the Reform: Catholic Music in the Twentieth Century*, http://www.musicasacra.com/pdf/chron.pdf, repr. from Robert A. Skeris, ed., *Cum Angelis*

The Revolution of the Lutheran Hymn

The conflict was resolved for a time in the Christian world by the Lutheran hymn or chorale, and the legitimate interests of professional and laity are harmonized beautifully whenever one of these is sung in liturgy.

Martin Luther saw the exclusion of the laity from the music of the liturgy as one of the most egregious corruptions that had overtaken the Roman Rite since apostolic times. Believing that, as a priestly people, all worshipers should proclaim the Word of God, he vigorously promoted vernacular hymn singing in his reformed liturgy, even recasting the traditional Ordinary prayers into strophic paraphrases that could be turned into hymns. He seemed not to care very much about the sources of his Lutheran chorale tunes, many of which are still sung today. Some early chorales are simply ancient Latin (Catholic) hymns whose melodies were metricized and adapted to German translations of the originals. Others derived from old German traditions of sacred folksong, including pilgrim songs, Crusader songs, *Geisslerlieder* (penitential songs), and fifteenth-century devotional songs typically associated with popular feasts such as Christmas. Others are *contrafacta*, with an entirely new text applied to a secular song. Still others have entirely original tunes and texts. Some of the melodies—"A Mighty Fortress" being perhaps the most famous—Luther composed himself.

The innovation was wildly popular, attested by a steady stream of new hymnbooks throughout the sixteenth century. John Calvin in Geneva permitted only metricized psalms to be sung in the austere Reform services and yet oversaw a significant line of such hymnals, crowned by the great third edition of the *Genevan Psalter* in 1562. Isaac Watts popularized an English tradition of metricized psalms in the early eighteenth century, and the Wesleys brought many of his texts and tunes and many of their own to America.

At first hymns were sung in unison, a cappella. But the riches of Western harmony proved too tempting to resist for long, and by the end of the sixteenth century, all the Lutheran and even some Calvinist publications began appearing with harmonizations in four voices,

---

Canere: Essays on Sacred Music and Pastoral Liturgy in Honour of Richard J. Schuler (St. Paul, MN: Church Music Association, 1990), 7. Anthony Ruff's book records many exceptions to this rule, particularly in chaps. 11 and 23. See *Sacred Music and Liturgical Reform: Treasures and Transformations* (Chicago: Hillenbrand, 2007).

with the popular tune in the top voice, in the guise that most Catholics today think of when they hear the word "hymn." It is here that the professionally trained musician and the lay amateur worshiper can come together in common cause.

O Sa-cred Head sur-roun-ded by crown of pier-cing thorn,

Example 10-2. The opening phrases of "O Sacred Head Surrounded."

Here is a very famous Lutheran chorale now become well-known even to Catholics, who, if they are fortunate, sing it on Palm Sunday and during Holy Week. The tune originally set a forgettable lament of unrequited love in the fifteenth century before Luther brought it into the temple, and since then it has known many religious texts, including this adaptation of a poetic meditation of Bernard de Clairvaux, and many translations of them.[3] Because J. S. Bach arranged the tune five different ways in his *St. Matthew Passion* (1727), one of his best loved works, it has become known as the "Passion Chorale." Thus its current association with Passiontide.

In its simplicity, the tune meets every requirement of indigenous popular song. Its range is one octave, comfortable for the average voice. Its rhythm seems plain to the point of dullness, mostly plodding quarter notes with the occasional eighths dividing a beat. Except for the long notes that articulate each phrase, those two note values, the quarter just twice as long as the eighth, comprise the entire duration range for the tune. There is no hint of syncopation or any other rhythmic subtlety. The phrases of the melody are rigidly periodic, each exactly eight beats, and of course match up perfectly with the meter and rhythm of the poem. There are two cadence patterns, the first ending on the weaker latter half of the measure, the second on the stronger, and these alternate with the regularity of a clock for the eight phrases of each verse of the hymn. In sum, the tune is a fine example of a typical folk melody that might be found in any number of religious traditions, well within the competence of the untutored faithful.

---

[3] George William Rutler, *Brightest and Best: Stories of Hymns* (San Francisco: Ignatius Press, 1998), 51.

What is there to attract the highly trained, sophisticated professional musician?

The arrangement. The secret of the chorale tradition's power lies in the particular manner of harmonization.

When "Be Not Afraid" and other melodies of the American folk-revival influence are set, it is a rather simple matter of choosing the chord to be played by the guitar or keyboard every measure or so. In this sense, the chord is a set of three or four pitches played at the same time that seem consonant with the fragment of melody that they accompany. As far as the harmony is concerned, it matters not a whit how those pitches are played. They might occur all at once in a strum, or individually in a fast guitar pick or leisurely keyboard arpeggiation. They are harmonies purely conceived, as simultaneous pitch classes. This is sometimes called the vertical dimension of an arrangement, from the custom of notating chords as stacks of notes in a vertical column, indicating that they are to be played all at once, since left-to-right relations in a score represent the passage of time. A tune such as "Be Not Afraid" written out with only chord symbols above the melodic notation is an arrangement perfectly adequate for performance.[4]

Bach's harmonization of "O Sacred Head Surrounded" in example 10-3, by contrast, is not merely a functional chord progression laid upon a preexisting melody; rather, it is a synthesis of four independent melodies sung together at the same time that harmonize one another by artful coordination. The vertical dimension of harmony is fused with the horizontal dimensions of four melodies in a weave that is the very soul of Western art music. This art is known as counterpoint.

---

[4] The arrangement of "Be Not Afraid" quoted in chap. 3 is a more elaborate translation into a keyboard idiom, which takes something away from the improvisatory aspect of the folk revival. A folk guitarist (or a good keyboard improviser) would need only the tune and the chord symbols to sing the song.

Example 10-3. Soprano, alto, tenor, and bass melodies from one of J. S. Bach's arrangements of the choral tune "O Sacred Head Surrounded" (German original: *O Haupt voll Blut und Wunden*), opening phrases.

Example 10-3 shows the original "Passion Chorale" tune arranged with the three new melodies invented by Bach and commonly known by the names "alto," "tenor," and "bass" after the parts of the choir that would sing them. Taken individually, each has pretty much the same simple character as the familiar soprano melody. All are rhythmically simple, melodically constrained, and matched to the same text as the soprano tune.

At the same time, each melody is its own. None merely shadows a commanding soprano melody at some fixed interval, as happens so often in the improvised harmonies of the folk revival. Indeed, at many points the melodies have independent rhythms, such as the alto's faster eighth notes in the first measure or the bass's in the third, and independent melodic contours in a special virtue of counterpoint known as contrary motion. Each melody is fun to sing because each one has its particular charms. The bass line is more or less in charge of the chords being made, and it has that powerful rising scale in the third measure. The tenor singer gets to move chromatically from A-natural through A-sharp to B (mm. 2–3) and effects a modulation, or change of tonal center, from D to B that is another peculiarity of Western music deriving from its harmonic language. The alto melody begins and ends on the same pitch, D, but singing this melody can be fascinating because the functional meaning of the two Ds differs, since it is the tonic or keynote at first but not at the end, something like a musical pun.

The mutual independence of the four melodies is an illusion, of course. In order to sound well together, their vertical combination of pitches must obey the rules of harmonic syntax, a grammatical constraint as powerful as that of any spoken language. The minor miracle of it all is that when they sound together, they create in their ensemble a progression of harmonies so logical and ordered that it is difficult to believe that it did not govern the composition of all four melodies. In some sense, it did. Western composition in the tradition of counterpoint, which includes such diverse figures as Palestrina, Bach, Mozart, and Vaughn Williams, is a continual tug of war between the vertical integrity of the harmonic progression and the horizontal integrity of the individual melodies. When the composer dupes us into believing that neither interest was compromised, the miracle occurs.

Example 10-3 shows two lines of chord symbols below the score, one the Roman numerals of traditional harmonic theory, the other the guitar symbols familiar from popular song charts. While the Roman numeral analysis does indicate the modulation to B minor, both systems understate the harmonic content of the passage. There is nothing to indicate, for instance, the delicious dissonance of the alto D sounding against the E in the main melody at the beginning of measure two, or the parallel running of bass and alto in measure three. But they do bring out one harmonic feature which instantly distinguishes this music from anything recent of popular origin: the harmonic rhythm.

The rate of chord (root) change in the passage is roughly every beat, or four per measure.[5] Compared to "Be Not Afraid" or anything similar, this is as the hare is to the tortoise. Bach's speedy harmonic rhythm has three salutary effects. The first is an obvious and intrinsic harmonic interest: rapid chord changes charge the music with an internal rhythmic intensity, and in fact turn the plain rhythms of the melody into a virtue because they articulate with clarity each change.

Fast harmonic rhythm frees the tune from the straitjacket of periodic phrasing, a second benefit. In popular-style tunes of the last forty years, the slow harmonic rhythm means that the progression cannot complete its syntax within the span of the melodic phrase, so the four-bar phrasing of the tune becomes the main cognitive hook for the listener, and as such must be rigidly consistent and unmistakably clear. But Bach's opening phrase with its six chord changes has all the grammar of a complete harmonic sentence. Lutheran hymns need no unnaturally long notes or harmonic functions needed to fill out the symmetry of phrase as in "Be Not Afraid," and many hymns, such as Ralph Vaughan Williams's "Down Ampney," can do very well without symmetrical phrasing at all. But even the many that do have melodies as periodic as "O Sacred Head Surrounded" have not the slightest hint of singsong triviality, owing to the third effect of Lutheran harmonic rhythm, a sacred semantic arising from its most delicate meter.

As we remember from our experiences with "Be Not Afraid," every chord change creates a powerful accent in the music, and since the folk-revival song subsists on slow harmonic rhythm, its chord changes define each measure in heavy-handed fashion. When the melody of the

---

[5] Two minor exceptions: the third beat of measure 1, which has two changes, and the first two beats of measure 3, both of which are B minor. The second case is mitigated, however, by the running bass, which changes the inversion of the B minor chord and counts in perception nearly as important as a change of chord root. For more on the complexities of harmonic rhythm, see Joseph P. Swain, *Harmonic Rhythm: Analysis and Interpretation* (New York: Oxford University Press, 2002).

folk song is itself rhythmically complex, syncopated, and moving off the strong beats, all may be well, but when, as in the "Celtic Alleluia," everything lines up with these slow harmonic changes, a nursery sing-song inevitably results.[6]

Since in Bach's arrangement *all* the beats enjoy the benefit of a chord change, they are all equally weighted in that regard, and the understated duple meter of the chorale comes from much subtler materials, such as melodic accents and chord functions. The very beginning, for example, is metrically quite vague; we are not confident of the metric pattern until perhaps the third measure. The very first harmony is D major, the tonic, and normally accented not only because of its tonic property but also because it is the first thing heard.[7] But the second chord has the highest melodic note of the phrase, and the leap up to it accents it even more. So which chord is heavier, more salient in perception? It is hard to say, which is why there is very little sense of meter at the hymn's opening. Without hearing clearly stronger and weaker beats, no meter can arise. In this quality, Bach's arrangement approaches the aesthetics of plainchant and classical polyphony.

The decline in hymn composition in the eighteenth and nineteenth centuries, despite the best efforts of certain Victorians and their successors, such as Vaughan Williams, correlates very well with a decline in contrapuntal skill, and in particular the speed of harmonic rhythm. "Shall We Gather at the River," "How Great Thou Art," and other similar chestnuts of American revival movements suffer badly from sentimentalism because their arrangements sustain a single harmony for measures on end, enervating every phrase of harmonic activity. Even venerable Catholic tunes such as the "Lourdes Hymn" (Immaculate Mary) can be utterly trivialized if the harmonization is not truly contrapuntal in a way that distracts from the tune's insistence upon the tonic note in each phrase of the verse.

These are the subtleties that fascinate the professional. With all the simplicity of their tunes, no true lover of music will ever tire of Bach's chorale arrangements. And he had many predecessors—Michael Praetorius, Johann Walther (Luther's assistant), Claude LeJeune—

---

[6] This is a review of the discussion in chap. 3.

[7] Cognitive scientists call this the primacy effect and have long recognized its influence in temporal groupings. See W. Jay Dowling and Dane L. Harwood, *Music Cognition* (New York: Academic Press, 1986), and David Butler, *The Musician's Guide to Perception and Cognition* (New York: Schirmer, 1992).

who, while not the masters of modern harmony that Bach was, are nonetheless prized by trained musicians for their peculiar archaisms and harmonic personalities absent from Bach.

In short, everyone is satisfied. This is the great symbiosis of the Lutheran hymn and its worthy descendants. In "O Sacred Head Surrounded," the average Lutheran who knows no more music than he is used to singing, but mightily enjoys that, gets a fine tune that is easy to sing. Worshipers with some musical tutoring might join the choir, where they may make a special contribution by trying one of the alto, tenor, or bass melodies that are beyond the competence of the main congregation. And the organist, a person of many years' musical study, will revel in playing all four melodies at once, each articulated as if it were sung alone, yet all sounding in glorious harmonic synthesis.

Protestant Hymns in Catholic Liturgy

The Lutheran solution to the conflict of lay congregation and professional musician that bedevils religious traditions exercised a terrific influence on many other Christian and even some non-Christian traditions. If Catholic readers were surprised to learn that "O Sacred Head Surrounded" was not originally Catholic, they may well be even more astonished to know that "Holy, Holy, Holy," "Jesus Christ Is Risen Today," "Now Thank We All Our God," "Alleluia! Sing to Jesus," "Praise to the Lord," and many other favorites sung at Catholic Masses the world over owe at least some of their origin to Lutheran and Anglican sources. Despite official Catholic prejudices against all manner of Protestant music that retarded the progress of congregational singing for centuries after the Council of Trent, in the end the genius of the Lutheran hymn proved too attractive to resist.[8]

But how to use it? Before the reforms of the Second Vatican Council, when Catholic congregational singing was desired by many but not

---

[8] Anthony Ruff presents evidence that "congregational vernacular hymnody was a part of the medieval Mass in many locales." Some of his evidence is equivocal because it derives from documents relating to the Divine Office rather than the Mass, and he does not show that any such hymns replaced the Mass propers as they do now, but later German sources are more convincing. This would indicate that with his musical reform of the liturgy, Martin Luther simply tapped into a popular impulse. See *Sacred Music and Liturgical Reform*, 567–73.

for the most part officially encouraged, hymns like these edged their way cautiously into the liturgy as unofficial appendages of the "Low Mass" (*Missa lecta*) that had no official music at all, sung over the celebrant's spoken liturgy, especially in Germany, home of the *Singmesse* (Singing Mass). They could cover processions in and out, as well as the reception of Communion if the official antiphon were not chanted, as it mostly was not. After Vatican II, the hasty and desperate search for music suitable for congregational singing seems to have carved into stone "the four hymns": entrance song, offertory song, communion song, and recessional. A generous interpretation of this practice is that they substitute for the traditional introit (entrance), offertory, and communion antiphons as provided in "option four" in the General Instruction of the Roman Missal.[9] Since the council, "the four hymns" spaced strategically through the liturgy is a pattern we may have grown accustomed to, but it remains an awkward compromise.

"What ought to be a central source of the Christian's liturgical and personal prayer—the Psalter—is at least eclipsed if not ignored when hymns are used."[10] One difficulty is that hymns cannot set the Ordinary and proper texts for a given liturgy; at best they can only paraphrase them.[11] The periodic phrase structure of most hymns requires a strongly rhymed and metered poetry, a characteristic of none of the prayers of the liturgy, not even the psalms. Although one can still hear them in German-speaking lands at least, this incompatibility rules out hymn-style settings of the *Kyrie, Gloria, Credo, Sanctus*, and *Agnus Dei* because, in the interest of catholicity, the General Instruction of the Roman Missal does not permit paraphrases of these prayers. It does permit paraphrases of the Mass propers, and in fact "option four" slides much further down the slippery slope to a "suitable liturgical song." But the awkwardness of paraphrase is seen in the advice of liturgical magazines, the weekly search by liturgists for the right hymns to reflect the "theme of the liturgy" on any given celebration. Paraphrase necessarily distances the hymn from the original text, and when that is done four times for each Mass, it is hardly surprising that

---

[9] See chap. 6 for details of this interpretation.

[10] Kevin Irwin, *Context and Text: Method in Liturgical Theology* (Collegeville, MN: Liturgical Press, 1994), 236–46.

[11] This point was made early on in the days of reform by Helmut Hucke, "Church Music," trans. Theodore L. Westow, in *The Church and the Liturgy*, vol. 2 of *Concilium: Theology in the Age of Renewal* (Glen Rock, NJ: Paulist Press, 1965), 124.

little liturgical coherence remains. When the proper antiphons from the Roman Missal are chanted, on the other hand, no such worries occur. The proper "theme" is built right in for every occasion.[12]

A second awkwardness derives from the musical characteristics of even the finest hymns of the Lutheran and Anglican traditions, best understood by contrast with plainchant. The hymn brings a kind of interruption of the liturgical action.[13] A chant appears to arise out of the silence naturally. Because its rhythm is, more or less, the rhythm of speech, it creates a continuity with spoken prayer that is seamless, and in fact in a fully chanted liturgy the plainchant is the essential medium of prayer. Any normal speech, such as the homily, interrupts the music, and not vice versa. When the organ sounds to introduce the hymn, a different sense of time, a measured time a little alien to liturgy, takes over. The fact that there has to be an introduction without singing shows the seam. When the celebrant's chanted preface to the Eucharistic Prayer leads to a strongly metric, hymnlike setting of the *Sanctus*, for example, this kind of awkwardness is unmistakable and unavoidable, because not only the beat but also the tonality must be set by the organ. Plainchant, by contrast, molds itself to the formless prayer. The chanted preface leads directly into the chanted *Sanctus* on the same tone, without interruption, an integral musical composition. A hymn imposes its simple but overpowering musical structure on the prayer and makes an artifact of it. These discontinuities are not exactly antithetical to the liturgy but can seem like something of a compromise in intelligence and disrupt an aesthetic unity of action.[14]

A third liturgical awkwardness of hymns is ironically an aspect for which they are rightly prized: their varied characters. Hymns can be loud, boisterous, processional marches, such as "O God Our Help in Ages Past" or "For All the Saints," structures that build to great climaxes, such as "Lift Up Ye Heads" or "Wake, Awake for Night is Flying," or lyrical contemplations, such as "O Sacred Head Surrounded" or "The King of Love."[15] Such characters have given birth to a modern litur-

---

[12] See also chap. 14 on the musical effects of the liturgical year.

[13] See comments of various authors in Ruff, *Sacred Music and Liturgical Reform*, 564.

[14] Other practical problems are discussed in William Mahrt, "The Place of Hymns," *Sacred Music* 137, no. 3 (Fall 2010): 4–5.

[15] These are some of the more common English titles for hymn tunes which may set a variety of texts. The tunes here are, respectively, *St. Anne* by William Croft, *Sine Nomine* by Ralph Vaughan Williams, *Macht Hoch die Tür* (traditional), *Wachet*

gical semantics. The entrance hymn must be full throated but the communion a quiet reflection. The recessional hymn, for which there is no analogue at all in traditional liturgy, is nothing more than a concession to a sensibility bequeathed to us by nineteenth-century novels, detective thrillers, and Hollywood movies that insist on a climactic ending. Plainchant knows none of these distinctions, as semantic reference is alien to it.[16] There are no characters of chant to contend with in liturgy. The description "rousing hymn" may be apt for "Lift Up Ye Heads," but "rousing Gregorian chant" just sounds silly. To be sure, the semantics of the Lutheran and Anglican are overwhelmingly sacred in the modern world, but each one brings with it a bit of worldly reference, an emotionalism inessential to the liturgical action.

Finally, one might remark that the hymn, while a brilliant solution to the problem of congregational singing, is a distinctly Western solution, because the harmonic language that makes the Lutheran hymn possible is a distinctly Western language. Indigenous musical languages of Asia and Africa are fundamentally monophonic—one melody at a time—and therefore cannot, at least by means of counterpoint, imbue a single composition with musical simplicity and sophistication at once.

These difficulties do not gainsay the significant advantages of a Lutheran-style hymn for liturgy, that is, "for considering such hymnody as an integral, canonical part of the liturgical order followed by a local church."[17] Its immense success in Lutheran and Anglican liturgies especially and the popularity of their hymnals over the centuries can only mean that we have here a natural means of divine praise. What is truly significant is the range of musical competencies the hymn can satisfy; in this, it is much like plainchant, which as we have seen can run from the nearly monotonic litany to the highly melismatic and thoroughly professional liturgical antiphons. This range was unintentionally demonstrated when the Episcopal Church in the

---

Auf by Philip Nicolai, *O Haupt Voll Blut und Wunden* (traditional), and *St. Columba* (traditional).

[16] See chaps. 7 and 12. Joseph Ratzinger remarks, "The cosmic character of liturgical music stands in opposition to the two tendencies of the modern age that we have described: music as pure subjectivity, music as the expression of mere will. We sing with the angels. But this cosmic character is grounded ultimately in the ordering of all Christian worship to *logos*." *Spirit of the Liturgy* (San Francisco: Ignatius Press, 2000), 155.

[17] Ruff, *Sacred Music and Liturgical Reform*, 589.

United States brought out with some fanfare its new national hymnal in 1982 to replace the venerable Hymnal 1940. A great cry went up from those worshipers of moderate musical training in the pews because the new hymnal pew edition printed only the main (soprano) melody for the hymns, whereas the 1940 edition had printed four-part arrangements, thus denying certain congregants the pleasure of singing the main tune on one verse, the tenor part on another, the bass on another. The editorial authorities had underestimated their congregations badly.

And the hymn is more than a synthesis of lay competence and professional musical aspiration. It allows the common worshiper a taste of musical grandeur such as enthralls the symphony musician or choral society singer. There is nothing quite like the experience of singing one of these proud hymns at the top of the lungs in a large, resonant church filled with like-minded worshipers, all driven and sustained by a great pipe organ whose accompaniment can grow more adventurous with each oncoming verse. This is perhaps as close as liturgical music ever gets to democracy. Save the organist in charge, everyone else present contributes equally, regardless of the quality of one's voice, because no one can hear an individual voice. Voices are heard only in the magnificent summation of sound. It is hard to deny that, as different from the ethereal plainchant as it may be, the hymn too may afford a foretaste of the heavenly chorus of praise when sung this way.

Part III

Building Traditions of Liturgical Music

Chapter 11

Primary Considerations

> For liturgical symbols to work, music included, there has to be a collective memory.
> Archbishop Rembert Weakland (1993)

The first two parts of *Sacred Treasure* have introduced some general aspects of the current state of affairs in Catholic liturgical music, some of the fundamental causes of its confusion, and the great treasure house of Roman Catholic musical traditions of times past. It is time now to put these understandings to some practical good effect: to consider building traditions of Catholic liturgical music for the Roman Rite in the future.

It may seem odd to speak of "building" a tradition in a church where traditions of two millennia are fundamental elements of doctrine and liturgy. Yet, with regard to music, we stand on barely broken ground. The great traditions of plainchant and polyphony that were the foundation of liturgical music for centuries had been moribund since the Enlightenment and were only in the incipient stages of revival when the Second Vatican Council was called. These revivals were summarily dismissed thereafter and replaced by one ill-advised adoption or experiment after another, attempts at founding that either have collapsed through the weakness of their materials or survive their aesthetic blight by sheer functionality, lack of any other choice, and ignorance of alternatives. Local parishes have experienced this series most pragmatically as a constantly changing repertory, a revolving door of the latest hits that are replaced, it seems, as soon as they are learned. The surest sign of this sorry state is the lamentable but continuing presence in churches of the missalette, that disposable "worship aid" whose repertory is about as lasting as the newsprint on which the booklet is printed. This was supposed to be a temporary fix, the prop holding up the building until a cornerstone of liturgical renewal and its music had been cut and fitted. But with only the vaguest directives from the episcopacy, most parishes have nothing close to what might be called a tradition of liturgical music. The prop has become a permanent symbol of the deficit.

Why Traditions?

Since most Catholics living in the Western world have experienced little of what traditions of liturgical music feel like, let us reflect on their nature a bit. Why indeed should building traditions be the means of renewing music in a parish?

A liturgical tradition embodies a symbolism of great richness and depth. Here is not the place to rehearse the importance of symbols for the Catholic tradition, but merely to agree with authorities ancient and modern that they are immense in virtually every dimension of Catholic life, in liturgy above all. Music may there be a symbol of particular power, since of all the arts it is the only one bearing and conforming itself to the Word of God. One of its powers is to mark the people of God as a distinct community that knows and sings a kind of music belonging properly to itself. Knowing the music is the sign of belonging to the community. The music also symbolizes the orientation of this community toward the Divine, and it is the primary action of giving thanks and praise. Finally, liturgical music can symbolize the bridge that liturgy builds between the present world and the next, the transcendence of time and space. Once again, music, whose composition entails the sculpture of time in a way that abolishes the necessity for space, has no equal among the arts in symbolizing this. "Liturgy . . . implies an encounter with the all holy, the sacred. If God is one of the participating actors through the action of the Holy Spirit, then the weight of that transcendent dimension has to be carried by the symbols and by the music in particular."[1]

An essential aspect of a musical tradition, perhaps of any tradition, is its constancy or stability. In some religions this means quite literally that the same chants are sung on each liturgical occasion. The richness of Catholic music history bestows a somewhat broader conception of stability, a stability of several musical languages made distinct from any in the secular world, a repertory of worthy compositions that serves the liturgical year in its abundant variety and yet evolves but

---

[1] Archbishop Weakland, address to the National Liturgical Music Convention in Melbourne, Australia, on April 19, 1993. Published as "The Song of the Church: Liturgy and Music," *Origins* 23, no. 1 (May 20, 1993): 13.

gradually, on the timescale of decades and generations, if not centuries.

A microtradition familiar to most contemporary Catholics that might illustrate this stability and its properties is the small set of Christmas carols. Mostly German, Austrian, or French folk melodies, or tunes such as "Silent Night" composed to sound like one, or Victorian products of the great revival of hymn singing prompted by the Oxford Movement in the nineteenth century, such as "Joy to the World" or "The First Nowell," these songs come around to Catholic parishes for three weeks every year at Christmastide. Even the boldest liturgist hardly dares to replace one of these favorites with a new composition. And yet, on the scale of the centuries, the repertory has evolved significantly. It is a like the sequoia tree, ancient, durable, ever there, but living and changing.

The annual return of the carols is a repetition characteristic of ritual. In the years immediately following the Second Vatican Council, the concept of ritual—and of its repetitions in particular—was, let us say, not highly prized. The antagonism seems to have been grounded in a functionalist account of the liturgy combined with inflated notions of liturgical creativity, and was perhaps even encouraged by a narrow reading of a brief passage in *Sacrosanctum Concilium* advising that "the rites should radiate a noble simplicity. They should be short, clear, and free from useless repetition" (SC 34).[2] The distance and experience of a few decades has miraculously rehabilitated rituals. Rembert Weakland, former Archbishop of Milwaukee and musicologist of no mean achievement, remarks how the "repetition of symbol is a very important part of that collective memory" essential to a traditional community.[3] Every time the Christmas carols are sung, they remind us of our past as a community simply because we have sung them before in just this way.

In other words, we have begun to rediscover the creativity of rituals. This is a touch ironic, since it was precisely in the name of creativity

---

[2] Everything depends on what is understood by "useless." See also Aidan Nichols, *Looking at the Liturgy: A Critical View of Its Contemporary Form* (San Francisco: Ignatius Press, 1996), 78. Another critique of the functionalist approach to liturgy is Joseph Ratzinger's "Theological Problems in Church Music," in *Crux et Cithara: Selected Essays on Liturgy and Sacred Music*, ed. Robert Skeris (Altötting: Alfred Coppenrath, 1983), 216–17.

[3] Weakland , "The Song of the Church," 14.

that liturgists frowned upon the "useless repetitions" of ritual in the years immediately following the Second Vatican Council. But cultural anthropologists knew that any forced spontaneity is absolutely deadening, that "the shortest way to creativity is habituation to technical means of expression and steady soaking in an historical context."[4] Musicians too have known this very well for as long as they have practiced instruments. The small sacrifices of personal creativity they make to learn rote scales and other slavishly imitative techniques buy the tremendous freedom to create interpretations of Bach and Mozart. For the parishioner, the creativity bought by ritual comes from the security of knowing the rite, a feeling of confidence akin to a well-worn family tradition. Turkey may be served at every Thanksgiving, and yet the tradition is always creative, with an element of novelty that must come from our being a year older if from nothing else. The gift of creativity in liturgical ritual, and certainly its music, is the same, arising from "an impunity, an absence of worry about the credibility of what is represented."[5] In this sense, tradition contains its own ratification.

Building traditions might finally banish the liturgical anxiety that has gripped most parishes the past four decades, the implicit threat that one will have to adapt or accommodate some new requirement with every visit to Mass. There is no more visceral symbol of this discomfort than the revolving door of musical repertory. For most of the year, the warm security of the Christmas carols is far, far away.

Tradition and Traditions

Because Catholicism is a historical religion that values the material world and the good things that occur in it, its regard for tradition is not monolithic, but plural. It recognizes that while the essential truths are immutable, certain aspects of their expression through liturgical action evolve over time. "For the Liturgy is made up of unchangeable elements divinely instituted, and of elements subject to change. These latter not only may be changed but ought to be changed with the passage of time, if they have suffered from the intrusion of anything out of harmony with the inner nature of the liturgy or have become less suitable" (SC 21).

---

[4] David Martin, *Two Critiques of Spontaneity*, 13; quoted in Nichols, *Looking at the Liturgy*, 53.

[5] Martin, *Two Critiques of Spontaneity*, 13; quoted in Nichols, *Looking at the Liturgy*, 56.

A tradition of liturgical music is therefore constructed on more than one level and in more than one dimension. There is the historical dimension: the *Gloria* could have been chanted in the eighth century, sung polyphonically at a solemn Mass in the sixteenth, and operatically in the eighteenth, but the words were always the same. The unchanging text is a core tradition governing lower-level traditions of musical setting. There is the geographical dimension: the *Gloria* may have been sung to the Ambrosian melody in Milan, the Sarum in Salisbury, and the Gregorian in Paris, but once again the local traditions are united in the words that are sung. And then there is what might be called the hierarchical dimension: traditions that hold within a parish, within a diocese, within a national conference, and within the worldwide church. Catholics live with this tension of a limited pluralism, and it is not considered a shortcoming or a weakness of the faith, but rather a natural consequence of the incarnation, which makes human history precious. Thus the instruction on inculturating the liturgy *Varietates Legitimae* proclaims:

> It [the liturgy] must be capable of expressing itself in every human culture, all the while maintaining its identity through fidelity to the tradition which comes to it from the Lord.[6]
>
> During the course of the centuries, the Roman rite has known how to integrate texts, chants, gestures and rites from various sources and to adapt itself in local cultures in mission territories, even if at certain periods a desire for liturgical uniformity obscured this fact.[7]

The "desire for liturgical uniformity" is to be taken seriously, however, because there is no greater symbol of the unity of the people of God than this. The recognition of a limited pluralism in liturgical traditions cannot justify limitless idiosyncrasy and disregard for how neighboring parishes, dioceses, and nations pray the liturgy.[8] "Liturgy

---

[6] Congregation for Divine Worship and the Discipline of the Sacraments, *Varietates Legitimae*: Instruction on Inculturation and the Roman Liturgy, March 29, 1994, http://www.adoremus.org/VarietatesLegitimae.html; originally published in *Origins* 23, no. 43 (April 14, 1994), art. 18.

[7] Ibid., art. 17.

[8] John D. Zizioulas believes this to be a modern corruption of practice in the ancient church: "It is very significant that, unlike what the churches do today in an age marked by a tragic loss of the primitive ecclesiology, there was never a celebration of the eucharist especially for children or for students, etc., nor a eucharist that could take place privately and individually. Such a thing would destroy precisely

celebrated as 'good for us' in a particular liturgical assembly within a particular local Church is not necessarily effective 'for the life of the world.'"[9] All bear some responsibility to the unity of the world church. Isolated practices and music accomplish isolation, and in a world where more and more of its Catholics travel to ever-farther reaches, it would seem to be a matter not only of catholic symbology but also of simple charity to make the liturgy ready to welcome the stranger.

A Simple Restoration?

The inevitability of the little traditions is partly why digging up and brushing off the repertory of Roman Catholic sacred music like some long-hidden musical Pompeii is hardly the simple solution to the contemporary crisis that it might seem. In his historical survey of this repertory, Anthony Ruff has described in detail three "problem areas" created by the new Roman Rite—active participation of the laity, the liturgical choir, and the position of the composer—and his ambivalent conclusions bespeak the complexities involved.[10]

There are severe practical problems. Traditional Roman Catholic sacred music is indeed a vast and complex repertory, with works ranging from the simple to the grandiloquent, and all manner of customs and controversies of performance. Neglect and distortion of plainchant, to take but one example, during the modern era since the invention of opera and downright rejection of it during the years following the Second Vatican Council have ensured that twenty-first-century Catholics, including most clerics, do not know the basics of this repertory. A revival means a great deal of relearning.

There are technical and financial difficulties. High Renaissance polyphony and the operatic repertory remain for the time being beyond the reach of virtually all but cathedral or large city parishes simply because they demand too many resources and musical skills.

---

the catholic character of the eucharist which was *leitourgia*, i.e. a "public work" for all Christians of the same city . . ." *Being as Communion: Studies in Personhood and the Church* (Crestwood, New York: St. Vladimir's Seminary Press, 1985), 151–52.

[9] Mary Collins, OSB, *Contemplative Participation:* Sacrosanctum Concilium; *Twenty-five Years Later* (Collegeville, MN: Liturgical Press, 1990), 20.

[10] Ruff, *Sacred Music and Liturgical Reform* (Chicago: Hillenbrand, 2007), chaps. 17–19.

That they exclude congregational singing is yet another concern. Despite the many bad ideas, dead-end roads, and poor advice that have plagued liturgical music since the council, active participation of the laity in the liturgy is perhaps the one reform in *Sacrosanctum Concilium* that everyone applauds. It is here to stay, although not without a more considered reflection of what it entails for liturgical music.[11]

There is the perennial problem of creativity in liturgical music. Gregorian chant and the other traditions comprise frozen repertories of dead, or classicized, musical languages. Is it artistically feasible to compose new works in them? What is the living liturgical composer to do?

Finally, it is not at all clear at this point how much of the traditional music that originated in Europe and the United States will work in non-Western lands. That much of it can be sung and has been sung beautifully in far reaches of the world is a matter of historical fact, but whether every people can learn it, and whether they should, is not a simple matter.

Pompeii was excavated to be visited and studied as a museum piece, an artifact of intellectual interest. The liturgy is an action to be lived by present Christians, redolent though it be of thousands of years of tradition, including musical tradition. The musical treasure is there and its virtues are deep. But in building traditions for the present and future church we cannot hope to reconstitute liturgies of the Middle Ages or any previous age, even though we may harvest their fruits. The project is more subtle than a restoration exercise in musicology or liturgical history.

What We Need to Understand: The Musical Symbol

To return to the fundamental premise, Catholic liturgy is an action founded on symbols. Indeed, it is a feast of symbols of all kinds: verbal, gestural, physical, and certainly musical. Understanding liturgical music means, in part, understanding the symbolic properties of music and how they interact with all the other symbolic properties of the liturgy.

Symbols mean things, so we require, first of all, some understanding of musical semantics, how music means.[12] Beyond the minimum of

---

[11] In short, this means that although they exclude congregational singing, we cannot conclude that they exclude the congregation. See chap. 18.
[12] See chap. 12: The Semantics of Sacred Music.

adequately carrying the liturgical texts, musical semantics should ensure the unimpeded communication, in the deepest sense, of the liturgy's holiness, "the summit toward which the activity of the Church is directed . . . the source from which all her power flows" (SC 10) and how this symbology perdures through generations. To do this, liturgical music must have a sacred semantic. Some liturgists in recent times have doubted the very existence of the category "sacred music," and if they are right, then any significant role for music in building liturgical traditions, or indeed in liturgy itself, is fictitious and doomed to a pathetic failure.[13] To avoid such catastrophic pessimism, we must know how these writers err, and above all how a sacred semantic in music can operate.

One essential property of all symbols is perdurability. The various liturgical innovations of recent years—interpolated blessings, banners, liturgical dances, and so on—so often appear forced and artificial because they vainly attempt to invent new symbols on the spot. But "new symbols" is almost a contradiction in terms, and so they have no power. Except for those rare objects attached to some cataclysmic event, such as the cross, we become aware that something is a symbol only after significant time has passed, time that allows the accrual of meaning that slowly creates the symbol.

In building a tradition of music, which is a language of symbols,[14] dedicated to the action of the liturgy, which is dramatized largely through symbols, the stability of the music is essential as it ensures the

---

[13] See Ruff, *Sacred Music and Liturgical Reform*, 26–28, for a survey of some of these. Fr. Ruff summarizes the objections as three. First, that the term "sacred music" dates to the nineteenth century; therefore, earlier times cannot have conceived of the notion. This Whorfian argument can be dismissed out of hand. Because there is no name for a category in a culture does not entail that the category, in absolute terms, does not exist. Claudio Monteverdi called *L'Orfeo* (1607) a *favola in musica*, not an *opera*, and Joseph Haydn called his Op. 17 *divertimenti* and not *quartetti*, but only the most obtuse music historian would refuse to call them "opera" and "string quartet," since they share every characteristic with those genres. Second, that the term has no reliable stylistic earmarks. As Ludwig Wittgenstein has shown, this can be true of any common cultural term, such as "game." Fortunately, we do not abandon useful semantic categories because of such elasticity and dependence upon context. Third, that conceiving a category of "sacred music" would limit composers. As will be shown in chap. 14, this is true only in cases of limited imaginations.

[14] Suzanne Langer, *Philosophy in a New Key: A Study in the Symbolism of Reason, Rite, and Art*, third ed. (Cambridge, MA: Harvard University Press, 1956).

stability of the tradition. But how shall we ensure the stability of musical symbols? By recourse to musical traditions that have already proved themselves capable of stability, and by observing their patterns. For if we are to build a tradition, our materials must be the strongest possible, unaffected by the superficial parade of fashions through time.[15] One such musical tradition, already bound to the liturgy, is the liturgical year.[16] This rich mine of symbols has been mostly neglected these last decades because some of its hallmarks—the proper antiphons—have been eclipsed by songs with generic all-season texts. This is a touch ironic, since Prosper Guéranger began blazing the trail to the Second Vatican Council back in the 1840s with his massive *L'Année Liturgique*, the first major contribution to the liturgical movement.

Finally, there is symbolism of the liturgical language. Liturgy is at root an action, but it is an action articulated principally through language. It is difficult to conceive of "giving thanks" (Eucharist) without words, as human languages attest. At minimum then, liturgical music must carry the sacred words, the liturgical texts, and—if this relationship is not to be entirely random—a happenstance of notes and words, then some account of liturgical language is in order.[17] The correspondence of musical and linguistic phrasing is so basic that it has already come up, for both good and ill, in the music already examined. But the very choice of language itself has an incalculable effect on the music that sets it, as long historical experience has shown, because the two symbolic systems of music and language must reach an intricate synthesis where each reinforces the other. Where our words come from, their form, their weight, and how they are understood will all affect the symbolic power and meaning of the music and the ultimate stability of the tradition.

What We Need to Understand: Three Eternal Conflicts

The sacred music traditions of all the major religions have wrestled with three fundamental conflicts of interest, tensions that seem intrinsic to the enterprise. The liturgical music of Roman Catholicism is no exception, and while there is no escaping these conflicts, the wise architect of tradition takes them into account.

---

[15] See chap. 13: Understanding Musical Symbols: The Infallible Judge.
[16] See chap. 14: Understanding Musical Symbols: The Seasons of Liturgical Music.
[17] See chap. 15: Understanding Musical Symbols: Language in the Liturgy.

The first is the conflict of musical creativity and tradition itself.[18] A healthy tradition is stable and conservative, while a healthy musical culture invents new works all the time. Since the reform, creativity would seem to have had the upper hand; indeed, many would say it has run amok. Mandating a hidebound repertory, however, is not what stability entails. For if we are to build a tradition and not a museum, it must be alive and growing. A more mature notion of musical creativity, both in composition and performance, must replace the adolescent kind that has hamstrung our liturgies since the council. Liturgical creativity and liturgical tradition are properly understood not in terms of prerogatives and competition but in terms of one enriching the other. Our history shows how this may be.

The second is the conflict of the "little traditions" of local culture and the catholicity of the worldwide church. Much of the writing on liturgical inculturation has taken its absolute virtue for granted and focused on how to get it done. The exemplary success of certain American parishes using gospel music has inadvertently promoted a simplistic approach to inculturation of liturgical music around the world: find the local pop music and set the words of the Roman Rite to it. History and recent experience have demonstrated how the worldwide diversity of liturgical music can enrich the Catholic tradition while exacting its price, how embracing local musics can bridge a chasm between the Gospel message and local culture, but also how it may exclude outsiders. Sorting out some of the complexities of the conflict between local traditions and catholicity demonstrates how a theory of a sacred semantic of music applies to the real world.[19]

The third conflict is that of the professional musician and the congregation, perhaps the most serious of all.[20] Every major religion at one time or another has seen its gifted sacred musicians at war with the natural desire of all, musically trained and untrained, to praise the Most High. In Catholic parishes, *participatio actuosa*—"active" or "actual participation" of the laity—is more vigorous now than at any time since antiquity, but it has also suffered from misunderstanding, extremes of which have marginalized organists and other music professionals, and from its simplistic translation as "congregational sing-

---

[18] See chap. 16: An Eternal Conflict: Creativity and Tradition.

[19] See chap. 17: An Eternal Conflict: Inculturation and Catholic Liturgical Music.

[20] See chap. 18: An Eternal Conflict: Congregational Singing and *Participatio Actuosa*.

ing." One can understand why the insistence of Catholics from the top to the bottom of the hierarchy on the importance of lay participation in the liturgy might be considered a case of John Henry Newman's vox populi, and rightly so, but the concept has been lamed through its own overstatement. A more nuanced conception will actually enrich the practice of it.

Building any tradition, consciously or unconsciously, liturgical or otherwise, is an enormous investment of effort and especially time—a great deal of time, decades and generations. Unwise investments, such as we have made too often since the council, show little for their efforts. Making the wise investments that, with time, will yield the richest fruit of living traditions of liturgical music is what the third part of this book attempts to promote.

Chapter 12

Understanding Musical Symbols: The Semantics of Sacred Music

> Just as Jesus would not let people hold onto moments of thrill and transfiguration, so artists who design their work so that thrill or sensation is its chief purpose are defective artists. This is especially obvious in church music, for its purpose is to assist the believer in his journey towards God, not to attach him to the sensations of this world.
> Eric Routley (1976)

No lament about the liturgical music after the Second Vatican Council is as ubiquitous and loud as the one about its propriety. The lament may take many forms: "It doesn't sound sacred," "It's inappropriate for Mass," "There's no solemnity," and so on. And it may have many particular stimuli: the use of guitar or piano, texts from secular sources, arrangements after the folk revival or jazz styles, and so on. But these are all laments about the same fundamental aspect of the music: its semantics.

Once there were those who, in the years directly following the council and especially in the United States, believed that such comments proved that reform was on the right track, that the desacralization of liturgical music was exactly what *participatio actuosa* at Mass required. After all, explicitly sacred forms and styles were irrelevant to the everyday experience of modern Catholics and therefore could not speak to them and invite their active participation. But such thinkers are few now. Four decades of experience, experiments, and trials and errors have shown the relevance theory to be bankrupt.[1] The renewal of the eternal search for transcendence depends upon the integrity of music more than any other liturgical element, save the Word and the sacrament itself.[2] Such transcendence can only arise through a proper musical semantic.

---

[1] See chap. 4.
[2] Judith Marie Kubicki, *Liturgical Music as Ritual Symbol: A Case Study of Jacques Berthier's Taizé Music* (Leuven: Peters, 1999), 23.

"Semantics" means the meaning in music. More specifically, it describes how music may refer to the real world beyond its own abstract and intangible sounds. For one pragmatic example, it is the semantic quality of the music that causes a match of melody and words in a song to be good or bad, that is, whether the sense of the words seems to fit the "sense" of the music or not. Semantics is the aspect of music that nonmusicians wonder about when they think about music in the abstract, if they are wont to do so, and in the limited field of musical aesthetics, a branch of philosophy, it is by far the dominant issue and has been since Plato. The question of whether music actually can mean anything, can refer to the outside world, and if so, how, has always been controverted and vexed, but rarely has the problem had such a practical import, affecting millions of worshipers every week, as in its application to the modern Roman Catholic liturgy.

There is one aesthetic school, sometimes called absolutism,[3] that maintains that music cannot refer to the outside world. The abstract sequence of sounds denoted by "c-r-o-s-s" in English points to a physical object, or a set of objects, or perhaps a physical activity in the world. The abstract sounds of music can never do this, so claims this school, even if the referent is not physical but an intangible one such as "love." The musical sounds can only refer to themselves in the sense that we hear the second phrase of "O Sacred Head Surrounded" as a literal repetition of the melody in the first phrase, or the ending as a transposed variant of the beginning, for so they are. And it does seem silly to ascribe any romantic narrative "interpretation" to abstract, instrumental works such as the keyboard fugues of Bach. But even the staunchest apologists for "absolute music" could hardly object when someone describes those same fugues as "learned" or points out how different is their effect when played on the piano instead of the organ, and yet learnedness and effect already imply something beyond the notes of the music.

Without denying that the significance of self-reference in music may indeed be not only true but also most useful in understanding things such as musical structure, it is yet reasonable to claim that music may have among its semantic effects some power to refer, to connote, to present, and to signify. Musicians of a liturgical bent and experience

---

[3] For an introduction to the contrast of absolutism and referentialism, see Leonard B. Meyer, *Emotion and Meaning in Music* (Chicago: University of Chicago Press, 1956), chap. 1.

in fact would simply dismiss the philosophical denial of musical semantics out of hand. If music never signified anything beyond its own sounds and their perceived patterns, then all our arguments over which music is appropriate for the sacred liturgy would be so much hot air. A psalm could be set to the tune of "Dixie" or "The Marine Corps Hymn" or "Mood Indigo" or "Stayin' Alive" without conferring the slightest disadvantage (or advantage) to its meaning or use. Whether the character of the music is "appropriate" for the psalm and the liturgy that sang it would be a foolish question. Without signification of some kind, music has no character.

There is no one in liturgy, and few in other musical circles, who would believe that music has no power to signify. Music may indeed have a strong character, and its propriety for liturgy is perhaps the issue central to all the controversies about modern Catholic liturgical music.

Semantic Range[4]

But the experience of musical semantics can be rather paradoxical. Consider the following experiment.

The members of a group independently choose music for a friend's wedding procession from a set of three unfamiliar compositions to be played for them: (1) J. S. Bach, Overture to the Fourth Orchestral Suite, slow section; (2) Beethoven, Symphony no. 3, second movement; (3) Chopin, any nocturne. I have run this test on groups of twenty-five and more, and the response on written ballots is unanimous: all choose the Bach, a fanfare with trumpets and timpani playing dotted rhythms in stately phrasing, to the exclusion of the Beethoven movement, slow and in a minor key and called *Marcia funebre* (Funeral march) to boot, and the Chopin, a reflective work for piano. The proper choice, which is to say the best semantic match for the wedding, seems absolutely clear. But then play any other instrumental work and ask the same subjects to write down a word, phrase, or sentence that expresses best "what the music means." Very likely, not even two ballots will be identical; most, in fact, will not even be very close in meaning to one another. Why is there an excellent semantic match in the first task, but none at all in the second?

---

[4] The following is a summary of the account of general musical semantics presented in Joseph P. Swain, *Musical Languages* (New York: Norton, 1997), chap. 3.

When we ask "What does the music mean?" we suspect that music, being a human invention, has a property analogous to another sound stream that is also a human invention: speech. But for the analogy to work, that is, for it to illustrate how music can signify or symbolize things in the way that speech does, we must leave aside one important power of speech, predication, and abandon a common misunderstanding about the nature of words: single meaning.

Predication happens in normal speech when we use sentences or sentence fragments to relate words to one another, or more precisely, to relate their meanings. "That hymn was great" relates a specific member of a set of things called "hymns" to a quality of value. Music can predicate but rarely, only in the most constrained of circumstances.[5] But there is a less ambitious form of meaning in speech—or in speech elements, really—familiar from word association games, and that is the "presentational" meaning of isolated words. Saying the word "monster" by itself to someone does not predicate it, but certainly conjures associations in the mind of the hearer. These are meanings too, and music can produce analogous ones. Play a chord on a pipe organ and certain associations will spring to mind; play the same chord on a piano to bring others quite distinct. When someone claims that a certain Chopin nocturne for piano (no words) expresses "loneliness," it may be a personal interpretation to be seconded or not, but it is not nonsense. The music is capable of such a presentational connotation.

To understand how such presentational meanings in music succeed or fail to match up with words in a song, we have to recognize that in speech the meanings of individual words are not singular and fixed. "Cross," for example, may denote (1) intersecting marks on a page, (2) a Roman means of execution, (3) to traverse a boundary or space, (4) to obstruct someone's plan, or (5) to pass the soccer ball in front of the net, and others besides. All common words are similarly polysemic.[6] This is not relativism. Polysemy does not claim that a word can

---

[5] Such a case would be the use of "character themes" or *Leitmotiven* in operas. See Swain, *Musical Languages*, 48–49, 58–61.

[6] Some semanticists would claim that *all* words are polysemic. The most famous proponent would probably be Ludwig Wittgenstein at the beginning of his *Philosophical Investigations*, trans. G. E. Anscombe (Oxford: Basil Blackwell, 1953), 4. See also David Cruse, *Lexical Semantics* (Cambridge: Cambridge University Press, 1986), 51, and Susumo Kono, *Functional Syntax: Anaphora, Discourse, and Empathy* (Chicago: University of Chicago Press, 1987), 2.

mean anything that one wishes at the moment. It means, rather, that instead of conceiving the meaning of "cross" as a singular fixed point in English, we should conceive of it as a space like a sphere, with infinitely many points within, but bounded by the mutual agreement of speakers using that language. The points within represent all the possible legitimate meanings of "cross"; the edge of the sphere delimits illegitimate meanings, that is, any uses of "cross" that the English-speaking community would find illogical, confusing, and otherwise unacceptable. The sphere is the *semantic range* of the word "cross."

If all common words have ranges of meaning, how then does a linguistic community speak with precision and communicate without undue ambiguity?

> Mark a cross where the client should sign.
>
> Do not cross. [traffic signal]
>
> We adore you, O Christ, and we praise you, because by your holy cross you have redeemed the world.

The matter seems quite simple. Fluent speakers of English know exactly which meaning of "cross" is intended because the context defines it for them. The physical environment of the traffic signal, the ritual in the liturgy, or merely the other words in the expression point to exactly one of the meanings of "cross" within its semantic range, and that is the meaning activated in the hearer's mind.[7] Appropriate usage and understanding of a word in English depends upon the interaction of the word's semantic range—its many possibilities—with the specific context of the moment.

Now we understand the results of the experiment. In the second case, when the group members were asked to write a "translation" into English of a musical passage without any other context, the great breadth of the semantic range of that passage allowed a plenitude of legitimate connotations to come to mind, so that the probability of any two subjects matching them is low. But in the first case, the task of choosing wedding music defined the context so precisely and the semantic ranges of the three compositions are so distant and different

---

[7] Again, some semanticists would quibble with "exactly one." But if we substitute "an extremely constrained set" of meanings, it doesn't affect the following argument.

from one another that there was no doubt about which must be the appropriate response. The analogy with spoken words is quite good. Asking a group to define "cross" without context produces some variety of responses. Asking "What's a cross?" while they are enjoying a soccer match in a pub would probably produce only one. It is an important truth about musical passages that their semantic ranges are typically vaster than those of even the most polysemous words, but this is a difference in degree, not in kind. The principle is the same.

Semantic Association

Before applying this universal experience of language to musical compositions with words, two more observations are worth making. First, just as the context points to the appropriate meaning of "cross" at the moment, "cross" for its part helps to form the context for all the other elements. "Cross" contributes to our knowing exactly which meanings of "mark" and "sign" are intended in the first sentence and "redeemed" in the last. In perception science, this is known as a feedback relation.[8] The context specifies "cross," and "cross" builds the context at the same time. Second, although the examples above all predicate "cross," context can activate specific meanings in presentational senses too. In natural speech, pure presentational uses are rare, so examples are a little strained perhaps, but the fact remains that uttering "cross" out of the blue while walking down a busy street will bring associations to the hearer's mind quite different from those if it were pronounced in the nave of a church.

That is partly because members of a language community hardly ever learn words abstractly, such as from a dictionary, but rather con-

---

[8] We have already cited this principle writ large in chap. 1, in the relation of Scripture and tradition and in Kevin W. Irwin's proposal for method in liturgical theology in *Context and Text: Method in Liturgical Theology* (Collegeville, MN: Liturgical Press, 1994). In perception science, the problem is quite old, summarized over fifty years ago by Floyd H. Allport in *Theories of Perception and the Concept of Structure* (New York: John Wiley and Sons, 1955). For a summary of feedback (or circular) perception with particular application to music, see Swain, *Musical Languages*, 77–81, where it is proposed that feedback mechanisms in speech and musical perception, constrained as they are by the necessity of real-time processing, are found in the temporary store known as working memory. Here bits of raw sensory information can be coordinated by experience to form the most coherent semantic.

cretely, in particular contexts. The mother tells the child, "Never cross the street without me," as she takes his hand and leads him to the other side. When older, he might hear her say, "We make the sign of the cross," and see the particular hand motions as they enter a church. We associate a new word with the situation that presents it and know from experience that its meaning is proper to that particular context. As we hear it used in other situations—some similar, some different, none identical to another—we form the concept of its semantic range, that set of semantic points legitimated by the language community. This is what it means to learn the lexicon of a language.

Semantic Distinction

Just as important, we learn where its boundaries are, where legitimate use of one word stops and another word takes over, where "warm" ends and "hot" begins.[9] Thus the semantic ranges of all our words are in some sense conceived in terms of their overlaps and discrete boundaries with each other.

An example of this principle of semantic distinction rather significant for Roman Catholics and other believers in the miracle of the virgin birth of Jesus occurs in the translation history of the famous verse from Isaiah 7:14: "Therefore the Lord himself will give you this sign: the virgin shall be with child, and bear a son, and shall name him Immanuel" (NAB). The word here translated as "virgin" is originally *almah* in the Hebrew of the sixth century BC, which had among the meanings in its broader semantic range "virgin," but also "young woman."[10] But the Jewish scholars who made the Greek translation of the Scriptures known as the Septuagint in the third century BC had a variety of Greek words of finer distinction to choose from, including *kore*, "young woman." But instead of any of these they chose *ha parthenos*, "the virgin." Their translation is not at all unfaithful to the Hebrew *almah*, but the scholars surely narrowed the meaning of the passage by

---

[9] Note that these boundaries can shift with context. In New England, "warm" denotes quite different temperatures, depending on whether it is spoken about the weather in January or July.

[10] Some scholars refute this claim with a contextual argument, that *almah* is never used in the Old Testament except where it is clear that an unmarried virgin is implied.

181

exploiting the specificity of a richer Greek lexicon.[11] They eliminated an ambiguity of the original and thus cleared the way for the prophetic tradition carried on in St. Matthew's Gospel (1:23). The point relevant for musical semantics in liturgy is this: that the specific meaning of the Greek *ha parthenos* has its basis, in part, in the existence of distinct words meaning something else.

Words and Music

How, then, does a composer imagine an appropriate musical setting of Psalm 23?

Like a word in a natural language, a passage of music has a semantic range. Generally speaking, the semantic range of the musical passage —its interpretative potential—is much broader than words in natural language because we rarely ask of music the same kind of specific reference that we routinely expect of language, but this difference is merely in degree and not in kind, as we understand from the wedding music experiment. The semantic range of the passage is still a set of (perhaps infinitely) many, but not unbounded, meanings.[12] If it were unbounded, the range would stretch forever, and we would have the situation posited by those who believe that music has no semantic value at all: the passage containing all possible meanings would be meaningless.

The composer then may imagine a musical passage that contains the meaning of "The Lord is my shepherd; I shall not want" within its semantic range.[13] The music is not a translation of the psalm verse, nor

---

[11] This is a very common situation in comparative linguistics and is the bane of translators. English, to take a more prosaic example, has "warm" and "hot," but Italian only has *caldo*, which must cover the same range of temperatures, and thus, as an isolated word, is less precise. *Una giornata calda* could be translated legitimately as "a warm day" or "a hot day," depending on the context of the utterance, as always.

[12] The difference between "infinite" and "unbounded" appeals to the spatial metaphor on which is based the idea of semantic range. A sphere, for example, has infinitely many points within it, and these points are bounded by the limits of the sphere. This means that there is also an infinity of points outside the sphere. In the same way, a lexical item may have infinitely many meanings within its semantic range, but there are infinitely many more outside the range (the "sphere") that do not qualify as legitimate meanings.

[13] Revised Standard Version. The New American Bible has "The Lord is my shepherd; there is nothing I lack." I have never heard a musical setting of this translation.

does it exclude many other possible uses, just as the meaning of "cross" as "mark" does not exclude its potential for meaning *how Jesus redeemed us*. The important thing is that the sense of the psalm verse resides well within the semantic range of the music, as close to the center as possible, and not outside it. The theme music for "Star Wars," for example, or Wagner's "The Ride of the Valkyries" would probably not do, for their semantic ranges, though broad, do not comprise "The Lord is my shepherd: I shall not want."[14]

Once the match is made, a feedback analogous to that of natural language comes into play. The words act as a specifying context for the musical passage, indicating which of its (perhaps infinitely) many meanings will be activated. The music means that "The Lord is my shepherd; I shall not want," at least in a presentational sense. At the same time, the music contextualizes the psalm verse, so that we understand the psalm through the music more specifically than before. Perhaps we gain an insight into what "I shall not want" really entails or feels like.

But this is to speak of the psalm setting as a mere song, a type of musical gloss on a poem. The composer is out to express the text in an original way through music, an admirable musical aesthetic born of sixteenth-century humanism and with us ever since. But it is not a liturgical aesthetic. We certainly do not sing the psalms at Mass primarily in order to understand their meaning better. We sing them because they are given to us to praise God in music. Musical images of shepherds, green pastures, banquets, and cups overflowing are beside the point.[15] The semantic that liturgy requires is not the songster's expression of text, but something much higher. "Therefore sacred music is to be considered the more holy, the more closely connected it is with the liturgical action, whether making prayer more pleasing, promoting unity of minds, or conferring greater solemnity on the sacred rites" (SC 112). In some sense, the best liturgical music deflects attention from itself toward the particular act in the sacred drama. The words sung are essential because they are the prayer, but,

---

[14] One can cite specific technical details of these pieces as evidence for this statement, such as cultural associations of their tempo, rhythmic figures, and orchestration, but the examples would not seem to be controversial for the purposes of illustration.

[15] The issue of "expression" in liturgical music has already been visited in connection with plainchant (chap. 7) and the Lutheran hymn tradition (chap. 10).

paradoxically, the music points not to them but to Whom they are directed. The musical semantic that liturgy requires is transcendence.

The Search for Transcendence

Imagine a Mass that takes place in a pub instead of a church. Everyone is dressed casually. The priest wears a sweat suit. A rock beat pounds loudly from the karaoke box and the singer on the pub stage moans, "God is my caregiver; I don't need nothing.'" As people arrive, the priest greets them with "Great to see you, sit down, have some bread and wine."

The cheer may be infectious and warm feelings of camaraderie may abound, but of course any social occasion is capable of these. And so, even assuming the most spiritual inclinations in the participants, few would find in this scene anything close to the kind of restoration we seek in religion. The proof is in the fact that despite all the wrongheaded ideas about reform that have denuded, deritualized, and impoverished the Roman Rite in many places over the last four decades, we have not come to this. On the contrary, traditional vestments never left, and solemn languages, decorum, churches, and music are on the rebound. Transcendence requires them.

In Eastern religions, transcendence can mean, simply, escape from the world. Christian liturgy has a more delicate task. We cannot reject the world because God created it and personally intervened to save it. Christian liturgy is therefore born of the world, and its elements, both real and symbological, are worldly things. But if "in the earthly liturgy we take part in a foretaste of that heavenly liturgy which is celebrated in the holy city of Jerusalem toward which we journey as pilgrims," we can never be satisfied with a liturgy that is only of earth (SC 8). It must transcend, build a bridge to the heavenly world. Thus the ancient vestments, the sacred spaces, the strange golden cups, and the elevated language act as crucial "not of this world" symbols. But music—intangible, invisible, creating its own flow of time free of the world's time—can outdo them all in its power to transcend.

In setting liturgical prayer to music, the composer imagines music that captures not so much its literal sense as its spirit as close to the center of its semantic range as possible. Good liturgical music contains within its semantic range not the meaning of the sung text but the meaning of the very action of liturgy that transcends this world and touches the next. In other words, like the other symbols of liturgy, its music must somehow transcend its earthly elements of physical sound and human language to become, at least symbolically, something that gives us the foretaste we seek. It can do this by exploiting the two properties of semantics analyzed above: distinction and contextual association.

Remember that the Greek *ha parthenos* must denote an unambiguous "virgin" in part because there are other Greek words denoting a "young woman, not necessarily a virgin," in the lexicon. If liturgical music is to connote the next world, it too must distinguish itself from the musics that are unambiguously of this world. The most straightforward way of doing this is to avoid secular musical characteristics.[16] What are these? If we regard, for the moment, only the Western tradition for the sake of simplicity and consider all the styles of music that we hear every day in our routines of living at the turn of the twenty-first century, three fundamental characteristics in common mark their secularity.

One is the presence of strong meter, the regular beat that organizes the rhythmic patterns of virtually all popular music of the twentieth century, jazz, and a great deal of art music. In pop particularly, since the advent of rock and roll in the 1950s, the relentless duple pattern is almost inescapable.

The second is harmony, the chords that have clothed most Western art music since the Middle Ages and popular music since the sixteenth century. Exceptions are few: some kinds of traditional folk singing, a rare treat these days, or the group singing at a sports event or at a birthday party. In the world of commercial popular music, harmonization is never even open to question.

The third is domination by instruments. It may seem odd to claim this in a culture where the word "song" is synonymous with "composition" in the minds of most, but the fact is that in the modern world songs come with instruments attached. The quaint scene of a crowd striking up a tune a cappella in the pub is fading fast, replaced by machines that supply an ersatz instrumental accompaniment now considered essential for popular song.

Such is *musica saeculae*, the music of the world: amplified loudly, constantly harmonized, with a clear, constant meter and a rich instrumental palette. Now let us imagine a music with all those things

---

[16] "Secular" from the Latin *saecula*, "the age."

removed. When the instruments and amplification are taken away, there are left pure human voices. Without harmony, they all sing the same single note at the same time. Without meter and regular beating, their music flows along like a quiet stream. Is such a music possible? Yes—it is called plainchant.

If plainchant is "given pride of place in liturgical services" in the Second Vatican Council's *Sacrosanctum Concilium*, if the other world religions say the same thing by their actions, surely it is because plainchant has this semantic property of distinction (SC 116). It is unlike anything we hear in our normal world. Therefore, it is capable of having at the heart of its semantic range the heavenly world. This is why plainchant is the most iconic sacred music on earth, why monastics in traditions from the Buddhist to the Byzantine labor to preserve its integrity.

And yet, like the other elements of the liturgy, plainchant comes from the world. If it were utterly alien, no one could sing it. In fact, it shares one crucial property with secular music: tonality, the organization of its various notes around a governing central pitch. Tonality makes plainchant perceptible to the human mind and able to be heard, learned, processed, and sung. That is why it hardly affects the semantic distinction of plainchant. Tonality is common, not only to secular Western music but also to all indigenous musics the world over, because it is a minimum prerequisite for musical perception and comprehension.[17] It is as basic to music as syntax is to speech, and neither one affects semantic distinction very much.

Transcendence in liturgical music requires a mark of distinction, characteristics that set it apart from the secular world, allowing it to signify the world beyond. It is a necessary condition, but not sufficient. The meaning of "cross" owes something to the fact that its semantic range is different from "line," but positive connotations can only come from contextual associations, how we hear and speak the word "cross." If "cross" may have for Catholics awesome connotations, that is because they hear and experience it in awesome contexts, such as the liturgy for Good Friday when even bishops fall to the ground before it, and all venerate it in solemn procession. In short, the semantics of an abstract expression are intrinsically traditional, arising

---

[17] The so-called atonal musics of twentieth-century modernism I do not consider indigenous. Rather, they are invented, artificial languages. See Swain, *Musical Languages*, chap. 6.

from habitual associations and usages of the community that understands it.

So it must be with liturgical music. The notes of a pipe organ in the soundtrack of a film or television show instantly remind Westerners of great cathedrals, solemn liturgies, weddings, and other things that happen in church because *that is where and how they have always heard this instrument*. Since perhaps the tenth century, the pipe organ had been the only instrument allowed in Christian churches and even in 1963 was the only instrument named in *Sacrosanctum Concilium*, the instrument that "can most effectively elevate people's spirits to God and things above" (SC 120). Why was it the only one admitted to church one thousand years ago? No one knows. To be sure, there is nothing intrinsically divine about the pipe organ or its sound, just as there is nothing intrinsically redemptive about the sequence of sounds in "cross." But now they are robust cultural associations, born of tradition and practice, and own therefore a sacred semantic.

Evolution of Sacred Semantics

These two properties of sacred semantics—distinction from unambiguously secular music and traditional association with sacred contexts—automatically arise in those religious traditions that fuse their music to their holy texts, which defend them as best they can from the corruption of change.[18] That is why plainchant is the prime exemplar of music possessing an irreproachable sacred semantic, for its essential musical characteristics, modes of presentation, and above all its liturgical associations have remained nearly untouched over the centuries. But Roman Catholicism from its ancient days never bound Scripture to a particular musical setting, never equated the truth of the Word

---

[18] One could persuasively argue that "semantic distinction" and "semantic association" are merely two different epistemic aspects of the same thing. Distinction refers to the semantic boundaries of a lexical item (word or passage of music, in this discussion) that are defined in part by the boundaries of all the other items in the language having similar "neighboring" meanings. "Warm" means, in part, "not hot" and "not cold." Association refers to the set of experiences that speakers or listeners must go through in order to acquire the knowledge of a semantic range. I find, for the moment, that while one could legitimately describe a "sacred semantic" as the product of "distinct associations," it is useful to have the two aspects to connote respectively the state of the language (distinction) and the process of learning it (association).

with the manner of singing it. Thus, the polyphonic elaboration of plainchant and other innovations have naturally arisen within the church's walls.[19] From without the walls, at many points in its history, liturgical music has known the intrusions of music from the world. The pipe organ may indeed have been one such intrusion. These are the sources of Catholicism's incomparable treasure of sacred music. But how did such richness accrue without compromising the tradition's distinction from the secular world while acquiring essential liturgical associations? How did the pipe organ recast itself from a Roman instrument signifying imperial power into the only officially recognized sacred instrument of the church?

Let us consider a number of historical case studies.

Polyphony constitutes a radical departure from plainchant. It vitiates the melodic simplicity of chant by adding simultaneous melodies to it, producing a rich harmonic texture of four, six, twelve, and more notes sung at a time. On plainchant's free flow, it imposes a steady, if gentle, meter in order to coordinate these melodies. And in some performance traditions, polyphony may employ instruments, although to be sure, plainchant may also be accompanied by the organ in some places. Despite these changes, classical polyphony owns a sacred semantic only slightly less iconic than plainchant.

It began with two great semantic advantages. Its first embodiment arose as a shadow melody to plainchant in the context of festival liturgies, and therefore from its beginning the liturgical associations were strong, as was its distinctiveness. The courts had nothing like it. But as centuries passed, its musical potential began to be applied to secular songs, and at the same time, folk tunes began to be heard as the slow foundation melodies, or cantus firmi, of polyphonic Masses. Now polyphony became controversial. Pope John XXII wrote in 1324 that certain polyphonic techniques "have brought into disrepute the basic melodies of the Antiphonal and Gradual" and yet allowed that polyphony did belong to the liturgy, "principally on solemn feasts at Mass and at Divine Office . . . but always on condition that the melodies themselves remain intact in the pure integrity of their form."[20] There was some agitation at the Council of Trent to get rid of it alto-

---

[19] See chap. 8.

[20] John XXII, *Extravagantes comunes*, bk. 3, chap. 1, quoted in Robert F. Hayburn, *Papal Legislation on Sacred Music, 95 A.D to 1977 A.D.* (Collegeville, MN: Liturgical Press, 1979), 20–21. For more details about this episode, see Edward Schaefer,

gether because some polyphonic Masses had used secular "lascivious" madrigal music within them. In other words, both the pope and the council fathers worried that polyphony had lost its semantic distinction, rendering it inappropriate for liturgy. What saved it, ultimately, was the invention of opera, which at a stroke defined a secular style so radically different in design and purpose from its precedents that anything with polyphonic character was left in the dust of the churches. This, ironically, restored the semantic distinction that had been blurred in the fifteenth and sixteenth centuries. Classical polyphony became a kind of ecclesiastical language analogous to Latin, safe from change and corruption.

Opera presents quite a different case study. Soon after its invention at the end of the sixteenth century, church composers began to use the new language to set psalms and eventually the Ordinary of the Mass.[21] The use of the pipe organ and an occasional chorus maintained a most tenuous musical link with the extant tradition; almost the entire weight of any sacred semantic of this operatic music depended upon the sacred texts. Again controversy erupted: this was theater music invading the church. It had no distinction as sacred music, and its sound did nothing to remind a worshiper of the divine. And in fact the only thing that distinguishes an aria from a Mass by Vivaldi or Mozart from an aria in one of their operas is the text. The controversy persisted through the nineteenth century at least, and in part prompted the famous *motu proprio* of Pope St. Pius X of 1903, which prescribed precisely what liturgical music seemed to have lost: the restoration of its distinctive sound and a renewal of its liturgical association.

Polyphony triumphed because it began with strong associations to the liturgy, never lost them, and after a period of compromise finally managed to stave off the musical temptations of the outside world. Operatic music began with no liturgical associations or symbologies working in its favor. (It did not need or particularly want them.) Its sound connoted boisterous crowds, carnivals, mythologies, assassination plots, seductions, heroisms, and other attractions of the theater. Composers tried to build a liturgical semantic into it on the strength of simply singing the sacred words. After three centuries, the effort had produced some remarkable concert works but succeeded in liturgy

---

Catholic Music through the Ages: Balancing the Needs of a Woshipping Church (Chicago: Hillenbrand, 2008), 64–71.

[21] See chap. 9.

only to the extent of its anachronistic choruses. Because of its constant use in the secular concert and theater world, there was no chance for the style to acquire a semantic range that did not include undesirable elements of every kind. Even the holiest texts with all their liturgical associations could not overpower the secular sound constantly reinforced by every musical experience outside the church.[22]

But how to explain then the resounding success of the great Lutheran hymns, which own a sacred semantic in the Western world hardly less archetypical than plainchant, and yet whose sources can be surprisingly secular?[23] The tune of "O Sacred Head Surrounded," one of the most famous, may be traced as far back as the fifteenth century as *Das macht ein Magdelein zart* (So does a charming maid).[24] In 1601 the same tune appeared in a collection of Hans Leo Hassler as *Mein G'müth ist mir verwirret* (My mind is confused) and was first set to spiritual words as the hymn *Herzlich tut mich verlangen* (Heartily do I desire) only five years later and by the familiar text *O Haupt voll Blut und Wunden* by 1647.[25] By the time J. S. Bach assumed the post of directing all church music in the city of Leipzig in 1723, it was well ensconced in Lutheran repertory. Why did not the tune's secular associations damn it from the outset as "inappropriate," as would shortly happen to operatic music, or as would surely happen if anyone today tried to use "Dixie" to set the "Glory to God"?

First of all, the semantics of European art music had changed a great deal from the fifteenth to the late sixteenth century, when opera arrived. Indeed, the change might be termed revolutionary. At the earlier time, there was far less distinction in musical idiom between music in the church and music in the court than at the later time.[26]

---

[22] To be precise, "every musical experience" for those who could afford such experiences. It is possible, even likely, that working-class people who on occasion heard operatic music in church thought it glorious. For them, it could only be associated with liturgy and thus would gain a robust sacred semantic.

[23] The earliest chorale tunes, if not composed by Martin Luther himself and his musical associates, were adaptations of Latin plainchants, German sacred folk songs such as pilgrim songs, and secular folk tunes made into *contrafacta*. See chap. 10.

[24] George William Rutler, *Brightest and Best: Stories of Hymns* (San Francisco: Ignatius Press, 1998), 50.

[25] Robert Marshall and Robin A. Leaver, "Chorale," in *The New Grove Dictionary of Music and Musicians*, sec. 11, "The Baroque Era, c1600–75," ed. Stanley Sadie (New York: Macmillan, 2001).

[26] "En composant Psaumes et Cantiques dans le style des chansons à la mode, les musiciens avaient accès à tous les milieux, car l'écart était alors très faible entre

Yes, forms and perhaps performance traditions were different, but the note-to-note musical syntax remained similar, since, after all, the entire polyphonic tradition of combining simultaneous melodies had sprung from the church. Only a small portion of "secular" music heard was harmonized at all. But the sixteenth century had developed the familiar syntax of functional harmony, which made it possible for the secular madrigalists and art song composers to build structures independent of the structural imitation, *cantus firmus*, and other compositional practices associated with the church. Opera rent the growing split completely asunder by forming a new musical style dedicated to a dramatic aesthetics that seemed antithetical to liturgy. So while the tune "O Sacred Head Surrounded" may have a secular origin, its sound was nevertheless hardly distinct from a good church hymn.

Second, folk tunes are notoriously promiscuous in their textual relations. Substitutions of one set of words for another in a given tune were commonplace. Thus it is usually impossible to speak of specific semantic associations for a folk tune. Having made many marriages to various texts, a tune's semantic range remains too broad to sustain much specific association.

This kind of continuous exchange occurred, third, because the humanistic aesthetic, which prescribes that the music of a vocal composition (the overwhelming majority of compositions before the seventeenth century) must express its specific text, had not yet arisen. This is a modern ideal, charming in its way and indispensable for the understanding of art music composed after 1600, but it is quite alien to plainchant and sacred polyphony and to the efforts of Luther and his musical assistant Johann Walther when they compiled their first collections of "sacred songs" in the 1520s.

Fourth, the musical clothing of harmony and arrangement can count much more heavily in semantic import than the tune itself, particularly if, as was common in the early Lutheran chorale harmonizations,

---

musique savante et musique populaire. Ces conditions, assez exceptionenelles dans l'histoire de la musique religieuse, ont grandement favorisé l'éclusion et le succès des Psaumes et des chants spirituels en français." (In composing psalms and canticles in the style of popular songs, musicians had access to all the [musical] devices, for the separation then between art music and popular music was very small. These conditions, quite exceptional in the history of sacred music, greatly favored the inclusion and the success of psalms and spiritual chants in French.) Denise Launay, *La Musique Religieuse en France du Concile de Trente à 1804* (Paris: Société Française de Musicologie, 1993), 57.

the tune was buried in the tenor voice.[27] The transformation of a single melody by harmonic arrangement is tantamount to creating a new musical work, much as a jazz arrangement completely transforms a Tin Pan Alley ballad.

In short, bringing the German folk tune *Das macht ein Magdelein zart* into Lutheran hymnody risked only the specific associations of a single tune, which had been already weakened into insignificance when the tune set one folk text after another. Furthermore, the tune did not differ in its melodic syntax from Latin hymns. Bringing opera into the liturgy, on the other hand, meant the importation of a distinct musical style that had strong semantic associations built into it. Opera arias could not be dressed up to cover their theatrical origins. They came all of a piece, and to tamper with their construction would denature them, undermining the qualities for which they were sought in the first place.

What have these history lessons to say to us who struggle with the question of what sounds sacred? They confirm distinction and contextual association as musical aspects that primarily determine the semantic range of a style, musical language, genre of composition, and so forth. When a type of music, originally and indubitably sacred, begins to mix in secular elements, it may acquire unwanted associations symbolized by those elements that blur the music's characteristic sacred sound, in whatever form that might be. When a type of music, originally and unmistakably secular, attempts to accommodate itself to the liturgy, it fails to acquire the necessary sacred semantic as long as it is perpetuated in secular activities, regardless of the holiness of the texts it sings, simply because it can never acquire any character to distinguish it from the profane.

When the social context, the context of actually using the music, changes, however, such a transformation from the secular to the sacred may successfully occur. The love song *Das macht ein Magdelein zart* could only become the passion hymn "O Sacred Head Surrounded" because the culture that composed it became something utterly other than what it was, with symbols of worldliness far different than the song had originally known. The outside world had moved on, while the song stayed in the same place, quite close to the musical idiom of

---

[27] The more familiar arrangement with the tune in the soprano voice, known as the *cantional*, did not appear until 1586 in Lucas Osiander's *Fünftzig geistliche Lieder und Psalmen*.

the church, as it happened, and acquired a new association and eventually the requisite distinction by default.[28]

This is exactly what may happen in the semantic evolution of words. "Vulgar" once meant, in English, "popular." Read the *Apologia Pro Vita Sua* of John Henry Newman, or most any other nineteenth-century prose, and one will find "intercourse" strewn throughout the work. It takes the modern reader aback a bit at first, but the old authors intended no prurience. The word meant "interaction," usually social, as in conversational exchange. In the last half century, however, the use of "intercourse" has been confined almost entirely to sexual matters. The newly restricted context relentlessly applied has greatly tightened the semantic range of the word so that now it is impossible to use the word in conversation unless one intends to talk about sex.

Successful *contrafacta*—old tunes outfitted with new, usually sacred texts—such as "O Sacred Head Surrounded" all have similar histories. So many favorite hymns coming from the Welsh, English, or German folk repertory lost their broader semantic ranges as their popular cultures changed, and yet because they were composed in simple, sturdy rhythms not dissimilar in character from those of Lutheran hymnody, a skilled harmonization was all that a convincing sacred semantic required. And the further the mass market popular music grew from such folk simplicity, the greater was the semantic distinction which those newborn hymns acquired. An extreme case is, once again, "O Sacred Head." Today we know it as the "Passion Chorale" because we never sing it but late in Lent, on Passion Sunday or on Good Friday, always with a Passiontide lyric that has become fairly fixed, and certainly no less because of its five different arrangements in J. S. Bach's *St. Matthew Passion*. But in Bach's day, its semantic range was still fairly broad, albeit sacred. He used the tune to open and close the magnificent "Christmas Oratorio," and it requires a little getting used to for moderns, even for seasoned Bach lovers, to hear the "Passion Chorale" dressed up with trumpets and timpani and sparkling string passages to conclude the joyous message of that work.

---

[28] Anthony Ruff is correct when he points out that many a "new musical development found its way into worship" through the centuries, but his conclusion that therefore there is no way to distinguish between sacred and secular simply does not follow. It is a historical fact that meanings of historical "developments" in music change through time, according to the principles of distinction and association described here, which he does not take into account. See *Sacred Music and Liturgical Reform: Treasures and Transformations* (Chicago: Hillenbrand, 2007), 26–27.

The Gray Areas

In another area, our liturgical reception of Bach has grown broader, not narrower: his instrumental music. In his own day, of course, organ music was well accepted as appropriate for liturgical contexts; that is why he composed most of it. Now, however, Bach's instrumental music of every kind—suite movements, unaccompanied pieces for violin, concerto movements, harpsichord works, music that Bach himself would never have dreamed of using in church—is regularly heard in many Christian churches as preludes, postludes, or music to accompany some ritual or mediation. Is this appropriate or not?

From a historical perspective, the case is similar to that of "O Sacred Head Surrounded." Although conceived in utter secularity, Bach's instrumental music experienced a shift of cultural context of radical proportions. First almost all of it was forgotten after his death for nearly a century, thus removing it from cultural circulation and any semantic reinforcement, secular or otherwise. By the time of its revival in the mid-nineteenth century, the Bach style was known by the preludes and fugues of the *Well-Tempered Clavier*, a few great church works such as the *St. Matthew Passion*, but above all as a thing sui generis, an inimitably learned contrapuntal art that traced its origins to the classical polyphonists such as Palestrina. If Bach had titled some instrumental movement as a gigue, a polonaise, or some other dance, it mattered little. The Bach "sacred" sound was there. This explains the possibility of using his church cantatas liturgically. They are undeniably operatic in their recitatives and arias, but their contrapuntal chorus movements, often with a great Lutheran hymn tune as their backbone, and the essential Bachian counterpoint excuses the cantatas because Bach did not write opera and, as a musical mind set apart, he does not now sound like opera.

From another perspective, however, there are those whose musical minds would protest the sound of a Bach gigue (or any gigue) in liturgy. These are not the common parishioner. These are the classical music lovers, especially the Bach lovers who have heard his music many times in those peculiarly modern secular contexts called concerts. Their associations of gigues are quite specific, and they can hear the distinctive musical qualities that say "gigue" and "dancing" and not "sacredness."

This history lesson teaches that the semantic context of music is no simple matter. We have here in the case of Bach's instrumental music at least two contexts that intersect and interact. One is the big context of the music's culture, history, and broad associations. The other is the little, immediate context of the situation, including the states of the participants and the personal histories that each brings to the liturgy. Plainchant is the archetypical sacred music not only because of its intrinsic musical character and its distinction from modern secular music of all types, but also because modern cultural experience of plainchant, however intermittent and limited, is monolithic. The experiences of other kinds of liturgical music will not always be so.

Conclusions

The first conclusion is actually a premise of the theory, introduced in retrospect as a means of review. There is nothing intrinsically sacred about any music or any kind of music, if by "intrinsically" one imagines a music divorced from all possible contexts, an empty signifier, as one could imagine a brand new combination of English morphemes combined in one's head to make a new word. Such a word would forever be a nonsense word, and such a music would also mean nothing beyond itself. In this sense, not even plainchant is intrinsically sacred, or ontologically sacred, to use Edward Foley's term.[29] If it were, there would be no desire and no need for any other kind of liturgical music anywhere in the world. But on the contrary, *Sacrosanctum Concilium*, while according plainchant a merited priority, implicitly recognizes the possibility of other worthy kinds of sacred music. The instruction for the implementation of its musical principles, *Musicam Sacram* (1967), makes this explicit:

> No kind of sacred music is prohibited from liturgical actions by the Church as long as it corresponds to the spirit of the liturgical celebration itself and the nature of its individual parts, and does not hinder the active participation of the people. (*Musicam Sacram* 9)

This premise in no way leads to the relativistic belief that, if a sacred semantic is not intrinsic, then any kind of music is therefore suitable for the liturgy. The conclusion simply does not follow from the premise. Just because no music is intrinsically sacred does not entail that a sacred musical semantic, however acquired extrinsically, may

---

[29] Edward Foley, *Ritual Music: Studies in Liturgical Musicology* (Beltsville, MD: The Pastoral Press, 1995), 173–89.

not have necessary qualities that certain compositions, genres, and styles never attain, thus making them unsuitable.

The second conclusion, then, is that music can certainly acquire a sacred semantic of significant power, bounded by community agreement and contexts both general and specific. This semantic is embodied in purely musical phenomena, which explains why a sacred text, by itself, is insufficient to imbue a composition with a sacred semantic.[30] Such a sacred semantic renders a music potentially appropriate for liturgy because the liturgical action is centrally located in the music's semantic range.

How is this sacred semantic acquired, then? By the fact of an exclusive, and therefore distinct, historical association with liturgy—the third conclusion. That the qualities of association and distinction are hard facts of the world makes the theory pragmatic. Why is the pipe organ "held in high esteem" as "the traditional musical instrument, the sound of which can add a wonderful splendor to the church's ceremonies and can most effectively elevate people's spirits to God and things above" (SC 120)? Because it is a historical fact that the pipe organ has been heard in Christian churches, chiefly in liturgical contexts and hardly anywhere else, for ten centuries. That is its exclusive association.[31]

It is true that associations may evolve and cultural contexts may change over time. As long as the music is a means of proclaiming the Word and is not the Word itself, it is theoretically possible for any kind of music to acquire a sacred semantic. Can the piano or electric keyboard, recently introduced to many churches to enliven the plodding harmonies of the praise songs and other popular idioms descending from the American folk revival, ever sound as sacred as the organ?[32] The answer is yes, in theory. But this would entail the piano not only replacing the organ as the predominant liturgical instrument in the West, but the destruction over time of all the piano's associations, reinforced through television and cinema and everyday experience, with saloons, bars, cocktail lounges, bordellos, concert halls, practice

---

[30] It also supports the rejection of a theory of liturgical music founded on liturgical principles alone. See chap. 1.

[31] Even the organ concert, a relatively recent phenomenon, almost always occurs in churches. Theater organs and harmoniums are quite different instruments with distinct timbres.

[32] One example, Robert Dufford's "Be Not Afraid," has a piano arrangement and is analyzed in chap. 3.

rooms, student recitals, children practicing at home, and all its other present roles in the secular world. As long as it retains those roles, it can never acquire a robust sacred semantic and never sound solemn in church, just as operatic Masses never did. In other words, while Edward Foley and like-minded theologians are right when they point out that no music is intrinsically (ontologically) sacred, any more than the utterance "mountain" must absolutely refer to a majestic geological formation that many like to climb, they miss the pragmatic reality that for centuries of speaking English, "mountain" has referred to—and will continue to refer to—that thing we like to climb, and there is nothing to be done about it. In the same way, for all practical purposes, the piano will remain a secular instrument for the foreseeable future, and the sound of the pipe organ may as well be ontologically sacred.

But a number of Welsh folk tunes, popular continental processional songs, and a significant body of baroque instrumental music, among other musics, have survived the test of time, with semantic ranges greatly altered, although not without showing compromising signs of their origins in most cases. And so, finally, we have not a semantic dichotomy, absolutely sacred or absolutely secular, but rather a continuum, a spectrum of "sacredness" that has plainchant at one end and military marches and rock music at the other, with the many other musical styles and genres of the Western world aligned at points between. The conception entails a choice of musics for liturgy, indeed, but hardly an arbitrary, whimsical, or capricious choice; rather, it is an intelligent choice, one conscious of the semantic range of each music and how it may interact with the specific context of the moment.

There is one last, inescapable conclusion about the semantics of sacred music: it cannot be instantly implanted in a music or invented on the spot. This is, of course, precisely what a good many well-intentioned liturgists have tried to do in these decades following the Second Vatican Council: to "design" a liturgical music that would instantly symbolize renewal. But a designer symbol, truly ex nihilo, is a contradiction in terms.[33] A concatenation of new sounds can never make itself understood to the community at large without a defining context, no more than a newly invented word could. Even the wholesale appropriation of a musical language for such a purpose is doomed

---

[33] Such new "symbols" as we have from advertisers, of course, are not really new at all, merely recombinations of older ones whose semantics are well known to the market at which the product is aimed.

to failure because it could bring with it no semantic except that which it had already acquired from contextual use in the culture, one that was certainly not liturgical. Robust musical semantics that can withstand the myriad eddies and buffets of the culture changing around them are inherently traditional, built on long practices and repeated uses, like ritual itself. This may seem an enormous handicap to those creative spirits hoping to compose the next great Mass, to missionaries confronting unfamiliar cultural contexts, and to other liturgical interests. But it turns out that tradition and history are not the limitations they seem. In fact, they have the answers.

Chapter 13

Understanding Musical Symbols: The Infallible Judge

> Truthful lips endure forever,
> the lying tongue, for only a moment.
> Proverbs 12:19

There are agnostics in the world who appreciate Roman Catholic liturgy a great deal more than many believers for one reason: its beauty. Some regard a solemn Mass as a consummation of the best of Western art, architecture, music, poetry, and drama, an aesthetic experience that Roger Scruton calls "insatiable" in the sense that one is drawn to it again and again, as one returns to any great work of art.[1] It is a simple fact that the efforts of artists to beautify the celebration of the liturgy over the centuries have yielded a great portion of the artistic patrimony of the Western tradition. Throughout history, aesthetic values have been bound to liturgical values very tightly.[2]

Music, being the most liturgical of all the arts, has always borne the most intense scrutiny and excited the most vociferous controversy about such values, as is still very much true today. The tradition has always held that liturgical music, first of all, must be held to the highest aesthetic standards because anything less will fail to uplift the spirits of worshipers. Pope Pius X, who wrote the most comprehensive and articulate summary of the principles of Roman Catholic liturgical music ever to come out of the Vatican in his *motu proprio* of 1903, states without hesitation that music "must be true art, for otherwise it will be impossible for it to exercise on the minds of those who listen to

---

[1] Roger Scruton, *The Aesthetics of Music* (Oxford: Clarendon Press, 1997), 369.
[2] Anthony Ruff views beauty in music as a kind of cultural function of liturgy: "The unfolding of cultural and artistic achievement is the natural result of healthy interaction between liturgy and human culture." *Sacred Music and Liturgical Reform: Treasures and Transformations* (Chicago: Hillenbrand, 2007), 16.

it that efficacy which the Church aims at obtaining in admitting into her liturgy the art of musical sounds."[3]

"True art" became the slogan for this principle. Pope Pius XII used it in both of his encyclicals concerning music, *Mediator Dei* of 1947[4] and *Musicae Sacrae* of 1955.[5] Then it appears in the first article on liturgical music in *Sacrosanctum Concilium* itself:

> Therefore sacred music is to be considered the more holy, the more closely connected it is with the liturgical action, whether making prayer more pleasing, promoting unity of minds, or conferring greater solemnity upon the sacred rites. The church, indeed, approves of all forms of true art [*verae artis*] which have the requisite qualities, and admits them into divine worship. (SC 112)

But what constitutes true art, and how is a composition to be identified as such? Because the Catholic tradition allowed developments in its liturgical music almost from the beginning, it has always faced this question whenever evaluating the steady stream of new liturgical music flowing throughout its history. Was the first polyphony true art? Were the edited plainchants of the Renaissance humanists true art? The operatic Masses of Mozart? The decades following the Second Vatican Council saw the near total eclipse of plainchant and most other traditional Catholic musics, as well as a flood of thousands of new compositions from every quarter. Are these true art? The controversy remains as fierce as ever.

No composer wants to admit that his creations are not true art. In earlier times, however, there were always minimum technical requirements that anyone aspiring to true art had to meet, as there are certain minimum physical skills that athletes must have if they wish to even consider entering the world of professional sports, before the evaluation of what they can do in a specific sport even begins. Burning desire to create new music, love of liturgy, and even prodigious natural

---

[3] Pius X, *Tra le Sollecitudini*, 2.

[4] "We cannot help deploring and condemning those works of art, recently introduced by some, which seem to be a distortion and perversion of true art and which at times openly shock Christian taste, modesty and devotion, and shamefully offend the true religious sense." *Mediator Dei*, 195.

[5] "If these prescriptions are really observed in their entirety, the requirements of the other property of sacred music—that property by virtue of which it should be an example of true art—will be duly satisfied." *Musicae Sacrae*, 45.

talent were all very well, but they could never replace the years of technical training that awaited every young composer. The popular image of the young prodigy striding upon the world's stage as an accomplished genius of musical composition finds precious few examples in history. Palestrina, Bach, Handel, Beethoven, and virtually all the great names we recognize took years of lessons when they were young.

Postmodern culture in the Western world has made such minimal standards obsolete. Edward Foley's *Ritual Music: Studies in Liturgical Musicology* (1995) is just one prominent example of a new and pervasive relativism that undermines the relevance of technical mastery. The first salvo is fired in the name of democratization, a softening up that is hard to resist: "It is important to recognize that untrained musicians—ordinary people—very definitely have something to say about the quality of our worship music."[6] Exactly what ordinary people might be capable of saying beyond "I don't know much about art, but know what I like" is left unsaid, but that matters little to populist sympathies. This attack is broadened in scope with the charge of cultural elitism: "The assertion that musical judgments can only be made by competent musicians becomes particularly unacceptable when we move outside Western culture. In many traditional societies . . . it is not the degreed or specially trained musicians who ultimately judge the quality of the music. It is the people."[7] If this picture of traditional societies proposes that all music comes from all the society's members equally, without recognition of extraordinary musical talent, then it is as naïve as it is romantic. If it does allow for objective talent, then it ignores the fact that, with degrees or not, a society's gifted musicians are the ones who decide which music is to reach the wider world through performance, a far more powerful act of musical criticism than anything "the people" are likely to say thereafter.[8] But Foley's main thrust here is antiprofessionalism, and it appeals to a democratic culture, regardless of its accuracy or practical wisdom.

---

[6] Edward Foley, *Ritual Music: Studies in Liturgical Musicology* (Beltsville, MD: The Pastoral Press, 1995), 129.

[7] Ibid., 130.

[8] For more detailed examples of this cultural dynamic, see Joseph P. Swain, "Musical Communities and Music Perception," *Music Perception* 11, no. 3 (Spring 1994): 307–20.

Such relativism has made the controversy about what constitutes "true art" more complex that it used to be. Before postmodernism, one asked at first two questions of a new composition: "Is it great music?" and "Is it appropriate for the sacred liturgy?" Now these cannot even be entertained as yet. Ahead of them lie "Is beauty a liturgical value?" and "Is beauty objective?" and "Isn't the judgment of liturgical music entirely individual?" Only if we survive these can we ask, "Is it true art?"

Liturgy and Beauty

Must the liturgy be beautiful? The most radical of the Protestant reformers in the sixteenth century believed that the great music, architecture, and decorative arts of the Catholic tradition were diabolical instruments that distracted worshipers from what should be the center of their attention. And so ornate churches in Geneva were stripped down, great pipe organs ripped out, and music simplified down to nearly monotonic, unharmonized melodies for psalms—for a while. Within a century, the harmonies were restored along with the organs, and by the nineteenth century, great neo-Gothic structures of Methodist and Presbyterian denomination sprouted all over the United States. Beauty, it seems, is hard to resist.

Pope Benedict XVI opposes puritanism head-on by understanding beauty as proceeding from the very nature of liturgy as an expression of creed, of the timeless principle of *lex orandi, lex credendi*:[9] "This relationship between creed and worship is evidenced in a particular way by the rich theological and liturgical category of beauty. Like the rest of Christian Revelation, the liturgy is inherently linked to beauty: it is *veritatis splendor*."[10] The argument is simple. Everything that happens during Mass is part of the sacrificial offering that is the liturgy and its

---

[9] "The phrase ascribed to Prosper of Aquitaine *ut legem credendi lex statuat supplicandi* ('the law of prayer grounds the law of belief') has become something of a theme statement for many contemporary authors concerned with liturgical theology, often preferring this original formulation to the shortened *lex orandi, lex credendi* ('the law of prayer is the law of belief')." See extensive historical background to this principle in Kevin W. Irwin, *Context and Text: Method in Liturgical Theology* (Collegeville, MN: Liturgical Press, 1994), especially p. 3 and notes, and its specific application to Catholic liturgical music in Edward Schaefer, *Catholic Music through the Ages* (Chicago: Hillenbrand, 2008), 24–29.

[10] Benedict XVI, *Sacramentum Caritatis*, art. 35.

mystery, and therefore everything—language, act, and their musical setting—must be as good as we can make them, imperfect though they always will be. "The beauty of the liturgy is part of this mystery; it is a sublime expression of God's glory and, in a certain sense, a glimpse of heaven on earth. . . . Beauty, then, is not mere decoration, but rather an essential element of the liturgical action, since it is an attribute of God Himself and His revelation."[11]

Additionally, beauty is right and just because the liturgy is an offering of ourselves. If in the Mass we offer ourselves without reserve as an essential element of the sacrifice, then the artifacts of the liturgy must likewise hold no reserve. But if these things we have made—music, building, decorative art, mode of speech, decorum, behavior—hold nothing in reserve, they must perforce be the best that we have and can do, and therefore must aspire to beauty even if we do not always achieve it.

Lastly, and most pragmatically, liturgy should be an "insatiable" experience, infinitely renewable. Worshipers should want to come repeatedly and to seek repeatedly. Like any masterwork of art, it must satisfy for a time and then enrich with reacquaintance.

Absolute Beauty

The most common and pernicious postmodern argument against the foregoing is that notions of musical goodness and beauty and true art are merely conventions of culture. They have no objective measure and cannot even be identified objectively. Therefore, in pragmatic terms if not absolute terms, such notions have no relevance to the evaluation of a liturgical composition. A popular song pithily expresses this subjectivism: "Everything is beautiful in its own way." Every artifact establishes its own terms of beauty, its own standards, and then, naturally enough, fulfills them. Claiming that everything is beautiful has the same effect as claiming that everything is art: the statement defines those categories out of existence, since there is no longer any mark of distinction which sets the limits of the term.[12] If art and beauty own marks of distinction, they cannot be everything. Practically speaking, then, postmodern beauty does not exist.

---

[11] Ibid., art. 35.
[12] The second definition of "define" in the *New Shorter Oxford English Dictionary* (1993 edition) reads, "determine or indicate the boundary or extent of."

The quotidian experiences of every musical culture in the world contradict this view. Everywhere there are young people who spend a lot of money to study music with renowned teachers, who sacrifice time, effort, and spirit to learn instruments and singing, who practice hundreds and thousands of hours before presenting themselves as musicians. Their goals—exquisite tone, accurate intonation, proper expression, etc.—are held in common by members of that culture. That is why every society has expressions for "musical talent" and recognizes its most gifted members. If goodness in music were so subjective, what causes such unanimity? What is "renowned" in a teacher? And why bother studying, training, and perfecting when perfection has no meaning beyond the self? One person's intonation should be as good as another's, but the relativist idea that precision of pitch doesn't really matter for music would be ridiculed every place on earth. Agreement about repertory is equally impressive. Of all the musical works produced in a culture, most are discarded with hardly a second hearing, some survive for a short time, and a very, very few are preserved from one generation to the next. If there were no common notions of goodness in music, there could be no such Darwinian pattern of survival, since the randomness of individual preferences could never reach such a consensus by chance. And this is why postmodernism, fortunately, has almost no impact beyond the theorist; no practicing musician gives this extreme relativism a second thought.[13]

But the views and experiences of those in the actual business of making music scarcely bother postmodern thinkers. If every musical behavior within a culture contradicts them, it is because the entire culture has been trained by convention to value certain musical attributes over others. Common notions of true art are made common by a great peer pressure, an irresistible force of consensus. Entire musical communities have been conned into believing in value systems that have no basis in reality. The classics of any repertory canon are merely the selections of dominant cultural trends and strains, perpetuated by habit and vested interest of institutions. Absolute beauty has nothing to do with it.

---

[13] Ruff is forced to admit with the rest of us that "it is notoriously difficult to define artistic excellence and authentic artistic progress, particularly in the context of widely varying cultures," but fortunately that fact does not prevent him from averring that "such difficulties need not prevent one from embracing these ideals." *Sacred Music and Liturgical Reform*, 17.

The argument is not logically controvertible and not falsifiable. One can always insist that however the culture behaves, such behavior is convention, not a response to anything absolute outside or beyond. Since convention is nothing more than cultural consensus, the argument reduces to a tautology.

But if not controvertible, the cultural construct argument is made utterly improbable once history is brought into the discussion. For cultures change and indeed are in continual evolution. This much is a truism. So then cultural trends and vested interests also change. Fashions come and go. Pop songs hit the charts and then disappear. The Boston Symphony Orchestra, surely a vested interest in music, was dominated by Germans after its founding in 1880, by the French in the 1920s, and by Americans after World War II, but these changes of local culture did not prevent the orchestra, as measured by the very loud speech of its programming, from thinking throughout this time that Mozart, an Austrian, was a pretty good composer, worthy of presentation again and again, year in and year out. The two centuries in the Western world since Mozart have witnessed paradigmatic alterations of worldviews on every dimension, and yet, through all this upheaval, Mozart's music has been treasured as a true art by every culture, every nation throughout the whole world that has come to know it.

If postmodern critics respond that this continuity is simply a peculiar tradition of reverence, a kind of cultural habit, hard to kick, which proves nothing about the quality of Mozart's music, what shall they say to historical cases of revival, such as that of J. S. Bach or Palestrina? Bach's music was but marginally known in his lifetime and then mostly forgotten for about a century after his death.[14] During this time, there could not have been any "constructs," peculiar traditions, or cultural habits of keeping his music alive. Then Felix Mendelssohn's heroic resurrection of the *St. Matthew Passion* in 1829 proved something of a sensation. By 1850 a new Bach Society planned the publication of all his works, most of which had never been heard by anyone alive. Remember that Bach in his own time was merely one of hundreds

---

[14] I refer to European culture at large. Certain of the keyboard works, such as the *Well-Tempered Clavier*, were maintained by pedagogues, and a very few isolated connoisseurs tried to keep alive a small number of vocal works, but by and large Bach's music was ignored by the newly forming musical concert culture. Certainly there was nothing like the Bach reputation that we know today.

of hardworking eighteenth-century opera or church composers, and a good number of these caught the interest of the early nineteenth-century in the incipient revival of early music. Yet of all these, Bach's music was the only one of its time to achieve a kind of apotheosis, invading every aspect of musical life, forming the staple of all conservatory training and the instruction for most instruments wherever in the world Western music was practiced. How to explain this remarkable consensus? Opposite to Bach's conquest of a culture that had no prior interest in him is a case of the complete collapse of a music that had every political and cultural support: Soviet music. Rarely has any music enjoyed for so many decades the explicit promotion of all the cultural powers that be with such pitifully little to show for it now. John Henry Newman takes the same position to explain how a consistent Christian doctrine could survive so many errors and heresies that "would but have broken up the Church the sooner, resolving it into the individuals of which it was composed, unless the Truth, to which they were to bear witness, had been something definite, and formal, and independent of themselves."[15]

Insisting that all such phenomena result from coincidence and cultural prejudice, not absolute universal qualities of the music, is logically defensible, much the same as insisting on the purely coincidental recovery of diabetics after the administration of insulin is also logically defensible. But the empirical probabilities of both stances are close to zero, and we can safely leave postmodern relativism to the credulous theorists in their academies. True art does exist.

Identifying True Art

But if there is such a thing as "true art," how can we account for the diversity of musical styles, each with its own apparent standards of goodness, that is, its own theory of beauty? The relativists seem correct when they point out that we do not hold jazz to the same harmonic standard that Mozart observed, and yet we judge some of its compositions to be as excellent, albeit in different ways, as his. If we claim that the grammar of jazz is not the same as the grammar of Mozart and

---

[15] John Henry Newman, *An Essay on the Development of Christian Doctrine*, sixth ed. (Notre Dame, IN: University of Notre Dame Press, 1989), 348; first published in 1878.

therefore cannot be directly compared, can they not respond in kind that the same is true of Gregorian chant and the "Celtic Alleluia?"[16]

Let us pursue the grammar analogy further. Assume that a principal goal of human language is communication. Communication, one abstract purpose of language, is therefore one objective measure of success or goodness of someone's use of language or speech, or even of an entire language. How well does this person or this language communicate? Now it is obvious that different languages achieve this purpose by different means, and so we have a rich diversity of speech in the world. But it is also obvious that the degrees of accomplishing an effective communication can vary. No one can reasonably say that the communication skills through speech of a three-year-old are as good as those of an educated adult. Linguists agree that a pidgin, a first-generation mixing of two languages, is a clumsy and syntactically immature form of speech, whereas a creole, a second-generation hybrid, is as mature and effective as either of its parent languages. The Romans recognized that the Greek language was superior to Latin in its ability to express certain philosophical distinctions because Greek has definite and indefinite articles while Latin does not.[17] And native speakers of any language can inhibit understanding through grammatical and lexical error, as any teacher of writing well knows.

Even though languages differ in construction, sound set, lexical emphases, and many other respects, it does not follow that no generalized judgment about the quality of an utterance can be made, at least with respect to the general purpose of communication.[18] Rather, the diversity of languages arises from a sufficiently abstract purpose to which all languages aspire, perfect communication, and for which they have different solutions. Diversity does not exclude the existence of such an abstract principle; in fact, diversity is better explained by its existence, by virtue of its abstraction. Composers strive to make their music beautiful; that they do so in different ways does not exclude the possibility of an abstract and absolute principle of beauty, even if we cannot find the words or concepts to define it consciously and rationally, even if none of them succeeds perfectly.

---

[16] The metric properties of these are compared in chap. 3.

[17] Personal communication, Andrew Keller, former Associate Professor of Classics, Colgate University.

[18] Language may have other purposes, of course, such as artistic purposes, diversion, social behavior. This fact does not blunt the argument.

Why, then, does it seem unfair or even impossible to compare compositions of different styles? Why the discomfort if we claim that the "Celtic Alleluia" is not good enough for the sacred liturgy, while the plainchant *Alleluia pascha nostrum* most certainly is? Is Ted Williams a greater athlete than Jack Nicklaus? The hitter and the golfer approach the ideal of athleticism by different means, and therein is the difficulty. If we could agree on what "athleticism" means, then we could answer. Different musical styles likewise try to do different things. In other words, they try to approach the ideal of beauty by different paths, and indeed this is one of the distinctions of their style systems. If we could agree on the nature of musical beauty, we could evaluate. But such agreement seems remote, as the philosopher of language Ludwig Wittgenstein discovered with much more mundane concepts, because of its abstraction.[19] Still, even though we cannot articulate the ideals of beauty, this does not mean that the ideals do not exist. Considering the nature of musical style can give us some confidence that we can identify beautiful compositions, if not articulate their nature.

A musical style system is founded on the musical materials that the composer has at hand. These are musical languages. Every musician acquires an intuitive knowledge of the musical language (or, in recent times, several languages) of the parent culture. A musical language, technically speaking, is a set of discrete pitches and durations that combine according to rules of syntax to create the hierarchical organizations of tones that we call music, and these often are endowed with semantics appropriate for specific contexts or uses.[20] By analogy, a musical language might be imagined as a box of tools and materials that the musician uses to build things called compositions. Every musician in the same time and place gets the same box, as did Johann Sebastian Bach and George Frederic Handel, born within fifty kilometers and one month of one another in central Germany in winter 1685. It is quite possible, indeed common, to build compositions that sound quite different from one another, *within the limits of the language*, even though they come from the same box, and the inestimable and yet remarkably contrasting music of Bach and Handel makes a textbook case for this phenomenon. But if one musician builds a great palace lasting for generations and another musician a lean-to that falls flat with the next cultural wind, we can rightly say that the first is a supe-

---

[19] *Philosophical Investigations*, trans. G. E. Anscombe (Oxford: Basil Blackwell, 1953), 4.

[20] Joseph P. Swain, *Musical Languages* (New York: Norton, 1997), especially chap. 8.

rior composition. If we are very clever, we might be able to say why the first survived for so long or why the other blew into oblivion even though the same materials and tools were available to both builders. It is often a matter of musical engineering, which is why technical analysis can be revealing, but the governing concept is that one composition exploited superbly the musical language at hand and the other did not. And that is one measure of good and bad. We should never fear to hold a piece of liturgical music to the standards it adopts for itself—its musical language and the potentials of that language.

Pragmatically, in the real world of choosing music for a given purpose, whether it be a concert or a campfire songfest or a solemn Mass, we are content to evaluate, within the comparatively well-defined criteria of musical languages, their potentials and purposes. We know more or less intuitively what plainchant is capable of, and we measure a composition not against the most absolute beauty or notion of true art, but against a more local one that represents the perfection of plainchant. The same is true of popular songs, jazz, or any other expression of a musical language. In local terms, this produces value systems for times and places that are pragmatically indistinguishable from true absolute values, except that they require a contextualization. The context of the music constrains what is needed and provides a measure for the music's value. In music for the Roman Catholic Mass, that critical context is the liturgy.

The Liturgical Context

This is why *Sacrosanctum Concilium* states as an opening principle that "sacred music is to be considered the more holy, the more closely connected it is with the liturgical action, whether making prayer more pleasing, promoting unity of minds, or conferring greater solemnity upon the sacred rites" (SC 112). The principle is dual. Goodness in musical art per se, "true art," is an absolutely necessary condition for liturgical music: no combination of other liturgical aspects—text, community appeal, ease of learning, etc.—can save fatally defective music. But while a necessary condition, goodness or beauty is not sufficient. Simply stated, not all good music makes good liturgical music. Here considerations of text, communal participation, theological rightness, musical symbolism, solemnity, and transcendence all come into play. While we may hesitate to say whether and why *Alleluia pascha nostrum* is a greater work than "Celtic Alleluia" according to purely musical criteria because the two works are composed in different styles, we can and must be courageous when it comes to deciding whether they are appropriate for the particular context for which they are intended: the sacred liturgy.

In 1983 the American Bishops Committee on the Liturgy published "Music in Catholic Worship," a revision of an earlier statement, "Liturgical Music" (1972). The statement was never approved by the vote of the American Conference of Bishops. If *Sacrosanctum Concilium* is analogous to the United States Constitution in terms of authority, and the instruction *Musicam Sacram* (1967) is likened to approved congressional legislation, then "Music in Catholic Worship" might correspond to a congressional committee report. Nevertheless, because it remained the only guideline on liturgical music ever issued by American bishops, it has enjoyed considerable prestige and influence in the American Catholic Church during the postconciliar period.[21]

On the question of absolute goodness, the committee at first assents to the tradition: "Only artistically sound music will be effective in the long run. To admit the cheap, the trite, the musical cliché often found in popular songs for the purpose of 'instant liturgy' is to cheapen the liturgy, to expose it to ridicule, and to invite failure,"[22] a truth that has been fairly corroborated by much of what has happened in recent decades. But fast on the heels of this bold statement of principle is another that emasculates the first completely:

> We do a disservice to musical values, however, when we confuse the judgment of music with the judgment of musical style. Style and value are two distinct judgments. Good music of new styles is finding a happy home in the celebrations of today. To chant and polyphony we have effectively added the chorale hymn, restored responsorial singing to some extent, and employed many styles of contemporary composition. Music in folk idiom is finding acceptance in eucharistic celebrations. We must judge value within each style.[23]

This feeble and innocent attempt to evade the problem of comparing apples and oranges by dismissing it altogether nullifies the principle of absolute quality by giving the compositional hack and the sentimental

---

[21] In November 2007 the full conference of the American bishops did finally approve a revision of the document, retitled "Sing to the Lord." The changes, particularly those in the passages under discussion here, are minor.

[22] "Music in Catholic Worship (1972, 1982)," chap. 11 in *The Liturgy Documents*, vol. 1, 4th ed. (Chicago: Liturgy Training Publications, 2004), art. 26.

[23] Ibid., art. 28.

pastor an indefeasible weapon: if any song is criticized on grounds of musical aesthetics, including the most objectively technical aspects, the composer may always claim that the criticisms are irrelevant because he has composed the piece in a new style with new standards.[24]

Musical style is given the impregnable armor of the most destructive relativism: "Style and value are two distinct judgments."[25] Far beyond admitting that it is hard to compare the goodness of compositions from two distinct styles, the committee claims that musical style systems cannot be evaluated at all. This is dubious even on purely musical grounds. We have good, objective, technical reasons for stating without hesitation that plainchant makes lousy dance music, and that statement is an evaluation. But when the extramusical context of the sacred liturgy enters the discussion, the committee's principle crumbles completely.

Consider the good old song "Dixie." Once a military marching song for soldiers of the Confederacy during the American Civil War, it lives on as a kind of anthem for traditional culture in the southern United States. As a marching song, it is an excellent example of its style, a mid-nineteenth-century popular song idiom with strong duple meter and a rousing, singable melody. "Music in Catholic Worship" must approve this song for the liturgy, with suitable word changes, of course,

---

[24] Robert I. Blanchard, writing in the contentious wake of the famous Milwaukee meeting of the Church Music Association of America in 1967, warned against precisely this attitude: "We must be careful not to canonize certain styles of music. But we have to be just as careful not to allow ourselves to be fooled into believing that every possible musical style is equally capable of a genuine liturgical expression and experience." See "Church Music Today—the Center Position," in *Crisis in Church Music?* (Washington, DC: The Liturgical Conference, 1967), 66.

[25] It is remarkable that this bald relativism is somewhat toned down in the update of "Music in Catholic Worship" called "Sing to the Lord," which the American bishops approved as a "guideline" in November 2007. Article 136 of the new document reads, "Sufficiency of artistic expression, however, is not the same as musical style, for 'the Church has not adopted any particular style of art as her own. She has admitted styles from every period, in keeping with the natural characteristics and conditions of peoples and the needs of the various rites.' Thus, in recent times, the Church has consistently recognized and freely welcomed the use of various styles of music as an aid to liturgical worship." Since no reasonable person acquainted with music would ever equate "sufficiency of artistic expression" with "musical style," it is difficult to know what point is intended by the sentence, except to disguise while preserving the relativism of "Music in Catholic Worship." See Helen Hull Hitchcock, "Bishops Approve Three Liturgy Items at Busy Baltimore Meeting," *Adoremus Bulletin* 13, no. 9 (December 2007–January 2008): 4, and William Mahrt, "Sing to the Lord," *Sacred Music* 135, no. 1 (Spring 2008): 44–51.

perhaps to "Glory to God in the highest," because "We must judge value within each style" and never the style itself. Well, within its military marching style, "Dixie" is a very fine piece.

It is easy to understand why the committee tried to make the argument. The members wished to shield all the musical experiments going on in the euphoric days following the council with an armor invulnerable to the arrows of technical criticism already blackening the air. But there is nothing of substance to the argument, as "Dixie" quickly proves. Musical styles are born of musical languages with certain potentials, including semantic potentials, which is why "Dixie," or any song like it, fails any current test of liturgical propriety. Once the criterion of the liturgy enters, one can most reasonably ask, "Are these potentials appropriate for the liturgy? Can this style possibly accommodate the transcendence of the liturgical action?" In short, musical languages and the style systems they generate are subject to contextual criticism just as well as are individual compositions. No work composed in a style whose semantic range cannot accommodate the transcendence that is a paramount goal of every liturgical celebration, no matter how excellent an exemplar of its style, can qualify as liturgical music. This is not snobbery; Chopin fails just as badly as "Dixie." On the other hand, that some style such as polyphony or plainchant has a robust semantic of transcendence does not guarantee that all or even most compositions in that language are good enough for the liturgy. There are reasons why we remember Palestrina and not his colleague Ingegneri, nor, for that matter, the Cecilian imitators of the last two centuries, whose mediocre polyphonies still clog the repertory of the Vatican choir.

Now we may return to the founding dual principle in *Sacrosanctum Concilium*, that sacred music worthy of the liturgy must intrinsically have musical goodness and beauty and at the same time be appropriate for the specific context that is the liturgy. We return with renewed confidence that such true art objectively exists, somehow beyond and outside the human prejudices of time and place, and with confidence that judgments about sacred music can be made with rationality enough to ground our traditions.

But before postmodernism such confidences were not lacking, and yet the history of musical criticism is a litany of gross errors of contemporaneous judgment. The stories about the premature interment of Beethoven or some other master are the ones passed around as the most amusing, but far more frequent than shortsighted underestimations are the overly zealous promotions to the compositional pantheon:

Telemann, Bononcini, Salieri, Spohr, Raff, and many, many other names who ranked at the top of their classes in their times but who today are found in the second tier or worse. The freshness of a new composition, its sheer surface novelty, not to mention the critic's temptation of being the first to acclaim a new musical saint, makes such promotion hard to resist. The list of Nobel Prize winners in literature tells the same sad story. The greats of yesterday most often become the lost and unremembered of today. So what is the good of our confidence in true art, if contemporary judgment is so fallible?

First, let us disabuse ourselves of two quite illogical and yet common myths about artistic value in history. The first is a kind of historical romanticism that believes in some past golden age of artistic achievement. Back then, in the Middle Ages or the eighteenth century or whenever you will, they knew how to compose and standards were high, as compared to today, when all musical technique and good taste have gone to the dogs. The historical evidence is quite otherwise. Masterworks in the eighteenth century were composed at about the same rate as any other time, including the present century, well under one percent of all compositions, in my estimation. If everything we hear from some past century seems great, it is because only the great have survived for us to hear. The other myth is a kind of Catholic hubris, particularly associated with the aging generation of the Second Vatican Council, and believes that anything composed before 1960 is inadmissible because it symbolizes some awful Ghost of Church Past, while only contemporary music can speak to contemporary people. If the romantic myth fails logically because every classic was once new, the contemporary myth logically condemns the very idea of tradition, since what counts as "contemporary" changes with every passing year, every passing day. Neither recognizes an essential historical process that acts on the history of theology as well as on the history of music, a process that John Henry Cardinal Newman called "development," now better known as "discernment."[26]

The Classical Judgment

The historical process works quite simply. First, a composer writes a new work. Because it is new, it will have musical features that no one has ever heard before: melodies, harmonies, rhythmic patterns, word

---

[26] Newman, *An Essay on the Development of Christian Doctrine*, 29–30.

settings, etc. If they are sufficiently interesting, they capture the attention of the current audience, that is, the audience contemporary with the composer, because of their sheer novelty and qualities of immediate attraction. "Men care most for the song which is newest to the singer" states Plato, quoting Homer, in *The Republic*.[27]

In almost every case, these attractions will weaken with familiarity and the passage of time, either because with repeated hearings we realize that those things that interested us initially were in fact not so fascinating after all, or because other new works have arrived on the scene that are fresher and therefore more appealing for the same reason that the first work once appealed to us. "We like to welcome the goods that novelty can bring, and our openness to this thought itself does something to increase the stress on what we do know from the side of what we do not."[28] Every music lover has had the experience of being thrilled on some first hearing of a work, only to wonder on the fifth hearing what all the fuss was.

Some few works, however, may last to the next generation of listeners, a new audience, before they fade into historical oblivion. And an extremely rare composition may never fade, but maintain and even strengthen its attraction known from its first contemporary audience for other audiences generations hence, and even in different places and cultures. Why? What causes it to survive?

On one point the postmodernists are correct. Every work of art is a product of culture, and the fixation of interest on a Beethoven or a Cézanne is an act of culture. Where they err is in supposing that such acts are arbitrary, so that one could substitute Wagenseil for Beethoven without changing the industry of cultural adulation. The acts are not arbitrary. They are caused by the presence of universal qualities in the music itself, qualities that indeed require a cultural training to comprehend but which themselves transcend contemporary cultural values, qualities that have the power to enthrall not only the first generation of listeners but also the second and third, long after sheer novelty has worn off.

Because it is so much less abstract, the survival of a classic film may be more immediately grasped than that of a musical composition.

---

[27] Plato's Republic, trans. G. M. A. Grube (Indianapolis, IN: Hackett, 1976), 424c, p. 90.

[28] Anthony Saville calls this historical process "loss by displacement." *The Test of Time: An Essay in Philosophical Aesthetics* (New York: Oxford University Press, 1982), 113.

Casablanca is certainly a product of its time. Its World War II plot is laced with Allied propaganda, themes of heroism, self-sacrifice, and romantic love; its use of language, its social roles, and everything about it bespeak its origins in America of 1942. There were many other films made that year with similar characteristics, and several, such as *Reap the Wild Wind*, had casts as famous and earned comparable box office receipts. But within a generation *Reap the Wild Wind* was forgotten, viewed today only by film historians and John Wayne fanatics, perhaps, while *Casablanca* continues to fascinate its fifth generation of viewers. It shows the hallmarks of its very particular origin while seeming to be for all time. That is why we call it a classic film. Indeed, for theologian David Tracy, these universal qualities of classicism, these "certain expressions of the human spirit so disclose a compelling truth about our lives that we cannot deny them some kind of normative status. Thus do we name these expressions, and these alone, 'classics.'"[29] While musical compositions are neither true nor false in any logical sense, the universal appeal of a musical classic across nations and histories, "its kind of timelessness as permanent timeliness,"[30] surely denotes qualities that resonate potentially in all listeners, true art, and thus denotes some inexpressible truth about humankind.

This is true in part because a classic can speak to all, albeit in different ways, in a faint echo of the Pentecost event. Because film makes constant reference to the real world, *Casablanca*'s capacity to appeal to different levels of appreciation and to reward viewing after viewing is easy to see. The first time, one is caught up in the battle of good and evil, represented by the resistance and the Nazis, intertwined with the triangular love story. Next time, one appreciates the moral conflicts of the jaded hero who must choose between satisfying himself and the greater good of his community and world. Then, on the third viewing, one can savor all the short stories of the minor characters—the delightful emigrant German couple and the lecherous chief of police—that are told within the larger plot. And finally the technical genius of the film's composition may be studied almost forever, to say nothing of the interactions of the various levels of plot and character.

The four-voiced Lutheran chorale, with its simple tune on top and its intricately woven tapestry of accompanying melodies, is a kind of

---

[29] David Tracy, *The Analogical Imagination: Christian Theology and the Culture of Pluralism* (New York: Crossroad, 1981), 108.
[30] Ibid., 102.

musical composition where this kind of intrinsic multivalent interest is transparent and systematic.[31] There are some masterworks aimed at the connoisseur to be sure, but they are rare, especially in sacred music. Even when they are not obvious, as in the chorale or *Casablanca*, the universal qualities of the musical classics in the Western canon satisfy every interest to some degree. With a contrapuntal intricacy and harmonic depth that few can comprehend in toto, the *Mass in B Minor* of Bach also has orchestral splashes and mighty bursts of choral singing that can thrill most anyone.

What exactly are these universal qualities in music? Philosophers and critics since Plato have tried and failed to enumerate them, but once again, the failure of articulation does not in the least entail that they cannot exist. The universal qualities of true art are the simplest and best explanation of the demise of Soviet music along with its regime, the explosive resurrection of Bach, and the dynamics of culture preservation in general. It explains why hit parade radio programs change their listings every week, the drop-offs never to be heard again, and it explains why some choral societies have insisted on performing Handel's *Messiah* annually for over two hundred years.

No, we need not be defeated by our inability to articulate or adequately theorize about these universal qualities of music. We only need to be assured of their presence in a composition when we consider its suitability for liturgy. We need a litmus test, and we have one. It is history.

The history of music grants to its readers some basic truths about the worth of compositions, empirically verified. The first is that it is most natural for an artist to create in ways that will attract his contemporaneous audience. Before twentieth-century academicism created a hothouse for them, composers who were so far "ahead of their time" that their hearers could not understand them were also out of work and soon in the dustbin of cultural history. The romantic image of the neglected genius is a myth. It is therefore quite unremarkable when a new song makes a splash, even if it be rather mediocre. That is the natural order in the arts.[32]

The second historical truth is that the splash almost always subsides to nothing. Nearly all musical compositions pass into cultural oblivion

---

[31] See chap. 10.

[32] This is not to say, of course, that all new compositions do make a splash. Many, perhaps most, are so poor as to fail even in pleasing their contemporaries.

once their spawning generations have also passed away. They lacked the universal classical qualities that have the power to reach beyond their first and only hearers.

The passage of time is therefore a kind of "corrosive force"[33] or indefatigable winnower that separates the multitudinous chaff from the rare and precious wheat, and this is precisely what benefits the inheritors of a musical tradition. History itself is the sieve, the famous test of time, that reveals the tradition's true treasures. Newman, speaking of developments in Christian doctrine, uses history in the same way:

> We prove them by using them, by applying them to the subject-matter, or the evidence, or the body of circumstances, to which they belong, as if they gave it its interpretation or its colour as a matter of course; and only when they fail, in the event, in illustrating phenomena or harmonizing facts, do we discover that we must reject the doctrines or the statements which we had in the first instance taken for granted.[34]

Compositions are proved similarly, in performance and practice, in repetition and study, and, in the case of liturgical music, in the grueling "body of circumstances" of the sacred liturgy. Tracy, in seconding Newman, notes that this historical test may occur even in the sense of a single person revisiting a classic, but it is history just the same:

> If, even once, a person has experienced a text, a gesture, an image, an event, a person with the force of the recognition: "This is important! This does make and will demand a difference!" then one has experienced a candidate for classic status. If one's own experience has been verified by other readers, especially by the community of capable readers over the centuries, the reflective judgment should prove that much more secure. If the experience is verified at a later period of life, when a new but related understanding of the same classic occurs with the same force of revelatory power, then, once again, a reflective judgment upon the realized experience of this text, event, gesture, image, symbol, person—this structured expression of the human spirit—is rendered yet more plausible, still more relatively adequate.[35]

---

[33] Saville, *The Test of Time*, 80.
[34] Newman, *An Essay on the Development of Christian Doctrine*, 101.
[35] Tracy, *The Analogical Imagination*, 115–16.

History, then, can identify a classic as litmus identifies an acid, and the older the work, the stronger the color. Thus we may satisfy one criterion, the criterion of greatness, of the dual principle in *Sacrosanctum Concilium*.

But the *Mass in B Minor*, for all its musical excellence, will probably never engage the Roman Catholic liturgy. Remembering all the while that great music is not necessarily great liturgical music, can we ask the history of music *in liturgy* to identify true art? Remembering that a classic is a classic in part because it somehow remains above the fray of continuing cultural change, transcending its originating context to adapt somehow to all contexts, can we discover a category of *liturgical classic* that contains not only great works of music but also those which transcend their original liturgical births to adapt to the liturgy as it changes through history? Rembert Weakland explicitly rejected such a prospect during the first great swell of postconciliar liturgical reform, speaking at a conference of liturgical musicians in 1967: "We cannot go backwards in time to find an art-music that will satisfy the liturgical demands of today. . . . They will fail because the treasury of church music we are asked to preserve, whether it be chant, polyphony, Mozart, or Bruckner, is the product of a relationship between liturgy and music that is hard to reconcile with the basic premises of the constitution itself."[36] If his assumption that the set of liturgical classics is void, that there can be no such thing as liturgical classics in principle, then our reliance on history to identify true art is worthless, as is, in fact, the ideal of a liturgical tradition of any substance.

Weakland's argument was quite simple: liturgy after Vatican II is reformed and different, and we cannot expect liturgical music conceived with older liturgies in mind to meet its needs. But the argument assumes two things: first, that no liturgical music can ever have universally liturgical "classic" qualities that would enable it to adapt to liturgical reforms and new contexts; second, that the postconciliar liturgy is not merely superficially different but substantially other than any preconciliar liturgy.

The euphoria of the 1960s and its extravagances are understandable now, but viewed from the calmer distance of more than four decades, few historians of liturgy describe *Sacrosanctum Concilium* as a radical

---

[36] Weakland, "Music and Liturgy in Evolution," in *Crisis in Church Music?* (Washington, DC: The Liturgical Conference, 1967), 4.

document, a complete revolution.[37] The christocentric action of celebrating "the paschal mystery: reading those things 'which were in all the scriptures concerning him,' celebrating the Eucharist in which 'the victory and triumph of his death are again made present,' and at the same time 'giving thanks to God for His inexpressible gift' in Christ Jesus, 'in praise of His glory' through the power of the Holy Spirit" holds as true in the eighth century as in the sixteenth as in the twenty-first[38] (SC 6). Not even *Sacrosanctum Concilium*'s promotion of "active participation" is a new element, although it is certainly emphasized as never before. Active participation as an essential aspect of liturgical music certainly makes us hear and evaluate traditional repertory with new ears, but only the constricted translation of *participatio actuosa* as "congregational singing" would rule out significant portions of the traditional repertory on technical grounds.

If the *novus ordo* is not a radical break with the past, but essentially the same action and form in a new rite, then to agree with Weakland one must presume an impossibly precise congruence between musical style and liturgical form. The very character and the semantic range of plainchant, for example, must be so well matched to the rite contained in the 1962 Missal that it fails the 1970 Missal. But we have seen how music, in the general case without any accompanying text or lyric, has a semantic range of enormous breadth and little precision.[39] If plainchant fits liturgy like a glove, it does so because it conforms so well to the diction of the liturgically proper text as no other musical style does. To claim that plainchant cannot set a liturgy with a three-year cycle of readings, with two biblical readings ahead of the gospel instead of one, with intercessory prayer after the gospel, or with any other of the technical changes is patently ridiculous, and to claim that it fails some generalized "spirit" of the new liturgy denies the essential oneness of the Roman Rite throughout history.

For classic music to be classic liturgical music, it must have the power to direct the open mind toward God, to reflect faithfully the liturgical action, and to permit *participatio actuosa*, among other things. If a type of music has inspired liturgy in the past, there is no reason a

---

[37] For example, see Avery Dulles, "Vatican II: The Myth and the Reality," *America* 188, no. 6 (February 24, 2003): 7–11.

[38] Internal quotations are, respectively, Luke 24:27; Council of Trent, Session 13, Decree on the Holy Eucharist, chap. 5; 2 Cor 9:15; and Eph 1:12.

[39] See chap.12.

priori to suppose it cannot do so in the present, because these necessities have always inhered in liturgy.[40] If classic music survives because its qualities mold themselves again and again to a changing culture, there is no theoretical reason to doubt, and every historical reason to believe, that classic liturgical music can do as well with a continually changing liturgy.

The history of liturgical music can fairly divide its repertories into two groups: those that have passed some liturgical test of significant length and those that have not. In the first group, there is plainchant front and center. Even with the exclusion of the "corrupt" period following the Council of Trent, its history of many centuries reveals a musical language that apparently changed very little despite many liturgical accretions. Works were passed down for many generations, and they continued to work their transcendence, evidently, through the centuries of liturgical change. Classical polyphony has a shorter history, but nonetheless gripped the liturgical imagination strongly enough to withstand the attacks of the most traditional reformers who wished to eliminate it at Trent. Allowing for differences in certain doctrinal emphases in its texts, we might also admit the best of Lutheran chorale tradition to this group as the first great liturgical experiment in congregational singing, since the Lutheran liturgy differs from the Roman only in minor details. In the second group are the operatic Masses of the eighteenth through twentieth centuries, a genre which was born and lived in controversy over its liturgical propriety, and the popular styles since the Second Vatican Council, which experienced the same kind of history, albeit so short and with such inconsistency of repertory that their surpassing the test of time cannot yet be known in any case.

This is why it makes sense that *Sacrosanctum Concilium* names Gregorian chant as the one music retaining "pride of place in liturgical services" and gives polyphony the first nod among other possibilities (SC 116). This is why it recognizes that other kinds of music are liturgically possible but withholds any specific recognition. No other large repertory has withstood as well the historical winnowing, but that is not to rule out that one well might.

---

[40] This is true even of *participatio actuosa*, despite its new prominence at the Second Vatican Council, as long as one does not translate the phrase as "congregational singing."

Contemporary Classics?

We who now find ourselves in the historically curious position of having to build traditions of liturgical music also find that our most reliable ally in this momentous project, the cognizance of the traditional repertory of Catholic music, is probably at the lowest level among practicing liturgical musicians as at any time in history. And so parishes rely on the only instincts they have left, their intuitions about contemporary music, to choose the foundations for their traditions. But the warning of history is clear: parishes who build only on a foundation of recent music are building their houses on sand. As they have experienced for forty years, what they build quickly comes quickly down, to be replaced by newer music ad infinitum, acting just like its surrounding secular culture.

But a total resignation to the historical repertory, while a safer and much more promising route to success than any other, leaves one very human difficulty: what is the contemporary composer to do? Why did the conciliar fathers insist that "composers, animated by the christian spirit, should accept that it is part of their vocation to cultivate sacred music and increase its store of treasures" (SC 121)? Indeed, how can a tradition live without growing? What is the living composer's response to the burden of classicism?

Tracy's "new but related understanding" alludes to the essential act of the theologian, not simply to know the classic texts and doctrines but to interpret them. In music, too, interpretation, properly understood, turns out to be the insight required for the peace and prosperity of all liturgical musicians. Such interpretation begins with the repertory of symbols, the largest collection of which is the liturgical year.

Chapter 14

Understanding Musical Symbols: The Seasons of Liturgical Music

> It is nevertheless wonderful how the succession of year after year diminishes not one atom of the freshness and vehemence of those impressions, and each new beginning of the cycle of mystic seasons seems to be our first year.
> Prosper Guéranger (1841)

In the middle of the nineteenth century, the founder of what would become the most important center for the recovery of Roman Catholic plainchant—the Abbey of St. Pierre at Solesmes—Prosper Guéranger, secured his reputation as one of the fathers of the liturgical movement not with any study of music but with a nine-volume reflection on the ancient practice of the liturgical year.[1] In his introduction he writes:

> The ecclesiastical year . . . is neither more nor less than the manifestation of Jesus Christ and His mysteries, in the Church and in the faithful soul. It is the divine cycle, in which appear all the works of God, each in its turn: the seven days of the creation; the Pasch and Pentecost of the Jewish people; the ineffable visit of the Incarnate Word; His sacrifice and his victory; the descent of the holy Ghost; the holy Eucharist; the surpassing glories of the Mother of God, ever a Virgin; the magnificence of the angels; the merits and triumphs of the saints. Thus the cycle of the Church may be said to have its beginning under the

---

[1] Prosper Guéranger, *L'Année Liturgique*, 15 vols. (Paris: H. Oudin et Cie, beginning in 1841 [unfinished]). Guéranger evidently wanted the study to include fifteen volumes, but completed only nine before he died in 1875. The remaining six were completed by another Benedictine under Guéranger's name. The first volumes were contemporaneous with his *Institutions Liturgique*. See a review of Guéranger's other writings in Kevin W. Irwin, *Context and Text: Method in Liturgical Theology* (Collegeville, MN: Liturgical Press, 1994), 19 and following.

patriarchal Law, its progress under the written law, and its completion under the Law of love.[2]

More than one hundred years later, Guéranger's conception was recalled by *Sacrosanctum Concilium*, the liturgical constitution of the Second Vatican Council:

> Within the course of the year, moreover, it [the church] unfolds the whole mystery of Christ, from the incarnation and nativity to the ascension, to Pentecost, and the expectation of the blessed hope and of the coming of the Lord.
>
> Thus recalling the mysteries of the redemption, it opens up to the faithful the riches of her Lord's powers and merits, so that these are in some way made present at all times; the faithful lay hold of them and are filled with saving grace. (SC 102)

Owing to human limitations of sense and time, the manifold mysteries of God are too rich to be contemplated in a single Mass, though it be the consummate prayer of the church. Each and every Mass re-presents the paschal mystery of Christ's sacrifice for our salvation in conjunction with the gift of himself in the Eucharist. This is the great drama of Catholic faith. But for us to begin to comprehend this central mystery in its fullness, we must witness and participate in another drama, "the sublimest that has ever been offered to the admiration of man,"[3] coincident with the drama of the Mass but played out on the timescale of the solar year. This is the liturgical cycle.

Thus each Mass contains the universality of the paschal mystery and manifests a particularity of that mystery at the same time. Consider the introit, offertory, and communion antiphons proper for the Fourth Sunday of Advent (Cycle A in the reformed 1970 calendar):

> Let the clouds rain down the Just One, and the earth bring forth a Savior. (Isaiah 45:8)

> Rejoice, O highly favored daughter! The Lord is with you. Blessed are you among women, and blest is the fruit of your womb. (Luke 1:28, 42)

> The Virgin is with child and shall bear a son, and she will call him Emmanuel. (Isaiah 7:14)

---

[2] Prosper Guéranger, *The Liturgical Year*, trans. Dom Laurence Shepherd, OSB, vol. 1, *Advent* (Westminster, MD: Newman Press, 1948–50), 9–10.

[3] Ibid., 14.

The particular mystery here is the incarnation, but even more specifically, the significance of its anticipation. The Mass begins with a prophecy that already resonates with double meaning in two kinds of time: the great time scale of God's plan through history, within which lives his prophet Isaiah in the dark time awaiting the light of salvation; and the time of our own moment, the expectation that the actual solemnity of the incarnation will occur for ourselves within the very week. The offertory introduces yet another time scale, the earthly life of Jesus, conflating the greeting of the angel to Mary with the greeting of her cousin Elizabeth. The quotations are so famous and beloved that we need no other cue to link them back to Isaiah's prophecy heard in the introit. Then the communion antiphon recalls another Isaiah passage foretelling that angel's greeting with the name Emmanuel, while at the same time reminding everyone present of the gospel passage from Matthew 1:18-24 proclaimed earlier. The opening prayer of the celebrant, the collect, conjoins these multivalent signs of the mystery of the incarnation to the mysteries of sacrifice and resurrection present in every Mass, without which all such anticipations lose all significance:

> Lord, fill our hearts with your love, and as you revealed to us by an angel the coming of your Son as man, so lead us through his suffering and death to the glory of his resurrection, for he lives and reigns with you and the Holy Spirit, one God, for ever and ever. Amen.

And because the entire liturgy is celebrated late in December, among the shortest days of the year, but at that point in the solar cycle when days begin to lengthen once again, the biblical histories and symbols take on sensible and visceral correspondence to the physical being of the faithful.[4] In analogous ways, each day of the liturgical year, according to its proper prayers, "opens up to the faithful the riches" of the particular mysteries of faith, "made present at all times" (SC 102) by symbols of text, music, color, and liturgical art, always in conjunction with the universal themes of Christ's passion, resurrection, and thanksgiving in the Eucharist.

---

[4] One of the more interesting problems of inculturation of the liturgy is reconciling such a northern symbological scheme with Catholics who live in the southern hemisphere, where, of course, the days are at their longest and about to shorten. See Joseph Ratzinger, *The Spirit of the Liturgy*, trans. John Saward (San Francisco: Ignatius Press, 2000), 105.

This single instance of the Fourth Sunday of Advent offers but a glimpse of the liturgical year's complex representation of the divine temporal order and its evangelical power. Its genius seems present from the historical beginnings of Catholic liturgy: "The content of the [earliest Easter] celebration went beyond the death itself to proclaim the total mystery of the Cross in all its dimensions, from incarnation to parousia."[5]

It is a mistake both common and natural to suppose that the year takes its form from the life of Jesus, with his Advent placed at the top of the cycle, followed immediately by his birth at Christmas, the early days of his ministry, the journey to Jerusalem during Lent, and the passion, resurrection, ascension, and Pentecost all in due course.[6] It is natural because these historical events in the earthly life of Jesus are so important to the historical nature of Christianity. But already this coincidence of time scales seen in this single Sunday makes it impossible to read the liturgical year biographically, just as we cannot read the gospels that way. The forty days of Lent and the fifty of Easter reproduce actual time spans that Jesus lived among those events, however symbolic and inaccurate they may actually be, whereas the period between Christmastide and Lent can only symbolize years to make any sense. Interwoven time frames explain why the Feast of the Annunciation on March 25 can be nine real months ahead of Christmas but also in the midst of our contemplation of his passion.[7] For those who read the Divine Office, this passion is recalled every Friday with the singing of the penitential Psalm 51, regardless of the time of year. The transfiguration is commemorated twice each year, on the Second Sunday of

---

[5] Thomas J. Talley, *The Origins of the Liturgical Year*, 2nd ed. (New York: Pueblo Publishing, 1991), 13.

[6] This mistake has been long lamented. In sympathy, liturgical historian Adolf Adam quotes another, R. Berger: "There is a widespread tendency . . . to understand the liturgical year as a representation of the life of Jesus: from the expectation of his birth, through his incarnation, public ministry, suffering and resurrection, to his sending of the Spirit and second coming. Anyone can immediately see that this approach does not account for details of the liturgical year. But it is not even verifiable if we look only at the broad lines of this year." See Adolf Adam, *The Liturgical Year: Its History & Its Meaning after the Reform of the Liturgy*, trans. Matthew J. O'Connell (New York: Pueblo Publishing, 1981; originally published as *Das Kirchenjahr mitfeiern* [Freiburg: Herder, 1979]), 29.

[7] "Because March 25 usually falls in the Easter penitential season, and the sobriety of this season seemed incompatible with the joy proper to the feast, the old date of December 18 was observed for a long time in Spain, while the Church of Milan celebrated it on the last Sunday of Advent." Adam, *The Liturgical Year*, 153.

Lent and on August 6 in the sanctoral calendar (cycle of saints), with different emphases in each case. The church insists that it is the mysteries—including those without historical representation, such as the Trinity, not only the earthly events—that we commemorate.[8]

Even thinking about the liturgical year as a succession of pastoral "themes"—expectation, incarnation, repentance, resurrection, evangelization, and so on—is too neat for the calendar. Such themes will not be confined to their time slots. With obvious symbolism, end-of-the-world readings dominate the month of November, the end of Ordinary Time that concludes with the relatively new solemnity of Christ the King on the last Sunday of the liturgical year.[9] But as the following First Sunday of Advent proclaims a new liturgical year, end-of-the-world readings and references continue uninterrupted, again because we are meant to await the coming of the Savior in more than one time frame. "There is no contradiction because even in the eschatologically oriented period the first coming of Christ is not forgotten, but rather both aspects are present."[10] Even the tone of a season can be broken, as the Glory to God rings out on the Solemnity of the Immaculate Conception in the midst of solemn Advent, as the Lenten transfiguration episode concludes when Jesus charges Peter, James, and John "not to relate what they had seen to anyone, except when the Son of Man had risen from the dead" (Mark 9:9). By the reformed calendar of 1970, the Holy Thursday liturgy ends Lent, but fasting and works of penance continue through Saturday until the great vigil of Easter.

The Seasonal Symbols of Liturgical Music

Therefore, one of the most important jobs of Catholic music, as "an integral part of the solemn liturgy" (SC 112), is somehow to articulate the liturgical year in its sumptuous complexity, to symbolize the universals and the particulars of its nature.

This is one of the most important reasons why the repertory of Roman Catholic liturgical music is unmatched on earth. From at least the time of our earliest musical sources, the liturgical year has been a source of incomparable richness. The great majority of liturgical compositions were not intended for some generic, all-purpose Mass, but

---

[8] See ibid., 25, on the origins and nature of the "idea-feasts."
[9] Ibid., 28, reports that the tradition of beginning the sacramentaries with Advent dates from the tenth century. The Solemnity of Christ the King dates from 1925.
[10] Ibid., 133.

for a liturgy of a particular season if not a particular day in the calendar. Gregorian proper chants and the cantatas of J. S. Bach set texts that had been assigned to their particular feasts long before their creators came onto the scene. And so as the liturgy evolved through the centuries, particularly in the elaboration of the sanctoral cycle, the repertory of liturgical music grew with it.

But how does it cooperate with the manifold symbolism and time frames of the year? If we conceive liturgical music, as do Buddhist priests and Muslim imams, as really a form of heightened speech appropriate for addressing God, of the same substance as the holy words, then there is little problem. All the content and symbology of the liturgical year is in the words of its prayers, proper and Ordinary, through their respective particular and universal properties. The antiphons of the Fourth Sunday of Advent do their work merely by being written as they are, and singing them creates an effect of heightened presence and sacredness, nothing more. But this conception of liturgical music is alien to Roman Catholicism, which has historically treated its music as having symbolic and therefore semantic qualities distinct from the holy words that it sets. Catholicism has always asked its music to do more than carry the prayers up to God. Music solemnizes and glorifies these prayers with its own appropriate subtextual significance, the wordless commentary running below the liturgical stage. This semantic potential of liturgical music complicates its role in the articulation of the liturgical year quite a bit.

Centuries ago, a Catholic entering a cathedral church just in time to hear the choir sing the plainchant introit *Rorate coeli* (Heavens, let the Just One come forth) in late December would have instantly felt that it was the Fourth Sunday of Advent if he had not realized it beforehand, even if he could not understand the words. Not merely that it was the Advent season, or some time close to Christmas; no, the precise moment in the liturgical year would have been conveyed by the plainchant. How could this be? Surely the melodic shapes of *Rorate coeli* are not a timepiece code for the liturgical calendar? Music generally lacks such a specific semantic range, does it not? Well, yes, generally, but this is not a general case. If this Catholic parishioner had attended every Fourth Sunday of Advent Mass since childhood, he would have heard this same melody then, *and only then*, every year of his life. An association born of the mind and musical perception would have grown up, and just as the slightest whiff of turkey with a particular spice can instantly recall long-ago memories of childhood Thanksgiving, so can a melody learned in childhood and associated with some unique annual event recall that event for that person forever. An unconsummated symbol, the melody of *Rorate coeli*, has been filled with meaning for all Catholics who share this experience: the meaning is "the beginning of Mass for the Fourth Sunday of Advent." Just as any utterance used consistently in a specific circumstance will acquire the distinct meaning appropriate for that circumstance, so can a melody if the context is similarly circumscribed.

So it is quite possible for music to symbolize very specific and yet abstract biblical themes, such as Isaiah's prophecy of the Just One raining down from heaven, if the music is heard only in connection with that text and none other. The power of this symbol might be exploited at liturgical moments beyond the introit, such as an organ prelude on the same melody, or a newly composed congregational psalm response that recalls its shape, or in the singing of Palestrina's magnificent five-voice motet *Rorate coeli*. The message would in each case be the same: "This is the Fourth Sunday of Advent—let the heavens rain down the Just One."

That is but the beginning of music's symbolic power. The Catholic liturgical cycle has obvious climactic moments, like any great drama, that cry out for this kind of specific, unique musical setting: Christmas, the institution of the Blessed Sacrament on Holy Thursday, the Ascension, Pentecost. Seasonal music will not do for these, because the sense of climax, of spiritual arrival, is a moment, a discrete event, not a generic period of time. The opening notes of the Easter Proclamation *Exsultet iam angelica turba caelorum* (Rejoice, heavenly powers; sing choirs of angels) would be utterly enervated of their incomparably joyous thrill were they heard at many other times of the year, rather than once and once only, at the end of the penitential season, sung in a darkness illuminated only by candles in the hands of the faithful.

The forty years since the Second Vatican Council's reform of the liturgy have seen little such specificity because the propers of the traditional calendar have been largely abandoned. Recently, composers have attempted to make up a bit for the near total absence of seasonal music composed in the first two decades after the council, but popular American hymnals such as *Gather* and *Ritual Song* still have no settings for Isaiah's prophecy of the Just One.[11] This is no surprise, given the constraints of popular-style music.[12] The four-bar phrase structure

---

[11] The closest that these collections can approximate for the offertory is the traditional *Ave Maria*, and for the communion, "O Come, Emmanuel."

[12] See chap. 3.

alone would require deforming these brief antiphons into some kind of quatrain with extra verbiage that could only cloud their interrelations.

Instead, seasonal music has aimed at less specificity, not at matching the symbology of a particular feast or Sunday but at matching a general theme or tone of a season, in rough analogy, perhaps, to the traditional liturgical colors of the altar and celebrant. This is done almost entirely by exploiting "option four" of the General Instruction of the Roman Missal, the substitution of the day's proper antiphons by "another liturgical chant that is suited to the sacred action, the day, or the time of year," the practice that has maintained the hegemony of the "the four hymns" over the common conception of music at Mass.[13] In this way, "O Come, Emmanuel" may be sung on any Sunday of Advent, even though its verses properly belong only to the last seven days when the "O" antiphons frame the *Magnificat* at each Vespers.[14] "O Come, Emmanuel" then comes to sound like the Advent season, not any particular Sunday in it, not only because of its magnificently appropriate hymn text, but because, again, Catholics hear its music only during Advent and at no other time. In the same way, the General Instruction of the Roman Missal allows a "seasonal antiphon" for the responsorial psalm.[15]

It is difficult to say with much precision what the tune of "O Come, Emmanuel" means for the season, other than the general theme of Advent: a hopeful expectation of the Savior. It is true that the hymn's text has a rich lode of symbolic treasure: the exile of Israel, the Key of David, the law of Mount Sinai, the Daystar, and so on, but the collection of them is not specific to any particular liturgy in Advent. It is specific only to the season of Advent, and individual elements receive no reinforcement or symbolic correspondence from a given liturgy except fortuitously. Seasonal hymns or antiphons can never have the same precision of articulation as true propers, because their semantic ranges must encompass the entire season, with all its themes and symbols. Being so much larger, their semantic ranges are more diffuse.

---

[13] For text of the regulation and more details, see chap. 6.

[14] So called because each antiphon for the *Magnificat* in the seven days preceding Christmas eve begins with an "O" acclamation: "O Wisdom," "O Key of David," etc.

[15] General Instruction of the Roman Missal (Collegeville, MN: Liturgical Press, 2011), art. 61.

The semantic principle at work here is simply this: the more specific the attending context of a piece of music, the tighter and more precise its semantic range.[16] Assuming a consistent usage, a true proper will eventually come to mean the specific feast to which it belongs, while another piece used variously through a season will acquire a broader semantic for the season.

The most successful case, by far, of a musical sound that symbolizes a liturgical season is the repertory of Christmas carols. It is a stable and robust repertory of songs that no European or American parish would do without, and it is instructive to understand why this season has acquired such a strong musical hallmark while others have not. Christmas carols had been part of popular culture in Europe and America for centuries, but generally excluded from liturgies by both Protestant and Catholic authorities until the eighteenth century in Europe and the nineteenth century in England, where they became an armament in the liturgical renewal following the Oxford Movement. (The popular "Service of Lessons and Carols" dates from 1880 in Truro, England.) They also, less fortuitously, became allied with the interests of the marketplace in the twentieth century, as a visit to any shopping place of the period has proven.[17] Christmas carols therefore occupied a singular niche in modern Western culture, a musical repertory that was truly popular and yet had strong religious overtones. They stood ready to fill the liturgical void at Christmastide quickly when Catholic liturgical reformers promoted congregational singing in the mid-1960s. Unlike the music of the folk-revival movement, which tried unsuccessfully to fill the void at other liturgical seasons, the style of many Christmas carols is close to that of the polyphonic Lutheran hymn, combining a sacred semantic range with ease of singing. Although some carols would never be appropriate for liturgy (e.g., "Deck the Halls"), owing to their words and, to lesser extent,

---

[16] An application of the theory laid out in chap. 12. It is true that some traditional proper melodies are heard more than once during the year, accompanying different texts. In such cases, the semantic precision is inversely proportional to the number of such *contrafacta*, but the semantic principle still holds.

[17] Perhaps the single ironic benefit of the recent self-censorship of "political correctness" in Western culture has been the near banishment of the more sacred carols from the shopping malls, lest their explicit references to God and his Son offend agnostic, atheistic, and non-Christian spenders. For liturgy, this is a good thing, because it prevents their sacred semantic from erosion caused by association with the secular world and, more specifically, a consumerist society.

their musical styles, a significant number now occupy a permanent place in the seasonal repertory. Some other songs, such as "Jesus Christ Is Ris'n Today," "Come Holy Ghost," and a few Marian hymns, have acquired close associations with other solemnities of the year, but generally speaking, Catholicism does not have sets of seasonal carols comparable to the Christmas carols, because no other repertory of deep popularity could maintain a sacred semantic against the onslaughts of secular culture during the last two centuries.

Might it be possible to build traditions of Advent carols, Lent carols, and Easter carols analogous to the tradition of the Christmas? The theory of seasonal semantics sketched above suggests a straightforward strategy: for each season, select a small and unique repertory of appropriate songs or hymns, and sing them, consistently, year after year, only during their respective seasons. In a generation, or two at most, the repertory of Easter, Lent, and Advent carols will have been established.

It is easier said than done.

The selection of music upon which to build the tradition is critical. As we have painfully experienced with many years of revolving-door repertory, only the very best music will survive the test of time and have the power to satisfy the spiritual hunger of generation upon generation. It is not easy to find song texts which both meet the musical requirements of congregational singing, an integral musical structure, and also symbolize the season with accuracy and depth. Even the Christmas carols may falter here. While it is true that the great second verse of "Hark! The Herald Angels Sing" captures the mystery of the incarnation about as closely as anyone could wish—"Pleased as man with man to dwell / Jesus our Emmanuel"—other favorites, such as "Away in the Manger," have little more substance than Christmas candy.[18] This is to say nothing of the great puzzle of identifying music of the highest value.[19] Misjudgments are costly. Jettisoning a piece after three, four, or five years because no one can stand to sing it any longer means a loss of three, four, or five years of investment in the building project. Without very wise choices, it will never reach a com-

---

[18] Owing to a jejune understanding of semantic theory coming from the schools of "political correctness," editors of many missalettes and hymnals have altered this line to read "Pleased as man with *us* to dwell," which not only ruins the play on the word "man" but changes and dilutes the meaning of the incarnation.

[19] See chap. 13.

fortable level of stability; rather, it will be like a wall whose stones keep falling away.

What will be the geographical scope of the new carol traditions? Parochial? Diocesan? National? The smaller the scope, the less internal stability they will enjoy, owing to the modern transience of the people who must sustain the tradition. The greater the scope, the more difficulty in finding agreement about the selection.[20] The Christmas carols enjoy a unanimity born of their widespread cultural origins and long history, which also ratified their intrinsic value. Can today's multicultural world possibly replicate that unusual phenomenon?

Lenten carols should obviously reflect the main themes of repentance and spiritual renewal, Advent carols the anticipation of the incarnation, and so on. But as we have seen, such thematic categorization is rarely so pat in the actual liturgical cycle. If the songs are faithful to themes, they must step out of season. A synopsis of the parable of the Prodigal Son, "O Father We Have Wandered," long rehearsed during Lent, should appear also in mid-September of year C when that parable is read on the twenty-fourth Sunday of Ordinary Time. Would it seem just too odd to sing "O Come, Emmanuel" on March 25, the solemnity of the Annunciation? If we do so with all such shifts of time frame, what happens to the semantic association built up between the music and the time of year? Does "O Father We Have Wandered" begin to sound less Lenten because we sing it elsewhere, or just out of place, like a Christmas carol sung in July?

The same identity crisis can arise from the time-honored tradition of using *contrafacta*, or different sets of words with a given tune.[21] In the *Gather Comprehensive* hymnal, for example, "O Father We Have Wandered" is set to the same tune that most English-speaking Christians know as "O Sacred Head Surrounded," sung during Passiontide. Are such strong Passiontide associations to be transferred, and thereby weakened, by bringing them to bear on the general theme of penitence?

The thematic approach to seasonal music seems completely lost in Ordinary Time, which has no obvious unifying theme, or rather,

---

[20] Susan Benofy has chronicled the failure of one such attempt. See "The Birth and Death of a National Hymnal—1973–1976," part I in *Adoremus Bulletin* 13, no. 1 (March 2007): 4, 8; part II, "Seeking a 'Core Repertoire,'" in *Adoremus Bulletin* 13, no. 2 (April 2007): 11, 13.

[21] See chaps. 10 and 12 for details on the history and nature of *contrafacta*.

whose themes may change from Sunday to Sunday. Indeed, the determination of "the theme of the Mass" often becomes contentious. Correspondences among the readings may be too abstract, distant, or even at odds, apparently. Often enough, there seems to be no song that fits very well. The resulting all-too-common feature of "the four hymns" at Ordinary Time, then, is a rather random offering of Christian songs that simply praise God, such as "Praise to the Lord" or "We Gather Together" or any number of more recent popular-style songs that may actually praise the gathering instead. Now there is nothing amiss in simply praising God, since that is a primary purpose for the liturgy corresponding to human nature, but, in comparison to the potential symbolic depths of true proper musical settings, such as those in the Fourth Sunday of Advent, the generic hymn seems to be a loss of a great opportunity for spiritual nourishment.[22]

Seasonal Ordinaries

Another opportunity missed not only in recent decades but throughout much of the Catholic tradition of liturgical music is the reflection of the liturgical cycle through musical settings of the Ordinary prayers: *Kyrie, Gloria, Credo, Sanctus,* and *Agnus Dei.* The suggestion would appear to contradict itself. These prayers are sung at every Sunday Mass regardless of the season. How could they reflect the liturgical cycle at the same time?

In one instance, this occurs with the omission of the *Gloria* during the seasons of Advent and Lent. The absence of this joyful canticle marks the penitential character of these times, and its return in the vigils of Christmas and Easter, accompanied by the ringing of church bells, provides two of the most dramatic moments in the liturgical year.

Articulating the liturgical cycle entails a change of some kind. Musically speaking, Advent must sound differently from Christmastide. Here is where the Roman Catholic tradition of treating its sacred music as semantically distinct from the prayers it sets may bear some of its fruit. The words of these five Ordinary prayers may not change, but the musical setting may change with the season. The same prin-

---

[22] This seems particularly true in view of the Second Vatican Council's desire to bring Catholics closer to the actual Scriptures, which are the basic source of texts for the propers of the Roman Missal.

ciple of creating a context to define a semantic range, as that which has defined Mass propers and seasonal hymns, can work with Ordinary prayers. If a diocese provided that a different setting of *Kyrie eleison* be sung for Advent, for Christmas, for Lent, and so forth, and if they were sung with consistency year after year, within a generation that diocese would have a repertory of *Kyries* that connoted, or "felt like," Advent, Christmas, Lent, and all the rest.

The generous collection of Ordinaries found in the *Graduale Romanum*, the officially approved source for plainchants of the Roman Rite, hints here and there at such a seasonal strategy. The first set is entitled *Tempore Paschali* and designates one setting of the *Kyrie* for Sundays and another for feasts and memorials of the Easter season.[23] Another group of all Ordinaries except the *Credo* is designated for the feasts of the Apostles, another for solemnities and feasts of the Blessed Virgin Mary, another for Sundays of the year, another for Sundays in Advent and Lent, and another for weekdays in Advent and Lent.[24] Most of the Ordinary settings have no seasonal designation at all. Obviously, this is no thoroughgoing provision for the entire liturgical year, but the principle of a musical association is clearly there, and there is no reason why each season could not have its distinctive ways of singing the Ordinaries of the Mass.

Such a program may well be too ambitious for many places, although it certainly would be well within reach of any parish with a decent choir and knowledgeable director. But there are less ambitious means of accomplishing the same effect to a smaller degree. Rather than reflect each season distinctly, a program could aim to reflect more general tones, with plainer settings for Ordinary Time, solemn ones for Advent and Lent, and festive ones for Christmas and Easter, thus reducing the learning from five complete Ordinaries to three.

An even simpler alternative would exploit the special qualities of the church organ, "the traditional musical instrument, the sound of which can add a wonderful splendor to the church's ceremonies and can most effectively elevate people's spirits to God and things above," in the estimation of the Second Vatican Council (SC 120). Only one plainchant setting of each of the five Ordinary prayers need be learned. The seasonal distinctions would then be made by the organist.

---

[23] *Graduale Romanum*, "Pro dominicis," 710–11, and "Pro festis et memoriis," 711–12.

[24] Ibid., 725–27, 741–44, 748–51, 764–66, 767–68, respectively.

Once again, in Ordinary Time a simple modal accompaniment would do. In Advent and Lent it might be best to leave the organ off altogether, analogous to the omitted *Gloria*, rendering the plainchant in its purest, barest form, a kind of musical sackcloth that is still beautiful. And then the festival seasons would call for an exuberant harmonic arrangement. In each season the congregation would sing an unchanging melody setting unchanging words, while the musical vestment would move with the season.

The point of "seasonal" Ordinaries? Here, the power of music to provide a semantic range distinct from the words of the prayers can accomplish what the words by themselves would find most difficult: to symbolize the different time frames and historical referents that the liturgical year makes possible. The universality of the paschal sacrifice and Eucharist of each and every Mass is symbolized by the sameness of the words in these Ordinary prayers. They are always prayed; this drama is always played out. A distinct musical setting, disturbing this intimacy not in the least, enriches the universality of the liturgy with the particularities of the season, however blurred they may seem in such a verbal context. The liturgy would then own all the advantages: the specific symbolism of true propers and the more general affect of seasonal liturgical music.

Chapter 15

Understanding Musical Symbols: The Languages of Liturgy[*]

> One advantage of the traditional Latin ritual was that it could be performed by the most diverse groups and individuals, surmounting the divisions of age, sex, ethnicity, culture, economic status, or political affiliation.
> Victor Turner, anthropologist (1969)

Sacred music depends on language more than does any other kind of music. Part of this dependence is ontological. The purpose of sacred music is to praise, to give thanks, and to petition the infinite God in a mode that is beyond speech and yet remains a kind of speech. Words, sacred words, are essential to this purpose. The broad, vague semantic range of music alone, while also essential, is insufficient.

The other part of the dependence is structural. The syntactic and semantic relations of the sentence bind the tones into coherence. Take away the words from a plainchant of any religion, or from a piece of Roman Catholic classical polyphony, and the composition completely disintegrates, reduced to meaningless, meandering sequences of tones. The power of the great *Exsultet* chant that blesses the new light of Christ on the Easter Vigil comes mostly from its poetry, for the latter portion of its music is little more than a reiteration of common chanting formulas that are heard every Sunday of the year during the preface to the Eucharistic Prayer, a paradoxical illustration of why liturgy must be sung, since the music here is nonetheless essential for the *Exsultet*'s effect. The more modern Lutheran hymns, operatic settings, and popular folk sacred songs all enjoy a more robust, purely musical integration through harmonic structural techniques, and yet the vast majority of them cannot survive on their music alone.

The words chosen to sing at a liturgy are therefore an essential aspect of all liturgical music. This is why controversies over new

---

[*] Some passages in this chapter appeared as "Liturgical Latin Reconsidered," *Adoremus Bulletin* 9, no. 3 (May 2003): 13. Used by permission.

translations, texts, and usages continue to this day, as they have recurred throughout the centuries of the Roman Catholic tradition. This history has been driven by two issues: the use of traditional, classical language, primarily Latin, and the sources of the texts regardless of language.

Primary Sources

By far the greatest source of words for liturgical music for most every Christian tradition is the book of Psalms. This collection of 150 poetic prayers, many of which are traditionally ascribed to King David, enjoys a preeminence born of history and tradition. St. Paul advises the Christians of Colossae: "Let the word of Christ dwell in you richly, as in all wisdom you teach and admonish one another, singing psalms, hymns, and spiritual songs with gratitude in your hearts to God" (Col 3:16). Praying the Psalms was and still is the heart and soul of monasticism in both Eastern and Western traditions, the stricter orders singing the entire Psalter every week. Unison psalm singing by the entire congregation was the only kind of liturgical music allowed by John Calvin in his radical reform, and "lining out," a simple psalmody comprising a leader intoning a pair of psalm verses echoed immediately by the assembly, may still be heard in Scotland and the American South. It was the art of the psalm paraphrase that made the names and hymns of Isaac Watts and John Wesley immortal.

Early on, the Roman Catholic Mass was dominated by psalm singing. What we know today as the introit (entrance), offertory, and communion songs were once complete psalms, framed by other biblical sentences known as antiphons. As the liturgy coalesced into a single action elaborated by prayers proper to the occasion and the gradual addition of the Ordinary chants (*Kyrie, Gloria, Credo, Sanctus, Agnus Dei, Ite, missa est*), these liturgical psalms shrank to single verses, still surrounded by their antiphons. This happened also to the psalm sung between the readings, called the gradual or tract, depending on the liturgical season. The missals issued after the Second Vatican Council augmented the gradual tradition with a responsory psalm for cantor and congregation (the "responsorial psalm"), although only in the cases of the shortest psalms is it sung completely through.[1]

---

[1] It should be noted that singing the gradual remains an option for the Roman Rite. "In the dioceses of the United States of America, the following may also be

The historical precedence of the Psalms is logical, given Christianity's origin as a sect of Judaism and whose earliest liturgies owed much to Jewish practices.[2] Jesus and all his immediate disciples heard and sang psalms their whole lives. As the faithful developed their theological identity, particularly in regard to the Holy Trinity, these essentially Jewish prayers began to be concluded with a Christianizing epilogue known as the lesser doxology: "Glory be to the Father, the Son, and the Holy Spirit, as it was in the beginning, is now, and ever shall be, world without end."[3]

But history alone cannot explain the classic status of the Psalms, without which they would have fallen by the wayside, as did many other Jewish practices that were maintained for a time by the early church, only to be abandoned eventually. "In their prayed poetry, the Psalms display the whole range of human experiences, which become prayer and song in the presence of God. Lamentation, complaint, indeed accusation, fear, hope, trust, gratitude, joy—the whole of human life is reflected here, as it is unfolded in dialogue with God."[4] Only the christological is lacking, but even that may be remedied when the Psalter is read as all the Old Testament is read by traditional Christianity, as a grand prophecy to be fulfilled in the gospels.

As poems, however, the Psalms do not resonate with modern popular culture. Their metaphors are of the land, the desert, the geography of Palestine, nature, primitive agriculture, sacred history (especially the Exodus), and war. In their original Hebrew they do not rhyme systematically, nor have they isochronous lines or even meter, but they are instead organized by devices of parallelism. Thus, they correspond neither to modern poetic sensibility nor to modern musical structures. This has been well known since at least the sixteenth century, when even Calvin had to compromise their integrity by translating the Psalms into French and metricizing them for his best-selling

---

sung in place of the Psalm assigned in the *Lectionary for Mass*: either the proper or seasonal antiphon and Psalm from the *Lectionary*, as found either in the *Roman Gradual* or *Simple Gradual* or in another musical setting." General Instruction of the Roman Missal (Collegeville, MN: Liturgical Press), art. 61.

[2] See, for example, Joseph Ratzinger, *The Spirit of the Liturgy*, trans. John Saward (San Francisco: Ignatius Press, 2000), 139.

[3] A common translation of the most common Latin version of the lesser doxology, "Gloria Patri et Filio et Spiritui Sancto, sicut erat in principio et nunc et semper, et in saecula saeculorum."

[4] Ratzinger, *The Spirit of the Liturgy*, 139.

series of *Genevan Psalters*. Watts and Wesley did the same in English. In every case, of course, this reformation meant distortion.[5]

A thousand years in your eyes
    are merely a day gone by,
Before a watch passes in the night,
    you wash them away.
They sleep,
    and in the morning they sprout again
    like an herb.
In the morning it blooms only to pass away;
    in the evening it is wilted and withered.
 	
(Ps 90:4-6)
	A thousand ages in thy sight
	Are like an evening gone;
	Short as the watch that ends the
	    night
	Before the rising sun.
	Time like an ever rolling stream
	Bears all its sons away;
	They fly forgotten as a dream
	Dies at the op'ning day.
	
	(Watts, "O God Our Help In Ages Past")

These reformers understood that distortion in the form of regular phrase lengths and sturdy rhyme was the only way to adapt the Psalms to popular song forms—hymns—that the common, unlearned churchgoer could understand and quickly memorize. The only kind of music that can faithfully follow every poetic contour of the Hebrew or of a close translation is plainchant.[6]

Following the Psalms in prestige and propriety for sacred music are the canticles, a much smaller group of poems drawn from both Old and New Testaments. In Eastern celebrations of the Divine Office, the Nine Canticles, which include the Canticle of Moses (Exodus 15:1-19) and the Canticle of the Three Children (Daniel 3:57-88), occupy a prominent place. In Roman Catholic tradition, the three gospel

---

[5] Anthony Ruff notes that "an important German example of such metrical psalmody is the Catholic metrical Psalter, with all 150 psalms in rhymed meter with melodies, first issued by Fr. Kaspar Ulenberg in Cologne in 1582. It was often reprinted into the nineteenth century." It is unclear what role, if any, these psalms played in the Mass. See *Sacred Music and Liturgical Reform: Treasures and Transformations* (Chicago: Hillenbrand, 2007), 578.

[6] Classic polyphony, because of its extremely subtle metric structure, can also accommodate close translations without any distortion of the text. However, that same metric structure requires that the text be presented very slowly, requiring a long time for the singing of a single psalm, and so polyphonic settings of complete psalms are rare. They are too impractical.

canticles—the Canticle of Zechariah (traditionally known as the *Benedictus*, Luke 1:68-79), the Canticle of Mary (*Magnificat*, Luke 1:46-55), and the Canticle of Simeon (*Nunc dimittis*, Luke 1:29-32)—figure in three of the major offices: Lauds, Vespers, and Compline.

The biblical psalms and canticles taken together stand behind the lion's share of Catholic liturgical music for the past two millennia, particularly if all the popular adaptations and paraphrases are included. And yet both the Divine Office and the Mass draw liberally from other biblical sources for their music. Gospels and apostolic epistles are sung directly in classical or vernacular languages whenever the readings from the Lectionary are chanted, as they should be in a solemn celebration. Direct quotations from them and from other biblical books may also appear as introit, offertory, and communion antiphons.

Secondary Sources

Some essential Mass texts are not directly taken from Scripture, however, but are redactions or adaptations of it. The *Gloria* (Glory to God in the Highest) is a prose hymn stemming from the proclamation of the angels in the Gospel of Luke (2:14). The *Sanctus* (Holy, Holy, Holy) stitches together bits of Isaiah (6:3), the Gospel of Mark (11:9; cf. Matt 21:9), and the book of Revelation (4:8). The *Agnus Dei* (Lamb of God) derives from John the Baptist's salutation to Christ (John 1:29). Other Mass texts paraphrase the Scriptures, and others are freely composed. The line between free invention and paraphrase is difficult to draw precisely in some of the Mass propers. The text of the offertory antiphon *Vir erat*, for example, comes from the book of Job but is not a faithful quotation.[7] And the words of the *Credo* (I Believe in One God), composed by one Patriarch Paulinus of Aquileia in the eighth century following the proclamation of the Council of Nicea in 325 AD, do not appear in the Bible at all.

What warrants the appearance of nonbiblical texts in the sacred liturgy? Why should the Mass and Divine Office need anything other than the Word of God? John Henry Newman supplies the principal answer: a tradition of developing doctrine. As centuries pass and the

---

[7] The antiphon has "quem Satan petiit, ut tentaret: et data est ei potestas a Domino" [whom Satan sought to tempt: and he was given power by the Lord]. This text does not appear in the book of Job, but concentrates a more detailed account. I thank Fr. Jerome Weber for suggesting this example.

depths of the Scriptures are discerned with ever-greater clarity, new truths, which never contradict but build upon more ancient ones, are revealed to the faithful, truths that have their roots in Scripture but grow forth at some remove. These find musical expression in the liturgy. It is true that the primary purpose of liturgical music is latreutic, not didactic, but we worship what we believe to be true—*lex orandi lex credendi*—and so the development of doctrine beyond the literal text of Scripture must give rise to prayer that acknowledges it.[8]

The first explosion of such development was set off by the revelation of the New Testament itself. Just as the Psalter commemorates the salvation of God's people in the Exodus story, so must Christian liturgical music commemorate the salvific events of the Gospel. But because it is almost entirely prose, the New Testament lends itself to musical setting even less well than the Psalms. To be sure, there are some canticles and hymn texts, but for popular usage even these must be translated and metricized. Thus, the following hymn text adapts the Pauline proclamation of the Logos:

Because of this, God greatly exalted him and bestowed on him the name that is above every name, that at the name of Jesus every knee should bend, of those in heaven and on earth and under the earth, and every tongue confess that Jesus Christ is Lord, to the glory of God the Father. (Phil 2:9-11)	At the Name of Jesus Ev'ry knee shall bow, Ev'ry tongue confess him King of glory now; 'Tis the Father's pleasure We should call him Lord, Who from the beginning Was the mighty Word. (C. Noel)

The Sacramentary used to celebrate the Mass, and any good hymnal for that matter, has texts that praise the Trinity, Mary and the saints, and the Eucharist, as well as other songs that reflect upon themes of the New Testament. And so we have the repertory of Christmas carols and Easter carols that rarely quote the Bible while recalling the Gospel accounts. Liturgical actions too, such as the collects and prayers over

---

[8] For a history of this relation, see Kevin W. Irwin, *Context and Text: Method in Liturgical Theology* (Collegeville, MN: Liturgical Press, 1994).

the offering, the sources of the Gregorian chant tradition, are typically expressed with nonbiblical language, as New Testament prayers directly associated with the Eucharist are very few.

And then there have arisen from time to time new devotions and prayers, such as the Canticle of St. Francis and the *Stabat Mater*, which is sung in many versions in the Stations of the Cross devotion. This is to say nothing of specific petitions and praises: *Veni Creator Spiritus* (Come Holy Ghost), "For All the Saints," and this following curiosity are all examples:

> "Come, follow me," says Christ the Lord, "All in my way abiding;
> Deny yourselves and hear my word, obey my call and guiding.
> O bear the cross what e'er betide; take my example for your guide."
> (Johann N. Scheffler; trans. C. W. Schaeffer)[9]

Every age brings new perils, new joys, new saints, and therefore new prayers.

Biblical adaptations, free recompositions, and nonbiblical prayers are motivated by the faith and doctrine that stand behind them. Most of these needs were long met by the plainchant tradition, which sings prose with ease and covers most any liturgical action. But elaborate plainchants were not for the common congregant, and so the great flowering of hymnody through the centuries also responded to the development of doctrine and changing devotional emphases, within the liturgy and without.

There is, and always has been, a conflict between the constant and praiseworthy upwelling of spiritual devotion lifted to God in the popular hymns and song forms on the one hand and orthodoxy on the other.[10] Recalling how the Eastern and Western Christian churches finally sundered over a single word, *filioque*, in 1054, we realize that words are important and orthodoxy can be a subtle and learned thing. This is why most popular expressions found homes in saint's day processions, devotional fraternities, domestic use, and other extraliturgical devotions through most of the history of the church and why the numerous sequences and popular tropes that had indeed seeped into the Mass over centuries were omitted from the new missals published

---

[9] The full text appears in *Hymns, Psalms and Spiritual Canticles*, compiled, edited, and arranged by Theodore Marier (Belmont, MA: BACS Publishing, 1972), no. 134.

[10] For more on this conflict, see chaps. 10 and 18.

after the Council of Trent, beginning in 1570. Because such accretions could obscure the paschal action of the liturgy, historically such texts were kept at arm's length. And so the wisdom of the Second Vatican Council fathers only reflected the long tradition when they approved article 121 of the liturgical constitution: "The texts intended to be sung must always be in conformity with catholic doctrine. Indeed, they should be drawn chiefly from the sacred scripture and from liturgical sources." This is simple prudence. We pray as we believe and we believe as we pray.

But prudence was largely ignored. After the council, the general anxiety to do something dramatic very quickly led to hasty translations of the Latin Ordinary prayers into vernacular languages and the practical suppression of the propers and their music, replacing them with hundreds of new songs. What are these song texts like?

Some composers of popular liturgical music, to their credit, have bravely carried on the traditions of paraphrasing the Psalms, adapting salient gospel passages, such as the Beatitudes, or resetting traditional texts, such as the Canticle of St. Francis. The musical problems of the folk-revival style remain to undermine the positive effects of such worthy texts, of course, but such compositions have at minimum tried to carry out the wishes of article 121.[11]

Others have not done so. The article's "chiefly" allows the occasional invention that is neither biblical nor liturgical.[12] Composers are to rely on biblical and liturgical texts simply to guarantee "conformity with catholic doctrine."

Perhaps that safeguard is not strong enough. Quoting the Bible without sufficient context can be a dangerous thing, as the fundamentalists have taught us so well. Thomas Day has criticized with some justice what he calls the "I am the voice of God" song, which features the biblical text, usually the words of Jesus himself, "usually without quotation marks, in a somewhat bored, relaxed, almost casual style. This is startling and unprecedented in the history of Christianity."[13]

To be sure, there are a small number of traditional hymn texts that use

---

[11] See chap. 3 on the technical problems of the folk-revival style and its descendants.

[12] The original Latin is *potissimum*, which might also be translated as "most of all."

[13] Thomas Day, *Why Catholics Can't Sing: The Culture of Catholicism and the Triumph of Bad Taste* (New York: Crossroad, 1992), 64.

the Savior's words or paraphrases of them, as does the last hymn quoted above, "Come Follow Me." But there the author has taken care to insert right at the beginning the key phrase "says Christ the Lord," which confesses the lordship of the God-Man and at the same moment makes the congregation singing the hymn declare, "This is not me talking."

From a near conflation of believers in God with God himself in the "I am the voice of God" song, it is but a short step to self-idolatry:

> I myself am the bread of life
> You and I are the bread of life,
> Taken and blessed, broken and shared by Christ
> That the world might live.[14]

Even the most charitable reading of this paraphrase of John 6:51 cannot avoid the impression of the congregation abrogating to itself some salvific power of the Eucharist. From here it is hard to imagine a greater offense, except to forget about the author of the liturgy completely:

> We come to share our story, we come to break the bread,
> We come to know our rising from the dead.[15]

This refrain, set to a "traditional Hawaiian" tune, has five verses to go with it, within which the first person plural "we" is sung nine times. Singing the refrain six times around the verses would bring the total of "we"s to twenty-seven iterations. "God," "Christ," "Lord," and "Jesus" never appear at all, the author evidently satisfied with a few unidentified uses of the second person singular, such as "your people." There is an "Alleluia" in the final verse. The refrain credits no one else for "our rising," appears instead to make ourselves the agent of the sacrament, and leaves unanswered why "our story" should be central

---

[14] Refrain of "Bread of Life," by Rory Cooney. © 1987, OCP Publications, 5536 NE Hassalo, Portland, OR 97213. All rights reserved. Used by permission.

[15] Refrain of "Song of the Body of Christ," by David Haas (Chicago: GIA, 1989). It is true that the title of a work, especially an instrumental work (no words), contextualizes what is heard to some extent, so we may be grateful that the egocentrism of this lyric may be mitigated somewhat. However, it is my experience that congregants remember the words that they sing far better than the title that they do not.

to the liturgy, or indeed, of the slightest interest to anyone outside the congregation.

Who is worshiped in these songs? What do they imply about who God is, who we are, the origin of the liturgy, and the proper relationships that obtain between creature and Creator? "It appears that the congregation is in love with itself."[16] If *lex orandi lex credendi* is a true principle, if we believe that if we pray something often enough we come to believe it, then the 1992 Gallup poll finding that "only 30 percent of those [American Catholics] surveyed believe they are actually receiving the Body and Blood, soul and divinity of the Lord Jesus Christ under the appearance of bread and wine" is hardly surprising.[17] Such lyrics should never come anywhere near the liturgy.

Why, then, do they? In part because "the four hymns" of the liturgy have become the dominant form of new liturgical music in the Western world, and their content is largely uncontrolled. To review the history a bit, the so-called entrance, offertory, communion, and recessional "hymns" are technically replacements for the proper introit, offertory, and communion antiphons for the specific Sunday or feast.[18] Since the 1960s, it is almost the universal practice in the United States to overlook the traditional instruction to sing psalms at these places in the liturgy and use the fourth option, "a suitable liturgical song similarly approved by the Conference of Bishops or the Diocesan Bishop."[19] In short, we find ourselves in the midst of one of those periods like the Middle Ages when the upwelling of popular sacred music overwhelms the liturgy. While medieval tropes and sequences obscured the central action as moss hides a rock, by sheer weight of textual elaboration, today's songs may obscure it by a kind of doctrinal fog.

Composers, because they are not often trained theologians, rely on episcopal offices for guidance, and when that fails, on the reigning liturgical *Zeitgeist*. If they understand from experience and proclamation that "Liturgy, as the public worship of the church, celebrates who we are and who we are called to be because of God's love for us in

---

[16] Day, *Why Catholics Can't Sing*, 66.

[17] A New York Times poll of 1994 found similar results. Both polls are critiqued by James D. Davidson in "Yes, Jesus is Really There," *Commonweal* 138, no. 17 (October 12, 2001): 14–16.

[18] Any music after the dismissal "Go in peace" is a modern invention with little liturgical precedent.

[19] See chap. 6 for complete text and details.

Jesus Christ," then it is no wonder that "we" is the center of worship in their lyrics.[20] How very far this seems from the Second Vatican Council's vision of liturgy: "The liturgy, then, is rightly seen as an exercise of the priestly office of Jesus Christ. In the liturgy the sanctification of women and men is given expression in symbols perceptible by the senses and is carried out in ways appropriate to each of them. In it, complete and definitive public worship is performed by the mystical body of Jesus Christ, that is, by the Head and his members" (SC 7). Song texts that are secularist, merely humanist, and insidiously idolatrous will persist as long as this defining teaching of *Sacrosanctum Concilium* remains unknown. *Lex orandi lex credendi.*

Sacred Classical Language

In the nineteenth and twentieth centuries, the use of the Latin language in the Roman Rite became a live issue. Many in the liturgical movement favored following the Protestants and introducing vernacular languages to pray the Mass. It was probably the single most contentious issue in the discussions surrounding *Sacrosanctum Concilium*, the first major document approved by the Second Vatican Council, and while articles 36 and 54 preserved the preeminent role of Latin in the sacred liturgy, they also provided enough exceptions to the norm to leave the defenders of liturgical Latin with only a Pyrrhic victory and to spark the explosion of vernacular translations and uses of the Roman Rite in the 1960s.[21] Indeed, for some time it appeared that ecclesiastical Latin would entirely disappear from active use on the face of the earth, except in an office in Vatican City where the most important documents were translated into Latin. It would thus resign its honored position as the classical sacred language of the Roman Catholic Church and join Sumerian, Old English, and the countless other lost tongues of humanity that are truly dead.[22]

---

[20] Mark Francis, *Shape a Circle Ever Wider: Liturgical Inculturation in the United States* (Chicago: Liturgy Training Publications, 2000), 20.

[21] See chap. 2 for the texts of these articles.

[22] Although ancient Greek, Latin, Sanskrit and other religious languages are often called "dead," they are still in active use as long as they are maintained in religious rites. I prefer the term "sacred classical" or just "classical." "Dead" languages are those such as Old English that have no role whatever in human activity, except perhaps in the lives of a few scholars who only read and never speak them.

The effect of this demise on the treasury of traditional sacred music could have been disastrous. Because virtually all plainchant of the Gregorian tradition, classical polyphony, and symphonic Masses of later centuries set the Latin text, a total insistence on the vernacular and only the vernacular would have locked up almost all of this treasure in the archives for good.

And then a strange thing happened. Interest in liturgical Latin began to revive, most notoriously within the schismatic Society of St. Pius X led by Marcel Lefebvre, but also in choir schools and other places where the sacred treasures of Roman Catholic music were practiced, and in quiet requests in various parts for permission to use the so-called Tridentine Mass, last published in the 1962 Missal. *Ecclesia Dei Adflicta* of Pope John Paul II (July 2, 1988) began to allow its celebration in limited circumstances. In 2007, Latin made headlines when Pope Benedict XVI released his *Summorum Pontificum*, making this "extraordinary Roman Rite" available wherever there could be found a priest competent to celebrate it.[23] What brings on this resurrection of this "dead" language?

In its formative stages in the first centuries of Christianity, the sacred liturgy was a polyglot affair, with prayers, psalms, sermons, songs, and acclamations in a mixture of Hebrew, Greek, Aramaic, and Latin, among other tongues, depending on the time and place of the celebration. But in the Roman Empire of that time, Greek and Latin were politically and culturally the dominant languages, and they became the most common ones for the liturgy.[24] Later in the church of Rome, Latin, as "the sole language of culture," slowly took over the majority

---

[23] Many commentators read this as a return of the Latin Mass and a rejection of the conciliar reforms. Nothing could be further from the truth. It was always permitted to any priest since the council to celebrate the Mass in Latin as long as he used the *novus ordo*, the new rite of the 1970 Missal that put in concrete form the ideals of the *Sacrosanctum Concilium*.

Contrary to popular belief, the council had nothing to say about the priest facing away from the people, postures, or a number of other features associated with the "old Mass." The aspect of active participation by the congregation is more complex, however, and would seem to require reevaluation should the Tridentine Rite become widespread.

[24] Even then, Aidan Nichols points outs that "that outstanding student of patristic language Christine Mohrmann had described the whole of the earliest eucharistic terminology" in a dialect of Greek distinct from everyday Greek. *Looking at the Liturgy: A Critical View of Its Contemporary Form* (Francisco: Ignatius Press, 1996), 101–2.

of prayer in the Mass during a period that extended from the third to sixth centuries.[25] At that time, Latin was the vernacular language of Rome and its environs, less so as distance from the western capital city increased. But while local variants continued for centuries, St. Jerome's Latin Bible, the Council of Nicaea, and the maturity of liturgical traditions gradually fixed liturgical prayers and readings in a permanent state. The everyday speech of the surrounding culture, of course, had no such anchors and continued to evolve slowly into medieval Latin, Tuscan, Venetian, Occitan, French, and all the other romance descendants of classical Latin.[26] Thus, liturgical Latin evolved by standing still, linguistically speaking, into a classical sacred language. Like all languages, Latin gathers its semantic store through its associated usages from real life, and if that usage is limited to the Divine Office and Mass, it will seem more and more "sacred" with each passing century.[27]

This development mimicked similar ones in all the major world religions. "It is sometimes forgotten by the advocates of a vernacular liturgy that our Lord as a Palestinian Jew never attended a strictly vernacular service in His life. Alike in the temple and the synagogue the Jewish services in Palestine were in the liturgical Hebrew, which was not understood by the people without special instruction."[28] The Jews have their ancient Hebrew, the Hindus their Sanskrit, the Muslims their seventh-century Arabic, the Byzantines their biblical Greek, the Orthodox churches their Church Slavonic. In every case, these languages, used in the holiest rites of their respective religions, were once vernaculars but now are utterly foreign to their modern adherents. This fact places the aftermath of the Second Vatican Council in an odd

---

[25] Joseph A. Jungmann, SJ, *The Mass of the Roman Rite: Its Origins and Development*, first ed. 1951, trans. Francis A. Brunner, 2 vols. (Westminster, Maryland: Christian Classics, Inc., 1986), 44.

[26] "Classical" in the sense that it was fixed. The Latin of Rome in the fourth century AD was already markedly different from the Latin at the time of Augustus and Tiberius Caesar when Jesus lived, just as today's American English is markedly different from Shakespeare's or John Winthrop's, from which it descended.

[27] Until the time of the Enlightenment, Latin was used elsewhere by the educated classes in all kinds of academic writing and a steadily diminishing stream of literature. But literate people were a small minority, and most of those were clerics of one sort or another. Most people who heard Latin heard it in church or used by churchmen.

[28] Gregory Dix, *The Shape of the Liturgy* (London: Dacre Press, 1945), 616.

perspective: the abandonment of Latin, the Roman Church's classical liturgical language, made Catholicism the one world religion without one. The eighteenth-century London cultural critic Joseph Addison once wondered why intelligent men and women of his time paid good money to hear three-hour dramatic presentations—Italian operas by Handel, Vivaldi, etc.—in a language that none could understand. We might ask the same question of the world's religions. Why have sacred languages?[29]

Gravitas

Consider the following oration:

Four score and seven years ago our fathers brought forth on this continent, a new nation, conceived in Liberty, and dedicated to the proposition that all men are created equal. Now we are engaged in a great civil war, testing whether that nation, or any nation so conceived and so dedicated, can long endure. We are met on a great battle-field of that war. We have come to dedicate a portion of that field, as a final resting place for those who here gave their lives that that nation might live. It is altogether fitting and proper that we should do this.	Eighty-seven years ago our predecessors started a new nation on this land based on Liberty and the idea that everyone is created equal. Now we are fighting a big civil war to see if any nation founded on these ideas can last for long. We are meeting on a great battlefield of that war. We have come to dedicate part of that field as a cemetery for those who gave their lives here so that the nation would live. This is a good thing to do.

It is essential to understand that Abraham Lincoln's Gettysburg Address, given in the left column, is in English, but it is not in the vernacular. Lincoln spoke in his own vernacular, a rhetorical form of nineteenth-century American English. This is no longer spoken in the United States. No one says "four score" in normal conversation to

---

[29] I recognize that vernacular languages are frequently used in all these religions, of course, but no world religion has completely and purposefully abandoned its tradition of sacred language in the way that Roman Catholicism nearly did after the council, unless one counts the 1979 Book of Common Prayer in the United States and its analogues elsewhere.

mean "eighty"; most Americans would not even understand it. "Final resting place" would be understood by most Americans today, but is clearly poetic, not vernacular, to be uttered in very particular circumstances, such as a funeral oration.

The right column presents a translation of Lincoln's address into today's vernacular American English. Nothing of the original literal meaning is lost; indeed, this version is more readily comprehended by the average American than Lincoln's original words. But the speech has lost instead most of its impressive weight. The Gettysburg Address is as close to Sacred Scripture as American political discourse comes, yet to sense this quality we must hear the original, old, even anachronistic expressions and turns of phrase. "Eighty-seven" has the same literal meaning (denotation) as "four score and seven" but not the same connotations, connotations which have symbolic power that comes in part from recognizing that we are hearing a historical language, a voice from the past. This psychic distance of Lincoln's language, the sense that it is not right there, that all is not on the surface, that we might have to think and work a little to open ourselves to its evocative allusions, is all part of its solemn affect. Linguist and bishop Peter Elliott comments on the rightness of the occasional esotericism in liturgical translation: "The slightly incomprehensible word 'oblation' sets up the mystery of the sacrifice. The very fact that it is not directly accessible suggests a meaning that is mysterious, something inviting us to go further, something provoking wonder, leading us deeper into the Mystery of Faith."[30]

And that is why no one attending a civil Memorial Day commemoration would prefer hearing a vernacular version of the Gettysburg address over the original, even though some of the original's literal meaning might escape comprehension. "Rites that do not allow a sense of distance deny *to the people*, paradoxically, a means of appropriating the act of worship, crippling them just at the point where they could be taking off Godward by a leap of religious imagination."[31] In its quotidian informality, the vernacular destroys almost all sense of

---

[30] Peter Elliott "Liturgical Translation: A Question of Truth," *Antiphon* 10, no. 3 (2006): 228–38; repr., *Adoremus Bulletin* 13, no. 4 (June 2007): 4. Aidan Nichols points out that sociologists have been aware of this for some time: "A certain opacity is essential to symbolic action in the sociologists' account, so that to attempt to render symbols wholly transparent is, to their mind, a thoroughly misguided proceeding." *Looking at the Liturgy*, 61.

[31] Nichols, *Looking at the Liturgy*, 65; emphasis in the original.

there being a ceremony at all.[32] For this reason, thousands of Anglican Christians mourned the loss of the "rolling sentences" of Tudor English and left their congregations when the Rite II order of worship came to dominate the latest revisions of the Book of Common Prayer.[33] They could not bear to face the loss of their sacred language—Tudor English—and its replacement by the lamest of vernacular translations. Roman Catholics know this drama well, for they played it out in the 1960s. The rash translations of the International Committee on English in the Liturgy were not only inaccurate but common. Banality choked poetry. Latin is poised to reappear in the Roman Rite because it provides the gravity, solemnity, and beauty that centuries of association with the divine liturgy, that is, tradition, endow a sacred language.

Understanding

Immediacy of comprehension has always been the primary, if not sole, argument of proponents of the vernacular. "The Council's call for full, active participation by congregations created the context for the present problem. This pastoral goal was closely linked to the need for comprehension, which resulted in a swift transition to a vernacular liturgy throughout the United States."[34] And there are surely circumstances when a direct, unmediated comprehension of what is spoken is for the best, such as in homilies or the Scripture readings at Mass. When we hear in the parable of the Prodigal Son that while the son "was still a long way off, his father caught sight of him and was filled with compassion. He ran to his son, embraced him and kissed him" (Luke 15:20), or when we hear that when Jesus appeared in Emmaus, "he took bread, said the blessing, broke it, and gave it to them. With that their eyes were opened and they recognized him" (Luke 24:30-31), nothing less than an instant and effortless understanding of the events

---

[32] Again, Bishop Elliot: "We imagine that we are conveying everything—nothing is concealed, no mysteries here—when in fact very little is being conveyed at all. When this happens, the Mass becomes boring, especially for the young." "Liturgical Translation: A Question of Truth," 4.

[33] "Rite II" in the United States; in England, "Series 3." See Buchanan, "The Winds of Change," in *The Oxford Guide to The Book of Common Prayer: A Worldwide Survey*, eds. Charles Hefling and Cynthia Shattuck (New York: Oxford University Press, 2006), 236.

[34] Miriam Therese Winter, *Why Sing? Toward a Theology of Catholic Church Music* (Washington, DC: The Pastoral Press, 1984), 5.

portrayed will allow their full power to strike.[35] But Bishop Elliot's comment on translation, as well as a great deal of human experience, suggest that "understanding the Mass" is a much richer phenomenon than the surface meaning of utterances.

A parable of a Vietnamese immigrant. One Sunday, a reporter from the New York Times appeared at the solemn Mass at St. Patrick's Cathedral in New York City. A lifelong agnostic, he had nevertheless scheduled an interview the next day with the Cardinal Archbishop of New York regarding certain recent political pronouncements, and he thought it might be wise to hear what the Archbishop had to say in his homily. Since he was a very fine writer, he understood every word spoken in the English-language liturgy. In his homily, however, the Archbishop did not speak on any political issue, but on true poverty of spirit, since the gospel reading was Luke 18:10-13, the story of the Pharisee and the tax collector, and the reporter from the New York Times went home unsatisfied. At the same Mass, not far from the reporter in the large cathedral, there happened to be a young woman who had emigrated from her native Vietnam and had arrived in New York the preceding day. She knew not a word of English. But her heart lifted when the Archbishop intoned and the choir and congregation sang *Gloria in excelsis Deo*, and she bowed her head reverently during the consecration, gave a radiant smile to all nearby during the sign of peace, and received the sacrament, the first in her new country, with moist eyes. She felt at home. Who, the reporter or the immigrant, better understood the Mass?

The vernacular argument stands on one dimension of understanding: the direct comprehension of the literal meaning of the words spoken. This dimension is hardly trivial, as the two gospel passages just cited attest, but it is singular and forgets that prayer is an action of many dimensions. Whether the prayer is spoken or sung, whether the priest holds his hands over the chalice or in the *orans* position, whether the congregants pray along or simply respond "Amen," the time of day, the season of the year, the scent of incense, the sound of bells, all these are part of the prayer. The prayer is an action, and in this action the literal meaning of its words may take second place to what happens, to how it is prayed. Christ did not command, "Say this in memory of me," but "Do this in memory of me" (Luke 22:19). This

---

[35] Jokes work in an analogous manner. If you have to translate a joke that you are hearing in a foreign language as you hear it, you will never laugh at the punch line.

is why most attentive Catholics can recall the gospel reading of the last Mass they attended but cannot recall what the collect or post-Communion prayer asked for. It is important to understand, right away, what the gospel says; at other points of the liturgy, it is more important that prayer is done with due solemnity. This is how the Vietnamese immigrant understood the essential action that is the liturgy without understanding a single word of it, while the reporter, who comprehended without effort every utterance, missed everything.

In retrospect, it is hard to see why the direct comprehension argument, the readings and homily excepted, swept away liturgical Latin to near extinction. Even in the days of the council, and well before it, cheap paper and printing had put missals with facing translations of the Latin in the hands of Catholics throughout the developed world. Today's technology makes liturgical materials more flexible than ever. If a Latin plainchant were presented and distributed like the following, who could reasonably object that the people cannot understand what they sing?

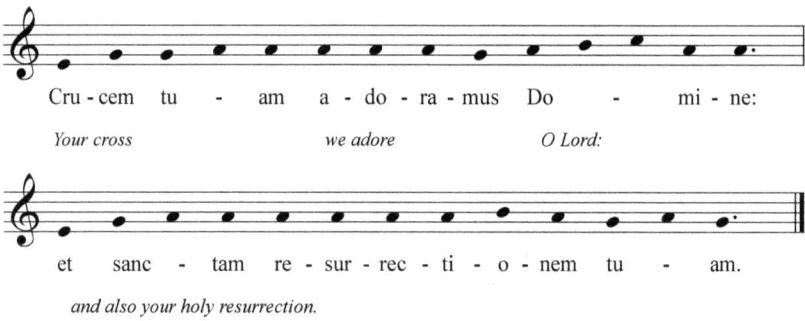

Example 15-1. Latin plainchant *Crucem tuam* with translation below.

Perhaps the psychic distance of Latin betokens a relationship between God and man that we, in the hubris of our times, like the popular song texts above, no longer wish to acknowledge. Perhaps direct comprehension is a kind of accidental stalking horse for what the vernacular has become: a political symbol that is particularly potent for those who came of age during or just following the Second Vatican Council? Vernaculars represent openness, reform, and renewal; Latin represents the old ways, the Church reluctant to divulge its secrets. The symbolism is not rational. Symbols seldom are.

Do such attitudes explain a number of common misunderstandings about liturgical Latin? The worst of these, which has known little contradiction from the episcopacy, is that the council banned Latin. This assumption naturally leads to the conclusion that the restoration of Latin is a rejection of the conciliar reforms and thus to the prejudice just outlined. Another misconception is that parishioners would be forced to "learn" Latin if it were restored to the liturgy, a task too onerous to impose. The fact is that liturgical Latin does not require the learning of the entire language in anything like the way one learns French in order to study or work in France. The commitment to learning the three short Ordinary prayers recited at every Mass—the *Kyrie*, the *Sanctus*, the *Agnus Dei*—amounts to a grand total of three Greek and thirty-two Latin words, less than a week's vocabulary assignment for a single lesson in a language course. Is this really beyond us? Are Jewish children who learn key Hebrew responses in their yeshivas, Hindus who study Sanskrit at summer camp, and Orthodox who can sing the *Trisagion* really so much cleverer than Catholics?[36]

The Moving Target

The revision of the 1979 Book of Common Prayer for Anglicans was not the first such revision, although it was the most radical by far. No, that book replaced the 1928 Book of Common Prayer, which in turn replaced one published in 1892. The succession traces back to the foundational books of 1662 and 1549, the latter proudly proclaiming that it had replaced the Latin of the Roman Church with "the vulgar tongue." Why so many revisions? Some were made to accommodate changes in liturgical form and practice, but others were required by the nature of vernacular language. The 1789 version published at the dawn of the American republic, for example, substituted "Our Father, who" for "Our Father, which," and "those who trespass" for "them that trespass."[37]

---

[36] Some might point out that those world religions are not evangelical in the way Christianity is supposed to be, arguing that the vernacular is necessary for the spread of the Gospel message. Surely the message itself is best conveyed in the vernacular, always and everywhere, but liturgical Latin seems not to have retarded in the least the explosive periods of evangelization that the histories of northern Europe, Latin America, Africa, and southeast Asia reveal. Moreover, as we have seen, the message is more than words.

[37] Marion J. Hatchett, "The Colonial States of America," in *The Oxford Guide to The Book of Common Prayer: A Worldwide Survey*, ed. Charles Hefling and Cynthia

For the vernacular is constantly on the move, intrinsically unstable. By definition, the vernacular is the plain, everyday speech of ordinary people, a system in constant flux. The only guarantee that a vernacular tongue of a given date and place can provide is that it will not be the vernacular eighty, fifty, twenty years hence. Just look at the preceding paragraph: "vulgar" in 1549 meant "popular," and it surely does not mean that now. And so, once a classical liturgical language is abandoned for the sake of direct comprehension by means of a vernacular, the task of maintaining the liturgy in the vernacular never ends. The 1979 Book of Common Prayer is not the last word by any means, for in 2029 its language will no longer be vernacular, and so keeping the Anglican liturgy in the vernacular will require a new revision. Catholics have learned this hard lesson only recently. Even now, translations of the Psalter, Lectionary, and Missal have gone through several versions, none in concordance with any approved translation of the Bible, and all fraught with controversy, because changes in language always elicit strong feelings.[38] The anguish that the English-speaking Catholic Church in 2011 suffered over the first Missal revision since 1970 is but the harbinger of many conflicts about translation. This is the eternal fate of liturgical vernaculars.

A classical liturgical language, such as ancient Greek, Church Slavonic, or Latin, on the other hand, brings with it the gift of stability. Its only context, the only place where it is used, is liturgy, and so it does not change as street language changes. "Lift up your hearts" may lose its force over time and require a new translation to get it back: "Fire up your hearts" or "Launch your spirits" are perhaps just around the corner. Or, who knows, perhaps it may take on some salacious connotation someday. But *sursum corda* will never change its meaning and will always have the same gravity and solemnity of expression as long as its context remains singular, as part of the invitation to the eucharistic prayer of the Mass. This is why Pope Pius XII declared Latin to be "an effective antidote for any corruption of doctrinal truth."[39]

Shattuck (New York: Oxford University Press, 2006), 179.

[38] This confusing state of affairs is explained by Susan Benofy in "Singing the Mass: We Cannot Say That One Song Is as Good as Another," *Adoremus Bulletin* 13, no. 8 (November 2007): 3–5.

[39] Pius XII, *Mediator Dei*, art. 60.

And because classical liturgical languages are never used apart from liturgy, they offer another gift: neutrality. Latin is nobody's native speech. In that sense, it is foreign to everyone, even those who pray in it, and operates at some remove from everyone's experience.[40] That is precisely its virtue for liturgical solemnity: "In the East, mystery in worship is maintained largely by the iconostasis.[41] In the West, the Latin language functioned as a kind of iconostasis of language. Coupled with the celebration of Mass *ad orientem*, the Roman Rite retained the sense of a holy mystery that the East maintained through the universal liturgical paradox of concealing so as to reveal."[42]

When a Japanese and an American converse in English, the relationship between the conversants is not quite equal. The American holds a position of authority in respect of his native knowledge of American English, a knowledge that the Japanese would not dream of questioning. That is why, a professor of German once related, Valerie Giscard d'Estaing, President of France, and Helmut Schmidt, Chancellor of Germany, chose to speak English during their summit meetings even though d'Estaing knew German and Schmidt knew French. Neither wanted to concede the linguistic advantage to the other, so they chose a neutral language, that is, one in which neither was a native authority.[43] When the Japanese Catholic attends an English Mass in the United States, he worships with that kind of linguistic disadvantage. Though it does not entail that they "understand" the liturgy any better, as the parable showed, the Americans present at the Mass are linguistically closer to the great prayer of the Mass.

Let us move to St. Peter's Basilica, Vatican City, on Trinity Sunday of 2002 at the High Mass at 10:30 a.m. There are devout Catholics there of every color and size, from every corner of the earth. The processional hymn is a *Te Deum* sung to the tune of "Holy God, We Praise Thy Name." There are verses in Italian, English, German, and French, each of which favors a small segment of the congregation. The only music

---

[40] This might be true even for those who know a foreign language well. I read German quite well, for example, and when hearing the saccharine commentary in the Bach cantatas and passions, I am not so sorry that it is not my native speech.

[41] The iconostasis is a screen that stands between the altar and the congregation. In some Orthodox rites, doors are opened to allow viewing during the Eucharistic prayer.

[42] Elliot, "Liturgical Translation: A Question of Truth," 3–4.

[43] Related in the class given by Professor Bruce Duncan at Dartmouth College in 1976.

that unites us all in song—that is, for those of us who have been taught to sing them—are the Latin chants for the *Sanctus* and *Agnus Dei*. For Latin is a neutral language. It is the native property of no nation, of no culture, of no person.

And as such it rightfully owns, paradoxically, the title of the universal language of the church.[44] Latin's position recalls what Lazar Ludwik Zamenhof hoped for his brainchild, Esperanto, his designer language invented at the turn of the twentieth century, which Zamenhof hoped would become the world's common language and thus an agent for world peace. "I have given my all for a single great idea, a single dream—the dream of the unity of humankind."[45] As an artificial language, it could be native to no one but must be learned as a second language by all and thus confer a linguistic equality on all. As long as the world knows no native common speech, vernaculars in liturgy can only unite individual linguistic communities at best, and they must at the same time isolate one from another in the wider world. As global migration increases apace, more and more parishes will experience linguistic divisions, and by using one vernacular or another, they will put someone in attendance in the second tier.[46] Or, like St. Stanislaus in Toronto, they might offer one Mass in English and the rest in Polish each weekend, so that many parishioners never meet one another in the great public work that is the liturgy. Latin, the neutral and universal sacred language, is the only reasonable choice for a language to symbolize the essential unity of the Roman Rite throughout the world.[47]

---

[44] As such, at least one church historian has argued that Latin is a unifying symbol: "While it seemed to express the timelessness of the Church, its uniformity had also helped unify the diverse ethnic and language groups that made up the American Catholic Church." See Gerald P. Fogarty, "North America," in *Modern Catholicism: Vatican II and After*, ed. Adrian Hastings (New York: Oxford University Press, 1991), 326.

[45] Pierre Janton, *Esperanto: Language, Literature, and Community*, ed. Humphrey Tonkin, trans. Humphrey Tonkin, Jane Edwards, and Karen Johnson-Weiner (Albany: State University of New York Press, 1993), 24.

[46] This is true even in macaronic (mixed language) liturgies in which any expressions unknown to some congregants are used. If the *Gloria* is sung in Spanish and the psalm in English to accommodate two linguistic groups within a parish, that means only that the English speakers will be excluded from the *Gloria* and the Spanish speakers from the psalm. The exclusions are momentary, but no less real.

[47] The objection that Latin would be a Western cultural imposition on the non-Western parts of the world will not stand scrutiny, because it confuses cultural his-

This is an ideal solution to be sure, but one that can be executed in small steps, compromises, and concessions to the human realities of language learning and local circumstances. The fathers at the Second Vatican Council wrote such prudence into *Sacrosanctum Concilium*.

> A suitable place may be allotted to the vernacular in Masses which are celebrated with the people, especially in the readings and "the common prayer," and also, as local conditions may warrant, in those parts which pertain to the people . . .
> Nevertheless care must be taken to ensure that the faithful may also be able to say or to sing together in Latin those parts of the ordinary of the Mass which pertain to them. (SC 54)

This is a vision of macaronic liturgy, a liturgy with words in a variety of tongues. The idea was criticized in the early aftermath of the constitution's promulgation as being somehow nonsensical to mix in a single liturgy, for example, Latin and English, even though Catholics have known such polyglot liturgies from the beginning.[48] The proponents of the vernacular who claim that it is strange and too difficult to worship God in a foreign language forget that "amen" and "alleluia" are all foreign words, while "hallowed be Thy Name" is an archaism. These cause no trouble. Why not? Because we have heard them since our youth and so they have become, for all practical purposes, part of the English language that we know. If Catholics the world over could bother to learn and teach their children the thirty-five words comprising the *Kyrie*, the *Sanctus*, and the *Agnus Dei*, chanted to the simple plainchant settings published in Pope Paul VI's little collection *Jubilate Deo*, in a generation those chants would feel just as comfortable as "Amen." Idealistic? It has already happened in the rural parish of St. Malachy's in upstate New York and in many other humble places.

---

tory with living culture. To modern Westerners, Latin is no more comprehensible than any of the world's languages if they are unknown to the hearer. From the hearer's point of view, the comprehensibility of a language has nothing do to with its cultural origin.

[48] Hastings, for example, commented that the vernacular "did not at first include the canon of the Mass, but the momentum of change was such in the early post-conciliar period—moreover, the absurdity of retaining an isolated island of Latin was so obvious—that this quickly followed." "The Key Texts," in *Modern Catholicism: Vatican II and After*, ed. Adrian Hastings (New York: Oxford University Press, 1991), 63.

It is a start. And what do we gain by such sacrifices? We unlock the sacred treasury of all the sublime settings of those texts in the Catholic tradition, releasing them from their imprisonment to do their work of uplifting hearts and spirits. Our children will regard them as their own. And for those three moments in the liturgy, at least, the whole world could praise God with one voice.

Liturgical tradition is a building of symbols. A language is a system of symbols, symbols united by rules for the purpose of communicating meaning. In its immediacy of words, a language symbolizes precisely what we believe and how seriously we believe. In its history and tradition and poetry, the language, taken as an entire edifice, can confer something of the transcendence authored by the liturgy. And when sung, the language creates the exalted language with which God meant us to pray. Nothing affects the vitality of a tradition of liturgical music more than its language.

Chapter 16

An Eternal Conflict: Creativity and Tradition*

> And it must still be, for us as descendants of those two grandmothers [Athens and Jerusalem], with that melody that we learn to sing, and from that counterpoint that we go on to compose melodies of our own. To be tone-deaf to the tradition is, therefore, to be unable to hear the voices of the past or the present—or of the future.
>
> Jaroslav Pelikan (1984)

Some twelve centuries ago, monastics in northern Europe began to experiment with an invention that would change the course of Western music and set it apart from all other musics of the world. They wrote down on parchment the melodies that they chanted in liturgy.

By symbolizing in precise concrete form something that is essentially abstract and fleeting in experience, notation renders music as an object of leisurely contemplation and opens its beginning, middle, end, and every significant detail to conscious inspection and comparison. Freezing musical motion—much as photography freezes action—allows different melodies to be fitted harmonically and performed simultaneously in ever more complex fashions. Combining simultaneous melodies is the essential and distinctive compositional approach of the Western tradition. It is no exaggeration to say that Western harmonic invention from the simplest guitar song to the grandest conception of J. S. Bach owes its existence to those monastics.

They had no such end in sight. They merely wished to ease the burden of memorization born by church singers. As the Roman liturgy and its music had become ever more elaborate through the early Middle Ages, the amount of rote learning required by singers had grown with it. So the earliest types of notation are believed to have simply reminded singers what they were supposed to have already learned. But devising notation that could represent pitches precisely

---

* Some passages in this chapter appeared in "Creativity and Tradition," *Pastoral Music* 25, no. 6 (August–September 2001): 10–13. Used by permission.

enough to avoid relying on a monk's memory developed logically, if not smoothly, from the original impetus. Guido d'Arezzo, who invented the do-re-mi system of sight-singing notation in the eleventh century, claimed that before notation it took a minimum of ten years to train a singer for liturgy. When singers acquired the ability to sing a notated chant *that they had never heard before*, truly a new world opened before their eyes.

But there is a little more to the story, for if the monastics only wanted to get the singers to avoid wrong notes and ugly dissonances, there are ways much less radical than inventing notation. They had another purpose in mind.

Music learned by rote in a pure oral tradition normally changes over time as it is passed from generation to generation. In improvisatory traditions this happens rapidly, but even in those sects where monastics make every effort to preserve what is handed on exactly as it was, some incremental change is inevitable, given enough time. The ninth-century monastics of northern Europe wished to resist this irresistible force because they believed that could create a symbolic uniformity of liturgical plainchant throughout the Carolingian realm. They sought catholicity in liturgy, a universality of no small symbolic import, and still very much in contention in the modern Catholic world.

The monastics' success in providing a uniform liturgical repertory, while far from perfect, was nevertheless unparalleled in the history of any music to that point. Here is where Western music really parts company with the rest of the world. The thousands of individual chants that characterize the liturgical year crystallized into the foundational repertory of church music for the next ten centuries. But their success, like many other technical innovations, threatened to make obsolete the very musician who seemed to benefit most: the composer. For by making the chant repertory standard and constant, the good monks removed almost all occasion for new liturgical composition.

An Eternal Conflict

The invention of notation in the West did not create the conflict of a religion's traditions and a musician's creativity. Such has been an occupational hazard of everyone involved in sacred music in every religion since the beginning. Tradition subsists on continuity and preservation of the past; creativity means that a new thing has arisen, and the creation of music seems of all the arts to be the most reminiscent of the Creator's original act, because new music needs no physical material and appears from the mind ex nihilo. So it is a worthy thing to compose for the Most High, but what need can there be for another setting of *Kyrie eleison* when the Catholic tradition overflows with them?

If notation did not create this conflict, it dramatized it in a particularly ironic way. The Coptic singer whose vocation was to preserve every pitch and nuance of the chant that was taught to him by his master, whose vocation was the same down through the generations, may not feel the conflict very much. He came to terms with the nature of his labor of love long ago. But the Catholic composer has been conscious of new possibilities and responsibilities in liturgical composition ever since the Western church adopted the view that a musical setting of a biblical passage was not one in being with the Scripture, that changes and new musical settings were possible. For the composer of integrity, the vast richness of the repertory made possible by notation can never be far from his thoughts. How does the composer remain faithful to this tradition without burying his talent in the ground like the unworthy servant? How can he fulfill the promise of a divine gift of musical creativity in the presence of the sacred treasure?

The conflict of creativity and tradition is sharper now than ever before in the history of Western music because of the modern era's extreme demands on the creativity of an individual artist, demands first articulated by nineteenth-century romanticism that have become more stringent ever since. The turn of the nineteenth century saw the spread through Europe of a new social phenomenon, the public concert, an event, strange in the eyes of the non-Western world, where middle-class folk paid money to contemplate music for itself, rather than merely hearing it as an appendage to a liturgy or a civic celebration. Concerts naturally created a healthy demand for performance music, and soon impresarios discovered that it was popular and economical to perform certain older works by composers who might even have died, composers that had come to earn the constant admiration of musicians and the general public. Thus the musical classic came into Western consciousness for the first time.[1] A repertory of such classics grew up quickly, founded at first on the works of Beethoven,

---

[1] In previous centuries the norm was, by and large, to hear new music at some specific occasion that called for it. J. S. Bach's obituary claims that he composed a new church cantata for every Sunday service for five years, even though the liturgical cycle was one year long. Music was generally not recycled or "classicized"

Mozart, and Haydn, but augmented rapidly by the great talents of Chopin and others of his generation, and then by the revival of Bach. The repertory, however valuable in itself, exerted a new pressure on living composers who had to compete with the dead for the first time in history. But how could a young composer compete with Beethoven, whose prestige rivaled the Deity's? By changing the terms of the competition, of course—that is, by changing the style of the music so that direct comparison was difficult, and by taking advantage of the intrinsic interest of novelty.[2] And so the pace of innovation in composition increased dramatically by the middle of the nineteenth century.[3]

This economic pressure coincided very nicely with the romantic elevation of the composer from one of society's mere craftsmen to an Artist, with all the romantic attributes of divine inspiration and eccentricity—one set apart by talent and vocation. The composer qualified as an Artist because he was no slave to tradition or convention but wrote his music according to the inspiration of original ideas. The more original the ideas, the greater the Artist. One reads this constantly in the criticism of Robert Schumann and other apologists for his generation and in virtually all analysis of Beethoven, well into the twentieth century, as the composer who broke the iron shackles of academic forms and gave himself over to pure musical expression. The force of this radical individualism is stronger than ever today, fueled by academic theories of "conceptual art." Even popular music, which remained for much of the twentieth century immune from the infection, has now constructed a canon of classics, against which newcomers must react and be measured.

The appearance of entirely new systems of melody, harmony, notation, and musical production, and the thorough reconsideration of what might count as art music in the twentieth century, all developed

---

but discarded, a practice that corresponds to the lower status of the composer as a craftsman, not an artist. One does not save old shoes or wedding cake.

This new consciousness of a musical past coincides with the nineteenth-century predilection to historicize almost any aspect of human civilization. See Jaroslav Pelikan, *The Vindication of Tradition* (New Haven: Yale University Press, 1984), 45.

[2] It is surely no accident, to take one example, that in the two or three decades following Beethoven's death in 1827 the production of those musical genres in which Beethoven's success was most obvious and most public—symphony, piano sonata, string quartet, concerto—all dropped off precipitately.

[3] A more detailed discussion of this history may be found in Joseph P. Swain, *Musical Languages* (New York: Norton, 1997), chap. 6.

directly from nineteenth-century conceptions of individualism and creativity. Composers invented such systems out of thin air in order to set themselves apart in the competitive field, to make themselves artistically distinct. The result in the world of art music has been the alienation of the greater public and the isolation of composers in academia. Although it was not, this might have been predicted, for the result is the natural consequence of radical individualism. Imagine a novelist who, to create the totally original novel, goes far beyond the invention of plot and character and designs a totally original language, with original syntax and lexicon, in which to write the novel. The novel indeed may attain a new depth of originality, but no one will be able to read it. Taken to its logical extreme, radical individualism becomes complete artistic isolation.

Obviously, an attitude that nearly makes an apotheosis of individual creativity is completely opposed to the spirit of the liturgy and renders the conflict between such creativity and liturgical tradition virtually irreconcilable. To begin to reconcile them, we must realize first that the modern myth of individual creativity is historically and culturally aberrant, and then adopt a more mature, historically informed, and pragmatic conception of musical creativity that obtains not only for most of Western music history but throughout the rest of the world as well.

Creativity and Interpretation

Consider the maestro of the Boston Symphony Orchestra conducting a performance of the *Missa Solemnis* of Beethoven. He determines the tempo at every moment, which critically affects the impact of the music. He judges the balance, the relative volumes of all the singers and instruments, which ones are to be in the perceptual foreground and which in the background. He decides how loud is the forte, how soft the pianissimo, whether a chord is to be punched incisively or broadened out, and a thousand other matters of musical articulation. Yet he would never dare to alter a single note of Beethoven. Is the conductor a creative musician?

Consider the soprano soloist in the same performance. She directs much of her musical energy to the execution of the soprano melodies exactly as Beethoven wrote them. She generally follows the conductor's tempo, but she can move a phrase here, prolong a note there, and then the orchestra must follow her. Decisions about when to breathe, whether to glide or jump from one note to the next, and what precise tone color to use are all hers. Is the soprano a creative musician?

Consider a violinist in the orchestra. Every note that he plays is foreordained; indeed, his many years of exacting training have refined his ability to execute all the thousands of pitches and durations composing the *Missa* as precisely as Beethoven wrote them. Nor has he any choice about how loud or how fast to play them. Every bow stroke and even fingering has been determined by his section leader. Yet, the sound coming from his violin is like a fingerprint, precisely matched to no other's in the world, his and his alone. Is the violinist a creative musician?

Yes, they certainly are, and all consider themselves so. How? Theirs is not the *Missa Solemnis* in the way that a painter creates his painting or the author his novel, but because music is a performing art, musicians' contributions are as necessary as Beethoven's to the fleeting existence in real sound of this thing we call the *Missa Solemnis*. Their relation to it is naturally different from the composer's but nonetheless essential. They create the performance and bring the *Missa Solemnis* into the sensible world for a moment. And their contributions are fully individuated, never the automatic and abstract executions of a computer algorithm or a machine. For performing artists, this individuation satisfies completely their creative instincts. There is no demeaning, no loss of identity or purpose, in faithfully following another's notes as perfectly as possible, in replicating all the pitch and duration patterns that Beethoven imagined, as all other past performances have tried to replicate, as all future performances will try to do. Rather, in perceptive musicians the feeling is one of being honored with the privilege of creating with the master, since every one of these numberless recreations of Beethoven's vision is a unique and irreproducible instantiation of the *Missa Solemnis*.

The musical performance in this sense is analogous to a liturgy. The author of the liturgy is God himself through the sacrifice of his Son, but it nonetheless cannot exist on earth without human collaboration, a privilege that is his gift. And just as the violinist, the soprano, and the conductor restrain and control their creative acts, each according to his or her proper role, so do the human participants at a liturgy. Just as no violinist, singer, or conductor wishes to stand out unduly from all past and future performances of the *Missa Solemnis* by being too loud or out of synch with his colleagues, through error of any kind, so should no celebrant, lector, or cantor want to shine the spotlight improperly on himself in the liturgy. Instead, all sacrifice their individual creative wills and profiles for the sake of the communities of performers, listeners, and worshipers. Individualism is banished, subsumed into the great wholeness that is the musical performance and the liturgy alike. And yet, the creativity of all is saved because all are interpreters.

A first violinist retiring from the Boston Symphony was interviewed on radio and half-jokingly referred to his fellow violinists in the section as "hardened criminals," but not even the most unsentimental regard for the music will deter the professional from his first responsibility: to interpret it. Ironically, this essential role of interpreter is a consequence of the same notation that supposedly froze the music into an unchanging objective state. Western notation, for all its admirable economy, flexibility, and precision, is not a recording device that produces the same exact output again and again; rather, it is an outline, a detailed sketch of the composer's idea that yields infinitely many performances, each one different from the last. The performer's role is greater than a mechanical translator of spots on paper into sound. The performer, even the section violinist in the *Missa Solemnis*, determines thousands of musical details that the composer could not include in the score. While many of these by themselves may fall below the limen of perception, taken together they shape the total performance decisively and constitute what we call an interpretation of the work.

In this, once again, musical tradition is akin to the theological: "The heart of any hermeneutical position is a recognition that all interpretation is a mediation of past and present, a translation carried on within the effective history of a tradition to retrieve its sometimes strange, sometimes familiar meanings."[4] Nor is interpretation an option for the theologian of integrity: "The classics, with their two notes of permanence and excess of meaning, always demand interpretation, never mere repetition nor simplistic rejection."[5] If the analogy is substantial, it begins to reconcile the most afflicted of those caught in the conflict of tradition and creativity: the composer. For while performance interpretation indeed saves the creative instincts of all participating musicians, the composer creates on an altogether different plane. It is the

---

[4] David Tracy, *The Analogical Imagination: Christian Theology and the Culture of Pluralism* (New York: Crossroad, 1981), 99.
[5] Ibid., 154.

composer who sets out what the players and singers must interpret. But how is the composer then an interpreter? What is there to interpret? In David Tracy's theological method, the modern theologian creates new classics by building on the old through authentic interpretation. John Henry Newman called the same thing "development":

> A true development, then, may be described as one which is conservative of the course of antecedent developments being really those antecedents and something besides them: it is an addition which illustrates, not obscures, corroborates, not corrects, the body of thought from which it proceeds.[6]

Composers of Roman Catholic liturgical music throughout history have done the same.

Catholic Traditions of Musical Interpretation

When those ninth-century monastics first recorded a plainchant on parchment, they created a blueprint for new sacred compositions.

Example 16-1. Late eleventh-century polyphony on a traditional *Kyrie* melody.

The earliest centuries of polyphony consist entirely of compositions that experiment with adding melodies to plainchant. Notation made the experimentation possible by freezing the plainchant melodies, by making them hold still while various new melodies from the minds of composers could be superimposed and tested one at a time, a state made plain by the term that describes the technique: *cantus firmus*, or "fixed chant." No one knows who first thought of this marvelous idea, but it became the bedrock of liturgical composition until the Second

---

[6] John Henry Newman, *An Essay on the Development of Christian Doctrine*, sixth ed. (Notre Dame, IN: University of Notre Dame Press, 1989; first published in 1878), 200.

Vatican Council. It is easy to see why. The *cantus firmus* technique is a brilliant compromise, a reconciliation of the interests of tradition and creativity.

From the composer's point of view, there is nothing to complain about, no more than a jazz musician who is asked to improvise on a standard tune. The new piece begins with a plan, a single restriction: the plainchant melody is the prominent basis for the new work. Such a limitation would hinder no composer of integrity, excepting only those who have bought the myth of romantic individualism and total creativity. It certainly never bothered Josquin, Palestrina, Monteverdi, J. S. Bach, or even Beethoven, all of whom employed it to greater or lesser extent. Why should it? For a true artist, tradition's demand is a challenge to be met, an artistic hurdle to be bounded, not unlike the home-run fence or the lines of a tennis court. In providing a framework, the *cantus firmus* was the source of much music both new and wonderful. It was the way things were done.

And it saved the tradition. From the vantage point of traditional liturgy, little has changed, regardless of how radical a musical innovation the invention of polyphony represents in the historian's eyes. Polyphony can be understood as a kind of trope, a gloss on the original plainchant melody, which is present all the while. If the Mass for Christmas Day calls for the plainchant introit *Puer natus est* (A son is born), a polyphonic version will sound that same melody, perhaps in new rhythmic guise, and certainly with melodic adornments around it to grant a greater solemnity to the feast.

Instrumental genres, such as the organ prelude, adopted the same trick. Even with words absent, a well-known tune can communicate its traditional semantic import in the more abstract instrumental form.

The *cantus firmus* is the classic form of interpreting liturgical music in composition. Just as a theologian may gloss one classic text to produce another, Palestrina will choose a classic plainchant to decorate with his own original melodies to produce a masterpiece of polyphony that can stand the test of time and become a classic in its own right. The plainchant tradition remains alive, well, and true to itself, while Palestrina's compositional talent could not have borne more abundant fruit. The interests of the conflict of creativity and tradition feed one another, reconciled in a way that enriches both.

Palestrina's own career illustrates the analogy of development—building upon classics to create new ones—in Newman's notion of the development of doctrine. A great many of Palestrina's works are constructed with a *cantus prius factus*—that is, a preexisting plainchant melody or an entire polyphonic composition (such as a motet) that is in turn based on a preexisting melody. But there are a great many others which appear not to be composed in this way. His *Missa Papae Marcelli* (Mass for Pope Marcellus), famous not only for its music per se but because legend once credited it with convincing the council fathers at Trent to forbear abolishing polyphony, was composed freely, without a *cantus firmus* or other traditional material. How then does it respect the tradition and connect with the past and interpret it? By the time of its composing, about 1560, the style of composing liturgical polyphony using traditional plainchant melodies had been developing for centuries. More importantly, by the sixteenth century it had acquired a sound distinct from that of secular polyphonic genres, which took their constructive principles from their poetic texts and from rapidly emerging modern harmonic functions. From that moment, classical polyphony matured from being a means of composition dependent upon actual plainchants guaranteeing liturgical propriety to a sacred musical language in its own right with no explicit need for them. The polyphony of Palestrina and his greatest colleagues carries with it a sacred semantic earned from centuries of association with plainchant, even to the point of emulating its free rhythm. Its sound is now part of the tradition, and composers who use it need not trouble about including a plainchant, much as theologians who quote St. Augustine need not reference the Bible to justify their sources.

And so more recent composers could avail themselves of a variety of musical techniques and symbols to participate in the tradition. Maurice Duruflé played it conservatively when he prominently quoted some of the simplest and best known plainchant Ordinary chants for his *Requiem* op. 9 (1947). Ariel Ramirez, in his folk Mass *Misa Criolla* of 1964, sets the Ordinary prayers to very traditional polyphonic forms even while infusing them with Latin American rhythms never known in Palestrina.

Giuseppe Verdi contents himself with the sound of a chorus to sanctify his famous *Requiem* (1874), but here the device is insufficient to withstand the onslaught of too much opera. One could easily predict the same failure were *Pange lingua* or some other plainchant set to a rock band. Musical symbols merely appended like so much tinsel to a music essentially foreign to sacred tradition will never substitute for the thorough integration of the tradition and a new composition.

Prerequisites of Integration

What does a successful integration of the new and the traditional require?

There is no easy answer, just as there is no formula for great music. In the days of plainchant and polyphony, it seemed so much simpler because the dominant musical languages were already sacred. Integrating one's new ideas into the tradition meant simply following one's training. Since the invention of opera, the rise of secularism in the West, and the dominance of secular musical languages over classicized sacred ones, the problem is more complex. Modern compositional schooling is all over the map, diffuse, decentralized, and chaotic; total reliance on training or, in the case of popular liturgical styles, experience and intuition produces mostly the inappropriate or pitiful results that one would predict. Successful sacred composers must make extraordinary efforts not only to step outside themselves, but to step outside the confines of the modern world in order to engage the traditions of sacred music that stand decidedly apart from it.

To do this, first of all, aspiring church composers must be intimately familiar with the tradition in all its richness. Lack of such basic knowledge is perhaps the most ruinous fault of most efforts in popular liturgical styles since the 1960s. Hearing those songs, one has not the slightest impression that their makers ever heard a single plainchant or polyphonic work, ever studied any Langlais or Vaughan Williams; rather, they simply wrote what they knew, which was not very much. There is no musical sign of any connection with the tradition, no effort at integration, and barring that, there is little hope that the music will ever sound sacred. "Coming to terms with the presence of the traditions from which we are derived is, or should be, a fundamental part of the process of growing up."[7]

This process of familiarizing oneself with the past, which is part of every notable composer's education throughout Western history, should spark new composers' development of technique and imagination. It is always hard to say which of these essentials of composition should take precedence, for technique without imagination is barren, while imagination without technique is powerless. Most likely they develop together, one feeding the other, in most compositional minds. The technical aspect, at any rate, demands time and training from

---

[7] Pelikan, *The Vindication of Tradition*, 53.

which there is no escape. Young composers wishing to blend grand new ideas for Masses with the traditional plainchant propers must solve at minimum the architectural trick of how to do it, how to make the notes of new ideas fit the notes of the plainchant. This is the noble art of counterpoint, and it requires some years to master it.

Finally, composers must make an act of humility by submitting their creative wills to the needs of the sacred liturgy and all its participants. Composers of sacred music always find themselves in a contradictory situation, for in composing they promote themselves, but in composing for the liturgy they suppress all individuality, all idiosyncratic musical persona. At a concert, part of our intention is to appreciate the creative mind of a Mozart or a Beethoven, but at Mass, the music should ideally point away from its creator to the Creator alone.

If these prospects sound dismal to the ears of contemporary composers, well, sacred composition today is a vocation, almost a priestly calling, more so now perhaps than it has ever been. Dedication, learning, and personal sacrifice are its signs, as they are of any Christian ministry. Its earthly rewards are mostly invisible and intangible, though they may be great indeed.

The Living Tradition

But in the end, what need can there be for another setting of *Kyrie eleison* when the Catholic tradition has so many beautiful ones? Having made the personal and artistic sacrifices, having learned the counterpoint, having accepted the great commission, has the new composer anything to do?

Once again, history shows that the predicament is not really new. It is true that radical individualism's ever-soaring standard of originality is not only unhealthy in itself, but works at complete cross purposes to any tradition that must be essentially conservative. It is also true that an aspiring composer must choose between a kind of streetwise education in the popular world, which is utterly secular in every way, and an academic training in musical languages that few outside its ivory towers can understand. So the modern situation is perhaps more acute and confused than ever before, and yet we can learn from its precedents.

One lesson is to avoid overstating the presence of novelty in the past. We are mesmerized by the astonishing vision of J. S. Bach composing a new church cantata every week in his first years at Leipzig and we forget that the Lutheran Mass in which it was heard was mostly filled with well-worn traditional music. Certainly the famous Lutheran chorales that gave the congregation its mode of participation—something to sing—were all old chestnuts virtually without exception. Palestrina's 104 polyphonic Masses stand as a record for its time, but if we imagine that he used them as he composed them, that would work out to about two new Masses per year of his professional life. There was plenty of room for traditional plainchant too. Integrating with a healthy tradition is an incremental process, not the revolutionary *coup de musique* of the 1960s, whose chaotic instabilities many parishes still endure today. It is true that in many circumstances the answer to "What need is there for another *Kyrie*?" may be "Not much." Parishes are so starved for the familiar comfort of the Christmas carol that it is unlikely that any new ones will be urgently sought. And yet, a living tradition will provide occasions where new music is the only thing that will suffice.

This is because a living tradition, like a living, functioning language, must respond to its context of occurrence, and that is always changing. The world presents at every moment utterly new situations never before experienced, and so English routinely invents new words and even modifies its most common syntactic forms to express them.[8] The Catholic liturgy must touch the earthly world even as it transcends it and likewise evolves constantly, though slowly, in response. "For the liturgy is made up of unchangeable elements divinely instituted, and of elements subject to change. These latter not only may be changed but ought to be changed with the passage of time, if they have suffered from the intrusion of anything out of harmony with the inner nature of the liturgy or have become less suitable" (SC 21). So too its music. A completely static tradition is a dead tradition.

It would be untraditional, therefore, if a solemn Mass commemorating the September 11, 2001, attacks or some other great calamity did not offer at least one new liturgical composition commissioned for the occasion. There need be no original text. It could be a new *Kyrie eleison*, for that matter, and thus connect instantly with the tradition. The very

---

[8] It is arguable that the current overuse of the present processive and the verb "to be" derives from contemporary culture's infatuation with the experiential at the expense of the factual. "He is having to study a lot" and "We are needful of financial support," once considered awkward, now commonly replace "He has to study a lot" and "We need financial support."

fact of its newness creates a unique semantic attachment to the event commemorated that no older work could match, and its melodies come to refer to and even symbolize the spiritual anguish of that particular moment. In most such cases, the new work would pass from the liturgical scene with the passage of time, but in a few cases, the work might be great enough to pass the test of time and enter the tradition with a more permanent status. *Kyrie Pro Victimis 9/11* could live on, ever recalling its terrible generating event, but through its universal qualities finding resonance in all times, as does all great liturgical music.

That is but one way in which liturgical music meets the ever-changing context that is the world. There will always be such events joyful and sorrowful, on the global stage and in the local parish. There will be new propers for new saints. There is the particularity of the liturgical year, mostly unexploited by recent liturgical composition. Yes, even new Christmas carols are possible.[9] All these demand new music.

In touching the world this way, the composer who integrates the need of the moment with individual art, imagination, and skill and with the great tradition of liturgical music accomplishes something far greater than mere "relevance," the shallow attempt to attract congregants by appealing to their most common secular tastes. The work is symbolic of the liturgical action, of the tradition's past, of the community's present, of the promise of the future. In bringing our spirits from one to another, such music accomplishes a transcendence analogous to that of the liturgy itself.

---

[9] The commercialization of the Christmas season has encouraged a steady stream of secular songs, responding to each new cultural interpretation of its meaning. Fortunately, these have not found their way into the liturgy. Actually, carols throughout history have been popular songs that have been traditionally excluded from the liturgy until quite recently, and then only those with the most appropriate religious texts were admitted.

Chapter 17

An Eternal Conflict:
Inculturating Liturgical Music[*]

> Thus I will proclaim you, LORD, among the nations;
> I will sing the praises of your name.
> 2 Samuel 22:50

No matter how much it may despise the world we live in, no religion can escape from it entirely, if only because the raw materials of worship—music, gesture, and language above all—are human artifacts that originate in particular peoples in certain times and places. Every religious practice springs from a culture with its practices and tools of expression. But Christianity, like the Jewish religion from which it sprang, engages culture more deeply because it is a historical religion. Christians recognize that God created the world we live in, "found it very good" (Gen 1:31), entered into it to save his creatures who had fallen into sin, and continues to carry out his plan of salvation in part by earthly means, his disciples and saints.

That is why Christian liturgy is not a means of escaping the world, but rather a means of transcending and sanctifying it. Commemorating the holy histories of creation and salvation, the liturgy unites their signal events bound to specific times and places to a timeless reality:

> The foundation of the liturgy, its source and support, is the historical Pasch of Jesus—his Cross and Resurrection. This once-for-all event has become the ever-abiding form of the liturgy. In the first stage the eternal is embodied in what is once-for-all. The second stage is the entry of the eternal into our present moment in the liturgical action. And the third stage is the desire of the eternal to take hold of the worshipper's life and ultimately of all historical reality. The immediate event—the liturgy—makes sense and has meaning for our lives only because it

---

[*] Some passages of this chapter appeared in "Inculturating Liturgical Music," *America* 191, no. 6 (September 13, 2004): 14–17. Used by permission.

contains the other two dimensions. Past, present, and future interpenetrate and touch upon eternity.[1]

Such interpenetration depends upon cultural means, words and music being primary, which is why the history of liturgical reform has most often turned on the issue of liturgical language.[2] Musical languages, semantically much less precise, have been given freer rein. And so the liturgical composer, whose art of all the arts is best suited to symbolize the time bound and the timeless in a single creation, composes in a musical language originating in a specific culture of a specific time and place. The intelligibility of the sung liturgy depends upon the participants understanding that musical language.

What does it mean to understand a musical language? It means to know, intuitively, how the music works, even though a listener may not know the name of a single note, very much as one knows the grammar of a native speech, though a speaker may know nothing of verbs, nouns, and other explicit syntactic categories. The native listener senses musical tension and resolution, agrees with fellow members of a musical community on the most exciting moments, can hear errors in performance without having had a single music lesson, and learns and memorizes songs and melodies with ease, especially as a child.[3]

How does one come to this wondrous capability? Usually by growing up in a musical community, again, as one learns a native language. Bombarded daily by its characteristic patterns, the children of a culture absorb a musical language's subtle nuances without effort. American adults touring a foreign land in Africa or South Asia at first may make no sense of the musical language that they hear for the first time. But with patience they might gain a toehold in comprehension by using basic perceptions that obtain in all music: the articulation of silences, the natural gestaltist groupings of notes in neighborhoods of pitch or duration, the noticeable repetitions of motive. With experience, they learn the workings left unexplained by these "natural" laws, those that are almost purely cultural practices and preferences.

---

[1] Joseph Ratzinger, *The Spirit of the Liturgy*, trans. John Saward (San Francisco: Ignatius Press, 2000), 60.

[2] See chap. 16.

[3] On the nature of a musical community, see Joseph P. Swain, "Musical Communities and Music Perception," *Music Perception* 11, no. 3 (Spring 1994): 307–20.

Learning a new musical language is easier than learning a new natural language because the broad semantic ranges of musical gestures demand much less precision than the vocabularies of speech, and besides, with music one is not asked to produce ("speak") at a high level of sophistication unless one aspires to professional status. In short, one way or another, we come to musical comprehension by means of experience and an open mind.[4]

And so the liturgy becomes intelligible on a deeply symbolic level. The liturgical music of the church cannot be, and never has been, some mysterious art completely removed from the musical experience of the faithful. Wherever the church is found, its music must meet the understanding of its worshipers if it can ever hope to fulfill its purpose: "the glory of God and the sanctification of the faithful" (SC 112). Musical inculturation is therefore a necessary and potentially bounteous consequence of evangelization itself. But when we remember that every culture is flawed, it becomes obvious that musical inculturation cannot be the mere adoption of local styles, fitted to a vernacular translation of the Mass. "True inculturation entails conversion, a purification of those attitudes and practices in a given culture that do not conform to the gospel of Jesus."[5] So the matter is not so simple.

Pragmatics of Inculturation

Two of the chief documents of the Second Vatican Council, the constitutions on the liturgy, *Sacrosanctum Concilium*, and the church in the modern world, *Gaudium et Spes*, emphasized the encounter between Catholicism and world cultures and thus inaugurated a period of explicit analysis and theorizing about inculturation. But it had been already an ancient practice of the church. Chapter 15 of the Acts of the Apostles recounts the precedent at the Council of Jerusalem:

> Some who had come down from Judea were instructing the brothers, "Unless you are circumcised according to the Mosaic practice, you cannot be saved." Because there arose no little dissension and debate by Paul and Barnabas with them, it was decided that Paul, Barnabas, and some of the others should go up to Jerusalem to the apostles and

---

[4] Joseph P. Swain, *Musical Languages* (New York: Norton, 1997), 177–80.
[5] Mark W. Francis, *Shape a Circle Ever Wider: Liturgical Inculturation in the United States* (Chicago: Liturgy Training Publications, 2000), 60.

presbyters about this question. They were sent on their journey by the church, and passed through Phoenicia and Samaria telling of the conversion of the Gentiles, and brought great joy to all the brothers. When they arrived in Jerusalem, they were welcomed by the church, as well as by the apostles and the presbyters, and they reported what God had done with them. But some from the party of the Pharisees who had become believers stood up and said, "It is necessary to circumcise them and direct them to observe the Mosaic law."

The apostles and the presbyters met together to see about this matter. After much debate had taken place, Peter got up and said to them, "My brothers, you are well aware that from early days God made his choice among you that through my mouth the Gentiles would hear the word of the gospel and believe. And God, who knows the heart, bore witness by granting them the holy Spirit just as he did us. He made no distinction between us and them, for by faith he purified their hearts. Why, then, are you now putting God to the test by placing on the shoulders of the disciples a yoke that neither our ancestors nor we have been able to bear? On the contrary, we believe that we are saved through the grace of the Lord Jesus, in the same way as they." The whole assembly fell silent, and they listened while Paul and Barnabas described the signs and wonders God had worked among the Gentiles through them. After they had fallen silent, James responded, "My brothers, listen to me. Symeon has described how God first concerned himself with acquiring from among the Gentiles a people for his name. The words of the prophets agree with this, as is written:

> 'After this I shall return
>   and rebuild the fallen hut of David;
> from its ruins I shall rebuild it
>   and raise it up again,
> so that the rest of humanity may seek out the Lord,
>   even all the Gentiles on whom my name is invoked.
> Thus says the Lord who accomplishes these things,
>   known from of old.'[6]

It is my judgment, therefore, that we ought to stop troubling the Gentiles who turn to God, but tell them by letter to avoid pollution from idols, unlawful marriage, the meat of strangled animals, and blood. (Acts 15:1-20)

The account provides an outline for what would become the general pattern of accommodating peoples who are strangers to the Gospel

---

[6] Amos 9:11-12.

and its antecedent Jewish traditions. There is a conflict between some tradition of the church and a local culture, a "yoke" that obstructs conversion. The church gives up something, here a traditional external mark identifying God's chosen people, on the basis of an internal truth, God's grace. At the same time, it is made clear that certain things will not be compromised, even for the sake of conversion. This fundamental dichotomy finds its way into *Sacrosanctum Concilium*: "For the liturgy is made up of unchangeable elements divinely instituted, and of elements subject to change" (SC 21). Those latter elements "subject to change," interacting with local cultures, have given form to the twenty-three distinct liturgical rites that comprise Catholicism today.

How does this dichotomy apply to the inculturation of music? For liturgical music, since it is bound neither to the Scripture nor to traditional doctrines, would not seem to own any qualities that are "divinely instituted," except perhaps its own ontology in the human condition. What could possibly constrain the adoption of whatever kind of music that missionaries found to hand?

Limits of inculturating liturgical music are to be found in the nature of the liturgy itself. A single sentence of *Sacrosanctum Concilium* sums up the species of music that can be liturgical: "Therefore sacred music is to be considered the more holy, the more closely connected it is with the liturgical action, whether making prayer more pleasing, promoting unity of minds, or conferring greater solemnity upon the sacred rites" (SC 112). These characteristics are necessarily abstract, given the vagueness and flexibility of musical semantics. But getting hold of a semantic range of a thing often begins by defining what the thing is not, and so like St. James in Acts 15, we may infer some basic prohibitions.

The connection to liturgical action rules out music that interrupts or distracts from the central focus, "to celebrate the paschal mystery: reading those things 'which were in all the scriptures concerning him,' celebrating the Eucharist in which 'the victory and triumph of his death are again made present,' and at the same time 'giving thanks to God for His inexpressible gift' in Christ Jesus, 'in praise of His glory,' through the power of the Holy Spirit"[7] (SC 6). The temptations of

---

[7] Internal quotations are Luke 24:27; Council of Trent, Session 13, Decree on the Holy Eucharist, chap. 5; 2 Cor 9:15; and Eph 1:12.

musical egoism come quickly to mind. There is only one star of the liturgy, and it is not those who sing or play instruments. The references to prayer and the unity of spirit bind the music to the words of the liturgy itself, or at least to words that contribute directly to its action.[8] Music incapable of bearing these texts appropriately is inadmissible. Finally, the "conferral of greater solemnity," addressing directly the loudest complaint about some recent liturgical music, asks that the semantics of the musical composition make present to all the gravity of what they do. The apprehended significance of the music should not divide participants one from another, nor by invoking harmful referents in the world should it divide the worshiping community from the will of God. As liturgical historian Mark R. Francis has noted, the church has practiced a prudent selectivity in its encounter with culture at least since the fourth century, when ritual elements associated with pagan rites, such as the use of certain musical instruments, were kept out of the liturgy.[9] The liturgy is transcendent, and nothing less than a thoroughly sacred semantic can promise the foretaste of heaven that the faithful seek in it.

Success Stories

Surely the greatest achievement of musical inculturation of the Roman liturgy is the repertory that most people call Gregorian chant. Historians are uncertain as to whether the melodies of the oldest repertory, about six hundred Mass propers, originated in Rome or northern Europe or are a conflation of two traditions, but the confusion derives from an effort by Carolingian authorities to unify liturgical practice within Charlemagne's ninth-century empire by adopting a standard Roman Rite, in other words, by inculturating on a broad scale. To this core repertory were added the plainchant settings of the Mass Ordinaries and, from various nations, a continually increasing store of Latin hymns, tropes, and sequences, many of which were discarded by the Tridentine reforms in the sixteenth century, but many

---

[8] This interpretation is explicitly ratified in SC 121: "The texts intended to be sung must always be in conformity with catholic doctrine. Indeed, they should be drawn chiefly from the sacred scripture and from liturgical sources."

[9] Francis, *Shape a Circle Ever Wider*, 29. See also Geoffrey Wainwright, *Doxology: The Praise of God in Worship, Doctrine and Life: A Systematic Theology* (New York: Oxford University Press, 1980), 363.

of which continue to reside in the Roman liturgical books of today. "These churches have the distinction of being the first to adapt the classical Roman liturgy to the culture of their people."[10] In the course of time, the result was a synthesis of cultures. To us moderns, this music *e pluribus* certainly presents a singular sacred aspect that is archetypically Catholic.

Of Rome and Aachen, who inculturated whom? History hides any precise knowledge of the origins of the music, its native traditions, and the semantic distinctions, if any, of the local plainchant traditions with regard to popular music of the time. But from this and from other similar—if less spectacular—experiences, the Church has discerned the second key principle of inculturation, that of the "double movement":

> By inculturation, the Church makes the Gospel incarnate in different cultures and at the same time introduces peoples, together with their cultures, into her own community. On the one hand the penetration of the Gospel into a given sociocultural milieu "gives inner fruitfulness to the spiritual qualities and gifts proper to each people . . ., strengthens these qualities, perfects them and restores them in Christ." On the other hand, the Church assimilates these values, when they are compatible with the Gospel, "to deepen understanding of Christ's message and give it more effective expression in the liturgy and in the many different aspects of the life of the community of believers.[11]

Once again the give and take between Scripture and dogmatic tradition comes to mind. All the great plainchant repertories—Gregorian, Mozarabic, Byzantine, Orthodox—retell this story.

A modern American success story of inculturation would be the African American or "black gospel" tradition.[12] Originating in African

---

[10] Anscar J. Chupungco, OSB, *Liturgies of the Future: The Process and Methods of Inculturation* (New York: Paulist Press, 1989), 7.

[11] *Varietates Legitimae*, Instruction on Inculturation and the Roman Liturgy, art. 4, including the term "double movement." The internal quotations are from Pope John Paul II's encyclical *Redemptoris Missio*, December 7, 1990, art. 52, and from *Gaudium et Spes* (Pastoral Constitution on the Church in the Modern World), Second Vatican Council, promulgated by Pope Paul VI, December 7, 1965, art. 58.

[12] There is another, earlier type of gospel singing associated with the shape-note tradition and white congregations. This is not the common referent of the term "gospel music" today.

American Protestant congregations after the Civil War, the recordings of Thomas A. Dorsey and Mahalia Jackson in the early twentieth century made this eclectic music part of the popular experience of many Americans. In the years since the Second Vatican Council, gospel has been sung in the Roman Catholic Rite more and more commonly in those parishes where native listeners of that musical language worship. How do the principles of the changeable versus unchangeable elements and the double movement between culture and universal religious tradition play out?

In one case study of a predominantly African American parish in Los Angeles in 1982, Jaqueline DjeDje outlines the order of worship for the "Gospel Mass" as follows:

A. *Introductory Rites*

(V) 1. Entrance song (choir)
     2. Greeting by celebrant

     Penitential rite
(S) 3. "O Lord, have mercy" (choir)

     Rite of Blessing the sprinkling Holy Water
(S) 4. "Glory to God" (choir)
     5. Opening prayer by celebrant

B. *Liturgy of the Word*

     6. Reading by lector(s)
(S) 7. Responsorial song/ "Alleluia" (choir)
     8. Reading by lector(s)/deacon
(S) 9. "Alleluia" (choir)
     10. Homily by celebrant
     11. Announcements
     12. Welcome of visitors
     13. Profession of faith
     14. General Intercession: Prayers by lector(s)/deacon, and clergy

C. *Liturgy of the Eucharist*

     Preparation of gifts
(V) 15. Offertory song (choir)
     16. Prayer over the gifts

	Eucharistic prayer
(S)	17. Preface Acclamations: "Holy holy" (choir)
	18. Prayer by celebrant
(S)	19. Memorial Acclamations: "Christ has died" (choir)
	20. Prayer by celebrant
(S)	21. Concluding Acclamations: "Amen" (choir)
	Communion rite
(S)	22. "The Lord's Prayer" (choir)
	Rite of peace
(V/S)	23. "Reach out and touch" (choir)
(S)	24. "God's (He's) already here" (choir)
	Breaking of bread: Lamb of God
	25. Lamb of God by celebrant
(V)	26. Communion song (choir)
(V)	27. Meditation song (choir)
	28. Prayer after communion

D. *Concluding Rite*

    29. Final Blessing
(V)   30. Closing song (choir)[13]

Figure 17-1. Order of the Gospel Mass at Saint Brigid.

The musical numbers marked (S) for "set"—that is, obligatory text—are principally the Ordinary prayers of the Roman Rite, those that are sung or recited unchanging at every Mass in the world. Those marked with (V) for "varied" would correspond to the proper prayers for the day. DjeDje remarks that with these, "the choir is allowed free choice of special songs to sing," from which we may infer that it was customary at St. Brigid's to exercise "option four" of the General Instruction of the Roman Missal regarding the singing of "another liturgical chant that is suited to the sacred action, the day, or the time of year" rather than the official plainchant propers or other psalm settings.[14] In this, St. Brigid's is no different from the vast majority of American parishes.

---

[13] Jacqueline DjeDje, "An Expression of Black Identity: The Use of Gospel Music in a Los Angeles Catholic Church," *The Western Journal of Black Studies* 7, no. 3 (1983): 155.

[14] For the complete regulation and a discussion, see chap. 6.

DjeDje's study does not provide scores for the Ordinary settings, but the order of worship is close to that of another Mass setting that employs gospel styles for some of the prayers: *The Mass of Saint Cyprian* of Kenneth W. Louis (1999). In Louis's settings of the Ordinaries, the traditional texts undergo troping and formal deformation in order to accommodate a musical style that grew up with very different kinds of text. The *Kyrie* is a slight trope of the English text in use since the 1960s:

> O Lord, have mercy, have mercy on us.
> O Christ, have mercy, have mercy on us.
> O Lord, have mercy, have mercy on us.

The trope "on us" is sung once to round off a three-fold repetition of each invocation, which actually makes the composition more Tridentine than postconciliar in form. The *Gloria*'s long prose text does not easily accommodate the strong periodic phrasing of gospel musical syntax, and so the conservatory influence of careful through-composition nearly overpowers the gospel style here.[15] Louis resorts to making "Glory to God in the highest, and peace to his people on earth" into a refrain, sung twice between recitativelike passages for a soloist. The *Sanctus* uses a call-and-response form of soloist and chorus typical of the tradition. This requires a great deal of text repetition, stretching the text to more than two minutes of music, but then Palestrina often does no less. The *Agnus Dei* is the most improvisatory sounding of all, with the seemingly endless repetition of cadential phrases so typical of the tradition. It begins with the traditional English text and then begins to trope the invocation "Lamb of God" as the music continues for over four minutes. The recording has no music for the sign of peace, as does the Gospel Mass at St. Brigid's, so it is likely that this long setting is intended to cover that action as well as the fraction of the Eucharist.

The 10:30 a.m. Sunday Gospel Mass at St. Brigid's lasted longer than most American Masses, up to two hours, because of the nature of the gospel settings.[16] The exchange of peace often lasted fifteen minutes

---

[15] There is no setting of the *Credo* on the recording.

[16] DjeDje, "Change and Differentiation: The Adoption of Black American Gospel Music in the Catholic Church," *Ethnomusicology* 30, no. 2 (Spring–Summer, 1986): 228.

alone, and one might wonder whether the eucharistic prayer was still perceived as the climax of the liturgical action, since, as in a musical composition, the apportioning of liturgical time heavily influences the perceived significance of events. The music of Louis's *Mass of St. Cyprian* allows for limited congregational singing, such as during the call-and-response patterns or in the refrain of the *Gloria*, but DjeDje reports other forms of active participation in the music, such as hand clapping and religious swaying or dancing.[17] In the three years following the introduction of gospel music at St. Brigid's, attendance at the 10:30 a.m. Mass soared from two hundred to twelve hundred.[18]

Provided that the texts replacing the proper antiphons and the solemnity of the whole celebration are faithful to the "true and authentic" spirit of the liturgy, it is hard to argue with such success. Whether or not the antecedent music at St. Brigid's and similar parishes could be termed a "yoke," the advent of gospel music as authentic liturgical music has all the signs of effective evangelization. As with the evolutionary growth of the plainchant repertory, the Roman Rite has proved itself capable of receiving a musical language once foreign, integrating it without harm to the "substantial unity" of the liturgy, and both Roman Rite and gospel tradition are thereby enriched in the double movement of true inculturation (cf. SC 37–38).

Local Context

And yet the success of the Gospel Mass is problematic in one way. It provides a simple model for inculturating liturgical music: to make the liturgy relevant to a local people, in a missionary situation or in an established one, simply find the local folk music and set the words of the Roman Rite to it. The model has worked well in the Gospel Mass and the more occasional use of black spirituals in parishes with large proportions of African American Catholics in the United States. It cannot work everywhere, not even in most places, in the rest of the world. Why not?

First, there is the problem of semantic interference. There is no question about the sacred semantic of gospel music, for its roots, its customary associations and usages, are entirely spiritual, if not liturgical,

---

[17] Ibid., 231.
[18] Ibid., 228.

albeit Protestant. When sung at Mass, the gospel style may indeed connote unimagined aspects of the relationship between God and man, but as long as they are true, that is all to the good enrichment of Catholic liturgical life. But it is not hard to imagine the disastrous consequences if some well-meaning missionary to Caucasian communities in the American South were to choose "Dixie" as the best tune to inculturate the liturgy. A great marching tune it is, but one that comes with semantic baggage of militarism, slavery, and white supremacy acquired, as most musical semantics are acquired, through centuries of association with just those things.

Such errors of judgment are not to be completely eliminated by even the most thorough training and cultural awareness, essential as they are in the practice of inculturation. *Missa Luba* is one of the most famous of the early efforts at adapting African musical idioms to the Roman Rite. Composed by Joseph Kiwele of the Congo in 1953, it resounds with characteristic drumming, instrumentation, rhythmic patterns, improvisatory figures, and parallel harmony, all setting the Latin text of the Ordinary of the Mass. Despite its apparently irreproachable origins, "a certain uneasiness was felt by many [Africans] upon hearing this music, a cautious expression of which might be: One does not sing such a thing in church! This is all too understandable, since *Missa Luba* adapted songs of a social genre almost exclusively, which at least today are perceived as unsuitable."[19]

In India, where the hard Western distinction between sacred and secular culture all but disappears, semantic interference easily leads to syncretism. The "Church in India Seminar" that occurred in Bangalore in 1969 presented an Indian Rite Mass, including a celebrant in saffron robe and traditional gestures of reverence. "At the offertory there was the 'aarti', the waving around of a thali or brass platter filled with fruits, a broken coconut, some joss sticks and the bread and wine." Again, "there was considerable hesitation in accepting what seemed to many a gradual conversion of the liturgy into a poor imitation of

---

[19] Christopher Klein, *Messenkompositionen in Afrika: Ein Beitrag zur Geschichte und Typologie der katholischen Kirchenmusik Afrikas* (Göttingen, Germany: Edition Re, 1990), 52. "So äußert sich bei vielen ein gewisses Unbehagen beim Hören dieser Musik, die sich in der zurückhaltended Erkenntnis ausdrückt: So etwas singt man nicht in der Kirche! Das is nur allzu verständlich, da die MISSA LUBA fast ausschließlich Lieder eines 'sozialen' Genres adaptiert hat, die zumindest heute als unpassend empfunden werden."

Hindu temple of worship. . . . Moreover, could these gestures and symbols be extricated from the myths, superstitions and errors in which they were embedded? The 'aarti' was not really an offertory, but a rite for driving out evil spirits."[20] In this intensely Hindu society with a small minority of Catholics practicing the ancient Syro-Malankara and Syro-Malabar rites along with the Roman Rite, the rich tradition of Hindustani and Karnatic classical music is bound historically, textually, and by musical association to Hinduism, as is most Indian art and classical literature. One scholar documents how the simple songs with congregational refrains called *bhajan* and also *kirtan* (hymns) have been used in Catholic liturgy, but because these genres have Hindu roots, it would seem impossible to eliminate their syncretic referents.[21]

Second, technical characteristics of native music or language may refuse to cooperate with the Roman liturgy. Expedito Magembe was a music teacher at the Roman Catholic seminary at Gaba, Uganda. "When composing new hymns Magembe ensures that the tone, accent and duration of each syllable of the text follows as closely as possible the speech tones. There is, however, one exception where at the word *akaggyawo* the second syllable *-ka-* should be long because it is followed by a double consonant *-gg-*. This shows that Magembe, although a Muganda, still has difficulty setting established liturgical text to music."[22] As indicated, a common problem is that some tone languages, such as Chinese, Thai, and certain African languages, the pitch contour—rising, falling, steady, etc.—of a syllable determines the meaning of the word. In the Tiv nation within Nigeria, "it is impossible, therefore, to sing different words to the same tune and have it make linguistic sense, for different words have different tonal inflections and the tunes must conform in pitch placement and direction to the tonal placement of the words. Song is literally heightened speech, intensified speech. Every stanza of a hymn, then, has a different text but also a different tune."[23] This could be a blessing in disguise,

---

[20] Benny M. Aguiar, "India and Sri Lanka," in *Modern Catholicism: Vatican II and After*, ed. Adrian Hastings, (New York: Oxford University Press, 1991), 377.

[21] Stephen F. Duncan, *A Genre of Hindustani Music (Bhajans) as Used in the Roman Catholic Church* (Lewiston, NY: Edward Mellen Press, 1999).

[22] Catherine Gray, "Compositional Techniques in Roman Catholic Church Music in Uganda," *British Journal of Ethnomusicology* 4 (1995): 144.

[23] John Worst, *A Nigerian Journal* (Grand Rapids, MI: Calvin College, 1984), 55–56. See also, Klein, *Messenkompositionen in Afrika*, 39–41.

discouraging, for example, poor strophic paraphrases of the Latin Ordinary prayers to accommodate easy verse-refrain musical settings. But lengthy through-composed pieces are not as easy for congregations to learn, and in many parts of Africa, strophic forms are the only traditional options.[24]

A third problem with simply setting the words of the Roman Rite to local folk music is that in many modern cultures of our increasingly globalized village, what constitutes the local folk music is no longer a discrete category. Consider Japan. The "indigenous" music that most Japanese grow up with today is entirely Western classical music and the latest popular sounds from America. Advanced programs of traditional Japanese music are rare, and in any case that music no longer resonates with the populace at large. The "traditional" 春の海 (*haru no umi*, "Sea of spring") that most Japanese associate with New Year was actually composed in 1928 and has a completely Western harmonization. The ancient music that is occasionally heard in Japanese society consists almost entirely of Shinto music for births, New Year, and special anniversaries, and of Buddhist chant at funerals. An evangelist determined to inculturate local music into the liturgy would choose between an obvious musical syncretism, Western pop in the guise of its failed, anemic Christian church idioms, and Western classical tunes, such as "Ode to Joy."

Consider Ghana. "The church hymn seems to be the most performed Western music in Ghana. . . . Hymn-tunes are on the lips of school children, workers and, even, farmers, every day. It is very common to hear a farmer humming a hymn-tune while tilling the land."[25] Has the Lutheran-style hymn become the local folk music of Ghana? It would seem to satisfy every criterion for folk music that any anthropologist could wish for. Consider Trinidad, where the Anglican hymns brought by the British colonizers still shake the church walls.[26] Consider Wukari, another region in Nigeria, where "the traditional music is Jukun, a style of elaborate solo melody with slips, slides, rapid little turns, and chorus responses together with very fast and intricate

---

[24] Gray, "Compositional Techniques in Roman Catholic Church Music in Uganda," 144.

[25] Asante Darkwa, "The New Musical Traditions in Ghana" (dissertation, Wesleyan University, 1974). Quoted in Klein, *Messenkompositionen in Afrika*, 21.

[26] Personal communication, Dr. Patrick and Mrs. Grace Kendall (natives of Trinidad), May 2006.

rhythms. But this music is in danger of disappearing. It is not easily learned by the congregations and can only be perpetuated by highly skilled singers. Besides, younger people tend to shun this traditional music in favor of the more modern sounding women's choir or the more Western-sounding four-part music."[27] Are the younger generation's preferences to be scorned because they are not "native enough"?

Evidently, some would do just that. A professor at the Southeast Asian Graduate School of Theology, I-to Loh, lectured the Hymn Society of Japan, admonishing its members to give up their longstanding traditions of Western melodies and words in their Christian services. "The great majority of Asian Christians have internalized Western hymns so much that it is difficult for them to develop their own traditional hymns. . . . It is our fundamental and highest duty to utilize these gifts and develop them to their utmost potential so that we may be faithful stewards in witnessing to our faith. . . . When we see God face-to-face and God asks us, 'What have you done with the Asian culture that I have given you?', how do we answer God?"[28] An isolated ethnomusicological zealot? Another ethnomusicologist, Bernardo Illardo, working in Bolivia, has recovered and restored an archive of "Jesuit Baroque music," that is, a repertory of European operatic-style sacred music introduced into Bolivia in the seventeenth century and, as happened in many of the colonies in Latin America, brought to a very high standard of performance and composition by native Bolivians. Professor Illardo explains that "one of the main enemies of this music were proponents of the post-Vatican II liturgy . . . they felt that the music was tied to the Latin Mass and traditional liturgical practices and tried to eradicate it and replace it with post-Vatican II guitar music and drums . . ."[29] So here in the Far East and Latin America is the spectacle of foreign advisors telling the local communities that the liturgical music that they have loved for generations is not native enough for their own liturgies. Could colonialism itself have preached with such condescension?

In a delightful scene from Ang Lee's great comic film *Eat, Drink, Man, Woman*, the oldest sister of the Taiwanese family at the center of

---

[27] Worst, *A Nigerian Journal*, 20.

[28] Hisashi Yukimoto, "Church Musician Encourages Asians to Eschew Western Harmony," *Ecumenical News International Daily News Service*, September 21, 2006.

[29] George Neumayr, "Defying the Multiculturalists," *Catholic World Report* 17:8 (August/September 2007), 36.

the story, a recently converted and enthusiastic Christian, witnesses her new husband's baptism by immersion. As he rises from the water, the large congregation solemnly bursts into song: Beethoven's "Ode to Joy"! In other scenes, the oldest sister is shown listening to Verdi's *Requiem* and high Renaissance polyphony on her headphones as she travels to and from her school. Lee's portrayal of the inculturation of religious symbolism finds many corroborations from the real world, as we have witnessed in Ghana, East Asia, and Latin America. In Uganda, "Christian hymnody is now so much part of Christian worship and Baganda life that it could be called 'indigenous' music. Hymns have even replaced traditional lullabies and work songs; they are now sung by house girls when ironing or hoeing."[30]

These communities appear to sense instinctively the need for a music that is extraordinary, more particular to the mysteries that they commemorate in the liturgy than any music they have known. In other words, they feel that the music must be semantically distinct. In the face of this sacred task, affects of culture become expendable. And so "ordinary people, including a wide section of Westernized Africans, have not been taken up by campaigns for African Authenticity, adaptation, indigenization, or simply Africanization. One reason for this may be that 'inculturation' seems to imply a return to an outmoded and irrelevant past, when people would rather move forward towards modernity."[31] Even in Los Angeles, "it is noteworthy that some members of Saint Bernadette who were black indicated that they did not want to be considered as black Catholics nor would they like the church to be regarded as a black Catholic church."[32] These communities know what some liturgists have forgotten, that culture is not an unequivocal good, that every culture requires conversion, the "turning toward" God, "a purification of those attitudes and practices in a given culture that do not conform to the gospel of Jesus."[33] "For the

---

[30] Gray, "Compositional Techniques in Roman Catholic Church Music in Uganda," 153.

[31] Patrick A. Kalilombe, "Africa," in *Modern Catholicism: Vatican II and After*, ed. Adrian Hastings (New York: Oxford University Press, 1991), 314.

[32] DjeDje, "Change and Differentiation," 230.

[33] Francis, *Shape a Circle Ever Wider*, 60. Geoffrey Wainwright concurs in *Doxology: The Praise of God in Worship, Doctrine and Life*, 363. Wainwright also refers to the first of H. Richard Nieburhr's fivefold typology of relations between Christ and culture, "Christ against culture," which obtains when a society at large is "totally dominated by values which run directly counter to God's kingdom," 390.

reign of God which summons us transcends all the achievements of every culture."[34] Cultural identity pales before Catholic identity. This is a kind of denial of culture that never sits well with postmodern relevance theorists but certainly resonates with the self-denial that all Christians are called to practice. "And everyone who has given up houses or brothers or sisters or father or mother or children or lands for the sake of my name will receive a hundred times more, and will inherit eternal life" (Matt 19:30; cf. Mark 10:29; Luke 14:26).

Inculturation and Catholicity

And so we have the paradox of a Christianity at once historical and essentially countercultural, and living this paradox in liturgy is a kind of sacrifice that Catholics suffer from time to time and place to place. The liturgical "elements divinely instituted" may quite literally contradict cultural norms and seem utterly strange, as Robert Schreiter describes:

> For example, questions about the eucharistic elements: How is one to celebrate the eucharist in countries where Muslim theocracies forbade the production or importation of fermented beverages? What was one to do in those cultures where cereal products such as bread were not known? Or how was one to celebrate baptism among the Masai in east Africa, where to pour water on the head of a woman was to curse her with infertility?[35]

Catholics profess that "He was made Man," and not a generic man, but a particular one who lived and died in first-century Palestine. This means that, by a kind of divine historical accident, certain cultural artifacts of that time and place take on sacramental significances that resist inculturation of any kind. "It is important that the individual rites have a relation to the places where Christianity originated and the apostles preached: they are anchored in the time and place of the event of divine revelation. . . . The Christian faith can never be separated from the soil of sacred events, from the choice made by God,

---

[34] Mary Collins, OSB, *Contemplative Participation:* Sacrosanctum Concilium; *Twenty-five Years Later* (Collegeville, MN: Liturgical Press, 1990), 20–21.

[35] Robert J. Schreiter, *Constructing Local Theologies* (Maryknoll, NY: Orbis Books, 1985), 2. Quoted in Francis, *Shape a Circle Ever Wider*, 65.

who wanted to speak to us, to become man, to die and rise again, in a particular place and at a particular time."[36]

Consider the elements of unleavened bread and grape wine, chosen by Christ as the vessels to contain himself. For Jews, these things have associations and resonances that many of us will never quite appreciate fully because they operate at a certain remove from our formative cultural experiences. For Japanese, home of rice and sake, that remove is that much greater. The preeminence of the Psalms in liturgy, with all their Jewish references and desert metaphors, is another example. There is nothing to be done about these things except to educate ourselves. Our conversion exhorts us to put on certain strangenesses and learn their significances, now immeasurably greater than any cultural value, through their function in the divine liturgy. "From the outset, Father Novel made it known to parishioners that as a Josephite [priest], his mission was for the welfare of black Catholics and that Saint Brigid would be a black Catholic church with a black cultural expression in its worship service and liturgy. Subsequently, those who could not adapt to the changes . . . departed for other congregations which had programs suited to their values."[37] In the end, all the beautiful and good things that may define a culture also divide it from another. The cost of a defiant cultural identity may indeed be high: "Just as a eucharist which is not a transcendence of divisions within a certain locality is a false eucharist, equally a eucharist which takes place in conscious and intentional isolation and separation from other local communities in the world is not a true eucharist."[38]

The conscious sacrifice of cultural symbols in liturgy, by contrast, is rewarded by catholicity, the openness to all comers upon which the tradition is founded. "Because it is catholic, the Church overcomes the barriers which divide humanity: By baptism all become children of God and form in Christ Jesus one people where 'there is neither Jew nor Greek, neither slave nor free, neither male nor female.'"[39] The logical extreme of such thinking is the *eschatos*, the end of time when all earthly culture becomes superfluous, subsumed into the kingdom

---

[36] Ratzinger, *The Spirit of the Liturgy*, 163–64.

[37] DjeDje, "Change and Differentiation," 228.

[38] John D. Zizioulas, *Being as Communion: Studies in Personhood and the Church* (Crestwood, NY: St. Vladimir's Seminary Press, 1985), 257.

[39] Gal 3:28, quoted in *Varietates Legitimae*, art. 22. Zizioulas makes the same point, using the same passage in *Being as Communion*, 157.

of God. In this view, the necessity of inculturation is a temporary state, a condition of our journey on earth. Yet while the earth remains, it is permanent, made necessary by local conditions that never entirely disappear, despite the shrinking global community, and also made necessary in an ontological sense by the original sin that prevents us from being as selfless as we might be. The church has always encouraged liturgical inculturation as the work of the missions,[40] but in the end, "the recovery of eschatological participation in sign, word, gesture, contemplation, and song depends paradoxically on our learning to distance ourselves from our own cultural assumptions."[41] A step on the road toward complete evangelization, when the Gospel has been brought to the whole world, inculturation is best carried out with one eye toward that day of a common celebration.

What contribution can liturgical music make toward this end? As worldwide inculturation progresses and the sacred treasure of liturgical music is enriched, how good it would be to develop a music that was neither theirs nor ours but belonged to everyone and allowed the catholic celebration for which we long. It would seem impossible to find such a music anywhere on earth. Its musical language cannot have identifiers particular to one nation or even one part of the world. Its rhythm must allow for all the speech patterns of the world. Its tonal elements cannot be too strictly located within the octave, in order to accommodate the variety of native pitch systems.

"To make it easier for Christians to achieve unity and spiritual harmony with their brothers and with the living traditions of the past," the Sacred Congregation for Divine Worship, under the direction of Pope Paul VI, published in 1974 a small collection of "Gregorian"

---

[40] In order to support the introduction of local customs everywhere into the liturgy, proponents sometimes make much of the fact that the word "especially" was added to this sentence in the original draft of article 38 of *Sacrosanctum Concilium*: "Provisions shall also be made, when revising the liturgical books, for legitimate variations and adaptations to different groups, regions, and peoples, especially in mission lands, provided that the substantial unity of the Roman Rite is preserved." But the historical fact is that inculturation is most associated with evangelization because that is where it makes the most sense. Once the double movement has occurred, it is no longer necessary for either a new congregation baptized into the church or the church as a whole.

[41] Don E. Saliers, "Symbol in Liturgy, Liturgy as Symbol: The Domestication of Liturgical Experience," in *The Awakening Church: 25 Years of Liturgical Renewal*, ed. Lawrence J. Madden (Collegeville, MN: Liturgical Press, 1992), 82.

chants that they hoped would stand as a core repertory for the world.[42] The pope believed that if everyone could do just this much, we could celebrate in some sign of full communion. The stratagem failed to catch fire: there was too much competition from local initiatives.

Perhaps the difficult experiences of the last four decades around the world will encourage a reconsideration. The hue and cry of Western cultural imperialism may go up at the mere suggestion, but the charge no longer has substance. Cultural imperialism occurs when one culture imposes its values upon another, replacing the indigenous values. The fear that this might happen with the music of Latin plainchant presumes that Latin plainchant is a cultural commonplace in the West. Once it surely was, centuries ago, but how can anyone reasonably argue that it remains so, when hardly anyone has ever heard a chanted liturgy or could sing a Gregorian melody to save one's life? For virtually all Roman Catholics in North America or Europe, a liturgy sung entirely in plainchant would be as strange and as countercultural an experience as for the Catholic in India or Ghana. Historically speaking, the traditional plainchant repertory is fundamentally Western and is in fact the ancestor of virtually all of Western art music; culturally speaking, from the present day, it is a neutral music, immanently worthy and yet a stranger to all. In this regard, it has something owned by no folk music anywhere: intrinsic liturgical value without the cultural or nationalistic mark that alienates outsiders.

Moreover, plainchant is the most economical of all musics. Requiring no expensive instruments or electronic equipment, it subsists on the natural human voice. While the quality and rich variety of chanting always profits from professional expertise, the simplest plainchants are well within the range of everyone, and beginning them requires only a reasonably knowledgeable celebrant. Many are easily memorized, a particular advantage for societies not yet addicted to printed music. The poorest community can own this treasure, as it may own all spiritual riches that do not rot away, and can be justly proud of it.

Remember that the most fundamental music of all world religions is plainchant. If there is any universal sacred musical idiom born to "make disciples of all nations" (Matt 28:19), plainchant has it. The

---

[42] *Voluntati Obsequens* (Vatican City: Sacred Congregation for Divine Worship, April 14, 1974).

musical characteristics of the plainchants in *Jubilate Deo* provide the proof.[43] Their modes (scales) are not the major and minor scales of the West, nor exactly the modes of the non-Western world. Within the octave, they can tolerate some imprecision, and since plainchant need not be harmonized, there are no tuning problems to trouble the monophonic communities of the non-Western world. Its quality is at once neutral and universal. Long dead as an "indigenous" music of any locality, plainchant indeed, like the divine liturgy itself, is the property of no one, or rather, its musical idiom owns the sacred quality that belongs to all the major world religions. In some deep sense, then, it is already familiar to all.

"Music has the privilege of being able to cross linguistic barriers, and so can be a powerful symbol of unity in worship."[44] So wrote Joseph Gelineau, an ardent proponent of liturgical reform both before and after the council. He was describing the simplest plainchant formularies, an excellent solution, though perhaps not the only one, to the eternal conflict of catholicity and local culture that will confront the church until the end of time.

---

[43] The collection includes Ordinary prayers most useful for the eucharistic liturgy in settings that are easy to learn and a few other common devotional works.

[44] The citation context is: "If, for the former, one ought to look for a musical language most suitable to the faithful, should one not be guided as much as possible by the traditional melodies for use by celebrant or deacon, for reading from Scripture or verses of the psalms? Technically it is noteworthy that those formulas of the sung word are the most widely used parts of the ecclesiastical repertoire and, by their very nature (though with all necessary transpositions), most easily adapted to various languages. In this way the liturgy would retain a certain universality in its most invariable and sacred parts. Music has the privilege of being able to cross linguistic barriers, and so can be a powerful symbol of unity in worship." Joseph Gelineau, SJ, "The Role of Sacred Music," in *The Church and the Liturgy*, trans. Theodore L. Westow (Glen Rock, NJ: Paulist Press, 1965), 61–62.

Chapter 18

An Eternal Conflict: *Participatio Actuosa* and Congregational Singing*

> O if I could only make the faithful sing the *Kyrie*, the *Gloria*, the *Credo*, the *Sanctus*, and the *Agnus Dei*, like they sing the litanies and the *Tantum ergo*. That would be to me the finest triumph sacred music could have.
>
> Giuseppe Cardinal Sarto (later Pope St. Pius X, 1894)

The Second Vatican Council promoted the active participation of the laity in the sacred liturgy in its liturgical constitution *Sacrosanctum Concilium*. This much is universally recognized and generally acclaimed by anyone interested in the contemporary Roman Rite. The Latin expression *participatio actuosa* or one of its declinations appears twelve times, scattered throughout the 130 articles of the constitution, a constant presence.[1] One could certainly argue that the particular reforms of the liturgy most notable and real—among them the option of using vernacular languages, the responsorial psalm, the addition of the memorial acclamation to the eucharistic prayer, the encouragement of local traditions—are different means of realizing this single priority.

Three of those twelve occur in chapter 6 (arts. 112–21), "Sacred Music," and a fourth occurrence, found in article 30 in the first chapter on general principles of the liturgy, speaks of "acclamations, responses, psalmody, antiphons, and songs" as means of promoting active participation by the people. There is no doubt that the council fathers looked to liturgical music as a chief means of involving the congregation in the liturgy to a universal degree unimagined before the council.

---

* Some passages in this chapter appeared in "St. Mark in Venice: a Liturgy without Hymns," *Pastoral Music* 30, no. 6 (August–September 2006): 33–34. Used by permission.

[1] The formulation in art. 26 uses the term *actualis participationis*.

But while there is hardly any disagreement about the council's general intent or about the intrinsic spiritual value of a congregation that becomes an essential part of the liturgical action, fierce debates have raged over what, in practical terms, *participatio actuosa* means for music at Mass.[2] One extreme view would translate *participatio actuosa* as "congregational singing" pure and simple: worshipers do not participate in liturgical music unless they sing it.[3] The opposite view holds that *participatio actuosa* is primarily an internal attitude, a type of spirituality determined by the formation of worshipers and their capacities for reflection upon the sung prayer.[4] Admirers of the tradition and the historical repertory of Catholic liturgical music are loath to throw out this treasure in favor of Masses so simple in composition that everyone can sing them throughout. Ardent reformers have sometimes characterized such admiration as an excuse to oppose reforming the liturgy. Trained musicians find themselves caught in the crossfire.

---

[2] For a fine survey of some of the protagonists of various points of view following the council, see Anthony Ruff, *Sacred Music and Liturgical Reform*: Treasures and Transformations (Chicago: Hillenbrand, 2007), chap.17.

[3] Edward Foley comes close to stating this. He writes, "Apart from the composition, whether or not the congregation sings the music is key in assessing something of the music's symbolic causality." *Ritual Music: Studies in Liturgical Musicology* (Beltsville, MD: The Pastoral Press, 1995), 153. Philip Harnoncourt wrote even more categorically right after the council: "Kirchenmusik, die in eine Form gefaßt ist, daß das Volk sich am Vollzug der ihm zustehenden Teile nicht aktiv beteiligen kann, ist unerwünscht. Die Kirchenmusik beginnt grunsdsätzlich beim Gemeindegesang." (Church music that is conceived in a form that does not share with the people a role in those parts belonging to them is not desired. *Church music begins essentially with the singing of the congregation.*) "Neue Aufgaben der katholischen Kirchenmusik (I)," in *Die Kirchenmusik und das II. Vatikanische Konzil*, ed. Philipp Harnoncourt (Graz, Austria: Verlag Styria, 1965), 59; emphasis in the original.

[4] Mary Collins, theologian: "The quality of lay liturgical participation the moment requires is contemplative, or mystical. I choose the term to press our understanding beyond what we have commonly understood by the call for full, conscious, and active participation. Contemplatives are attentive to presence. They are present to the mystery within which all life is lived. They are alert to and wait for manifestations of the sacred within the mundane. They see the traces of divine grace even in the shards of human brokenness and absurdity. They are awed by the evidence all around them that God slays and then gives life when all hope for life is gone." *Contemplative Participation:* Sacrosanctum Concilium; *Twenty-five Years Later* (Collegeville, MN: Liturgical Press, 1990), 82.

Once again, a principle of liturgy—*participatio actuosa*—must come to terms with the realities of music if such controversies are to be resolved. Liturgical scholars, historians, and pastors have certainly meditated at length on how to interpret *participatio actuosa*. But which of those interpretations of *participatio actuosa* might the real world of music making actually sustain?

The Documents and Common Sense

Some partisans of the debate have tried to corral the term *participatio actuosa* into their camps with an etymological argument about what the Latin constituents of the term have meant and how they should be understood and translated in modern languages.[5] "Should *actuosa* be rendered 'active' or 'actual'?" is perhaps the most common of these questions. But an etymological argument will not likely persuade many. The council fathers themselves were not, by and large, philologists who would have been familiar with the historical details of Latin words. In a consistent and yet limited linguistic context such as the Second Vatican Council, the best way to understand the meaning of a significant term is to observe how it is used throughout, because the immediate meaning of any lexical item is delimited by its immediate context in a complex feedback network.[6] The meaning of *participatio actuosa* within the context of *Sacrosanctum Concilium* and the following instruction for sacred music, *Musicam Sacram* (1967), is what we need to know. Usage within those documents, not in Latin dictionaries, is primarily where we will find what the council fathers intended for us to understand.

Assume that the council fathers intended *participatio actuosa* to mean "congregational singing," that singing by the congregation is the one true sign of its participation in the liturgy, that there is no other satisfactory way of participating in liturgical music except by singing. "The people will almost always join in the singing," trumpets Bernard

---

[5] One such argument, quite sophisticated, may be found in Colman E. O'Neill, "The Theological Meaning of *Actuosa Participatio* in the Liturgy," in *Sacred Music and Liturgy Reform: Proceedings of the Fifth International Church Music Congress, Chicago-Milwaukee, August 21–28, 1966*, ed. Johannes Overath (Rome: Consociatio Internationalis Musicae Sacrae, 1969), 89–108. A summary of this is in Ruff, *Sacred Music and Liturgical Reform*, 363–64.

[6] See chap. 12.

Huijbers, who in *The Performing Audience* provided the *magna carta* for this extreme interpretation.[7]

But if the council fathers had intended *participatio actuosa* to be satisfied by singing alone, how could they have written that "choirs must be diligently developed" in Article 114 or that composers should not create works that "can be sung not only by large choirs but also by smaller choirs" in Article 121? Why should they have insisted that "all (*sive minister sive fidelis*) taking part in liturgical celebrations . . . should do all that pertains to them, and no more" (SC 28) and, as a primary example, that "members of the choir also exercise a genuine liturgical ministry" if such pertinences were identical to those of the congregation? And in the interests of semantic distinction and precision, why did they not write the perfectly explicit Latin verb *canto / cantare*, "to sing" if that is indeed what they wanted?

Now assume that the council fathers intended *participatio actuosa* to denote an entirely interior disposition, a rapture of devotion when surrounded by the singing of the celebrant or the choir. "Silent listening to the choir singing Gregorian chant or polyphonic Mass parts represents an entirely legitimate form of *actuosa participatio*."[8] But how then could they have encouraged "acclamations, responses, psalms, antiphons, and songs" in Article 30 as a primary means of liturgical participation, or fostered "religious singing" (*cantus popularis religiosus*) so that the "voices of the faithful may be heard" in Article 118?

Any legitimate close reading of *Sacrosanctum Concilium* yields a meaning of *actuosa participatio* that lies somewhere within these extremes while excluding neither of them absolutely. *Musicam Sacram*, following the council by only four years, makes this interpretation quite explicit:

> This participation
> (a) Should be above all internal, in the sense that by it the faithful join their mind to what they pronounce or hear, and cooperate with heavenly grace,

---

[7] Bernard Huijbers, *The Performing Audience*, trans. Ray Noll et al, 2nd ed. (Cincinnati: North American Liturgy Resources, 1974), 7.

[8] Johannes Overath, "Die liturgish-musikalischen Neuerungen des zweiten vatikanischen Konzils," in *Geschichte der katholischen Kirchenmusik*, vol. 2, ed. Karl Gustav Fellerer (Kassel: Bärenreiter-Verlag, 1976), 377. This quotation is translated by Ruff, *Sacred Music and Liturgical Reform*, 362.

(b) Must be, on the other hand, external also, that is, such as to show the internal participation by gestures and bodily attitudes, by the acclamations, responses and singing.

The faithful should also be taught to unite themselves interiorly to what the ministers or choir sing, so that by listening to them they may raise their minds to God.

One cannot find anything more religious and more joyful in sacred celebrations than a whole congregation expressing its faith and devotion in song.[9]

The conciliar authority is loudly supported by all kinds of common sense. From the musician's and music lover's point of view, to insist that the only way of participating in music is to perform it is absurd, flying in the face of millennia of human experience. There is a hint in these debates at times that performing is somehow morally superior to listening, on some higher ontological plane, or at least more satisfying, so that to exclude the congregation from singing on any occasion is uncharitable. Nothing could be further from the truth. As a violist, I have performed Beethoven's *Missa Solemnis*, and as an audience member, I have listened to it. Both experiences were thrilling and unforgettable, and each offered perspectives unavailable to the other. Neither was absolutely superior, and if offered one last chance either to perform or hear the work before death, the choice would be painful. There is certainly no inferiority in the listening experience, as concert series subscribers prove with their money. Indeed, without denying for a moment the joy of making music, to be musically educated means above all to know how to listen.

This accords with the common experience of liturgy in general. Liturgy is constituted of words and actions. There are actions that are performed en masse, such as the opening sign of the cross, and there are others performed only by the celebrant and his ministers while everyone else attends. There are words that are sung or recited all together, such as the many acclamations, and other words, such as the Scripture readings and eucharistic prayers, which are spoken by one person while everyone else listens. Who would suggest that congregants hearing the proclamation of the Gospel do not participate in the

---

[9] *Musicam Sacram*, Instruction on Music in the Liturgy, given March 5, 1967, http://www.vatican.va/archive/hist_councils/ii_vatican_council/documents/vat-ii_instr_19670305_musicam-sacram_en.html, arts. 14–16.

reading? "It is forgotten that the first *actuositas* of man is to listen to the Word, to make resound within its deepest meaning, to allow the Word to illuminate, inundate, reassure and guide the soul of the believer." When considering the Word united to melody, "in fact, music with its beauty comes to transform itself into a numinous symbol connatural with the Word."[10]

Congregational Singing in Religious Traditions

The most immediate impetus for the Roman Rite to promote congregational singing came from the Reformation, when it became a hallmark of Protestant liturgy. The Council of Trent responded to the wave of popular religious music appearing all over Europe in the sixteenth century by resisting it, because the council feared that by adopting that sign of the Reformation as its own, the actual errors of the Protestants might gain some measure of credibility by association. Nevertheless, congregational singing, usually in the form of hymnody, crept into Catholic liturgies in various places, particularly in Germany, and with the revival of plainchant in the nineteenth century it became a cornerstone of the liturgical movement.[11]

Yet the image of the Protestants as champions of the priestly people who all sing the entire liturgy is somewhat overdrawn. Luther's own German Mass provided for the justly famous chorales to be sung by the congregation to be sure, but also preserved polyphonic Mass propers and Ordinaries, sung in Latin by trained choirs. There was a division of liturgical labor, and an absorbed, devotional listening was an integral part of Lutheran liturgical experience from the organ prelude onward. Had Lutheranism taken the radical stance on congregational singing, J. S. Bach and his many colleagues would have had no jobs. The Calvinists tried to insist on pure congregational psalm singing without even organ accompaniment, never mind polyphonic arrangement, and yet by the end of the sixteenth century, the great collections such as the *Genevan Psalter* appeared in harmonized ver-

---

[10] Gastone Zotto, "Il Primato dell'Ascolto nella Celebrazione del Rito Liturgico," in *Amen Vestrum: Miscellanea di Studi Liturgico-Pastorali in Onore di P. Pelagio Visentin*, ed. Alceste Catella (Padua: Edizione Messaggero, 1994), 457. Quoted in Ruff, *Sacred Music and Liturgical Reform*, 372. Translation here is mine.

[11] As Ruff has noted, this creep antedated the Reformation, in some localities by centuries. See *Sacred Music and Liturgical Reform*, 567–73.

sions. Today their descendant churches regularly have choirs and specialized music for them.

At the opposite pole was the late medieval Roman Mass, which provided for no official participation of the congregation. Slowly, in experimental and irregular steps, congregational song secured a place, at first de facto and then finally de jure in the twentieth century.

The Protestant and Catholic experience both show that extreme positions on the point of congregational singing, however liturgically and theologically justified, do not sustain practice for long.[12] Eventually, the tradition moves toward the center, a liturgy in which the congregation fulfills its spiritual desire and exercises an essential role in participation by singing some of the time, while celebrants, cantors, and choirs retain distinct liturgical roles for themselves.

This Christian experience finds analogues in the other world religions. Once, the *piyyut*, the principal form of Jewish liturgical hymn, was the province of the professional cantor, the *hazzan*. Later, its poetic forms became simplified and in Spain often adopted popular Arabic melodies to allow more congregational participation. Maimonides opposed the use of these *piyyutim* in liturgy. Hindu rituals were once dominated by the *dhrupad*, a north Indian composition sung by soloists on fairly complex melodic and rhythmic patterns, but waves of religious fervor in the sixth and twelfth centuries brought with them the *bhajan*, a much simpler liturgical music allowing at least a responsory refrain from the lay participants. And despite condemnation by Islamic authorities, the *qira'a bi'l-alhan*, the chanting of the Qurʾan to popular melodies rather than to the prescribed cantillation formulas, spread throughout the Arabic-speaking world from the ninth to twelfth centuries.

An Eternal Conflict

The forces driving this dynamism of congregational music are two. On the one hand is a desire, apparently innate in all human societies, to praise God with music, in song. "Man remains an image of his

---

[12] The late Middle Ages is certainly a long period, but Ruff demonstrates that popular and even vernacular chanting had made incursions into the liturgy of the Mass perhaps as early as the ninth century. See *Sacred Music and Liturgical Reform*, 568–72. Congregational participation seems to have been common in the early church, and gradually declines with the elaboration of the liturgy and the specialization of trained choirs.

Creator, and retains the desire for the one who calls him into existence. All religions bear witness to men's essential search for God"[13] (CCC 2566). Prayer in song seems like a hot spring boiling under the surface of the earth: it may be stopped up for a while, but it will surely well up at some unexpected time and place.

The stoppers, on the other hand, are usually the religious or liturgical authorities who would limit congregational song in the liturgy. It is easy to accuse them of a territorial selfishness, insecurity, and Pharisaic pride, and sometimes those charges are true. But more often the motives for their wariness are most legitimate, and it is important to understand what they are.

The most intrinsic constraints on congregational singing are technical. Because the vast majority of congregants have little or no formal musical training, congregational liturgical music must be simple. The Jewish *piyyutim*, the Hindu *bhajan*, and Japanese (Buddhist) *wasan*, however distant their grounding theologies, have obvious compositional strategies in common that allow quick and easy learning, particularly in societies and traditions of largely oral tradition. Refrains, isosyllabic poetry with simple rhyme schemes, corresponding periodic phrasing in the music, strong meter, and endlessly repetitive responses, as in litanies, are all ubiquitous. All take advantage of musical structures that exploit basic strategies of human cognition: rehearsal (repetition) and the hierarchical ordering of like forms. Clear beats combining into measures which combine into uniform phrases is only the rhythmic side of such strategies. Using the same musical motives, holding close to the tonic note, moving mostly by step, and ending each phrase with the same sound in a rhyme reinforces the cognitive structure melodically. It is no accident that article 30 of *Sacrosanctum Concilium* specifically recommends "acclamations" and "responses" as promising vehicles for *participatio actuosa*, that article 16 of *Musicam Sacram* concurs by listing them as a first priority in choosing congregational music for Mass. Acclamations and responses are texts so short that working memory alone, along with good will, suffices to learn their music at first hearing.

That is not so with the psalms and antiphons, and certainly not for the *Gloria* and *Credo*, which are all textually complex prayers that own none of the features required for a simple musical setting. The history

---

[13] Eph 1:5-6. See *Catechism of the Catholic Church*, art. 294.

of liturgical music shows how proponents of total congregational singing have struggled with them. Except for the lining out of psalms in certain Protestant Reformed congregations, which by most contemporaneous accounts produced an unholy din, the solutions all demand a deformation of the original texts. Metricization of the psalms, very common in Lutheran hymnody and its relatives, imposes a poetic structure which never existed in the Hebrew (or Latin translations) and brings the usual intractable problems of translating poetry. Converting the *Gloria* or *Credo* into strophic hymns amounts to the same deformation. Modern attempts to make pop songs out of them must impose a refrain such as "Glory to God in the highest" that interrupts the rhetoric, much as repeating "Four score and seven years ago" at intervals would disfigure the Gettysburg address. In short, congregational singing of the more complex liturgical prayers removes them further from the Scriptures or traditional texts from which they spring.

It also removes them, not always but often, from professional levels of musicianship, those qualities regarded as essential to good performance: getting the right notes (accuracy), singing in tune (intonation), moving together in rhythm (ensemble), and so forth. Here the division between the trained musician and the average member of a musical culture becomes uncomfortable.

To be sure, the tacit musical knowledge of the untrained should never be underestimated. Like the tacit understanding of a native language that allows any native speaker to create complex and original utterances and to spot the foreigner's errors without being able in the least to explain why they are wrong, the musical knowledge that one accumulates merely by growing up in a musical society is so vast that, again as in speech, an entire field of study, music psychology, has grown up to study how it is done. It is this native ability that makes congregational singing even possible. And yet, however estimable it may be, that ability is of a different order when compared to the ability of a gifted member of a musical society who has explicitly and formally studied music for twenty years and more. For music is a most exacting and difficult art. The story of Carl Weinrich, the Princeton organist who refused to perform any work that he had not practiced for ten years, may be exaggerated in fact but not in its message.[14] Professional musicians, like professional athletes, may enjoy an occasional

---

[14] Personal communication with Thomas Frost, a former student of Weinrich's.

victory but know that total control and mastery of their art will forever remain something to strive for without hope of ever attaining it in this world.

The history of religions certainly has its episodes where liturgy has been trampled upon by musical virtuosity. Criticism of the florid improvisations of the *hazzanim*, the cantors of Jewish liturgies, rose up in sixteenth-century Europe not far ahead of similar complaints about operatic singing at Mass in the seventeenth century. But surely since the Second Vatican Council the pendulum has swung far to the other side. The zealous infusion of simple song into Catholic liturgy since 1965 has alienated in too many places the professionally trained church musician. The image of a Joe Dimaggio or a Ted Williams being assigned to coaching Little League baseball for the rest of their days, sentenced for the crime of being really good, comes close to what some of these musicians must feel. Some have swallowed their better judgment and cooperated in great charity as best as their consciences allowed; others have left.

"Well, let them go" seems to have been the response of episcopal policy, and, to be sure, zeal for a mistaken notion of democracy in the church, an urge to level anything and everyone, would hold that the exit of musical professionalism is for the best. But such theory has run head-on into the experience of the last forty years, into the hard fact that music is a difficult and exacting art. Conditions in most places are bad. The prophecy of a completely simple liturgical music has been proved false.

It has failed because liturgy must be beautiful, and talented people who study music for twenty years and more are doing nothing more than training themselves to make beauty. That is the sole end of musical training. Now there is no contradiction in musical beauty and musical simplicity, and musical professionalism has no monopoly on the creation of beautiful compositions and performances. Many of our greatest plainchants and hymns have arisen from plain folks living in dim anonymity. But it is extremely difficult to create something that is at once simple enough for anyone to sing and at the same time has the universal qualities of lasting beauty, if only because the latter is so difficult even given the widest terms, never mind the constraints of simplicity. Congregational singing, by its untutored nature, must exclude certain great musical resources of beauty, techniques refined by the passing of centuries. This asceticism does not make great congregational music impossible, of course, as we know from history, but it does make it rare. And any proponent of broad congregational singing must be ready to accept, given the wildly variegated assembly from all walks of life that Thomas Day affectionately calls "the people," some pretty bad performances in the divine liturgy. God has not bestowed musical gifts democratically; not everyone can sing in tune.

Historically, popular movements to sing in praise of the divine, such as the Lutheran chorale, have originated outside authorized liturgy and worked their way into it. There is no conscious design to this process, no professional direction, and so such movements are unorganized, haphazard, purely popular, true upwellings of the spirit. The musical style for this singing is taken from the nearest thing at hand in the culture, popular music, which brings with it whatever semantic range it has already acquired as music used by the people.[15] In cultures where there is little explicit distinction between the sacred and secular—for example, Hindu culture until recently or the Christian Middle Ages in Europe—a popular style may adapt itself easily to a sacred rite without unwanted associations. But whenever a popular musical style has a distinctly secular semantic owing to its origins and cultural associations, connotations inappropriate for liturgy result. If contemporary Catholic liturgies in the United States seem drained of all solemnity and sacred character, little different from any other public meeting or, in the worst cases, from variety shows on television, it is because the liturgical styles of their music connote television and the rest of the secular world's traditional idols of money, power, and pleasure. Throughout history, religious authorities, from Maimonides to the Council of Trent to modern juridical Islam, have warned against the indiscriminate importation of popular music into their liturgies for precisely this reason.

In the long controversy over *participatio actuosa*, then, both the historical experience of world religions and the nature of congregational singing ratify the broad middle ground staked out by *Sacrosanctum Concilium* and *Musicam Sacram*. Simply put, the middle ground is that the congregation should not sing everything in the liturgy, nor should it feel obligated to do so, but it should sing some things. Exactly what those things are fuels the continuing debates on local and national levels. The documents wisely refrain from defining them, for they must be fashioned on the scene, taking the local context and

---

[15] On the meaning and nature of "semantic range," see chap. 12.

culture into account. For any number of reasons, some parishes will sing more than others. Anthony Ruff's *Sacred Music and Liturgical Reform* has in its final chapters a great deal of well-supported advice on this point, but necessarily conflicting criteria will make any solution provisional.

An Example from St. Mark's Basilica, Venice

Indeed, Catholic congregational singing will forever be a matter of making adjustments—minor ones, one hopes—in the light of experience. For the conflict between congregational singing and legitimate liturgical interests is indeed eternal and local, and theory can take us only so far. Case studies should loom large until the firm foundations of tradition are set. One most interesting example is the liturgy of the solemn Mass at the Basilica of St. Mark's in Venice. Here is a summary of the musical program for the liturgy as it was celebrated in the fall of 2005:

1. Introit. After an organ prelude, the choir sings a polyphonic setting of the Latin entrance antiphon for the day, with rousing organ accompaniment. The congregation stands, attending to the music and the substantial procession of at least a dozen ministers, followed by the incensing of the altar.

2. Invocation and greeting. These are chanted by the celebrant in Italian (the vernacular). The congregation responds in kind.

3. *Kyrie eleison*. Sung in Greek to a simple Gregorian melody, in the antiphonal manner, with the congregation answering the choir.

4. *Gloria in excelsis Deo*. Sung by the choir alone, usually in a Latin, polyphonic setting.

5. Prayer, chanted in Italian by the celebrant, followed by the first reading, which is spoken.

6. Responsorial psalm. A cantor intones the antiphon, to which the congregation responds. The cantor then chants the psalm in paired verses, all in Italian. After each pair sounds the congregational response.

7. Gospel acclamation. Following the second reading (spoken), the congregation sings a simple Alleluia, with the choir singing the

versicle. The gospel is read in spoken Italian, except at the Patriarchal celebration of the Vigil of the Immaculate Conception, when it was chanted in Italian.

8. *Credo*. Always the well-known seventeenth-century "neo-Gallican" Credo III of the *Graduale Romanum* sung in Latin in the antiphonal manner between choir and congregation. The programs indicate the texts to be sung by the congregation with bold print.
9. Offertory antiphon. A polyphonic composition for the choir accompanies the procession and incensing of ministers and congregation.
10. Prefatory responses are chanted in Italian between celebrant and congregation. Then the celebrant chants the preface in Italian. The choir follows immediately with a polyphonic Latin *Sanctus*.
11. The eucharistic prayer is spoken in Italian by the celebrant. The memorial acclamation, a chant in Italian that is the same each time, is sung by choir and congregation.
12. *Pater Noster*. Sung in Latin by choir and congregation to a traditional chant (again the Latin text is printed in the program).
13. *Agnus Dei*. Sung in Latin by choir and congregation to a Gregorian melody.
14. Communion antiphon. A polyphonic composition for choir.
15. Dismissal rites. Chanted in Italian by the celebrant with the congregation responding in kind.
16. The recession is accompanied usually by an exuberant piece for organ. Occasionally the choir sings as well. In the latter case, an organ postlude follows.

Most conspicuous by their total absence are the Lutheran-type hymns (the single occasion in fall 2005: on the Vigil of the Immaculate Conception, *O Sanctissima* was sung as a congregational processional hymn, replacing the entrance antiphon). To American and European Catholic music ministers who have for forty years fixated on "the four hymns" that replace proper antiphons, it must come as something of a revelation that a liturgy without them is even imaginable, never mind one as beautiful as this.

And yet, the absence of hymns means no loss of active participation by the congregation. Of the sixteen points of the liturgy listed above, the congregation sings in eleven and participates by active listening and watching in the other five. The continuous movement and varieties of sound keep one constantly engaged. (One American congregant confessed that she never noticed the hymns' absence.) The congregational singing seems dedicated and enthusiastic, despite the constant transience of the tourist component. Indeed, that Credo III, a long and through-composed chant sung from word sheets without musical notation, comes off as well as it does week after week indicates an earnest congregation indeed.

The division of liturgical labor relieves the congregation of the pressure to provide musical "variety" week after week. The most mobile texts, the propers, are left to the trained choir, which is professionally equipped to learn the hundreds of settings rapidly. The congregation does sing a new psalm antiphon each week, a single phrase of music, but otherwise sings the core of Ordinary prayers and acclamations that remain constant. Comfort level is high.

The liturgy at St. Mark's contradicts completely the stereotype of polyphony and plainchant as music that is, well, plain and always the same. The polyphonic settings at St. Mark's range from the sixteenth to twentieth centuries, the latter filled with all manner of dissonances and sophisticated rhythms that sound worlds away from Palestrina. And the chant has at least six modes of presentation: solo voice a cappella, choir a cappella, congregation a cappella, and then those three with various manners of accompaniment and harmonization. It would be hard to match this solemn Mass for sheer variety of musical sound and effect.

And that is why the broad middle ground of *participatio actuosa*, greater than a mere political compromise of opposing interests at Vatican II, is a conception superior—musically, liturgically, and theologically—to militancy of either total congregational singing or none. For both of those liturgies are impoverished by their limitation to a single form of congregational participation in music, either singing or contemplation. At St. Mark's, the experience is incomparably enriched by different kinds of participation in beautiful music, music worthy of the Most High. Worshipers do more than complete an assigned task or fulfill a role; they create a communal work of sacred art that the liturgy should be, an image of the proper diversity in the church itself, as described in its dogmatic constitution *Lumen Gentium*:

> In virtue of this catholicity each part contributes its own gifts to other parts and to the entire church, so that the whole and each of the parts are strengthened by the common sharing of all things and by the common effort to achieve fullness in unity. Hence it is that the people of God is not only an assembly of different peoples, but in itself is made up of various ranks. This diversity among its members is either by reason of their duties—some exercise the sacred ministry for the good of their brothers and sisters; or it is due to their condition and manner of life. (LG 13)

A violist in a string quartet is the one most often called upon to provide the routine accompanimental figures, the inner chord tones, and the rhythmic engines for the ensemble. For significant periods he plays nothing at all, silently attending to what surrounds him and waiting for the next cue to enter. This is no insult, no demotion, for he knows that the silence is as much a component of the total artwork of the string quartet as is any note played. It is true that the violist is rarely the center of attention. That starring role goes to the first violinist, and yet the first violinist can never say to the violist, "I do not need you" (cf. 1 Cor 12:21) The violist, however much in the background, is just as essential to the integrity of the string quartet as any other player.

The same is true of any liturgy where the musical *participatio actuosa* is shared according to the musical gifts that God has meted out to all present. "To one is given through the Spirit the expression of Wisdom, and to another the expression of knowledge according to the same Spirit; to another faith by the same Spirit; and to another gifts of healing by the one Spirit; to another mighty deeds; to another prophecy; to another discernment of spirits; to another varieties of tongues; to another interpretation of tongues. But one and the same Spirit produces all of these, distributing them individually to each person as he wishes" (1 Cor 12:8-11). For in the liturgy, as in any drama, roles are different, unequal yet essential. The celebrant cannot say to the laity, the lector cannot say to the congregation, the congregant cannot say to the choir, no one truly active can say to anyone else, "I do not need you."

Chapter 19

Foundations

> In the new freedom we need teachers above all. We need patience, and we need time.
>
> Francis P. Schmitt (1967)

The opening chapter of this book, "Liturgical Music Theory," proposed a model for reflecting upon the relationship between the sacred liturgy and its music analogous to the relation of Scripture and dogmatic tradition, that is, with one informing the other in an *"ongoing dialectical relationship* between *text* and *context."*[1] And so we have proceeded. We have used the source document in its historical context, *Sacrosanctum Concilium*, to interpret the realities of music in the context of the sacred liturgy. Now it is time to apply what we have learned about those musical realities to a rereading of the sixth chapter of that foundational document in order to understand better why it says what it says about liturgical music, in much the same way that a dogmatic truth informs the rereading of Scripture.[2]

---

[1] Kevin W. Irwin, *Context and Text: Method in Liturgical Theology* (Collegeville, MN: Liturgical Press, 1994), 56; emphasis in the original.

[2] There are still some who believe that no close reading of any council document will aid church renewal, because it is not to the text but to the "spirit of Vatican II" to which we must attend. A somewhat subtler argument contends that close reading is irrelevant because the final text was intended to placate minority views and ensure by its ambiguities that, according to Pope Paul VI's wishes, all conciliar documents would be approved by large majorities. It would seem to require very little imagination to see how any such attitude can lead only to chaos, with everyone having an equally legitimate claim on interpreting "the spirit" or "what the council really meant," just as analogous attitudes toward the Constitution of the United States would destroy American justice. All such foundational documents are the products of compromise, but the texts are the only basis for reasoned and even approximately objective interpretation of the event. Even though interpretation includes, even requires, a historical context, it is a responsible and highly circumscribed context that rules out, to take the extreme case, flat contradictions of

Sacrosanctum Concilium Revisited

Chapter VI: Sacred Music

> *112. The musical tradition of the universal church is a treasure of inestimable value, greater even than that of any other art.*

The constitution chapter opens with a vast spectacle, for the sacred treasure is not merely a repertory but a living tradition of enormous historical reach and cultural breadth. Here is the ratification of that critical turning point in the history of the Roman Rite which decided that liturgical music would not be one in being with the Word, but rather a means of offering that Word back to God. As such, it could take various forms and styles, growing with each century, as long as it remained faithful to the Word.

As vast as this spectacle may be, it is not unbounded, for traditions, by their very nature, have limits. Some things belong to the tradition and some do not, for if everything is, or may be, "traditional," the term ceases to mean anything. Here is a potential distinction to ground the semantics of sacred music.

As a treasure of inestimable value, the council fathers intended at the very least that the tradition not be ignored. And yet, in the years immediately following the council, the tradition was more than ignored: it was renounced, buried like the unworthy steward's charge, an unclean thing. One can only conclude that in this respect the liturgical reform outlined by *Sacrosanctum Concilium* was woefully misunderstood.

> *The main reason for this pre-eminence is that, as a combination of sacred music and words, it forms a necessary or integral part of the solemn liturgy.*

---

literal meanings in the text and other willful misinterpretations. The worldwide Synod of Bishops called in 1985 by Pope John Paul II to assess the state of renewal two decades after the council "came up with six agreed principles for sound interpretation." Among these: "3. The pastoral import of the documents ought not to be separated from, or set in opposition to, their doctrinal content. 4. No opposition may be made between the spirit and the letter of Vatican II." For fuller discussion of this issue, see Avery Dulles, "Vatican II: The Myth and the Reality," *America* 188, no. 6 (February 24, 2003): 8–9.

> *Sacred scripture, indeed, has praised sacred song (see Eph 5:19; Col 3:16). So have the Fathers of the Church and the Roman pontiffs who in more recent times, led by St Pius X, have explained more precisely the ministerial function of sacred music in the service of the Lord.*

Why is the tradition of sacred music a treasure of inestimable value? Because it is united to the words of the liturgy and to every specific act of praise and thanksgiving in a way that no other art or human artifact can be. Like words, music is an intangible reality that occupies no space but instead creates a time-world of its own within the normal time of our everyday existence, an icon of the liturgy's very action. In fact, the English translation "combination of sacred music and words" greatly understates the reality expressed by the document's original Latin *cantus sacer qui verbis inhaeret*, the music that inheres to and becomes an essential part of the prayer and thus an integral part of the liturgy. Therefore, the more closely the music can form itself to the nature of the words, the greater is its right to the name of liturgical music. And yet, the sacred words themselves, while essential to the liturgy, cannot by themselves guarantee a worthy composition. They are a necessary but insufficient condition. The organization of tones, the music qua music, owns its own essential qualities.

> *Therefore sacred music is to be considered the more holy, the more closely connected it is with the liturgical action, whether making prayer more pleasing, promoting unity of minds, or conferring greater solemnity on the sacred rites.*

The most important of these qualities, "connected . . . with the liturgical action" (*cum actione liturgica connectetur*), is abstract, especially given the vast semantic ranges of melodies without words. What does it mean for music to connect to the liturgical action? In the most pedestrian practical application, it means to coordinate with a physical movement, so that just enough psalm verses of the introit are sung to cover the entrance procession, the last antiphon dying away as the ministers reach their positions in the sanctuary. This is well and good, and liturgists have wagged many a finger in its favor in recent years.[3] But the connection must go deeper, surely, beyond merely accompanying the parades of the liturgy.

---

[3] See Irwin, *Context and Text: Method in Liturgical Theology*, 239.

Article 112 sets three desiderata for liturgical connection that begin to limit its understanding, that is, to define it. The first is "whether making prayer more pleasing," a somewhat flat translation of *orationem suavius exprimens*, "expressing prayer more sweetly" or perhaps "smoothly." The Latin more clearly points to the object of this desideratum: that prayer, itself and objectively, is to be made sweeter, not necessarily those who pray. If worshipers are delighted as well, so much the better, but their satisfaction is not the primary object of singing the liturgy.[4] The second desideratum is "promoting unity of minds" (*unanimitatem fovens*), *unanimitatem* having the sense of "concord." In the context of "liturgical action," this suggests that music draws the congregation to focus on what we believe and therefore on the singular object of worship, the paschal mystery. To what other purpose would unity of minds be directed?[5] This is the first strong hint of the necessity of a semantic distinction in sacred music, for if music is to foster a concord of faith, it must refer to it, however abstractly, to the exclusion of other things. Reference requires semantic power. The last desideratum confirms this necessity unambiguously: "conferring greater solemnity." Music connects with the liturgical action by proclaiming with every note that it is the most important action of our lives. We perform extraordinary things, such as presidential inaugurations and championship sports matches, with due solemn ceremony. Since the paschal mystery is greater by far, so must it have its greater solemnity, conferred in part by its music like no other in the world.

> *The church, indeed, approves of all forms of true art which have the requisite qualities, and admits them into divine worship.*

"The requisite qualities" again affirms that sacred words alone cannot ensure the integrity of a composition of sacred music. "All forms" again affirms that the sacred treasure is not a fixed repertory of com-

---

[4] Of course if the music is good and appropriate, worshipers must be delighted in the deep spiritual satisfaction of worthy and faithful worship. This delight is quite distinct from the moist eyes and spine chills that music, delightful in and of itself, can produce in those who love it.

[5] This interpretation is supported by the occurrence of the same verb *fovere* in art. 1 of the constitution, which states that the purpose of the constitution is "to encourage whatever can promote the union of all who believe in Christ."

positions but a tradition that, while certainly comprising a repertory, is capable of admitting new musical forms and new musical languages. But this is no relativistic invitation to all comers. To the contrary, "true art" proclaims the government of absolute truth and beauty over all experiments, developments, and growths of the tradition.

> *Accordingly, the sacred council, keeping to the norms and precepts of ecclesiastical tradition and discipline and having regard to the purpose of sacred music, which is the glory of God and the sanctification of the faithful, decrees as follows:*

This conclusion to Chapter VI's preamble, really the key article in the chapter, appears formulaic at first glance but actually amplifies its assessment of the role and power of music in liturgy. By alluding to adherence to "ecclesiastical tradition and discipline" it constructs an analogue with dogmatic tradition and its enormous prestige. Then, almost offhandedly, it defines the very purpose of sacred music, "the glory of God and the sanctification of the faithful," in a way that summarizes the more discursive exposition of the purpose of the sacred liturgy as a whole in articles 7 and 8 and makes the role of music in it parallel. Lastly, this purpose implies that music has the power of sanctification, not by itself, of course, but in its connection with the liturgical action.

> *113. Liturgical worship is given a more dignified character when the rites* [divina Officia] *are celebrated solemnly in song, with sacred ministers taking part and with the active participation of the people.*

The opening of article 113 affixes the conclusion to these inferences.[6] The mention of "sacred ministers" here implies a differentiation of roles in the liturgy and also that these ministers include in their offices a ministry of music of some kind, else there would be no assistance required. Here "active participation" (*acutose participet*) makes the first of its three appearances in the chapter. The conjunction of the term

---

[6] The plural "Divine Offices" in this context clearly denotes the eucharistic liturgy (Mass) as well as the set of prayer services often collectively referred to as the Divine Office: Matins or Vigils, Lauds, Prime, Tierce, Sext, None, Vespers, and Compline.

with "assistance of sacred ministers" hints again that the effort is cooperative, as in any drama, with clearly distinct roles. It may seem an obvious point that the people are to sing, and that is a fair interpretation in the light of what follows, but the actual text here is slightly ambiguous about who sings, for it uses the passive voice in the key phrase *sollemniter in cantu celebrantur*, particularly inasmuch as *cantu* may be easily translated as "chant" rather than "song."

> As regards the language to be used, the provisions of article 36 are to be observed; for the Mass, article 54; for the sacraments, article 63; for the Divine Office, article 101.

The cited articles warrant the preference for Latin with provision made for vernaculars for pastoral reasons.[7] Article 54, however, specifically approves that "the faithful may also be able to say or to sing together in Latin those parts of the Ordinary of the Mass which pertain to them," foreseeing the commonsense practicalities discovered in the last four decades' experience. Singing the same Ordinary settings week after week, a congregation, even an impoverished one with no printed materials, can master by oral tradition alone the *Gloria* and *Credo*, to say nothing of the shorter prayers, and at the same time establish a worldwide common prayer in a common language to common music.[8] Omitting mention of the propers would seem to presume a more highly trained body for their performance.

---

[7] Quoted in chap. 2.

[8] The Notre Dame study of liturgy corroborates this. "A clearer indication of the weakness of congregational singing is the fact that in only 12 percent of all Masses did the overwhelming majority of the people join in hymn singing; in another 18 percent at least two-thirds joined in. The singing of the common parts of the Mass (i.e. Kyrie or Gloria or Sanctus, etc.) was wholehearted at between a quarter and a third of the Masses. From this information, two things seem clear: The general level of congregational participation in the sung parts of the Mass is far from impressive, but the congregation does slightly better with repeated, familiar texts like the Sanctus than with texts which change from week to week, like hymns." Mark Searle and David C. Leege, "The Celebration of Liturgy in the Parishes," in *Notre Dame Study of Catholic Parish Life*, Report No. 5 (August 1985), ed. David C. Leege and Joseph Gremillion (Notre Dame, IN: University of Note Dame, 1985), 7. The solemn liturgy at St. Mark's in Venice, when the *Credo* is sung from memory by the congregation, is living proof of this common sense.

> 114. *The treasury of sacred music is to be preserved and cultivated with great care.*

This sentence has been emblazoned on the standard of liturgical traditionalists, but what exactly is "the treasury of sacred music (*Thesaurus Musicae*)"?[9] Anthony Ruff devotes a significant body of research to this question, and his conclusion that "the treasure of sacred music" cannot denote a fixed repertory of musical works is correct.[10] If the historical fact of growth and change in the repertory alone were not enough to convince, article 112 of this same document, which equates treasure with tradition, and certainly article 121, the exhortation to composers, must do so. But this truth is surely no license to jettison the historical repertory, as was attempted right after the council, since tradition by its very nature is a historical phenomenon. "New tradition" is nearly oxymoronic, possible only in relative terms, that is, in comparison with other, older traditions. To proclaim the invention of a tradition is pretentious and futile, for a tradition can only be validated with the passage of time, enough to fog the memory of any invention. Preservation and cultivating must therefore comprise the historical repertory, not as some immutable idol but as a resource for living liturgy and living composers. A tradition that cannot admit the growth of new repertory within its bounds is dead; a tradition that rejects its history destroys itself.

> *Choirs must be diligently developed, especially in cathedral churches. Bishops and other pastors of souls must do their best to ensure that whenever a liturgical service is to be accompanied by chant, the whole body of the faithful may be able to take that active part which is rightly theirs, as laid down in articles 28 and 30.*

The most immediate reading of this passage, to be supported by what follows in article 116, is that choirs have an important and distinct liturgical office in the reformed liturgy. A second reading might well infer that the function of church choirs is to support the congregation in their "active participation," which then can only be understood as

---

[9] *Thesaurus* is perhaps better translated as "treasure" rather than "treasury," which has connotations of place rather than the riches themselves.

[10] Anthony Ruff, *Sacred Music and Liturgical Reform* (Chicago: Hillenbrand, 2007), 357; see especially the analysis of magisterial documents in Part IV.

"singing." The two readings are not mutually exclusive: the distinct liturgical office of the choir has been multifaceted throughout history, and in the reformed liturgy it acquires a new facet, that of leading the congregation in song, while at the same time retaining its more traditional facets of chanting Mass propers, polyphonic Ordinaries, and so forth. The balance of the two readings is affected by the translation "rightly theirs," which might suggest that singing as much as possible is a "right" of the congregation. The Latin original *actuosam participationem sibi propriam* might have been rendered as "active participation proper to themselves" or perhaps "their own active participation," and that implies that there are musical moments reserved for other offices. There can be no doubt that the contradistinction drawn by the paragraph demands that the congregation be included in the music of the liturgy, but exactly how this is accomplished is yet ambiguous.

> *115. Much emphasis should be placed on the teaching of music and on musical activity [praxis musica] in seminaries, in the novitiates and houses of studies of religious of both sexes, and also in other Catholic institutions and schools. To impart this instruction teachers are to be carefully trained and put in charge of the teaching of sacred music.*
>
> *It is desirable also that higher institutes of sacred music be established whenever possible.*
>
> *Musicians and singers, especially boys, must also be given a genuine liturgical training.*

It is remarkable that, given the immense status and significance of the liturgy in Catholic theology and Catholic life and given the great importance of music within that liturgy just explicated, the council fathers thought this commonsense nuts-and-bolts advice necessary for *Sacrosanctum Concilium*. But if that is remarkable, how widely that advice has been ignored is astounding.[11] The average non-Catholic

---

[11] Nathan Mitchell reported in 1980 that although some seminaries had just begun to require some basic skills in sight singing and vocal training, in most seminaries, "pastoral music" was an optional elective at best. See "Liturgical Education in Roman Catholic Seminaries: A Report and an Appraisal," *Worship* 54, no. 2 (March 10, 1980): 137. Edward Schaefer has practical observations on the kinds of reform required for seminary education. See Helen Hull Hitchcock, "*Evangelia Cantata*: A Notated Book of Gospels; A Review-Interview with the Composer," *Adoremus Bulletin* 14, no. 1 (March 2008): 6.

American undergraduate music major will know traditions of Catholic music better than most priests.

> 116. *The church recognizes Gregorian chant as especially native to the Roman liturgy. Therefore, other things being equal, it should be given pride of place in liturgical services.*

This is one of the most often cited sentences in the entire chapter on liturgical music. The term "Gregorian chant" is not to be interpreted strictly as the relatively small set of northern European Mass propers dating from the seventh century, as academic chant historians might do, but rather as a commonplace for the range of Catholic plainchant in various places at least into the seventeenth century.[12] This explicit endorsement of a tradition within a tradition is carefully limited to the Roman Rite and thus avoids offending authentic historical traditions of other rites that are in communion with Rome now, such as the Armenian, or in the future, such as the Byzantine or Russian. The sentence also implies the continued use of Latin as a sacred language, in harmony with article 113, although it certainly does not forbid chanting in other languages or translating the original Latin texts of Gregorian chants.

The famous qualifier *ceteris paribus* (other things being equal) makes its appearance here to accommodate local conditions that might obstruct the use of plainchant or warrant its replacement by something more suitable for the sacred liturgy. In the light of both the theoretical nature of plainchant and experience since the council, it is difficult to imagine what these conditions might be in any general case. The American Gospel Mass, sung where the local people have grown up with an alternative musical language owning a true sacred semantic, might be judged a situation where "other things" outweigh the Gregorian advantages of biblical Mass propers specific for each Sunday: a universal and neutral language and a musical means to connect with the rest of the world.

In view of the general circumspection of the sixth chapter of *Sacrosanctum Concilium*, the explicit and sole ratification of plainchant as the church's musical language par excellence is astonishing and audacious. Assuming that the council fathers, by and large, could not have

---

[12] See chap. 7.

known in any detail about the technical advantages of plainchant—its free rhythm allowing natural conformance to any text, its liturgical efficiency, its cultural neutrality allowing smooth inculturation the world over, the enormous variety and complexity of repertory, its ease of learning in its simpler exemplars, and above all its utterly distinct and powerful sacred semantic, a kind of solemnity shared with all the world's major religions—their prescience is indeed a marvelous wisdom.

> *Other kinds of sacred music, especially polyphony, are by no means excluded from liturgical celebrations, so long as they accord with the spirit of the liturgical action as laid down in article 30.*

Yet another affirmation that the treasure of sacred music is no one repertory, not even plainchant, but an ancient tradition of worldwide provenance, forever capable of change and adaptation, a living thing. Why, amidst this main point of the sentence, amidst the "other kinds," is classical polyphony the only such alternative singled out?[13]

Cynics might argue that "especially polyphony" was the price the conservative wing of the council demanded for the rest of the sentence, and so it might have been. But that does not gainsay the unique qualities of the classical polyphonic repertory: a frozen musical language, historically preserved like the Latin language, whose sacred semantic is not only unimpeachable but, owing to its near-exclusive association with the Roman Rite, uniquely Catholic. There is no other style on the horizon that will share these properties in the near future, so it was certainly worth pointing out these special powers of the repertory.

But its mention nevertheless affects our understanding of active participation, indirectly cited in the reference to article 30: "To develop active participation, the people should be encouraged to take part by means of acclamations, responses, psalms, antiphons, and songs, as well as by actions, gestures, and bodily attitudes. And at the proper time a reverent silence should be observed." This is a curious near

---

[13] The document does not explicitly say "classical polyphony" in the sense that I have used it since chap. 8, but simply *polyphonia*. But only music theorists would understand "polyphony" to include any composition that combines simultaneous melodies in counterpoint from the Middle Ages on. Certainly in 1963, the council fathers had the repertory of the high Renaissance polyphonists in mind.

contradiction. Surely article 30 provides strong and virtually explicit support for congregational singing, and yet, "accords with the spirit," which constrains the choice of "other kinds of sacred music," cannot denote only congregational singing, else the promotion of polyphony makes no sense at all. And the list of means for active participation again implies the diversity of liturgical roles, since otherwise the people would just sing everything.[14]

> 117. *The standard edition of the books of Gregorian chant is to be completed. In addition a more critical edition is to be prepared of those books already published since the restoration by St Pius X.*
> *It is desirable also that an edition be prepared containing simpler melodies for use in smaller churches.*

This article implies more than a bit of housekeeping. Conciliar support for common editions of plainchant to use as a source, reference, and model backs up with action the "pride of place" awarded in article 116.[15] The second sentence refers to what became the *Graduale Simplex*, mostly simple antiphons and psalm tones that could be

---

[14] The wisdom of diversity of roles appears to be born out in practice. The Notre Dame Study: "Where the cantor sings less than 70 percent of the music, congregational participation rises sharply above that attained with any other kind of musical leadership. A similar phenomenon was observed with congregational singing itself. The congregation is much more likely to sing wholeheartedly if it is neither left to do all the singing nor virtually excluded by choir, folk group, cantor or other musicians. In other words, a sharing of the singing among different elements in the assembly would seem to be the most effective way of enhancing sung participation." Searle and Leege, "The Celebration of Liturgy in the Parishes," 7.

[15] This is corroborated by one of the prime movers of liturgical reform at the Second Vatican Council, Annibale Bugnini. See his *The Reform of the Liturgy 1948–1975*, trans. Matthew J. O'Connell (Collegeville, MN: Liturgical Press, 1990), 119–21, where he describes the intent of these publications in detail.

As a remarkable instance of contradictory interpretation motivated by zeal, Frederick R. McManus wrote four years after *Sacrosanctum Concilium*, "Article 117. The significance of the simple gradual, a direct fruit of Chapter VI, does not lie in the Latin texts and accompanying melodies. It lies rather in the principle: the first alternative to the proper chants of the Roman gradual is officially provided, and the door thus opened to greater diversity and adaptation." McManus, "Sacred Music in the Teaching of the Church," in *Crisis in Church Music?* (Washington, DC: The Liturgical Conference, 1967), 20. If McManus' assessment were true, however, the last sentence of article 116 which provides for "other kinds of sacred music" would have no sense.

learned with the minimal resources of rural or impoverished parishes. The council fathers saw no contradiction at all in the promotion of plainchant with the principle of *participatio actuosa*.[16] In short, article 117 provides the musical tools for any parish that wishes to reach beyond its parochial boundaries to the wider Catholic world by establishing a common tradition of liturgical music.

> 118. *Religious singing by the faithful is to be skillfully encouraged so that in devotional exercises as well as in liturgical services the voices of the faithful may be heard, in conformity with the norms and requirements of the rubrics.*

The explicit endorsement of congregational singing (*cantus popularis religiosus*), implicit at many other points in *Sacrosanctum Concilium*, arrives with four remarkable points. First, the watchword *participatio actuosa* is nowhere to be read in the article, implying yet again that the relationship between *participatio actuosa* and congregational singing is not that of a translation or an equation, but most likely that of super-class and subclass. *Participatio actuosa* certainly includes congregational singing as a prime element and evidence, but is not exhausted by it. Second, such singing "is to be skillfully encouraged." The best of efforts in any particular situation is what is worthy of the liturgy, and to achieve that for music in most cases demands professional direction. Third, we read once again in the last clause that there is no presumption that the congregation will sing everything, that more singing is not necessarily better liturgy. There is a division of labor, an assignment of roles in the drama. Finally, that "devotions and sacred exercises" (*piis sacrisque exercitiis*) comes ahead of "liturgical services" (*liturgicis actionibus*) reflects the typical solution for the historical tension of popular religious singing and the most solemn liturgies in every major religion. A simple, repetitive ritual such as the Stations of the Cross

---

[16] The Notre Dame Study agrees in its comment on those few parishes in the mid-1980s using plainchant: "but if the experiences of these parishes are anything to go by, there is no reason for thinking that chant will inhibit full congregational participation." Searle and Leege, "The Celebration of Liturgy in the Parishes," 7. Reaching further back, Aidan Nichols reports how "capacity crowds of two thousand and more who in the years 1937 to 1939 at Westminster Cathedral sang the *Ordinarium Missae* from the *Kyriale* . . . with a schola of male amateurs rendering the *Proprium Missae* remain in the corporate memory as testimonials to what could be done." Nichols, *Looking at the Liturgy: A Critical View of Its Contemporary Form* (San Francisco: Ignatius Press, 1996), 106.

can accommodate much more easily than the Eucharistic liturgy a simple, repetitive song that satisfies the innate desire to praise God with music.

> 119. *In some places, in mission lands especially, there are people who have their own musical tradition, and this plays an important part in their religious and social life. For this reason their music should be held in due esteem and should be given a suitable role, not only in forming their religious sense but also in adapting worship to their native genius, as indicated in articles 39 and 40.*

The article proclaims for music the ancient tradition now called "inculturation," with its traditional context of missions. The second sentence prefigures the more explicit doctrine of the double movement that appeared thirty years later in *Varietates Legitimae*. The new culture's music enriches the Catholic tradition even as the Roman Rite sanctifies the culture. The double movement and the constraint of the "suitable role" (*locus congruus*) together make it clear that the Roman Rite acknowledges cultural values as relative, in concordance with the most fundamental Catholic beliefs about fallen human nature. Not all local music is justified for the sacred liturgy, certainly not by the mere fact of its local authenticity.

> *Therefore, in the musical training of missionaries, special care should be taken to ensure that they will be capable of encouraging the traditional music of those peoples both in schools and in sacred services, as far as may be practicable.*

The article's conclusion strengthens the idea that inculturation is a relative value, mostly as a strategy of evangelization. To places already evangelized, traditionally Christian lands, no particular license is given to secular styles, and for good reason. Why replace traditional liturgical musics owning an explicitly sacred semantic with ones whose semantic ranges are compromised at best?

> 120. *The pipe organ is to be held in high esteem in the Latin church, for it is the traditional musical instrument, the sound of which can add a wonderful splendor to the church's ceremonies and can most effectively elevate people's spirits to God and things above.*
>
> *Other instruments also may be used in divine worship, at the discretion and with the consent of the competent territorial authority as laid down*

in articles 22 § 2, 37 and 40, provided that they are suitable, or can be made suitable, for sacred use, that they accord with the dignity of the sacred building, and that they truly contribute to the edification of the faithful.

The question of musical instruments in the sacred liturgy has been vexatious since the early centuries of the church when they were banned, perhaps in continuity with Jewish practice, which eliminated instruments as a sign of mourning after the destruction of the Temple in 70 AD, but more likely to keep Christian liturgical music semantically distinct from pagan instrumental music. Most religions restrict the use of instruments out of concern, conscious or not, to retain a sacred semantic in their rituals.

But it is a historical fact that instruments of various kinds have found their way into Catholic liturgies for at least ten centuries. This by no means eliminates the semantic issue, but conditions it. The council's praise of the pipe organ reflects the fact that this instrument, virtually alone, has acquired the connotation of "sacred instrument" by virtue of its exclusive employment within church walls.[17] No other instrument in the Western tradition can boast this history, and so the article mentions none, for in that respect violins, trumpets, and other symphonic instruments are compromised owing to their traditional associations with opera and secular music, to say nothing of piano and electric guitar, which were both born in the secular world of popular music and never left it.[18] The conditions that "the instruments are suitable . . . for sacred use, that they accord with the dignity of the sacred building, and that they truly contribute to the edification of the faithful" therefore warn that the indiscriminate importation of instruments into the liturgy can do harm because instruments are not

---

[17] In the nineteenth century certain kinds of organs began to appear as entertainment instruments, particularly in theaters and, in the twentieth century, cinemas. But these instruments are quite distinct in sound from the traditional pipe organ found in churches, and in any case the fashion never became sufficiently popular to threaten the sacred connotation of the pipe organ.

[18] This semantic appears to affect congregational singing. The Notre Dame study reports that "The presence of a choir was as effective in encouraging the congregation to sing as was the leadership of a cantor, and both of these were more likely to be associated with strong congregational singing than was the playing of a guitarist. Likewise, when the organ is played throughout the liturgy, congregational singing is likely to be more wholehearted than when a guitarist played." Searle and Leege, "The Celebration of Liturgy in the Parishes," 7.

semantically neutral. They bring the baggage of their origins, symbols whose harmony with liturgical symbols must be assessed. The assessment is obviously rooted in local culture and its musical symbologies. Within these conditions and perspectives then, the article opens the church door to those instruments around the world whose histories, necessarily different from those of the organ and piano, have provided them with semantic connotations appropriate for the Roman Rite.

In any case, the last phrase suggests that cultural assessment of instruments should aspire to more than setting a minimum standard for propriety to prevent unworthy connotations, by seeking sounds that complement the work of the liturgy and "elevate people's spirits to God." Both the English "edification" and the Latin *aedificationi* in the article refer to an act of building, the moral instruction of spirits, and not merely to their sensual pleasure. Instrumental sound and even purely instrumental music, such as an organ prelude, may do this in the same way as a religious icon, by pointing to objects of faith that may contribute to such building. But sound, being incomparably more abstract than the icon, does it not by referring to concrete saints and symbols in the gospels, but to memories and experiences brought to believers' minds by the sound's associations, however dim and inchoate, with spiritual encounters already experienced. Thus the present builds upon the past to make the spiritual edifice higher, closer to God, if the sound will allow it.

> 121. *Composers, animated by the christian spirit, should accept that it is part of their vocation to cultivate sacred music and increase its store of treasures.*

The last article's exhortation to living composers makes explicit in no uncertain terms what was implied in the first, that the treasure of sacred music is no dead and fixed repertory but a live tradition awaiting new riches. But their charge is not to create music in the way that the secular world has imagined since the nineteenth century, for the purposes of self-expression and self-fulfillment as an individual artist, but rather to "cultivate sacred music." Fulfilling the vocation of a composer of sacred music means far more than merely setting sacred texts, more than intending one's music for liturgy. It implies, like all Christian vocations, an inspirational relationship with the tradition, making its techniques and enormous symbological store one's primary resource for new composition.

> *Let them produce compositions which have the qualities proper to genuine sacred music, and which can be sung not only by large choirs but also by smaller choirs, and which make possible the active participation of the whole congregation.*

In reaction to the symphonic efforts in liturgical music of Giuseppe Verdi and others who thought only in terms of the monumental choir, the council fathers show here their intention to broaden the experience of sung liturgy far beyond the cathedral parish, beyond the well-endowed, to the whole world. The mention of small choirs and, one last time, *actuosam participationem* reflects again the diversity of liturgical roles and the expectation that different circumstances will require different kinds of liturgical music. Sacred music need not be uniform, except in its principles "proper to genuine sacred music."

> *The texts intended to be sung must always be in conformity with catholic doctrine. Indeed, they should be drawn chiefly from the sacred scripture and from liturgical sources.*

The principles of text are no less important than the principles of music.[19] In any lasting composition of liturgical music, both are essential and neither is sufficient. Despite this truth, this injunction, in particular its advice about the right sources for text, is probably the most widely flouted of *Sacrosanctum Concilium*'s sixth chapter on sacred music.

Rejected Mythologies

When the sixth chapter on sacred music from *Sacrosanctum Concilium* is read this way, not only on its own terms but also in the contexts of the whole document and the nature of sacred music itself, we can begin to clear the ground of mythologies that have choked the growth of traditions of Catholic music for parishes ever since the document appeared in 1963. These mistaken notions take many practical forms, but they can be grouped into three general mythologies: relevance, liturgical democracy, and false creativity.

---

[19] It is quite an ancient principle. Canon 59 of Council of Laodicea, 363–64 AD, forbids privately composed songs and noncanonical writings and restricts psalm singing to choirs, as a defense against Gnosticism. See Joseph Ratzinger, *The Spirit of the Liturgy*, trans. John Saward (San Francisco: Ignatius Press, 2000), 144.

Relevance in liturgy is the notion that the liturgy, an action built of symbols, can only engage worshipers by employing the symbologies of the contemporary local culture, by giving them what is familiar from their lives so that the liturgy can effectively respond and heal them. Music, preeminent among these symbologies, must be popular in style (*musica populi*), if liturgy is to have any hope of converting souls to the Christian life.

The first corollary of the relevance myth is that for anything to find a place in modern liturgy, it must be new: up-to-date translations, new rituals, and above all new songs. No music can be retained in liturgy for long; it soon becomes irrelevant and must give way to the latest. This leads to the next corollary, that anything old must be bad for liturgy. It is out of date and therefore cannot connect with contemporary lives. Further, old things are bad because they recall a bad time in the church, when liturgy was automatic and autocratic, ignorant of the needs of real people. Even old Scripture, insofar as it has provided words for sacred composers for centuries, has become suspect, to judge by the choices of contemporary composers. Musical styles precedent to the Second Vatican Council are of course totally inadmissible because they cannot reflect the new liturgy. The music of contemporary culture outside the church, the *saecula*, the culture of the age, is the only one to be promoted. Its music is good because it is relevant, and therefore it is beyond criticism. Indeed, criticism of it is dismissed out of hand as simply hostile to liturgical reform, irrelevant.

The relevance myth must embrace in principle the revolving door of the liturgical hit parade, songs that appear in missalettes one year and are gone the next, replaced by the next novelty. Not only has this practice proven to make liturgy a constant struggle for worshipers who never come to treasure anything musical, but it ironically symbolizes what Christians strive to free themselves of, the temporary things that "moth and rust destroy" (Matt 6:19) rather than the timeless and eternal. The relevance myth is therefore doubly antitraditional, in the sense of rejecting both the past, what has been tradition, and the very means of tradition itself, repetition and renewal of symbol. Relevance must disown the fundamental premise of *Sacrosanctum Concilium*'s conception of the sacred treasure as a living tradition.

Musical relevance opposes Christian tradition in yet another aspect. Music of any kind is a cultural artifact, and therefore any liturgical music comes from some culture, even though that culture may be long dead or only vestigial, such as the medieval European culture from which much Catholic plainchant has sprung. This fact, along with the comparative pluralism of the Catholic notion of liturgical tradition, has encouraged through the centuries, but particularly in the years since the council, the inculturation of local musics into the liturgy, a cultural relevance. But the esteem of culture is not unequivocal and cannot entail the uncritical adoption of local musical styles and practices, if only because Christianity recognizes that because of original sin no culture escapes fault, and its artifacts are not always good, its expressions not always true. Many things in the gospels are countercultural in a universal sense, and therefore so must be Catholic liturgy. Its music cannot be identical with that of any culture at large, past or present. There is always a critical distance between culture and a healthy tradition of Christian liturgical music.

But the fundamental desire of liturgical relevance—to ensure that liturgy spiritually nourishes all modern worshipers regardless of where they find themselves—is entirely laudable. A Catholic liturgy without connection to the real lives of the faithful is an impossibility and completely without meaning or value, so the intentions of the relevance myth are indeed worthy. The error is in the kind and depth of relevance that it seeks. If the symbologies of liturgy can only reflect worshipers' lives as they live them, then it is doomed to catastrophic failure since, after all, we are not satisfied with our lives as we live them. The very reason we attend liturgy is that we are incomplete, broken, and seek healing, as we confess in the penitential rite at every Mass. The sacred liturgy becomes relevant to people's lives not by reinforcing daily fare, but by convincing us of potential fullness, by revealing an existence beyond that of our lives as we live them that God's salvific power can achieve for us. "The celebration is not just a rite, not just a liturgical 'game.' It is meant to be indeed a *logike latreia*, the 'logicizing' of my existence, my interior contemporaneity with the self-giving of Christ. His self-giving is meant to become mine, so that I become contemporary with the Pasch of Christ and assimilated unto God. . . . The liturgy does indeed have a bearing on everyday life, on me in my personal existence."[20]

Its music therefore cannot merely symbolize where we are, but rather where we should be. It must transcend the age, the culture of the moment, to point to a greater reality than the one we know. Most often sacred music accomplishes this precisely by being clearly *not* of

---

[20] Ratzinger, *The Spirit of the Liturgy*, 58.

the age, or at least not *only* of the age, by having a character that is in some sense alien, even opposed, to the popular world without in the least respect lapsing into the modernist's self-idolatry of an entirely personal musical language. History shows that it is possible for a contemporary composition to create this, but as we have seen, the odds of success are long, and the accomplishment certainly requires more than merely adapting the local tunesmith's idiom to some sacred text. Since the invention of opera and the secularization brought by the Enlightenment, the church composer's obstacles have multiplied, since all the dominant contemporary musical languages of the Western world have been secular ones, bringing with them secular semantic ranges symbolizing the here and now.

The myth of liturgical democracy is less of a theoretical premise about liturgy than a set of attitudes: that because all liturgical roles are equally important, distinctions among them should be minimized if not eliminated; that because liturgy arises from the faithful in common, no special requirements for liturgical ministry should be necessary; that participation in liturgy is no longer a privilege, but a right; that decisions about liturgy, and certainly its music, should be subject to broad discussion if not a vote. The origins of such ideas, almost unimaginable a half century ago, are again most worthy: the strong promotion by the Second Vatican Council of the active participation of the people and the concomitant expansion of lay ministries. Few would criticize either development as long as they were executed as the council provided. But any reasonable interpretation of *Sacrosanctum Concilium*, certainly including its sixth chapter, must preserve both hierarchical ministry in the liturgy and the distinction of liturgical roles and functions. The good seed of the council has grown a little wild.

The practical damages to liturgical music come in the form of an extreme musical populism, so that the rights and potential contributions of the laity are exalted into a perverse antiprofessionalism, a barely hidden distrust of musical expertise. "Elitist" is the name called not only of living musicians but of the music that they might espouse.[21] The false egalitarianism ends up choking the growth of good congregational singing by asking people to sing music for which they are

---

[21] See James E. Frazier, "A New Choir School of the Roman Catholic Cathedral of the Madeleine in Salt Lake City," *The American Organist* 33, no. 3 (March 1999): 56–68.

unprepared and by denying them the professional guidance that they deserve. We recall the political chaos satirized by W. S. Gilbert in *The Gondoliers*: "When everyone is somebodee, / Then no one's anybody!"

But perhaps a worse effect, because it is more insidious, is the introduction of the notion of "liking" into the sacred liturgy, chiefly through its musical programs. Indeed, opining about whether one likes the liturgical music at a given parish, or even the liturgy as a whole, has become a new sport. In the context of both history and the nature of liturgy and its music, this is quite odd, as if one were to say, "I like the Constitution" or "I don't like gravity." We usually express likes and dislikes about things we have some measure of control over—food, music in the home, clothing—and the verb therefore implies some power to choose as a consumer. But Americans have not chosen the Constitution; it is simply there, like a mountain, and changing it is made very difficult by design in order to avoid damage by the ill-tempered fashion of the day. Similarly, it is rather pointless to like or dislike the *Credo* or the Our Father. So the expression of "liking" the liturgy, or more commonly its music, implies a control arrogated to ourselves because we believe the liturgy is really ours in the democratic sense, not God's and certainly not the whole world's.[22] Liking the music becomes a value, competing with beauty and liturgical propriety, and subject to a vote, since one's liking is completely subjective, beyond criticism, unquestionable. Who is to say that you shouldn't like a song? And so often the planning of music in liturgy resembles the planning for an outing to a restaurant: we generously try to accommodate everyone's taste and make sure that there is something for everyone to like when we get there. Parishes fortunate enough to celebrate

---

[22] In this vein Edward Foley, in *Ritual Music: Studies in Liturgical Musicology* (Beltsville, MD: The Pastoral Press, 1995), 185, comments, "No matter what a textbook might say about the excellence of a composition, if a community does not like it, it will be less effective in engaging its members in worship." In an extreme sense, he is right, of course. Liturgical music that no one can stand cannot be anything other than counterproductive. But the truism hardly implies that we should engage habitually in taking a poll and trying to please everyone's taste. Many people, when hearing the various Catholic musical traditions for the first time, may not "like" the music in the sense that they like the Beatles, but neither do they dislike it or find it offensive or, most important of all, think it inappropriate for the liturgy. Rather the opposite. That last criterion of propriety trumps popularity without question.

several Masses every weekend can offer a flavor for each; those with one liturgy with music may do with a smorgasbord.

And so the democratic liturgy that aimed to include everyone by granting equal status ends by dividing the faithful into camps. The paraphrase of St. Paul's first letter to the Corinthians is almost irresistible: "Each one of you is saying 'I am for Haugen,' and 'I am for folk music,' and 'I am for hymns,' and 'I am for plainchant'" (cf. 1 Cor 1:12). This is why *Sacrosanctum Concilium* has not one note, not one hint, about satisfying such tastes. That war without end can blight the liturgical action. This is not to say that emotional reactions to liturgical music are sinful or that individual worshipers should not have opinions about it, only to insist that the liturgy not be ruled by such considerations, but rather by what is true and proper to the liturgy.

The last myth to be rooted out is false creativity. Like relativism and the democratic liturgy, false creativity finds its origins in *Sacrosanctum Concilium* and in the general instructions and new missals that followed, good seed grown wild.

The principal origin is the appearance of alternatives and options in the sacred liturgy. Without pretending that the Roman Rite was ever uniform throughout the Western world, the presence in *Sacrosanctum Concilium* of language describing more than one way of performing the liturgy is itself certainly a watershed in the history of official liturgy.[23] Two obvious examples: the expressed preference for liturgical Latin, but with provision for vernacular languages (SC 36 and 54); and the similar preference for Gregorian chant, with other musical languages "by no means excluded from liturgical celebrations" (SC 116). Passages such as these, along with the delegation of liturgical authority to local bishops,[24] implied that liturgies did not have to be everywhere

---

[23] Joseph A. Jungmann describes the state of things in the Middle Ages, a period often caricatured as one of rigid liturgical uniformity: "Thus we find throughout the later Middle Ages a great variation in all those parts of the Mass-liturgy which were not fixed as a heritage of the ancient Roman sacramentaries—variation not only from country to country but from church to church, in fact, from Mass book to Mass book." *The Mass of the Roman Rite: Its Origins and Development*, first ed. 1951, trans. Francis A. Brunner, 2 vols. (Westminster, MD: Christian Classics, Inc., 1986), 97.

[24] SC 22 (2): "In virtue of the power conferred on them by law, the regulation of the liturgy within certain defined limits belongs also to various kinds of groupings of bishops, legitimately established, with competence in given territories."

and always the same, even in the ideal. The liturgical books of the *novus ordo* that soon followed only amplified the impression. There were three new eucharistic prayers included as alternatives to the time-honored Roman Canon. There are three versions of the opening rites (including a troped *Kyrie*), an option for replacing them by an aspersion rite, and many new prefaces to the eucharistic prayer. All these seem minor in comparison to the four options for the major propers of introit, offertory, and communion because the near-universal exercise of "option four" of article 48 of the General Instruction of the Roman Missal allowing "another liturgical chant that is suited to the sacred action, the day, or the time of year" affects the sensibilities of worshipers so greatly.

At some point these possibilities were transformed into obligations in liturgical minds. In other words, if a priest always prayed the Roman Canon because he preferred it, he was considered derelict in his liturgical duty. He should exercise more creativity by availing himself of the options in the liturgical books, so that the liturgy, like a good restaurant's menu, is not the same week after week. Variety, not just in service of the liturgical year or sacramental event but for its own sake, became a liturgical value.

From the obligation to exploit the possibilities of the *novus ordo* to make liturgical variety, it was but a short step to the freelance invention of liturgical text. The falsehood of this kind of "variety" can be seen clearly here in the merest comparison with other dramatic genres. Shakespeare patrons on their way to see a performance of *Hamlet* do not expect to hear the actors try to improve on the poet's original words, and in fact they would be outraged by any such attempt. Music lovers expect orchestra players to execute the notes of a Beethoven symphony exactly as he wrote them. Indeed, any other note is called a mistake.

These are among the sublimest works of art in the Western tradition, and for the Shakespearean actor and the classical violinist, the very idea of textual alteration would be sacrilege. The sacred liturgy is a greater work of art, yet many a modern celebrant would consider himself uncreative did he not edit the greetings and prayers to his own taste; "Individualism flourishes, and the liturgy may almost become the plaything of its celebrants."[25]

---

[25] Aidan Kavanagh, "The Conciliar Documents: Liturgy (*Sacrosanctum Concilium*)," in *Modern Catholicism: Vatican II and After*, ed. Adrian Hastings (New York: Oxford

> It is Holy Thursday and we are at the solemn evening Mass in a midwestern parish. The moment comes for the celebrant of the Mass, the pastor, to wash the feet of twelve parishioners, just as Christ washed the feet of the apostles at the Last Supper. During this deeply moving ceremony, the choir sings motets and alternates with the congregation, which sings hymns. Finally, this part of the liturgy comes to a close with the washing of the last foot. The music ends; you can almost sense that the congregation wants to weep for joy. Then, Father Hank (this is what the pastor wishes to be called) walks over to a microphone, smiles, and says, "Boy, that was great! Let's give these twelve parishioners a hand."[26]

In this, one of the most memorable of many memorable passages from *Why Catholics Can't Sing*, Thomas Day shows how great is the liturgical destruction when the myth of false creativity attains its full corruption. There is no reason, no explanation for the pastor's desecration of a transcendent moment with the insipid patter of a television talk show except that he must make himself the center of attention. Day calls this impulse egoism and narcissism, a psychological diagnosis. The moralist would simply call it pride.

The cardinal sin of pride has always been the enemy of liturgy, but it began to tempt as never before when the cultural forces of democratization combined with this spurious notion of liturgical creativity, opposite to the creativity of ritual, more akin to extemporaneous personal invention. Pride accounts for quite a number of the sad and embarrassing habits that ministers of liturgy have fallen prey to: the celebrant's informal chatter and jokes, the grossly amplified singers who eliminate all meaningful congregational participation, overly dramatic lectors, the music director's defiance of liturgical order by including a favorite piece that does not really fit, and above all the willful alteration of the very words of the Mass.[27] Every case has the same effect: a spotlight shines on the perpetrator. Those who associate such abuses with the liturgy's loss of solemnity are perfectly correct: there is a destruction of ritual that replaces its reassuring "absence of

---

University Press, 1991), 72.

[26] Day, *Why Catholics Can't Sing: The Culture of Catholicism and the Triumph of Bad Taste* (New York: Crossroad 1992), 50.

[27] These are all detailed in Day's chapter 5 of *Why Catholics Can't Sing*, "Ego Renewal."

worry about the credibility of what is represented"[28] with language or effect that distracts attention from what should be transcendent toward what is very, very ordinary at best.

The error is not in valuing creativity—for the liturgy, like the performance of Shakespeare and Beethoven, is a thoroughly creative act—but in understanding the order of creativity. A violinist in the back of the orchestra section believes in his own creative role in the performance because he knows he is essential to the life of the work. Without his contribution Beethoven remains silent marks on a page. Moreover, the violinist's sound is unique, exactly like no one else's, to say nothing of the numberless nuances of playing Beethoven's notes that are independent of the notation, that change with every execution. This is why we can claim that no two performances of the same Beethoven work, or of any musical work, are identical. Similarly, can any celebrant's recitation of the Roman Canon exhaust its meanings? There was a priest in Dorchester, Massachusetts, whose praying of the phrase "Have mercy on us all" toward the end of the eucharistic prayer had such a particular cadence and tone that it affected the meaning of the entire latter half of the prayer for those who attended to it. He understood what it means to interpret a classic, and this is the creativity of ritual. His congregation gained a new insight, a renewed spirit, and yet not a word had been changed.

Relevance, liturgical democracy, and false creativity, in their many manifestations, inspire the lamentations of the last four decades' liturgical practice. Those unhappy with the banalities, secularisms, and downright abuses of modern liturgy sometimes blame them on the Second Vatican Council. In the sense that all these mythologies find their original impetus in *Sacrosanctum Concilium* they are right, but the proximate cause of the trouble, certainly in the case of liturgical music, was not the council but the haste and curious cultural climate that led astray what were once good intentions. The hothouse of liturgical reform allowed extreme interpretations to feed one another, so that the newest, most "relevant" musical styles delighted the liturgical democrat by sidelining the musical professionals, the "elite," and at the same time opening a new, wide avenue of false creativity because the styles did not demand much skill or training. Adding new songs with

---

[28] Nichols, *Looking at the Liturgy*, 56.

original nonbiblical texts at a great rate seemed not only to intensify the creative individualism of the liturgy but to keep it constantly relevant. And so on. The snowball rolled down the hill all too fast.

Three Principles of True Art

With the ground cleared of misinterpretations, lasting traditions of Catholic liturgical music may arise on a foundation of three absolute principles of the true art: sacred musical semantics, absolute musical beauty, and *participatio actuosa*.

It seems a truism, but after forty years of wandering in the desert it nevertheless bears repeating: any lasting tradition of liturgical music must be founded on music that sounds sacred. Whatever the musical language, however that language is focused into style, wherever in the world it is sung, the music *qua musica* must have the action of the sacred liturgy at the center of its semantic range. Only then can it accomplish its function—"the glory of God and the sanctification of the faithful" (SC 112)—by symbolizing that transcendence, that true relevance Christians seek, that is, not the mere affirmation of our lives as we live them but a glimpse, a foretaste, of how our lives here and now may be transformed by Christ's salvation.

There are two elements to evaluate in a liturgical composition. The easier by far is the text. After all, the words of the liturgy are all laid out quite explicitly. A trained composer can set them to music. Only the literary saint or, much more commonly, the most egotistical and amateur composer would routinely reject the psalms, the gospel verses, and the traditional liturgical texts in favor of personal creations. But even scriptural texts cannot guarantee a sacred sound per se. The harder evaluation is the music.

"The music *qua musica* must have the action of the sacred liturgy at the center of its semantic range" is the music theorist's typically abstract formula, but it is meant to summarize common experiences of music. The tests of sacredness may be quite practical. Take a setting of the *Sanctus* in any language, or an Alleluia acclamation, or "another liturgical chant that is suited to the sacred action, the day, or the time of year." Remove its text or, better yet, imagine it vocalized (singing on "ah"). Retain any instruments; they too have semantic ranges. Now we have music *qua musica*, conveying its own presentational semantics without the benefit of words. What images, spaces, memories, and surroundings does it bring? Where has such music been heard before? In church, in the bar, on television, in the concert hall, at a football stadium, or during rice planting? Does it connote frenetic dancing in this world or some other world entirely? Does it engage the body or the spirit?

If the *qua musica* test fails, the holiest words from the Bible will not make the work a sacred composition fit for the liturgy, not because the words do not matter but because they are insufficient. The semantics of music, for all their abstraction, are too powerful. There is not the slightest doubt that the music of "Dixie" will completely eclipse any "glory of God" and certainly any sanctification of those singing it, even if it sets the *Gloria*.[29] And yet the same limit holds for the semantics of the music: essential, but insufficient. True art in liturgical music demands an intrinsic unity of all the excellences.

A lasting tradition of liturgical music perdures, persists through time. Therefore, its music must have those universal and absolute qualities which we cannot articulate in theoretical language, but yet which certainly exist and ensure the survival of the music beyond the moment, beyond the generation. A tradition cannot house music that we quickly tire of, but it can house that which engages us with a fresh message on every new encounter with it. In short, its music is beautiful and true art.

History has shown time and again that contemporaries of whatever age are the least qualified to judge the beauty of their own music because natural chauvinism for their own times leads to routine overvaluation of contemporary compositions. Contemporary compositions are like the children of a generation, and rare is the parent who can get enough critical distance from them to appraise them accurately. At the same time, history has shown itself to be the one reliable judge of musical beauty: the longer a composition is in demand, the more likely it is to own those universal qualities of greatness, because only those can satisfy the mercurial tastes of the changing generations by touching a more basic, deep sense of beauty.

"As offensive as it may be to some musicians, liturgical music, to carry the weight of the collective memory about the paschal mystery,

---

[29] I have done this experiment, setting the words of the *Gloria*, in Latin, to the tune and oom-pah accompaniment of "Dixie." The reaction from those who heard this: uproarious laughter.

is of its nature conservative in the best sense of the word."[30] Rembert Weakland, musicologist and former Archbishop of Milwaukee, spoke these words to the National Convention of Liturgical Musicians in Australia in 1993. It is an admirable admission of having come full circle, for shortly after the council in 1967 he wrote "We cannot go backwards in time to find an art-music that will satisfy the liturgical demands of today."[31] The utter rejection of history produced the revolving door of mediocrity, and since then many have repented of it, although few so honestly. "Conservative in the best sense of the word" means to hold to the truth, in this case the musical truths of truly great works. It cannot entail a reversal of the reformers' errors that completely dismisses the possibility of new works, for that turns the living tradition into a musicological museum. Catholicism has never done this. But in building traditions of liturgical music, the most secure foundation will be one of mostly older, tried-and-true works and musical languages. The brand new should never comprise a majority of the music in liturgy, barring some truly exceptional occasion. History shows that this too has never been done, that is, until after 1965. If natural circumstances and contexts, not the urgency of false creativity, generate new compositions by composers trained in the tradition, be sure that they will come and enrich the tradition.

The tradition is therefore the channel for true creativity, a creativity that, in the best sense of conservatism, denies the selfishness of radical individualism and responds instead to the tradition and its many

---

[30] Rembert Weakland, "The Song of the Church: Liturgy and Music," address to the National Liturgical Music Convention in Melbourne, Australia, in April 1993, *Origins* 23, no. 1 (May 20, 1993): 14. The eminent historian of liturgy Dom Gregory Dix concurs and points out with unforeseen irony that ill-advised changes come about as the result of clericalization: "Theology is a progressive technical science, and remains therefore always the professional preserve of the clergy and the interest of a comparatively small educated *élite* of the laity. Liturgy, on the contrary, is a universal christian activity, and so a *popular* interest; and therefore always remains a very conservative thing. It was the fact that the eucharist as a whole was a corporate act of the whole church which everywhere maintained the rigid fixity of the outline of the liturgy, through the conservatism of the laity. Changes in this outline only began when the rite as a whole had been partially 'clericalised' by becoming something which the clergy were supposed to do *for* the laity, and the laity for the most part had lost their active share in its performance." See *The Shape of the Liturgy* (London: Dacre Press, 1945), 7.

[31] Rembert Weakland, "Music and Liturgy in Evolution," in *Crisis in Church Music?* (Washington, DC: The Liturgical Conference, 1967), 4.

inspirations by interpreting them. This is the creativity of the Shakespearean actor and the symphony violinist, and it is also the creativity of the composer of new music referring explicitly to the tradition, becoming part of it, drawing worshipers into it, and therefore making possible the transcendence that they seek.

It might be interesting to try to argue that the absence of *participatio actuosa* in the seventeenth and eighteenth centuries caused the decline in liturgy of the period. In poor and rural parishes the liturgy, from the worshiper's perspective, surrounded the clear climax of the raising of the host and chalice with whispers, mysterious gestures, and prayers and readings in Latin. In the richer cathedral parishes the operatic Masses probably invited far more appreciation of virtuoso singing and far less interior prayer than had either the precedent plainchant or polyphony. In any case, surely it is the Second Vatican Council's revolutionary promotion of *participatio actuosa* that, more than anything else, caused the explosive revival of interest in liturgy among the laity. Catholics of all stripes care more about liturgy and its music, perhaps more than ever. "It was the best of times . . ." A lasting tradition of liturgical music must have *participatio actuosa* built right into it.

The chief mistake of the reformers in the 1960s, then, is once again not the principle but its application. The translation of *participatio actuosa* as "congregational singing" has actually retarded its progress and stunted the growth of liturgical tradition: by eliminating at times much of the historical repertory, by insisting on lowest common denominators of composition in the name of liturgical democracy, by asking the congregations to do much more than they are capable of. Parishioners then sense that much of the congregational singing they are asked to do is arbitrarily imposed and has become an onerous obligation rather than a welcome opportunity to do what they came for, to praise God in music. They are on edge, constantly on guard for the unexpected. Of course the liturgy obliges in many ways, but cooperation is virtually universal when the obligations seem natural and easy, a kind of sacred etiquette that only the boor would refuse, such as standing for the introit procession or responding "Amen" at the end of the Eucharistic prayer. But the revolving door is neither natural nor easy, and after forty years there is still a great deal of resistance, even in the soundest musical programs.

Participatio actuosa instead is the multifaceted concept that the council fathers wrote into *Sacrosanctum Concilium*. Yes, the semantic range of *participatio actuosa* certainly includes congregational singing, but it also includes responding deeply to sacred music sung by the cantor or choir or celebrant or played by the organist, attending as one silently attends to the readings from Scripture and the eucharistic prayer. It is the quality of total participation that is the proper measure, not some poll of how many are singing what percentage of the Mass. The constitution imagines active participation not on the model of a political democracy, where everyone's vote is the same regardless of personal qualification, but in the image of St. Paul's mystical body of Christ, where head and eye and foot have different roles to perform according to gifts given them by God, each distinct, each essential—no matter how lowly—to the integrity of the whole.

And so *Sacrosanctum Concilium* in its wisdom implies the first choice for actual congregational singing is not "the four hymns" but "acclamations, responses, psalmody, antiphons, and canticles"[32] (SC 30) and the Ordinary prayers that remain the same from Mass to Mass. Recall the solemn liturgy at St. Mark's Basilica in Venice.[33] Of the sixteen musical settings that comprise that Mass, the congregation sings in eleven of them, and ten of these are virtually the same every week.[34] Only the psalm response, a single musical phrase, must be learned on the spot. Variety? It is never missed; no one thinks of it. Instead there is the serene confidence of performing one's role as expected, of contributing an essential aspect to the sacred liturgy, even if it is a simple and heartfelt chanted "Amen." The real variety is appreciated, in the deepest sense, in the liturgy as a whole, an opulent musical variety of various solo voices, choir, organ, congregation, readings, and silence, and in the regular, mystical turning of the liturgical year.

The three essentials of liturgical music—a sacred semantic, beauty, and *participatio actuosa*—restore the good intentions of relevance, liturgical democracy, and false creativity to their origins.

True Art in Context

Even the most mathematically rigorous theory must deal with local context when it is applied. When the physicist meets the engineer, when the architect turns to the builder, the neat abstractions must

---

[32] I have substituted the English "canticles" for "songs," a better translation of the Latin *cantica*.

[33] The complete musical program is given in chap. 18.

[34] The exceptions would be those required by the change of season in the liturgical year, the substitution of a Lenten acclamation for "Alleluia," for example.

come to terms with messy realities on the ground. So it is with the foundation of traditions of liturgical music. Sacred semantics, beauty, and *participatio actuosa* will sound quite differently in different places.

In the first two cases, the variation of cultural measures of musical meaning and musical value is a patent truism in most people's experience. Every speech in the world demonstrates that the meanings we assign to a sequence of sounds are only valid for members of a single language community, and if it exists elsewhere, it will often as not mean something else. So the polyphony that provokes the association of "solemn Catholic music" in the Italian listener may merely seem to be "very pretty" in the Japanese. Particular hallmarks of beauty also vary with time and place. The trumpet screech that sounds horrible in Bach is brilliant in Armstrong. It may startle just a little that *participatio actuosa* will also find varying expressions around the world. It is true that every culture sings, but not in the same way, in the same circumstances, or even to the same extent. The staid congregation in rural New York State may be content with a minimum of singing and leave much to the choir, but at St. Paul's in Nairobi, Kenya, parishioners will complain if the choir sings by themselves more than a few prayers of the liturgy.[35]

The council fathers therefore made no absolute laws of practice in their liturgical constitution. Exception clauses are found at many a key point in *Sacrosanctum Concilium*. Awareness of local custom has informed the entire history of liturgical music and is the main premise of liturgical inculturation, and so alternatives accompany the practical recommendations for the predominance of liturgical Latin and Gregorian chant. Within the limits of the constitution, power is delegated to the local bishops, who, as the true *pastores* of the faithful, prudently judge and continually adjust the inevitable tensions and conflicts among the values of tradition and creativity, musical professionalism and congregational singing, catholicity and local musical custom. As with the engineer or builder, such fine tuning can be made only on site, and it may determine whether the edifice stands or falls.

And so, are all conciliar recommendations, all our theorizing and argument in vain? Certainly not. Local context does not entail relativism, the idea that because expressions of beauty and sacredness differ around the world, no absolutes for those categories exist, all judgments

---

[35] Personal communication from Fred Sisenda, May 2007.

about them are void, and bishops may do what they please. The fact that French people greet friends with a double kiss on the cheeks, Americans with firm handshakes, and Japanese with bows does not mean that no absolute principle of respect, expressed variously among the nations, operates behind them all.[36] Yes, it is probably futile to draw up a building plan good for every climate and terrain in the world, but that does not absolve architects of ensuring that their edifices stand against weather, rot, and other inevitable ravages of time. Relativism is the renunciation of all faith in absolute values, including, ultimately, God himself; sensitivity to local context, the pastoral judgment, is rather the prudential application of those absolute values. The music that brings to mind something of the Most High in Kenya may sound only "African" in France, but it still must have a semantic range and distinction for Kenyans analogous to that which Gregorian chant has for Frenchmen. What is everlastingly beautiful in the Andes may not sound like Bach, but it passes the same test of time. Even spiritual transcendence itself, intensely personal as it may be, cannot entirely reside in the subjective. The transubstantiation of the Eucharist is an absolutely transcendent action, whether any one person recognizes it as such or not.[37] Music and other liturgical symbols, being merely symbols, cannot be absolutely transcendent but may yet have the power, verified through sound reasoning and the empirical experience of lived history, to communicate a foretaste of heaven to those ready to hear it.

That is why it is a great error to conceive liturgical principles and pastoral concerns in opposition to one another, for the greatest gift any bishop can give his flock is a transcendent and worthy celebration of the paschal mystery. Prosper Guéranger, a founder of the liturgical movement, saw that the beauty and mystery of the liturgy are

---

[36] I realize that between the absolute condition of showing respect and the various expressions of it in different cultures there must be some kind of translation rule, also absolute. The empirical constraints on human behavior in many areas suggest that this indeed exists, and I leave it to professional ethicists to formulate it.

[37] "The paradox of ritual symbol is that in order for us to participate, the whole human being must be engaged through the senses (visible, acoustic, kinetic, and the like), while at the same time acknowledging that liturgical action signifies realities beyond immediate experience." Don E. Saliers, "Symbol in Liturgy, Liturgy as Symbol: The Domestication of Liturgical Experience," in *The Awakening Church: 25 Years of Liturgical Renewal*, ed. Lawrence J. Madden (Collegeville, MN: Liturgical Press, 1992), 74.

absolutely intrinsic to any pastoral good it might do.[38] Sacredness and the historical measure of beauty know no boundaries, even though their particular readings will change from place to place and time to time.

Liturgical Virtues

The appropriate semantics and the highest aesthetics of true art and *participatio actuosa* are essential qualities of Catholic liturgical music, but they will accomplish nothing without the proper disposition of faithful people, from bishops to pastors, professional musicians, and laity. This is not just a readiness to tolerate an occasional piece that is unfamiliar, but a conversion from certain entrenched attitudes and habits that have retarded lasting reform in the liturgy for decades. That these have not dulled the intense interest in the sacred liturgy that was awakened by the Second Vatican Council says a great deal about the stature of the liturgy in the spiritual lives of Catholics. Its reform is still the council's most sensible effect, and even the bitterest controversies over liturgy must mean that Catholics continue to care deeply about it. Indeed, it is a moral impulse, for the good of all, and therefore requires the development and practice of certain liturgical virtues, some of which have been the subject of this book. "The liturgy sustains the participated divine life that Christians properly denote the theological life, a life of faith, of hope, and of charity."[39] Perhaps the best frame for these liturgical virtues is indeed St. Paul's theological virtues.

"Love" (or *agape* or *caritas*) in St. Paul's first letter to the Corinthians is of course the very basis of Christian life, a constant regard for neighbor that comes from constant self-denial. In liturgy, love corrects the corrosive presumptions that the sacred liturgy is primarily about us and for us, and that its measure is how well we are pleased by it. Again, Archbishop Weakland's counsel to liturgical musicians:

> Liturgy, and thus its song, is not, first of all, entertainment. When young people say that liturgy is boring, they may be very correct,

---

[38] Irwin, *Context and Text: Method in Liturgical Theology*, 19.
[39] Jonathan Gaspar and Romanus Cessario, "'Worthy of the Temple': Liturgical Music and Theological Faith," *Nova et Vetera* (English edition) 3, no. 4 (2005): 674.

just as many necessary aspects of life are boring if one does not know anything about what is happening and cannot enter fully into the action. . . . Liturgy will always be boring if we do not see ourselves as involved, as the actors, as praying, as one with Christ under the action of the Holy Spirit. Liturgy demands faith and inner participation.

Nor is liturgy a therapeutic exercise. So often people will say: "But I don't get anything out of it." This personalistic view of every aspect of life, how it affects me, what I get out of it, pervades our culture. Liturgy is not a group therapy session. . . . The song that accompanies the liturgy can be one of just praise of God, with no concern about its therapeutic effect on the worshiping group.

Nor is liturgy a form of human intimacy, unless with Jesus Christ. In our culture people find intimacy that highest form of relationship that all seem to be seeking. Liturgy joins all gathered into a unity, but that oneness is deeply spiritual and not the kind that would go under the rubric of intimacy in today's world.[40]

Though celebrant, lector, musician, and congregant have various offices to perform, no one in any personal sense is important.[41] Actions that needlessly highlight the individual offend in the same way as would a singer who obstinately refuses to blend with the choir. They declare the temporary control and ownership of something that no individual person may own because it is a communal and universal action and, furthermore, authored by God. Liturgical charity instead entails that we surrender ourselves to the great communal action that is the liturgy, as symphony violinists surrender their personal liberty to the conductor. When we do so, we will perhaps realize a paradox like many in the gospels, in that such surrender of self brings more intimacy and personal spiritual satisfaction than one could possibly have imagined.

Charity therefore demands sacrifices of liturgical musicians that they typically are not trained to make, at every level of participation. The lay congregant and even the chorister must throw off attitudes promoted in the secular world as the routine behavior of individual prerogative. "Is this song *my* music?" or "Am I enjoying this?" can no longer be entertained.[42] The organist and director of parochial music

---

[40] Weakland, "The Song of the Church," 12–13.

[41] Thomas Day comments on liturgical "objectivity" at length in *Why Catholics Can't Sing*, 44–46.

[42] Humility in no way implies a musical sackcloth, that is, deliberately programming music that will offend or that is so culturally distant that no one can

refer first not to their own personal preferences but to the liturgical calendar and its traditional texts, while at the same time exercising the critical judgments given by their own gifts and training. Composers also discern this delicate balance, suppressing the composer's typical instinct for self-promotion and yet making the greatest art their skills will allow, at all times in reference to the tradition that they have inherited. They are not merely composers who happen to write music for church; they are liturgical composers. Their charge is a vocation. Indeed, all the musical roles of liturgy are vocational, insofar as they are divine calls to sacrifice something of one's individuality, not to say interpretative creativity, for the universal artwork of the liturgy.

If that universality, or catholicity, is to embrace the whole world, then not only the musical *personae* of individuals but even characteristics of parochial culture might be given up for the sake of languages and styles of music that signify the oneness of the liturgy and therefore the oneness of the body of Christ. "In addition to the universal councils of the Church, liturgical prayer, as the official prayer of the Church, is one of the most characteristic expressions in which the unanimity of the Church's faith . . . can be made external in a truly authentic manner."[43] "Universality, not uniformity" has become something of a justifying slogan for local prerogatives, but in an action that subsists so essentially on symbols, musical ones being preeminent of them all, how else would universality be verified if not on the uniformity of at least some of its symbols?[44]

---

understand it. Nothing in *Sacrosanctum Concilium* implies as much, and none of its preferred musics would have such effects.

[43] Edward Schillebeeckx, *Revelation and Theology*, vol. 1 (New York: Sheed and Ward, 1967), 218. This seems to be an abiding controversy among theologians. Bernard Häring wrote just a few years before, "The very diversity of liturgical languages and forms should make the essential structure of the liturgy, which should always be preserved intact, all the more conspicuous." See *The Johannine Council: Witness to Unity*, trans. Edwin G. Kaiser (New York: Herder and Herder, 1963), 61. Häring is correct in a certain Platonic sense that in observing many variant liturgies one would abstract the "essential structure." But few get to do this. Most experience a few variant liturgies in their travels, and what they notice is the discrepancies, particularly when they are of the egotistical sort just described.

[44] Mary Collins, for example, writes of the first millennium church, "Uniformity was not an unqualified value in this ecclesiology of communion; unity was." *Contemplative Participation: Sacrosanctum Concilium; Twenty-five Years Later* (Collegeville, MN: Liturgical Press, 1990), 13. What remains unexplained is how this unity is to be perceived, if not through the uniformity of at least some symbols.

When the townspeople of Chartres, France, saw fire destroy all but the western façade of their great Romanesque cathedral in 1194 and determined on the spot to build another, the magnificent Gothic church we know today, most of them had no prospect of ever seeing it finished. As they cut and transported stone, carved the thousands of figures, and stained the glass, all knew that they worked for the benefit of their grandchildren and generations beyond. Their efforts were powered by faith in the rightness of their project, charity for unseen generations, and above all by hope, even in the certainty that what they labored on could only be completed by others.

The building of lasting traditions of liturgical music requires this kind of hope, this "sure expectation of future glory," with the future understood not in terms of our own brief spans but on the scale of God's plan brought about through history.[45] The most astounding and costly error of the 1960s reformers was the notion that the vision of *Sacrosanctum Concilium* could have been realized in a few short years. That thinking persists in most places. If a congregation cannot learn a *Gloria* well enough to sing it effectively within a few weeks, the piece obviously "doesn't work." If liturgical Latin is unfamiliar, well, it will take too long to learn something about it. Such bad logic shortchanges *participatio actuosa* by denying the laity their chance to get used to things, to educate themselves to participate. It denies the sacred liturgy its proper status as a masterwork of art that, like all masterworks, works on many levels of appreciation and comprehension, that rewards study and long acquaintance with the constant refreshment of a classic. Impatience is hopelessness.

The hope of building traditions asks a complete change of orientation, from the week-to-week to the order of decades and generations. With regard to Catholic liturgical music, those who came of age after the council's liturgical reforms are lost generations. We have to accept this; it is our appointed role in liturgical history. Most of us have rarely experienced liturgy and liturgical music as the council envisioned it, certainly not on a regular basis, and, like the first builders of Chartres, we likely never will. Out of love and hope we plan and think and design instead for our own grandchildren.

---

[45] See Dante Alighieri, *Paradiso*, Canto XXV, 67. In *attender certo della gloria futura*, the first word might be understood as "waiting" in a more placid sense than the modern Italian *aspettare*, which is cognate with the English "expect."

Indeed, children should be kept constantly in mind. As we build our traditions, consider what it will be like to grow up with them, to experience musical prayer with no memory of its being uncomfortably new. Virtually no Catholic adults have had this experience. The child learns languages without prejudice, openly and innocently, both spoken and musical, as easily as he learns to walk, given enough time. Simple exposure to the sounds and contexts of usage are enough. Is liturgical Latin too much of a challenge for adults? Children who grow up hearing it every week will think it as natural as "Amen" and "Alleluia," two foreign words that even adults take as their own. Is a plainchant Mass too strange, too austere for us moderns? Children who grow up singing it will think it the most beautiful and natural way to pray, and its melodies will be with them through their whole lives, inexhaustible, because they are true art.

The sacrifices and hope required of our tradition building are not easy things, but parents endure such things for the sake of their children. When we sing the sacred treasure of our liturgical traditions not for ourselves but, like the first parents of Chartres Cathedral, for those who come after, and when we consider not so much what good it does for us, but what good it will do for them, perhaps it is not so hard. We know that we will not live to see the tradition's completion. To be sure, as liturgy and its music adapts to changing times and cultures in a way that a cathedral cannot, the work will end only at the Second Coming. No one beholds all the treasure, but that is no reason to be disheartened, because the treasure is made of many small and priceless gems of musical compositions set into the crown of the liturgy. Its beauty can always suffice for the moment.

And finally, or perhaps first of all, there is faith. Faith in liturgy means to take seriously what *Sacrosanctum Concilium* says of the liturgy in its prologue, that it is the "summit toward which the activity of the church is directed; it is also the source from which all its power flows" (SC 10). This image of spiritual power feeding on itself, again in analogy with Scripture and tradition, shows exactly what sustains liturgical traditions. We believe that it is among the most important actions of our lives, and therefore we handle it as a most precious work of art, with the reverence and all due solemnity that we grant to all our lives' most profound moments. At the same time, the power of that artwork cannot but invigorate our faith. Authentic traditions of liturgical music are sacred treasure because they participate so essentially in this mutual construction. With their words they express our faith, praise, and thanks and carry them all to God, and yet this very act in its sublimity creates in us an awe that inspires us to do it again and again in memory of him.

Bibliography

Adam, Adolf. *The Liturgical Year: Its History & Its Meaning after the Reform of the Liturgy*. Translated by Matthew J. O'Connell. New York: Pueblo Publishing, 1981. Originally published as *Das Kirchenjahr mitfeiern* (Freiburg: Herder, 1979).

Aguiar, Benny M. "India and Sri Lanka." In *Modern Catholicism: Vatican II and After*, edited by Adrian Hastings, 377–86. New York: Oxford University Press, 1991.

Allport, Floyd H. *Theories of Perception and the Concept of Structure*. New York: John Wiley and Sons, 1955.

Anderson, Emily, ed. *The Letters of Mozart and His Family*. Vol. 1. New York: St. Martin's Press, 1966.

The Benedictine Monks of Santo Domingo de Silos. *Chant*. Angel Records CDC 7243 5 55138 2 3, 1994.

Benedict XVI. *Sacramentum Caritatis*. Apostolic Exhortation on the Eucharist, Sacrament of Love. February 22, 2007. *Adoremus Bulletin* 13, no. 2 (April 2007): 3–10, and no. 3 (May 2007): 4–7.

Benofy, Susan. "The Birth and Death of a National Hymnal—1973–1976." Part I in *Adoremus Bulletin* 13, no. 1 (March 2007): 4, 8; Part II, "Seeking a 'Core Repertoire,'" in *Adoremus Bulletin* Vol. 13, no. 2 (April 2007): 11, 13.

———. "Singing the Mass: We Cannot Say That One Song Is as Good as Another." *Adoremus Bulletin* 13, no. 8 (November 2007): 3–5.

Blanchard, Robert I. "Church Music Today—the Center Position." In *Crisis in Church Music?*, 65–73. Washington, DC: The Liturgical Conference, 1967.

Buchanan, Colin. "The Winds of Change." In *The Oxford Guide to The Book of Common Prayer: A Worldwide Survey*, edited by Charles Hefling and Cynthia Shattuck, 229–38. New York: Oxford University Press, 2006.

Bugnini, Annibale. *The Reform of the Liturgy 1948–1975*. Translated by Matthew J. O'Connell. Collegeville, MN: Liturgical Press, 1990. Originally published as *La Riforma Liturgica 1948–1975* (Rome: CLV-Edizioni liturgiche, 1983).

Butler, David. *The Musician's Guide to Perception and Cognition*. New York: Schirmer, 1992.

Castelli, Jim, and Joseph Gremillion. *The Emerging Parish: The Notre Dame Study of Catholic Life since Vatican II*. San Francisco: Harper & Row, 1987.

Catechism of the Catholic Church. United States Catholic Conference. Liguori, MO: Liguori, 1994.

Chupungco, Anscar J., OSB. *Liturgies of the Future: The Process and Methods of Inculturation*. New York: Paulist Press, 1989.

The Cistercian Monks of Stift Heiligenkreuz. *Chant: Music for the Soul*. Decca B0011489-02, Decca B0012322-02, 2008.

Collins, Mary, OSB. *Contemplative Participation:* Sacrosanctum Concilium; *Twenty-five Years Later*. Collegeville, MN: Liturgical Press, 1990.

Concilium Tridentiunum Diaiorum. Edited by J. Massarelli. 9 vols. Freiburg, Germany: 1901–24.

Congar, Yves. *La foi et la théologie*. Vol. 1. *Le mystère chrétien*. Paris: Desclée, 1962.

———. *Tradition and Traditions*. Translated by Michael Naseby and Thomas Rainborough. New York: Macmillan, 1966.

Cooney, Rory. "Bread of Life." 1987. In *Heritage Missal 2007*, 537. Portland, OR: Oregon Catholic Press, 2006. Used by permission.

Crocker, Richard L. *An Introduction to Gregorian Chant*. New Haven, CT: Yale University Press, 2000.

Crouan, Denis. *The Liturgy Betrayed*. Translated by Marc Sebanc. San Francisco: Ignatius, 2000.

Cruse, David. *Lexical Semantics*. Cambridge: Cambridge University Press, 1986.

Davidson, James D. "Yes, Jesus is Really There." *Commonweal* 138, no. 17 (October 12, 2001): 14–16.

Day, Thomas. *Why Catholics Can't Sing: The Culture of Catholicism and the Triumph of Bad Taste*. New York: Crossroad, 1992.

Dei Verbum. Dogmatic Constitution on Divine Revelation. Promulgated by Pope Paul VI, November 18, 1965. In *Vatican Council II: The Basic Sixteen Documents*, translated and edited by Austin Flannery, OP, 97–115. (Northport, NY: Costello Publishing Company, Inc., 1996).

Dix, Dom Gregory. *The Shape of the Liturgy*. London: Dacre Press, 1945.

DjeDje, Jacqueline. "An Expression of Black Identity: The Use of Gospel Music in a Los Angeles Catholic Church." *The Western Journal of Black Studies* 7, no. 3 (1983): 148–60.

———. "Change and Differentiation: The Adoption of Black American Gospel Music in the Catholic Church." *Ethnomusicology* 30, no. 2 (Spring–Summer, 1986), 223–52.

Dowling, W. Jay, and Dane L. Harwood. *Music Cognition*. New York: Academic Press, 1986.

Dulles, Avery. "Vatican II: The Myth and the Reality." *America* 188, no. 6 (February 24, 2003): 7–11.

Duncan, Stephen F. *A Genre of Hindustani Music (Bhajans) as Used in the Roman Catholic Church*. Lewiston, NY: Edward Mellen Press, 1999.

Elliot, Peter J. "Liturgical Translation: A Question of Truth." Address to Sacrificium Laudis: The Medina Years (1996–2002) of the Research Institute for Catholic Liturgy, October 2005. *Antiphon* 10, no. 3 (2006). Reprint, *Adoremus Bulletin* 13, no. 4 (June 2007): 4.

Flannery, Austin, OP, trans. and ed. *Vatican Council II: The Basic Sixteen Documents*. Northport, NY: Costello Publishing Company, 1996.

Fogarty, Gerald P. "North America." In *Modern Catholicism: Vatican II and After*, edited by Adrian Hastings, 326–33. New York: Oxford University Press, 1991.

Foley, Edward. *Ritual Music: Studies in Liturgical Musicology*. Beltsville, MD: The Pastoral Press, 1995.

Ford, Paul R. *By Flowing Waters: Chant for the Liturgy*. Collegeville, MN: Liturgical Press, 1999.

Francis, Mark. *Shape a Circle Ever Wider: Liturgical Inculturation in the United States*. Chicago: Liturgy Training Publications, 2000.

Frazier, James E. "A New Choir School of the Roman Catholic Cathedral of the Madeleine in Salt Lake City." *The American Organist* 33, no. 3 (March 1999): 56–68.

Gaspar, Jonathan, and Romanus Cessario. "'Worthy of the Temple': Liturgical Music and Theological Faith." *Nova et Vetera* (English edition) 3, no. 4 (2005): 673–88.

Gather Comprehensive. 2nd ed. Chicago: GIA Publications, 2004.

Gelineau, Joseph, SJ, "The Role of Sacred Music." In *The Church and the Liturgy*, translated by Theodore L. Westow, 59–65. Glen Rock, NJ: Paulist Press, 1965.

Glymour, Clark. *Theory and Evidence*. Princeton, NJ: Princeton University Press, 1980.

Graduale Romanum. Tournai, Belgium: Desclée, 1974.

Graduale Simplex. Rome: Libreria Editrice Vaticana, 1967. Rev. ed., 1975.

Gray, Catherine. "Compositional Techniques in Roman Catholic Church Music in Uganda." *British Journal of Ethnomusicology* 4 (1995): 133–55.

Guéranger, Prosper. *L'Année Liturgique*. 15 vols. Paris: H. Oudin et Cie, beginning in 1841 (unfinished). Translated by Dom Laurence Shepherd, OSB, as *The Liturgical Year*, 15 vols. (Wesminster, MD: Newman Press, 1948–50).

Haas, David. "Song of the Body of Christ." GIA, 1989. In *We Celebrate Worship Resource*, no. 622. Franklin Park, IL: J. S. Paluch, 2004. Used by permission.

Handel, Stephen. *Listening: An Introduction to the Perception of Auditory Events*. Cambridge, MA: MIT Press, 1989.

Häring, Bernard. *The Johannine Council: Witness to Unity*. Translated by Edwin G. Kaiser. New York: Herder and Herder, 1963.

Harnoncourt, Philipp. "Neue Aufgaben der katholischen Kirchenmusik (I)." In *Die Kirchenmusik und das II. Vatikanische Konzil*, edited by Philipp Harnoncourt, 51–76. Graz, Austria: Verlag Styria, 1965.

Hastings, Adrian. "The Key Texts." In *Modern Catholicism: Vatican II and After*, edited by Adrian Hastings, 56–67. New York: Oxford University Press, 1991.

Hatchett, Marion J. "The Colonial States of America." In *The Oxford Guide to The Book of Common Prayer: A Worldwide Survey*, edited by Charles Hefling and Cynthia Shattuck, 176–85. New York: Oxford University Press, 2006.

Hayburn, Robert F. *Papal Legislation on Sacred Music, 95 A.D. to 1977 A.D.* Collegeville, MN: Liturgical Press, 1979.

Heritage Missal 2007. Portland, OR: Oregon Catholic Press, 2006.

Hesse, Mary. *The Structure of Scientific Inference*. Berkeley, CA: University of California Press, 1974.

Hiley, David. *Western Plainchant: A Handbook*. Oxford: Clarendon Press; New York: Oxford University Press, 1993.

Hitchcock, Helen Hull. "Bishops Approve Three Liturgy Items at Busy Baltimore Meeting," *Adoremus Bulletin* 13, no. 9 (December 2007–January 2008): 4.

———. "*Evangelia Cantata*: A Notated Book of Gospels; A Review-Interview with the Composer." *Adoremus Bulletin* 14, no. 1 (March 2008): 5–6.

Hitchcock, James. *Recovery of the Sacred*. New York: Seabury Press, 1974. Reprint, San Francisco: Ignatius Press, 1995.

Hovda, Robert W., and Gabe Huck. "Music: We Must Learn to Celebrate." *Liturgical Arts* 38, no. 2 (February 1970): 43.

Hucke, Helmut. "Church Music." Translated by Theodore L. Westow. In *The Church and the Liturgy*, vol. 2 of *Concilium: Theology in the Age of Renewal*, 110–33. Glen Rock, NJ: Paulist Press, 1965.

Huijbers, Bernard. *The Performing Audience*. Translated by Ray Noll et al. 2nd ed. Cincinnati: North American Liturgy Resources, 1974.

Hymns, Psalms and Spiritual Canticles. Compiled, edited, and arranged by Theodore Marier. Belmont, Massachusetts: BACS Publishing, 1972.

Irwin, Kevin W. *Context and Text: Method in Liturgical Theology*. Collegeville, MN: Liturgical Press, 1994.

Janton, Pierre. *Esperanto: Language, Literature, and Community*. Edited by Humphrey Tonkin. Translated by Humphrey Tonkin, Jane Edwards, and Karen Johnson-Weiner. Albany: State University of New York Press, 1993.

John Paul II. Speech of February 7, 2000, Vatican City. http://www.vatican.va/holy_father/john_paul_ii/speeches/2000/jan-mar/documents/hf_jp-ii_spe_20000227_vatican-council-ii_en.html.

———. *Vicesimus quintus annus*. Apostolic Letter on the 25th Anniversary of the Constitution *Sacrosanctum Concilium*. December 4, 1988. http://www.adoremus.org/JPII25SC.html.

Jungmann, Joseph A., SJ. *The Mass of the Roman Rite: Its Origins and Development*. 1st ed. 1951. Translated by Francis A. Brunner. 2 vols. Westminster, MD: Christian Classics, Inc., 1986.

Kalilombe, Patrick A. "Africa." In *Modern Catholicism: Vatican II and After*, edited by Adrian Hastings, 310–18. New York: Oxford University Press, 1991.

Kavanagh, Aidan. "The Conciliar Documents: Liturgy (*Sacrosanctum Concilium*)." In *Modern Catholicism: Vatican II and After*, edited by Adrian Hastings, 68–73. New York: Oxford University Press, 1991.

Kivy, Peter. *The Corded Shell: Reflections of Musical Expression*. Princeton: Princeton University Press, 1980.

Klein, Christopher. *Messenkompositionen in Afrika: Ein Beitrag zur Geschichte und Typologie der katholoischen Kirchenmusik Afrikas*. Göttingen, Germany: Edition Re, 1990.

Koenker, Ernest. *The Liturgical Renaissance in the Roman Catholic Church.* Chicago: The University of Chicago Press, 1954.

Komonchak, Joseph A. "The Struggle for the Council during the Preparation of Vatican II (1960–1962)." In *History of Vatican II*, vol. 1, edited by Giuseppe Alberigo, English version edited by Joseph A. Komonchak, 167–356. Maryknoll, NY: Orbis, 1995.

Kono, Susumo. *Functional Syntax: Anaphora, Discourse, and Empathy.* Chicago: University of Chicago Press, 1987.

Kraynak, Robert P. *Christian Faith and Modern Democracy: God and Politics in the Fallen World.* Notre Dame, IN: University of Notre Dame Press, 2001.

Kubicki, Judith Marie. *Liturgical Music as Ritual Symbol: A Case Study of Jacques Berthier's Taizé Music.* Leuven: Peters, 1999.

Kuhn, Thomas S. *The Structure of Scientific Revolutions.* 1st ed. 1962. Chicago: University of Chicago Press, 1970.

Langer, Suzanne. *Philosophy in a New Key: A Study in the Symbolism of Reason, Rite, and Art.* 3rd ed. Cambridge, MA: Harvard University Press, 1956.

Launay, Denise. *La Musique Religieuse en France du Concile de Trente à 1804.* Paris: Société Française de Musicologie, 1993.

Lockwood, Lewis H. *The Counter-Reformation and the Masses of Vincenzo Ruffo.* Venice: Fondazione Giorgio Cini, 1970.

London, Justin. *Hearing in Time: Psychological Aspects of Musical Meter.* New York: Oxford University Press, 2004.

Louis, Kenneth W. *The Mass of Saint Cyprian.* A Live Recording by the Holy Comforter—Saint Cyprian Catholic Church Gospel Choir and Orchestra. Chicago: GIA Publications, 1999.

Lumen Gentium. Dogmatic Constitution on the Church. Promulgated by Pope Paul VI, November 21, 1964. In *Vatican Council II: The Basic Sixteen Documents*, translated and edited by Austin Flannery, OP, 1–95. (Northport, NY: Costello Publishing Company, Inc., 1996).

Mahrt, William. "Practical Sacrality." *Sacred Music* 137, no. 4 (Winter 2010): 3–5.

———. "Sing to the Lord." *Sacred Music* 135, no. 1 (Spring 2008): 44–51.

———. "The Place of Hymns." *Sacred Music* 137, no. 3 (Fall 2010): 3–5.

Mannion, M. Francis. "Concert Masses: A Reply." *Liturgy 80* 19, no. 6 (August–September 1988): 10–11.

———. "Forum: The Need for an Adequate Liturgical Musicology." *Worship* 64, no. 1 (January 1990): 78–81.

———. "Liturgy and the Present Crisis of Culture." *Worship* 62, no. 2 (March 1988): 98–123.

———. *Masterworks of God: Essays in Liturgical Theory and Practice*. Chicago: Liturgy Training Publications, 2004.

Marier, Theodore. *English Chant Mass*. In *The Adoremus Hymnal*, 250–54. San Francisco: Ignatius Press, 1997.

Marshall, Robert, and Robin A. Leaver. "Chorale." In *The New Grove Dictionary of Music and Musicians*, section 11, "The Baroque Era, c1600–75," edited by Stanley Sadie. New York: Macmillan, 2001.

Martin, David. *Two Critiques of Spontaneity*. London: London School of Economics and Political Science, 1973.

McManus, Frederick R. "Sacred Music in the Teaching of the Church." In *Crisis in Church Music?*, 14–26. Washington, DC: The Liturgical Conference, 1967.

Meyer, Leonard B. *Emotion and Meaning in Music*. Chicago: University of Chicago Press, 1956.

Milner, Anthony. "Music in a Vernacular Catholic Liturgy." *Proceedings of the Royal Musical Association* 91 (1964–65): 21–32.

Mitchell, Nathan. "Liturgical Education in Roman Catholic Seminaries: A Report and an Appraisal." *Worship* 54, no. 2 (March 10, 1980): 129–57.

Morgenthaler, Sally. *Worship Evangelism: Inviting Unbelievers into the Presence of God*. Grand Rapids, MI: Zondervan, 1995.

"Music in Catholic Worship (1972, 1982)." Chap. 11 in *The Liturgy Documents*. Vol. 1. 4th ed. Chicago: Liturgy Training Publications, 2004.

Musicam Sacram. Instruction on Music in the Liturgy. Given March 5, 1967. http://www.vatican.va/archive/hist_councils/ii_vatican_council/documents/vat-ii_instr_19670305_musicam-sacram_en.html.

Neumayr, George. "Defying the Multiculturalists." *Catholic World Report* 17, no. 8 (August/September 2007): 36–37.

Newman, John Henry. *An Essay on the Development of Christian Doctrine*. 6th ed. Notre Dame, IN: University of Notre Dame Press, 1989. First published in 1878.

Nichols, Aidan. *Looking at the Liturgy: A Critical View of Its Contemporary Form*. San Francisco: Ignatius Press, 1996.

Niebuhr, H. Richard. *Christ and Culture*. New York: Harper, 1951.

O'Neill, Colman E. "The Theological Meaning of *Actuosa Participatio* in the Liturgy." In *Sacred Music and Liturgy Reform: Proceedings of the Fifth*

International Church Music Congress, Chicago-Milwaukee, August 21–28, 1966, edited by Johannes Overath, 89–108. Rome: Consociatio Internationalis Musicae Sacrae, 1969.

Ortony, Anthony, ed. *Metaphor and Thought*. Cambridge: Cambridge University Press, 1979.

Overath, Johannes. "Die liturgish-musikalischen Neuerungen des zweiten vatikanischen Konzils." In *Geschichte der katholischen Kirchenmusik*, vol. 2, edited by Karl Gustav Fellerer, Kassel: Bärenreiter-Verlag, 1976.

Pashler, Harold E. *The Psychology of Attention*. Cambridge, MA: MIT Press, 1998.

Pelikan, Jaroslav. *The Vindication of Tradition*. New Haven, CT: Yale University Press, 1984.

Pius X. *Tra le Sollecitudini*. Vatican City: 1903.

Pius XII. *Mediator Dei*. Encyclical of Pope Pius XII on the Sacred Liturgy. English version. Vatican City: November 20, 1947. http://www.vatican.va/holy_father/pius_xii/encyclicals/documents/hf_p-xii_enc_20111947_mediator-dei_en.html.

———. *Musicae Sacrae*. Encyclical Of Pope Pius XII on Sacred Music. English version. Vatican City: December 25, 1955. http://www.vatican.va/holy_father/pius_xii/encyclicals/documents/hf_p-xii_enc_25121955_musicae-sacrae_en.html.

Plato's Republic. Translated by G. M. A. Grube. Indianapolis, IN: Hackett, 1976.

Ratzinger, Joseph. *A New Song for the Lord: Faith in Christ and Liturgy Today*. Translated by Martha M. Matesich. New York: Crossroad, 1997.

———. *The Spirit of the Liturgy*. Translated by John Saward. San Francisco, Ignatius Press, 2000.

———. "Theological Problems in Church Music." In *Crux et Cithara: Selected Essays on Liturgy and Sacred Music*, edited by Robert Skeris, 216–17. Altötting: Alfred Coppenrath, 1983.

Ritual Song. Chicago: GIA Publications, 1996.

Ruff, Anthony, OSB. *Sacred Music and Liturgical Reform: Treasures and Transformations*. Chicago: Hillenbrand, 2007.

Rutler, George William. *Brightest and Best: Stories of Hymns*. San Francisco: Ignatius Press, 1998.

Sacrosanctum Concilium [Latin text]. *Constitutio de Sacra Liturgia*. AAS 56 (1964), 97–138. http://www.ewtn.com/library/councils/v2litlat.htm.

Sacrosanctum Concilium. The Constitution on the Sacred Liturgy. Promulgated by Pope Paul VI, December 4, 1963. In *Vatican Council II: The Basic Sixteen Documents*, translated and edited by Austin Flannery, OP, 117–155 (Northport, NY: Costello Publishing Company, Inc., 1996.

Saliers, Don E. "Symbol in Liturgy, Liturgy as Symbol: The Domestication of Liturgical Experience." In *The Awakening Church: 25 Years of Liturgical Renewal*, edited by Lawrence J. Madden, 69–82. Collegeville, MN: Liturgical Press, 1992.

Santayana, George. *The Life of Reason; or, The Phases of Human Progress*. Vol. 1. New York: Charles Scribner's Sons, 1905–22.

Saville, Anthony. *The Test of Time: An Essay in Philosophical Aesthetics*. New York: Oxford University Press, 1982.

Schaefer, Edward. *Catholic Music through the Ages: Balancing the Needs of a Worshipping Church*. Chicago: Hillenbrand, 2008.

Schillebeeckx, Edward. *Revelation and Theology*. Vol. 1. New York: Sheed and Ward, 1967.

Schmitt, Francis. "Leaning Right?" In *Crisis in Church Music?*, 52–64. Washington, DC: The Liturgical Conference, 1967.

Schreiter, Robert J. *Constructing Local Theologies*. Maryknoll, NY: Orbis Books, 1985.

Schuler, Richard J. *A Chronicle of the Reform: Catholic Music in the 20th Century*. http://www.musicasacra.com/pdf/chron.pdf. Reprinted from Robert A. Skeris, ed., *Cum Angelis Canere: Essays on Sacred Music and Pastoral Liturgy in Honour of Richard J. Schuler* (St. Paul, MN: Church Music Association, 1990).

Scruton, Roger. *The Aesthetics of Music*. Oxford: Clarendon Press, 1997.

Searle, Mark, and David C. Leege. "The Celebration of Liturgy in the Parishes." In *Notre Dame Study of Catholic Parish Life*, Report No. 5 (August 1985), edited by David C. Leege and Joseph Gremillion. Notre Dame, IN: University of Notre Dame, 1985.

Sing to the Lord: Music in Divine Worship. United States Conference of Catholic Bishops, November 2007. http://www.usccb.org/liturgy/SingToTheLord.pdf.

Snyder, Bob. *Music and Memory*. Cambridge, MA: MIT Press, 2000.

Strohm, Reinhard. *Essays on Handel and Italian Opera*. Cambridge: Cambridge University Press, 1985.

Swain, Joseph P. *Harmonic Rhythm: Analysis and Interpretation*. New York: Oxford University Press, 2002.

———. "Musical Communities and Music Perception." *Music Perception* 11, no. 3 (Spring 1994): 307–20.

———. *Musical Languages*. New York: Norton, 1997.

Talley, Thomas J. *The Origins of the Liturgical Year*. 2nd ed. New York: Pueblo Publishing, 1991.

Tracy, David. *The Analogical Imagination: Christian Theology and the Culture of Pluralism*. New York: Crossroad, 1981.

Varietates Legitimae. Instruction on Inculturation and the Roman Liturgy. Congregation for Divine Worship and the Discipline of the Sacraments. March 29, 1994. http://www.adoremus.org/VarietatesLegitimae.html. Originally published in *Origins* 23, no. 43 (April 14, 1994).

Voluntati Obsequens. Vatican City: Sacred Congregation for Divine Worship. April 14, 1974.

Wainwright, Geoffrey. *Doxology: The Praise of God in Worship, Doctrine and Life: A Systematic Theology*. New York: Oxford University Press, 1980.

Walsh, Michael J. "The History of the Council." In *Modern Catholicism: Vatican II and After*, edited by Adrian Hastings, 35–47. New York: Oxford University Press, 1991.

Weakland, Rembert. "Music and Liturgy in Evolution." In *Crisis in Church Music?*, 3–13. Washington, DC: The Liturgical Conference, 1967.

———. "The Song of the Church: Liturgy and Music." Address to the National Liturgical Music Convention in Melbourne, Australia, on April 19, 1993. *Origins* 23, no. 1 (May 20, 1993): 12–16.

Winter, Miriam Therese. *Why Sing? Toward a Theology of Catholic Church Music*. Washington, DC: The Pastoral Press, 1984.

Wittgenstein, Ludwig. *Philosophical Investigations*. Translated by G. E. Anscombe. Oxford: Basil Blackwell, 1953.

Wolff, Christoph. *Johann Sebastian Bach: The Learned Musician*. New York: Norton, 2000.

Worst, John. *A Nigerian Journal*. Grand Rapids, MI: Calvin College, 1984.

Yukimoto, Hisashi. "Church Musician Encourages Asians to Eschew Western Harmony." *Ecumenical News International Daily News Service*, September 21, 2006.

Zauner, Franz Bischof. "Die liturgische Konstitution und ihre Grundtendenzen." In *Die Kirchenmusik und das II. Vatikanische Konzil*, edited by Philipp Harnoncourt, 13–32. Graz, Austria: Verlag Styria, 1965.

Zizioulas, John D. *Being as Communion: Studies in Personhood and the Church.* Crestwood, NY: St. Vladimir's Seminary Press, 1985.

Zotto, Gastone. "Il Primato dell'Ascolto nella Celebrazione del Rito Liturgico." In *Amen Vestrum: Miscellanea di Studi Liturgico-Pastorali in Onore di P. Pelagio Visentin*, edited by Alceste Catella, 447–60. Caro Saluti Cardo 9. Padua: Edizione Messaggero, 1994.

Index

Abbey of St. Pierre, Solesmes, 34, 101, 223
Abbey of the Genesee, 83
Absolutism, 176
a cappella singing, 47n11, 99, 100, 107, 120, 123, 133, 144, 149, 185, 310
acclamation(s), 26, 72, 75, 86, 248, 283, 297, 300, 301, 304, 310, 322, 341
active participation. See *participatio actuosa*
Acts of the Apostles, 277–79
actual participation. See *participatio actuosa*
Adam, Adolf, 226
Addison, Joseph, 250
Advent, 50n50, 73n13, 96n2, 114–15, 224, 226, 227, 228–30, 232, 233, 234, 235, 236
aesthetics, 19, 72, 82, 136, 155, 176, 191, 211, 344; liturgical, 183
Africa, 7, 33, 35, 61, 64, 159, 255n36, 276, 286, 287, 288, 290, 291, 343
African American, 76, 281–84, 285
Africanization, 290
A German Requiem (Brahms), 139
Agnus Dei, 49, 75, 79, 96, 102, 111, 132, 133, 134, 139, 140n11, 157, 234, 238, 241, 255, 258, 259, 284, 297, 309
Aguiar, Benny M., 287n20
Alleluia, 102, 103, 111–13, 114, 115–16, 127, 245, 259, 282, 308, 337, 341n34, 348
"Alleluia! Sing to Jesus," 156
alternatim, 106
Amalarius, Bishop of Metz, 95
amateur, 57, 139, 150, 324n16
amateurism, 10, 38, 68, 84, 148, 337

Ambrose, St., 75
Ambrosian chant, 39, 96, 167
Ambrosian Rite, 81
American Catholic Church, 33, 210, 246, 258n44
American culture, 63, 64, 238
amplification of music, 57, 117, 185–86, 335
angel, 45, 129, 159n16, 223, 225, 229, 241
Anglican Church and traditions, 3, 61n1, 96, 119, 252, 255–56; hymns, 41, 46, 156, 158, 159, 288
Annunciation (feast), 226, 233
anthem, 119, 211
antiphon(s), 19, 26, 41, 72, 76, 77, 86, 102, 104, 110n15, 11n17, 116, 157, 158, 159, 171, 228, 230, 238, 239n1, 285, 297, 300, 304, 308, 310, 315, 322, 323, 341; *see also* communion, introit, offertory
antiphonary, 95
antiphony, 111
antiprofessionalism, 201, 311
Arab culture, 148, 249, 303
Aramaic, 248
architecture (church), 15–16, 107, 117, 199, 202
aria, 15, 138, 143, 189, 192, 194
Armenian Rite, 321
Armstrong, Louis, 342
Ascension, 224, 226, 229
Asia, 8, 35, 159, 255n36, 276, 289, 290
Athens, 261
"At the Name of Jesus," 242
"Ave Maria," 33, 147, 229n11
"Away in the Manger," 232

363

Bach, Johann Sebastian, 46n7, 85, 137, 138n6, 143–44, 166, 176, 177, 190, 193, 194, 201, 208, 228, 257n40, 261, 263n1, 269, 272, 302, 342, 343; *Mass in B minor*, 139, 216; "O Sacred Head Surrounded" arrangement, 150–56; revival of 205–6, 264
Baini, Giuseppe, 123
baptism, 62, 290, 291, 292
Beatitudes, 244
Beethoven, Ludwig van, 46n7, 139–41, 177, 201, 212, 214, 263, 264, 265–67, 269, 272, 290, 301, 334, 336
Benedicamus Domino, 104
Benedictus (Gospel canticle), 241
Benedictus qui venit, 134n18, 141
Benedict XIV, Pope, 135
Benedict XVI, Pope, 88n6, 202, 248
"Be Not Afraid," 42–49, 50, 51, 52, 53, 54, 56–57, 58, 151, 154, 196n32
Bernard de Clairvaux, 150
bhajan, 76, 147, 287, 303, 304
Bible, 17, 86, 101, 108, 148, 241, 242, 244, 249, 256, 270, 338; see also Scriptures
Blanchard, Robert I., 58n28, 211n24
Blessed Virgin Mary, 29, 58, 122, 155, 223, 225, 235, 241, 242
"Blowin' in the Wind," 58
Boethius, 9
Bolivia, 289
Book of Common Prayer (Anglican), 250n29, 252, 255, 256
Boston Archdiocesan Choir School, 11n13, 76
"Bread of Life," 245
Broadway, 48, 117
Bruckner, Anton, 218
Buddhist tradition, 101, 147, 186, 228, 288, 304
Bugnini, Annibale, 31, 37
Butler, David, 48n13
Byrd, William, 120, 124, 131n12

Byzantine, 25, 75, 91, 92n1, 96, 100n6, 186, 249, 281, 321

Calvin, John, 119, 149, 238, 239
Calvinism, 302; *see also* Genevan Psalter
cantata, 137, 143, 194, 228, 257n40, 263n1, 272
canticle, 29, 102, 104, 191n26, 234, 240–41, 242, 243, 244, 341; Gospel, 241; see also *Magnificat*
Canticle of St. Francis, 243, 244
cantor, 5n4, 31n11, 57, 68, 104n9, 111, 146, 148, 238, 266, 303, 306, 308, 323n14, 326n18, 341
cantus firmus, 121–23, 127, 191, 268–71
Casablanca, 215–16
Catechism of the Catholic Church, 4n3
catholicity, 29, 68, 78, 86, 157, 172, 262, 311, 342, 346; and inculturation, 291–95
Cecilian movement, 13, 34, 123, 212
celebrant, 41, 64n4, 68, 70, 134, 141, 147, 157, 158, 225, 230, 266, 282–83, 286, 294, 295n44, 300, 301, 303, 308, 309, 311, 334, 335, 336, 341, 345
"Celtic Alleluia," 51–57, 97–99, 113, 114, 127, 155, 207, 208, 209
Cessario, Romanus, 20n30, 344n39
Cézanne, Paul, 214
Chants of the Missal, 31
Charlemagne, 92, 96, 262, 280
Chartres Cathedral, 347–48
children and liturgy, 30, 34, 54, 55, 83, 167n8, 255, 259, 260, 276, 288, 347, 348
Chinese language, 92n1, 287
choir(s), 26, 32, 44, 68, 75, 76, 82, 96, 101, 106, 111, 153, 168, 228, 235, 253, 289, 311, 326, 335, 341, 342, 345; in classical polyphony, 129, 130, 133, 134; in Gospel music, 282–83; professional, 110, 120,

147, 156, 302, 303; schools, 11, 72, 76, 248, 331; and Second Vatican Council, 300–301, 319–20, 323, 328; and St. Mark's, 308–10; in symphonic masses, 141; Vatican, 212

Chopin, Frederick, 177, 178, 212, 264

chorale. *See* Lutheran, hymn

chorus and choral music, 62, 63, 72, 76, 137, 138, 140n9, 141, 160, 189, 190, 194, 270, 284, 288

Christian community, 8, 274, 280, 294; and inculturation, 281; and liturgy, 15, 20, 64n4, 73n13, 80, 83, 209, 332n22; nature of, 80–81; and tradition, 164–65

Christmas and Christmastide, 75, 96, 224, 226, 228, 229, 230n14, 234, 235, 269

Christmas carols, 65, 146, 149, 165–66, 230–33, 242, 273, 274

"Christmas Oratorio" (J. S. Bach), 193

christology, 239

Christ the King (feast), 227

chromaticism, 55–56, 64, 84, 135, 142, 153

Chupungco, Anscar, 281n10

cinema, 70, 103, 159, 214–15, 289, 326n17; film music, 103, 117, 187, 196

classic (status in art), 69, 142, 204, 213–21, 239, 263–64, 267, 268, 269, 336, 347

classical polyphony, xiii, xiv, 23, 24, 25–26, 40, 72, 93, 119–34, 136, 138, 155, 188, 189, 194, 220, 237, 248, 270, 322

Cold War, 61

Collect, 225, 242, 254

Collins, Mary, 5, 168n9, 291n34, 298n5, 346n44

Colossians, St. Paul's Letter, 238

"Come Follow Me," 243, 245

"Come Holy Ghost," 232, 243

Communion (sacrament). *See* Eucharist

communion antiphon, 14, 41, 85, 134, 224, 225, 241, 246, 309

communion song, 85, 157, 238, 283

composers, 6, 49, 50, 53, 68, 131, 191, 214, 216; and creativity, 65, 67, 91, 122, 135, 169, 207, 208, 221, 262–65, 267–70, 272, 274, 340, 346; and liturgical music, 134, 137–38, 168, 169, 189, 211, 276, 331, 346; and liturgical texts, 139, 140–41, 182–84, 229, 244, 246, 329; and Second Vatican Council, 26, 300, 319, 327, 329; and true art, 200, 207

compositional technique, 10, 54, 55, 67–68, 99, 110, 129, 153, 201, 271–72, 337, 339

concerto, 142, 143, 194, 264

Congar, Yves, 19

congregational singing, 11, 12, 27, 30, 31n11, 32, 40, 41, 44, 57, 58, 63, 72, 77, 84, 87, 156–57, 159, 318n8, 326; and gospel music, 285; and *participatio actuosa*, 23, 33, 39, 84, 145, 169, 219, 220n40, 231, 297–311, 340; and plainchant, 108, 110, 111, 117; and polyphony, 141; requirements for, 147, 148n2, 232; and Second Vatican Council, 23, 78, 323–26, 331, 341, 342

Consilium, 31

Constitution on the Sacred Liturgy. See *Sacrosanctum Concilium*

contrafacta, 145, 149, 190n23, 193, 231n16, 233

Coptic Christianity, 91, 96, 263

Corinthians I, St. Paul's Letter, 311, 333, 344

Council of Jerusalem, 277

Council of Nicea, 241

Council of Trent, 24, 29, 38, 77, 81, 119, 123, 130n9, 131–32, 135, 137, 138, 141, 145, 156, 220, 244,

365

279n7, 280, 302, 307; and classical polyphony, 119, 123, 130n9, 131, 132, 188, 270
counterpoint, 46n7, 127, 135, 138, 143n16, 151, 153, 159, 194, 261, 272, 322 (note 13)
creativity, xiv, 65, 68, 78, 165–66, 342, 346; false, 328, 333–37, 339, 341; and liturgical music, 84, 87, 121–22, 169, 172, 261–74, 340
Credo, 32, 49, 50, 96, 104, 105, 106, 120, 131, 132, 133, 139, 140n11, 141, 157, 234, 235, 238, 241, 284n15, 297, 304, 305, 309, 310, 318, 332
Credo III, 309, 310
Crocker, Richard L., 99n5
Crucem tuam (plainchant), 103, 254
cultural imperialism, 294
culture and language, 248–49, 258, 273n8; and liturgy, 10, 26, 35, 80, 86, 87, 144, 148, 167, 195, 198, 237, 275, 277, 279, 281, 282, 286, 288, 289, 290–92, 294, 295, 325, 327, 329–30, 346, 348; and music, 5, 46, 47n12, 59, 96, 121, 135, 136, 147, 172, 185, 192, 204–6, 208, 211, 214, 216, 220, 221, 276, 305, 307–8, 342; popular, 63, 77, 92, 95, 193, 231, 232, 239, 343, 345; postmodern, 201, 203

dance and dance music, 45, 54, 56, 76, 97, 113, 129, 135, 143n16, 170, 194, 211, 285, 338
Dante Alighieri, 136n2, 347n45
Day, Thomas, 11, 12, 33, 40, 244, 307, 335
Debussy, Claude, 97, 114
Deiss, Lucien, "Keep in Mind," 110, 115
Dei Verbum, 17n24
democracy, 63
democratization, 61–73, 84, 335; of liturgical music, 62–63, 66, 78, 201, 328

development (theological), 213, 217, 268
devotional music, 121, 145, 146, 147, 149, 243, 295n43, 302
dialogue Mass, 30
Dickens, Charles, 3
diversity of liturgical language, 346
diversity of liturgical music, 12, 75–82, 86, 172, 206, 207, 310, 311, 323, 328
Divine Office, 40n12, 91, 96, 104, 111n17, 131, 145, 156n8, 188, 226, 240, 241, 249, 317n6, 318
Dix, Dom Gregory, 80n6, 339n30
"Dixie," 177, 190, 211, 212, 286, 338
DjeDje, Jaqueline, 282–85, 290n32, 292n37
Dominican Rite, 81
Dorsey, Thomas A., 282
dramma per musica. *See* opera
drum, 286, 289
Dufford, Robert J., 42–43, 45
Duncan, Stephen F., 76n3, 287n21
Duruflé, Maurice, 270
Dylan, Bob, 44, 45, 64

Easter and Eastertide, 34, 75, 146, 226, 232, 234, 235, 242
Easter Vigil, 30, 103, 106, 227, 229, 237
Eastman School of Music, 66
Eat, Drink, Man, Woman, 289–90
ecclesiastical year. *See* liturgical year
egoism, liturgical, 12, 68, 84, 280, 335
elitism, 72
Elliot, Bishop Peter, 251, 252n32, 253, 257
England, 81, 96, 119, 139, 231
English Chant Mass, 110
English language, 109, 176, 179, 193, 195, 197, 249n26, 250–51, 257, 273; translating, 182n11
English, liturgical, 32n12, 75, 76, 109, 110, 146, 253, 256, 257, 258, 259, 284; Anglican use, 119, 252; psalms, 149, 240

Enlightenment, 34, 163, 249n27, 331
entrance antiphon. *See* introit
episcopacy, xiv, 7, 37, 84, 163, 246, 255, 306
Episcopal Church, 159–60
epistle, 140n11, 241
eschatology, 227, 292–93
Esperanto, 258
ethnicity, 78, 80, 237, 258n44
Eucharist, 3, 28, 70, 78, 79, 102, 167, 171n8, 210, 236, 242, 243, 248n24, 282, 295, 317n6, 325, 339; as center of liturgy, 9, 15, 19, 82, 117, 219, 223, 224, 225, 245, 257n41, 279, 284, 343; real presence in, 78, 246; validity of, 5, 291, 292
Eucharistic prayer, 68, 134, 158, 237, 256, 283, 285, 297, 301, 309, 334, 336, 340, 341
evangelization, 81, 227, 255n36, 277, 285, 293, 325
Exodus, 239, 240, 242
Exsultet iam (Easter proclamation), 229, 237
extraordinary Roman Rite. *See* Roman Rite

faith in liturgy, 348–49
feedback relation, 16–19, 180–81, 183, 299
Fifth International Church Music Congress (1966), 7
film music. *See* cinema
Foley, Edward, 5n4–5, 195, 197, 201, 298n3, 332n22
Foley, John B., 49, 51
folk music, xiii, 32, 38, 41, 46n8, 49, 57, 63, 64, 145, 148, 188, 190n23, 191, 192, 197, 333; and inculturation, 285, 288, 294
folk revival style, 41–59, 63, 67n6, 71, 84, 97, 110, 175, 196, 231; harmonic content, 151, 153, 154; semantics of, 244

"For All the Saints," 158, 243
Ford, Paul R., 110n15
four hymns, 41, 86, 157, 230, 234, 246, 341
France, 9n11, 101, 121, 136, 255, 257, 343, 347
Francis, Mark, 16n22, 277n5, 280
Franciscan, 117
Franck, César, 33
Frazier, James E., 72, 76n2, 331n21
free rhythm, 97, 100, 115, 117, 270, 322
fugue, 144, 176, 194
functional harmony, 47–48, 49, 54, 56, 67, 113–15, 116, 151, 154, 155, 270

Gaspar, Jonathan, 20n30, 344n39
Gather, 77, 229, 233
Gaudium et Spes, 37, 277
Gelineau, Joseph, 5n5, 295
General Instruction of the Roman Missal, 238n1; "option four," 15n21, 85–86, 157, 230, 246, 283, 334
General Synod on the Eucharist (2005), 24
Geneva, Switzerland, 149, 202
Genevan Psalter, 145, 149, 240, 302
Germany, 28, 136, 139, 157, 208, 257, 302
Gettysburg Address (Lincoln), 250–51, 305
Ghana, 76, 288, 290
G. I. A. Publications (Chicago), 76
G.I.R.M. *See* General Instruction of the Roman Missal
Glagolitic Mass (Janacek), 139n8
Gloria, 49, 50, 86, 96, 102, 104, 105, 106, 110, 120, 122, 131, 132, 133, 134, 137, 140n11, 146, 157, 167, 227, 234, 236, 238, 241, 253, 258, 259, 284, 285, 297, 304, 305, 308, 318, 338, 347; "De Angelis," 102, 105; and liturgical cycle, 234
Glory and Praise, 64

God (the Father), 3, 5n5, 8, 42, 134, 135, 137, 175, 184, 231, 245n17, 275, 289, 290, 291, 292–93, 307, 311, 343; desire to praise, 4–5, 83, 87, 91, 101, 145, 148, 183, 228, 234, 237, 243, 279, 303–4, 325, 340; in liturgy, 15, 19, 20, 58, 62, 73, 78, 80–81, 103–4, 117, 164, 187, 196, 203, 219, 223, 224, 225, 235, 238, 244, 246, 254, 259, 260, 266, 277, 280, 286, 301, 317, 327, 330, 332, 337, 341, 345, 347, 349; Word of, 16–17, 68, 149, 164, 239, 241, 242, 278, 314
Good Friday, 103, 186, 193
Gospel(s), 70, 102, 103, 134, 219, 226, 239, 240, 242, 244, 309, 327, 330, 337, 345; inculturating, 277, 281, 290, 291, 293, 294, 301, 330; message, 81, 242, 255n36, 277, 278; St. John, 5, 81, 103, 241, 245; St. Luke, 241, 253, 254; St. Mark, 227, 241; St. Matthew, 77, 87n5, 182, 225, 241, 291, 294, 329
gospel acclamation, 14, 308
gospel canticles, 240
gospel music, 15, 76, 172, 281n12, 282–86, 321
gradual (proper), 14, 111, 238
Graduale Romanum, 76n4, 85, 102, 103, 109, 235, 309
Graduale Simplex, 31, 73n13, 76n4, 85, 106, 110n15, 114, 146, 323
grammar, musical. *See* musical syntax
Greek language, 14, 181–82, 185, 207, 247n22; in liturgy, 108, 109, 248, 249, 255, 256, 308
Gregorian chant, xiii, 23, 25, 71, 72, 75, 76, 95, 119, 121, 122, 167, 169, 228, 243, 248, 280, 281, 294; aesthetics, 207; and modes, 56n23; and *participatio actuosa*, 300; performance, 112, 308, 309; and psalms, 15, 104, 105n9; revival, 13, 30, 33– 34, 293; Second Vatican Council, 23, 25–26, 31, 35, 39, 107, 110, 220, 321–23, 333, 342; semantics, 159, 343; terminology, 95–96, 99n5, 101; *see also* plainchant
Gregory Nazianzen, St., 23
Guéranger, Prosper, 34, 171, 223–24, 343
Guido d'Arezzo, 262
guitar, 42, 43, 44, 45, 46–47, 63, 64, 67, 151, 153, 175, 261, 289, 326

Handel, George Frideric, 46n7, 137, 138, 201, 208, 216, 250
"Happy Birthday," 100
Häring, Bernard, 346n43
"Hark! The Herald Angels Sing," 232
harmonic rhythm, 45–47, 50, 52, 53n19, 154–55
Harnoncourt, Phillipp, 5n7
harpsichord, 194
Hassler, Hans Leo, 190
Hastings Adrian, 36n23
Haugen, Marty, 71
Haydn, Franz Joseph, 76, 137, 139, 140, 141–42, 170n13, 264
hazzan, 303, 306
Hebrew language, 181, 239, 240, 248, 249, 255, 305; liturgical, 249
high Renaissance polyphony. *See* classical polyphony
Hiley, David, 99n5
Hindemith, Paul, 71
Hindustani music, 287
Hindu tradition, 76, 101, 147, 249, 255, 287, 303, 304, 307
Hitchcock, Helen Hull, 211n25
Hitchcock, James, 70n7
Hollywood, 56, 72, 115, 159
"Holy God, We Praise Thy Name," 79, 257
"Holy, holy, holy" (hymn), 41, 156
Holy Spirit, 17; in the Bible, 77, 278, 311; lesser doxology, 239; and

liturgy, 15, 164, 219, 223, 225, 226n6, 279, 345; and liturgical music, 8, 95, 96
Holy Thursday, 47n11, 227, 229, 335
Holy Trinity. *See* Trinity
Holy Week, 30, 150
Homer, 69, 214
homophony, 46
hope in liturgy, 347–48
"Hosea," 51, 55
Hovda, Robert W., 70n7
"How Great Thou Art," 155
Huck, Gabe, 70n7
Huijbers, Bernard, 299–300
humanism, 136, 138, 183, 191, 200, 247
hymn, 91, 97; Greek, 91; plainchant, 47n11, 280 101, 104, 111
hymn, congregational, 40, 75, 76, 77, 79, 99, 145, 147, 243, 247, 303, 335; Anglican, 41, 46, 158, 165, 288; Bach arrangements, 143n15, 149–56; Catholic use of, 8, 15, 26, 28, 30, 33, 58, 70, 72, 75, 156–60, 210, 287, 288, 302, 310, 318n8; contrafacta, 193–94; inculturation of, 29, 287–90; Lutheran, 39, 41, 73, 119, 121, 149–56, 231, 237, 288, 305, 309; recessional, 85n4; semantics, 158–59, 183n15, 190–93, 230, 232, 235; sources of, 148, 193–94, 238, 240, 241, 242, 244–45, 306
hymnal, 76, 110, 229, 232n18, 233, 242; national, 233n20
Hytrek, Theophane, 45

Illardo, Bernardo, 289
imitation (contrapuntal), 129, 130, 132, 138, 144, 191
Immaculate Conception (feast), 227, 309
"Immaculate Mary," 58
incarnation, 167, 224, 225, 226, 227, 232, 233

inculturation of liturgy, 86, 172, 225n4, 342; double movement, 281–82, 285, 293n40, 325; liturgical music, xiv, 275–95, 322, 325, 330
India, 76, 92n1, 286, 287, 294, 303
Indian Rite Mass, 286–87
individualism, 62–63, 264, 265, 267, 269, 272, 334, 337, 339
instruments, liturgical use of, 47, 69, 104, 186, 188, 280, 294, 325–27, 337; *see also* drum, guitar, keyboard, organ, piano
introit antiphon, 14, 41, 85, 96, 134, 224, 241, 246, 308, 309
Irwin, Kevin, 16n23, 19n28, 180n8, 202n9, 313n1
Isaac, Heinrich, 131n12
Isaiah, 181–82, 224–25, 229, 241
Islamic tradition, 61, 97, 101, 147, 303, 307
Italy, 33, 63

Jackson, Mahalia, 282
Japan, 76, 147, 257, 288, 289, 292, 304, 342, 343
jazz, 45, 47, 67, 99, 117, 132, 175, 185, 192, 206, 209, 269
Jerusalem, 184, 226, 261, 277–78; Council of, 277
Jesus Christ, 17, 77, 175, 181, 183, 246, 249n26, 252, 277, 278, 290, 292, 316n5; and liturgy, 4, 15, 16n22, 19, 20, 29, 116, 219, 223–26, 227, 237, 239, 241, 247, 253, 275, 279, 281, 292, 330, 338, 341, 345, 346; words of, 244
"Jesus Christ Is Risen Today," 156, 232
Jewish liturgical music, 92n1, 104, 147, 148, 239, 249, 292, 303, 304, 306, 326
Job, 241
John XXII, Pope, 188
John XXIII, Pope, 35

John Paul II, Pope, 24, 31, 37, 76, 119, 248, 281n11, 314n2
Josquin Desprez, 67, 120, 121–22, 269
"Joy to the World," 165
Jubilate Deo, 259, 295
Jungmann, Joseph A., 333n23

Karnatic music, 287
Kavanagh, Aidan, 30n9, 33, 38n29, 39, 84n1, 334n25
Kenya, 342, 343
keyboard, 6, 45, 47n9, 151, 196
kirtan, 287
Kiwele, Joseph, 286
Koenker, Ernest, 33, 34n21
Komonchak, Joseph A., 37
Korea, 76
Kraynak, Robert J., 62
Kuhn, Thomas, 14n18
Kyriale simplex, 31
Kyrie, 49, 75, 79, 86, 96, 102, 104, 108, 109, 111, 120, 131, 132, 133, 139, 140n11, 157, 234, 235, 238, 255, 259, 263, 268, 272–74, 284, 297, 308, 318n8, 334; and liturgical year, 235
Kyrie Pro Victimis 9/11, 273–74

laity, xiv, 3, 7, 20, 23, 32, 34, 35, 37, 38, 39, 87, 145, 148, 149, 147, 150, 156, 160, 168, 169, 172, 173, 297, 298n4, 303, 311, 331, 339n30, 340, 344, 345, 347
Langlais, Jean, 271
Lassus, Orlandus, 120, 123, 124
Latin America, 8, 64, 255n36, 270, 289, 290
Latin language, 31, 79, 107n11, 120, 121, 136n2, 137, 138, 139, 146, 147, 189, 207, 286, 288, 302, 338, 340, 347, 348; in classical polyphony, 302; disappearance of, 32, 38, 244, 254, 289, 333; neutrality of, 257–59; in *novus ordo*, 308–10; papal views on, 28, 29; and plainchant, 31, 47, 75, 76, 101–2, 105, 108–9, 111, 149, 190, 192, 280, 294, 342; as sacred language, 247–52, 256, 321; and Second Vatican Council, 23, 25, 26, 40, 84, 255, 299–300, 315–16, 318, 320, 323n15, 327; semantic value of, 237–38, 248–52, 255, 322
Latin Rite, 96, 104
lauda, 146
Lauds, 96, 241, 317n6
layperson. *See* laity
lectionary, 239n1, 241, 256
lector, 5n4, 68, 266, 282, 311, 335, 345
Lee, Ang, 289–90
LeJeune Claude, 155
Lent, 75, 96, 103, 193, 226, 227, 232, 233, 234, 235, 236, 341n34
lesser doxology, 19, 105n9, 239
lex orandi, lex credendi, 80, 202, 242, 246, 247
"Lift Up Ye Heads," 158, 159
lining out, 238, 305
litany, 106, 146–47, 159, 297, 304
liturgical books, 81, 88n6, 281, 293n40, 334
liturgical language, 24–25, 26, 27, 29, 32, 39, 69, 86, 108, 171, 237–60, 276, 346n43; *see also* vernacular language in liturgy
liturgical movement, 3, 13, 32, 33, 34, 35, 77, 80, 108, 123, 171, 223, 247, 302, 343
liturgical music education, 320–21
liturgical reform, xiv, 23, 31, 37, 38, 58n28, 63, 69, 77, 84n1, 87, 107, 123, 141, 218, 231, 276, 295, 323n15, 329, 336, 347
liturgical roles, xiii, 62, 103, 303, 323, 328, 331
liturgical season. *See* liturgical year
liturgical texts, xiv, 49–50, 91, 104, 145, 147, 170, 171, 238–47, 287, 328, 334, 337

liturgical variety, 9, 68, 81, 82, 310, 334, 341
liturgical virtue, 87–88, 279–80, 349; and pride, 335–36
liturgical year, xiv, 9, 65, 81–82, 85, 86, 96n2, 164, 171, 221, 223–36, 238, 253, 262, 274, 334, 341
liturgy, aesthetics of, 19, 72, 82, 155, 191, 202–3, 211, 344; conformity in, 27, 81, 324; confusion about, 9, 19; history of, 78, 169, 347; and laity, 20, 32, 34, 35, 37, 38, 39, 87, 148, 149, 168–69, 172, 297, 311, 331, 339n30, 340, 344, 347; "liking" of, 332–33; nature of, 14–16, 17, 18, 19–21, 62, 78, 83, 87, 116, 166, 273, 279, 328–37; pluralism, 167, 330; solemnity of, 16, 18, 31, 68–69, 88n6, 175, 183, 200, 209, 225, 252, 254, 256, 257, 269, 279, 280, 285, 307, 315, 316, 322, 335, 348; spirit of, 265, 285; unity, uniformity of, 79, 82, 86, 92, 167, 258n44, 262, 333n23, 346; values of, 8, 12, 19, 58, 87, 199, 202, 294, 334
Liturgy of the Word, 86, 282
Loh, I-to, 289
London, Justin, 53n19
"Lord Nelson" Mass (Haydn), 137, 142
"Lourdes Hymn" (Immaculate Mary), 155
Louis, Kenneth W., 284–85
love (*caritas*) of liturgy, 344–46
Low Mass, 5, 157
Lumen Gentium, 19n28, 37, 310–11
Lutheran, 302; hymns, 39, 41, 58, 99, 119, 149–56, 158, 159, 183n15, 190, 191, 192, 193, 194, 215, 220, 231, 237, 273, 288, 305, 307; Mass, 273; revival of liturgical music, 13
Luther, Martin, 148, 149, 150, 155, 156n8, 190n23, 191, 302

Madeleine Choir School, 72, 76, 331n21
madrigal (Italian), 132, 135, 189, 191
Magembe, Expedito, 287
Magnificat, 138, 230, 241
Mahrt, William, 73n14, 107n11, 111n17
Maimonides, 303, 307
Mancini, Henry, 56
Mannion, M. Francis, xiii n1, 20n29, 20n31, 51n17, 66
Marier, Theodore, 11n13, 76, 110, 115, 243n9
Mass for Pope Marcellus. See *Missa Papae Marcelli*
Mass in B Minor (J. S. Bach), 139n7, 216, 218
Mass of the Lord's Supper, 47n11
mass ordinaries. *See* Ordinaries Prayers of the Mass
McMahon, J. Michael, 73n14
McManus, Frederick R., 323n15
Mediator Dei (Pope Pius XII), 28, 30, 40n2
melisma, 104, 109, 159
memory and music cognition, 47, 106, 116, 147, 180n8, 304
Mendelssohn, Felix, 205
Messiah (Handel), 138, 216
meter (musical), xiv, 17, 53–55, 112–13, 114, 115, 116, 117, 127–29, 154, 155, 185, 186, 188, 211, 304; and harmony, 99, 100, 112–13; perception of, 52n18, 53, 54, 97–99, 100, 101, 115, 127
meter (poetic), 48, 49, 101, 150, 157, 239, 240n5
microphone, 57, 69, 72
Middle Ages, 146, 169, 185, 213, 246, 261, 303n12, 307, 322n13, 333n23
Milner, Anthony, 32
Minneapolis, 72
Misa Criolla (Ramirez), 270
Missa Dum Sunt Dies Pentecostes (Palestrina), 120–21, 132

missalette, 64, 77, 116, 163–64, 232n18, 329
Missal, Roman, 31, 41n3, 50n16, 75, 85, 158, 219, 234n22, 238, 243, 248, 254, 256, 333
Missa Luba (Kiwele), 286
Missa Papae Marcelli (Palestrina), 120, 123, 131, 270
Missa Solemnis (Beethoven), 139–41, 265–67, 301
missions, 25, 29, 63, 77, 81, 167, 198, 279, 285, 286, 292, 293, 325
Mitchell, Joni, 44
Mitchell, Nathan, 320n11
modal harmony, 64, 76, 115, 236
mode, church, 56, 64, 76, 103, 104, 115, 120, 142, 236, 295
modernism, 117, 186n17
monasticism, 95, 96, 186, 238, 261, 262, 268
monophony, 100, 107, 112, 159, 295
Monte, Filippo de, 71
Monteverdi, Claudio, 136n2, 170n13, 269
"Mood Indigo," 177
Morgenthaler, Sally, 70n8
motet, 120, 121, 124–29, 132, 134, 137, 138, 140n11, 143, 229, 270, 335
Mozarabic Rite, 96, 281
Mozart, Wolfgang Amadeus, 46n7, 76, 137, 139, 140, 142, 153, 166, 189, 200, 205, 206, 218, 264, 272
Musicae Sacrae Ministerium (Pope Pius XII), 28, 29, 30, 88n6, 200
musical community, 17, 201, 204, 276
musical language, 6, 9, 47, 77, 123, 132, 141, 159, 164, 192, 197, 206–7, 271, 282, 317, 331, 333, 337, 339; anachronistic, 137, 169, 322; evolution of, 136n2, 220, 270, 285; nature of, 208–9, 212; understanding of, 138n6, 144, 272, 276, 277, 321; universal, 293, 295n44

musical style, semantics of, 20n30, 42, 50, 92, 143, 175, 185, 190, 192, 197, 210–13, 244, 307, 322, 325, 346
musical syntax, 47, 77, 113, 114, 124, 153, 154, 186, 191, 192, 206–7, 208, 276, 284
Musicam Sacram, 32, 49n14, 195, 210, 299, 300, 304, 307
"Music in Catholic Worship" (1983), 210–12

Newman, John Henry, 3, 33, 173, 193, 206, 213, 217, 241, 268, 269
New Testament. *See* Scriptures
New York Times, 23
Nichols, Aidan, 6n8, 61, 83, 165n2, 248n24, 251n30, 324n16
Nigeria, 287, 288–89
Nonmetric. *See* free rhythm
Norbet, Gregory, 51
notation (musical), xiv; and congregations, 34, 310; in composition, 44, 45, 52n18, 53, 115, 121, 151, 268; interpretation, 99, 267, 336; invention, 9n11, 91, 92, 122n3, 261–63, 264
Notre Dame Study of Catholic Life, 5n4, 57, 64n4
novus ordo, 58, 76, 88n6, 134, 219, 248n23, 334; *see also* Roman Rite
"Now Thank We All Our God," 156

O'Carroll, Fintan, 51
"O Come, Emmanuel," 229n11, 230, 233
"O Father We Have Wandered," 233
offertory antiphon, 14, 41, 85, 96, 134, 224, 241, 246, 309
offertory song, 85, 157, 282
"O God Our Help in Ages Past," 46, 158, 240
Old Testament. *See* Scriptures
opera, 15, 33, 103, 117, 123, 132, 135–38, 141, 142, 148, 167, 168, 178n5,

189, 190, 191, 192, 194, 197, 200, 206, 250, 271, 306, 326, 331
opera Mass. *See* symphonic mass
option four. *See* General Instruction of the Roman Missal
oratorio, 137
orchestra, 62, 76, 78, 140n10, 141, 205, 216, 265, 266, 334, 336
Ordinary Prayers of the Mass, 49, 50, 64, 76, 77, 86, 157, 238, 244, 286; and congregational singing, 33, 25, 28, 75, 79, 141, 149, 255, 259, 288, 310, 318, 320, 341; Gospel music settings, 283–84; plainchant settings, 96, 104, 270, 280, 295n43; polyphonic settings, 120, 131, 134n19; operatic, 137, 139, 140, 189, 302; seasonal settings, 228, 233–36
Ordinary Time, 75, 227, 233, 234, 235, 236
organ, pipe, 66, 72, 76, 104, 188, 202, 302; J. S. Bach's, 143, 194; with hymns, 158, 160; and liturgical year, 235–36; with plainchant, 100–101, 111, 112, 115, 133; with popular music, 47; and Second Vatican Council, 196, 235, 325, 326, 327; semantics of, 112, 176, 178, 187, 189, 196, 197, 229, 236, 269; in Venice, 75, 76; at St. Mark's, 308, 309
organist(s), 6, 8, 12, 73, 75, 76, 101, 115, 156, 160, 172, 235, 305, 341, 345
original sin, 277, 293, 325, 330
Orthodox Church, 65, 86, 96, 147, 249, 255, 257n41, 281
"O Sacred Head Surrounded," 73, 99, 150–52, 154, 156, 158, 176, 190, 191, 192, 193, 194, 233
O Sanctissima, 309
Our Father, 111, 121, 255, 309, 332
Oxford Movement, 3, 165, 231

Palestine 239, 249, 291
Palestrina, Giovanni da, 10, 46n7, 67, 71, 82, 114, 120, 123–30, 132, 133, 136n2, 137, 138n4, 141, 153, 194, 201, 205, 212, 229, 269–70, 273, 284, 310
Palm Sunday, 150
Pange lingua, 47n11, 111, 270
"Panis Angelicus," 33
papal choir, 76, 96
parable of the Vietnamese immigrant, 253, 254
paraphrase of liturgical prayers, 102, 149, 157, 241, 245, 288, 333
Paris, 116, 167
Parsch, Pius, 32
participatio actuosa, xiv, 7, 23, 26–27, 29–30, 31, 32, 35, 37, 38, 39, 62, 69, 72–73, 84, 88, 145, 172, 175, 219, 220n40, 297–312, 324, 331, 337, 340–42, 344, 347; and plainchant, 110
paschal mystery, 15, 16n22, 19n28, 219, 223, 224, 236, 244, 275, 279, 316, 330, 338, 343
"Passion Chorale," 150, 152–53, 193
Passiontide, 103, 146, 150, 193, 225, 226, 233
Pater Noster. See Our Father
Paul VI, Pope, 31n11, 37, 259, 293, 313n2
Paulinus of Aquileia, 241
Pelikan, Jaroslav, 261, 264n1, 271
Pentecost, 77, 121, 215, 223, 224, 226, 229
perception of music, 17, 116, 180, 186, 228, 267, 276
phrasing, musical, 48, 52, 64
piano, 6, 45, 47, 145, 175, 176, 177, 178, 196, 197, 326, 327; digital, 76
Pius X, Pope, 297, 315, 323; *motu proprio*, see *Tra le Sollecitudini*
piyyut, 92n1, 147, 148, 303, 304
plainchant, 56n23, 68, 84, 92, 133, 160, 190n23, 283, 333; aesthetics of,

13n17, 17, 73, 155, 158, 195, 200, 208, 209, 211, 220, 237, 240, 243, 254, 294–95, 310, 340, 348; Council of Trent, 131; harmonizing, 110–16; modern use of 8, 58, 75–76; neglect of, 8, 23, 32, 37–38, 40, 58, 168, 200, 248; notation, 76, 262; performance, 236; and Plato, 176, 214, 216, 346n43

polyphony, 24, 121–22, 127–29, 138, 188, 268–72; revival, 32–36 123, 223, 259, 302; Second Vatican Council, 26, 31, 32–33, 39, 186, 321–24; semantics, 47n11, 159, 183n15, 186, 187, 190, 191, 197, 212, 219, 228, 235; tradition of, xiv, 28, 93, 95–117, 119, 163, 273, 280, 281, 285, 306, 329; translation, 109–10, 149, 150, 240, 254; see also classical polyphony

polysemy, 178–80

popular liturgical music, 25, 28, 29, 32, 40, 41–42, 48, 63, 64, 68, 70, 71, 75, 77, 84, 93, 145–60, 190n26, 196, 210, 220, 229, 231, 232, 234, 237, 240–44, 246, 254, 271, 302, 303, 307, 324, 329; see also folk revival style

postlude, 143, 194, 309

postmodernism, 201–6, 212, 214, 291

Praetorius, Michael, 155

"Praise to the Lord," 41, 156, 234

predication, 178

prelude, 143, 194, 229, 269, 302, 308, 327

processional song, 8, 76, 85, 134, 145, 148, 157, 158, 197, 243, 257, 308, 309, 315, 340

professional musician, 6, 7, 44, 59, 66–68, 72, 73, 76, 85, 110, 133, 136, 137, 139, 140, 148, 149, 150, 151, 155, 156, 159, 160, 172, 201, 267, 273, 277, 294, 298, 302, 303n12,

305, 306, 307, 310, 318, 320, 324, 331–32, 336–37, 339, 342, 344

proper(s) of the Mass, 8, 41, 58, 73n13, 85–86, 96, 104n9, 109n14, 110, 120, 131, 156n8, 157–58, 171, 219, 224, 225, 228, 229, 230–31, 234, 235, 236, 238, 239n1, 241, 244, 246, 272, 274, 280, 283, 285, 302, 309, 310, 318, 320, 321, 323n15, 334

Protestant churches, 9, 61n1, 65, 75, 136, 202, 247; and music, 11, 41, 58, 102, 119, 145, 156–60, 231, 282, 286, 302, 303, 305

Proverbs, 199

Psalm 23, 182–83

Psalm 42, 126

Psalm 51, 226

Psalm 92, v

Psalm 98, 145

psalm(s), 26, 86, 91, 95, 177, 202, 229, 238–41, 248, 258, 292n46, 302, 328n19, 337; antiphons, 116, 238, 246, 310; metricized, 41n3, 149, 192n27, 242, 244; paraphrase, 41n3, 102, 238, 241; plainchant, 76, 85, 104, 105n9, 106, 111n17, 133, 240, 283; operatic, 189; poetic structure, 102, 157, 304, 305; polyphonic, 121, 130, 132, 133, 191n26; responsorial, 14, 18, 75, 104, 210, 230, 238, 282, 297, 308; Second Vatican Council, 297, 300, 315, 322, 341; verses, 14–15, 18, 295n44

psalmody. See psalm

psalm tones, 15, 104, 109, 110n15, 323

psalter, 19, 77, 95, 157, 238, 239, 240n5, 242, 256; see also Genevan Psalter

publishers (music), 76

pub song, 62

Puer natus est, 269

Qur'an, 101, 148, 303

Ramirez, Ariel, 270
Ratzinger, Joseph, 16n22, 20, 61, 134n18, 159n16
recession, 309; hymn, 41, 85n4, 104, 159
recording and phonography, 6, 47n11, 95, 145, 282, 284
reference (extra-musical), 159, 176–77, 182, 316
Reformation, 91, 131, 302
refrain (in liturgical music), 31n11, 43, 49, 50, 52, 54n21, 56, 147, 245, 284, 285, 287, 288, 303, 304, 305
relativism, 14n18, 178, 195, 201, 202, 204, 205, 206, 211, 317, 333, 342, 343
relevance, liturgical, 61, 69–72, 116–17, 175, 203, 274, 291, 328–31, 336, 337
Renaissance, 119, 200
Renaissance polyphony. *See* classical polyphony
Requiem (Berlioz), 140
Requiem (Brahms), 139
Requiem (Duruflé), 270
Requiem (Verdi), 140, 142, 270, 290
responsorial psalm. *See* psalm
Revelation (book of), 241
revolving door, 64–65, 72, 85, 163, 166, 232, 329, 339, 340
ritual, 61, 69, 84n1, 86, 101, 107, 134, 165, 166, 179, 194, 198, 237, 280, 303, 324, 326, 329; creativity in, 335–36, 343n37
Ritual Song, 229
Rochester, New York, 66
rock music, 41, 54, 99, 117, 184, 185, 197, 246, 270
Roman Catholic Church, diversity of music, 75–82, 86, 96; doctrinal development, 16–18, 268; musical icons of, 95, 119, 228, 234; prejudices, 23–24, 107; repertory, 6, 10, 11, 12, 13, 33, 39–40, 65, 66, 72, 75, 77, 84, 86, 91, 92, 93, 96, 108, 110, 111, 119, 120, 132, 133, 138, 139, 145, 163, 164, 166, 168, 172, 199, 212, 219, 220, 221, 227, 228, 232, 235, 262, 263, 280, 285, 287–90, 294, 298, 314, 316, 317, 319, 322, 327, 340; and Scripture, 16–17, 187; state of music, 3, 67, 83–88
Roman Rite, 7, 14, 41, 58, 76, 109, 140, 149, 163, 167, 168, 172, 184, 209, 219, 235, 238n1, 247, 302; "extraordinary," 88, 248, 252, 257, 258; inculturating, 280, 282, 285, 286, 287, 288, 293n40, 325; Second Vatican Council, 297, 314, 321, 322, 325, 327, 333
romanticism, 56
Rome, 38, 70, 76, 77, 79, 81, 82, 87, 101, 248, 249, 280, 281, 321; *see also* Vatican
Rorate coeli (plainchant), 228–29
Routley, Eric, 175
Ruff, Anthony, 7n10, 13, 14–15, 16, 18, 19, 28n7, 32, 34n22, 108n12, 156n8, 168, 170n3, 193n28, 199n2, 204n13, 240n5, 303n12, 308, 319
Russian rites, 96, 321

Sacram Liturgiam, 37
sacred concerto, 137
sacred symphony, 137
Sacrosanctum Concilium, v, 3, 4, 7, 24, 28, 31, 34, 37, 38, 39, 41, 42, 165, 224, 247, 347, 348; authority of, 36, 210, 212, 218, 342; composers, 78, 327–28; inculturation, 81, 277–79, 293n40; liturgical language, 24–25, 29, 248n23, 259; liturgical roles, 27, 62, 331; music in liturgy, 11, 13, 14, 16, 21, 27, 32, 34–35, 58, 63, 79, 81, 87, 110, 186, 187, 195, 200,

375

209, 220, 313–28, 329, 333, 336, 341, 346n42; *participatio actuosa*, 62, 169, 219, 297, 299, 300, 304, 307, 340; nature of liturgy, 4, 13, 15, 19; and traditional repertory, 26, 82, 84
saint, 81, 123, 146, 147, 213, 223, 227, 242, 243, 274, 275, 327, 337
Saliers, Don E., 293n41, 343n37
Samuel (2), 275
Sanctus, 49, 75, 79, 96, 102, 111, 120, 132, 134, 140n11, 141, 142, 157, 158, 234, 238, 241, 255, 258, 259, 284, 297, 309, 318n8, 337
Sant' Anselmo (monastery, Rome), 101
Santayana, George, 11
Santo Domingo de Silos (monastery), 71, 95
Sarum Use, 96, 167
Saville, Anthony, 214, 217
SC. See *Sacrosanctum Concilium*
Schaefer, Edward, 5n4, 13, 18, 80n5, 107n10, 109n14, 138n4, 320n11
Schillebeeckx, Edward, 346n43
Schmitt, Francis, 70–71
Schreiter, Robert, 291
Schubert, Franz, 33, 76, 139, 140, 142
Schuler, Richard J., 24n2, 26n4, 28n7, 76, 133n16, 142n13, 148n2
Schumann, Robert, 264
Schutte, Daniel L., 51
Schwake, Gregor, 33
Scotland, 238
Scriptures, 15, 16–17, 18, 26, 61, 86, 91, 101, 107, 180n8, 181, 187, 219, 234n22, 241–42, 244, 251, 252, 263, 279, 280n8, 281, 295n44, 301, 305, 313, 315, 328, 329, 341, 348; New Testament, 102, 121, 240, 242–43; Old Testament, 102, 121, 146, 181n10, 239
Scruton, Roger, 199
season, liturgical and music, 9

Second Vatican Council, xiii, 4, 8, 19, 21, 40, 61, 62, 84, 87, 165, 166, 171, 224, 229, 234n22, 247, 249, 254, 259, 277, 336; and liturgical music, 11, 23–38, 39, 42, 57, 63, 86, 107, 109n14, 116, 141, 156, 163, 168, 175, 186, 197, 200, 213, 220, 235, 238, 244, 281, 306, 329, 344; and *participatio actuosa*, 145, 297, 299–302, 331, 340
secularism, 247, 271, 336
secular music, characteristics, 185
self-reference (music), 176
semantic association, 137, 180–81, 187n18, 191, 192, 228–29, 233, 285–86
semantic distinction, 91, 92, 103, 106, 107, 159, 181–82, 185, 186, 187, 188–90, 191, 192, 193, 195, 196, 203, 229, 234, 236, 270, 281, 286, 290, 300, 307, 314, 316, 322, 326, 343
semantic range, 177–80, 181, 182, 183, 184, 186, 187n18, 190, 191, 192, 193, 196, 197, 212, 219, 228, 230, 231, 235, 236, 237, 277, 279, 307, 315, 325, 331, 337, 340, 343
semantics, 42, 47, 50, 56, 169, 175–98; presentational, 178–79, 180, 183, 337; sacred, 42, 47n11, 73, 91, 119, 134, 138, 139, 140, 142, 144, 154, 170, 172, 187–93, 195–97, 231–32, 270, 280, 285, 321, 322, 325, 326, 341, 342; shift, 143–44; spirit of, 40, 64, 313n2; stability of, 170–71
Septuagint, 181–82
sequence, 243, 246, 280
Shakespeare, William, 132, 249n26, 334, 336, 340
"Shall We Gather at the River," 155
Sicut cervus (Palestrina), 125–30, 132
"Silent Night," 165
"Sing a New Song," 51, 55
Singmesse, 157

"Sing to the Lord" (American Bishops), 210n21, 211n25
Snowbird Statement (1996), 13
Snyder, Bob, 47n13
Society of St. Pius X, 248
sociology and liturgy, 61
solemnity, 68–69
Solesmes. *See* Abbey of St. Pierre
sonata, 140n11, 143, 264n2
song leader. *See* cantor
"Song of the Body of Christ," 245
Spain, 95n1, 226n7, 303
Stabat mater, 145, 243
St. Agnes Parish, Minneapolis, 76, 140, 142n13
"Star Wars" theme, 183
Stations of the Cross, 243, 324
St. Augustine, 3, 5, 9, 129, 270
"Stayin' Alive," 177
St. Benedict, 95
St. Bernadette's Church (Los Angeles), 290
St. Brigid's Church, Los Angeles, 283–85, 292
St. Gregory Nazianzen, 23
St. Gregory the Great, 95, 96
stile antico, 136, 138; *see also* classical polyphony
stile moderno, 136; *see also* opera
St. James, 227, 278, 279
St. Jerome, 108, 249
St. John, 227
St. John the Baptist, 241
St. Louis Jesuits, 64
St. Louis Jesuits Mass, 49
St. Malachy's Parish (Sherburne, NY), 68, 73n13, 75, 111, 259
St. Mark's Basilica, Venice, 83, 105, 111, 308–10, 318n8, 341
St. Mary's Parish, Hamilton, NY, 68, 75
St. Matthew Passion (J. S. Bach), 150, 193, 194, 205
St. Patrick's Cathedral (New York), 253
St. Paul, 238, 333, 341, 344
St. Paul, Minnesota, 72
St. Paul's Church, Cambridge, Massachusetts, 83
St. Paul's Church, Nairobi, 342
St. Peter, 227, 278
St. Peter Claver, Minneapolis, 76, 140
St. Peter's Basilica, Rome, 79, 82, 119, 257
strangeness, 107, 110, 116–17, 292
string quartet, 311
Strohm, Reinhard, 136n3
strophic forms, 101, 102, 116, 147, 148, 149, 288, 305
St. Simeon's Church, Venice, 75, 105
St. Stanislaus Church (Toronto), 258
St. Stephen's, Vienna (Stefansdom), 140
suite (dance), 143n16, 177, 194
Summorum Pontificorum (Benedict XVI, 2007), 88n6, 248
symbols, liturgical, 9, 40, 41, 42, 57, 61, 70, 79, 84, 86, 163, 164–69, 262, 274, 277, 287, 292, 295, 302, 329–31, 343, 346
symbols, musical, 117, 169–71, 175–260, 261, 270, 276, 295, 302, 327, 337, 343
symphonic Mass, xiii, xiv, 76, 93, 123, 135–37, 139–42, 167, 168, 189, 190n22, 194, 197, 200, 237, 220, 248, 270, 289, 306, 340
symphony, 142, 264n2, 334
symphony concerts and orchestras, 62, 143, 160, 205, 265, 267, 340, 345
syncretism, 286–87, 288
syntax, musical. *See* musical syntax
Syro-Malabar Rite, 287
Syro-Malankara Rite, 287

Taiwan, 76, 289
Te Deum, 79, 257
television, 71, 95, 117, 187, 196, 307, 335, 338

test of time, 65, 197, 217, 220, 232, 269, 274, 343
Tin Pan Alley, 33, 41, 56, 192
Thanksgiving (holiday), 166, 228
The American Organist, 72, 331n6
"The First Nowell," 165
"The King of Love," 158
"The Marine Corps Hymn," 177
The Mass of St. Cyprian, 284–85
tonality and tonal center, 43, 45, 100n6, 113, 114, 126, 128, 153, 155, 158, 186, 304
tone languages, 287–88
tract (Mass proper), 14, 238
Tracy, David, 215, 217, 221, 267, 268
tradition, xiii–xiv, 9, 10, 20, 25, 36, 39, 41, 47n12, 64, 189; carol, 146; composition, 153; and creativity, 27, 65, 186, 198, 261–74; dogmatic, 16–17, 18, 20, 241–42, 313; gospel music, 281–86; liturgical, 148, 164–71, 187, 212, 213, 229, 230, 231n16, 232–34, 238, 240–41, 249, 252, 324, 325, 328, 329–30, 337–47; performance, 6, 191; of religious music, xiii, xiv, 147, 149, 150, 151, 156, 158, 171–73, 186, 187, 188, 220, 243, 244, 248, 279, 280, 281, 287, 288–89, 289, 297, 298, 302–3, 304, 305; repertory, 26, 37, 205, 217, 218, 221, 260, 317, 319, 321, 322, 327; in Roman Catholicism, 13, 25, 73, 163, 182, 200, 202, 210, 238, 292, 293, 314–15; Western, 11–12, 185, 199, 326, 334
Tra le Sollecitudini (Pope Pius X), 13, 24, 28, 29–30, 32, 189, 199
transcendence, 8, 69, 71, 88n6, 117, 137, 142, 164, 175, 184–86, 209, 212, 220, 260, 273, 274, 275, 280, 291, 292, 330, 335, 336, 337, 340, 343
transfiguration, 175, 226–27

translation (of liturgical texts), 7, 40, 50n16, 109, 149, 150, 238, 239n3, 240, 244, 247, 252, 253, 254, 256, 277, 305, 329
translation (of Scripture), 181–82
Tridentine reforms, 280
Tridentine rite (1962), 75, 88n6, 248, 284
Trinidad, 288
Trinity, 8, 17, 79, 227, 239, 242
Trinity Sunday, 81, 82, 257
trope, 50, 243, 246, 269, 280, 284, 334
true art, 199–209, 212, 213, 215, 216, 218, 316–17, 341–44, 348; three principles of, 337–44

Uganda, 287, 290
universal qualities (of masterworks), 206, 214–18, 274, 306, 338, 346

Varietates Legitimae, 81, 167, 281n11, 325
variety of liturgical music, 68
Vatican, xiv, 23, 28, 30, 34, 35, 36, 38, 76, 119, 123, 130, 199, 212, 257, 321
Vatican II. *See* Second Vatican Council
Vaughan Williams, Ralph, 154, 155, 158n15, 271
Venice, 75, 136, 147n1; *see also* St. Mark's Basilica
Veni Creator Spiritus, 243
Verdi, Giuseppe, 140, 142, 143, 270, 290, 328
vernacular language in liturgy, 7, 23, 25, 27, 28–30, 31n11, 32, 35, 40, 75, 108–9, 145, 147, 149, 156n8, 241, 244, 247–59, 277, 297, 303n12, 308, 318, 333
Vespers, 96, 230, 241, 317n6
vestments, liturgical, 117, 184
Victoria, Tomas Luis de, 120, 124
Vienna, Austria, 76, 139, 140
virgin birth, 181–82, 185

Virgin Mary. *See* Blessed Virgin Mary
Vitry, Phillippe de, 9n11
Vivaldi, Antonio, 138, 189, 250

Wagner, Richard, 183
Wainwright, Geoffrey, 290n33
"Wake, Awake for Night is Flying," 158
Walker, Christopher, 51
Walsh, Michael J., 37n25
Walther, Johann, 155, 191
Ward, Justine, 33
Watts, Isaac, 149, 238, 240
Weakland, Rembert, 163, 164n1, 165, 218, 219, 339, 344
Weber, Jerome F., 34n19, 95n1, 241n7

"We Gather Together," 234
Weinrich, Carl, 305
Well-Tempered Clavier, 194, 205n14
Wesley, John, 148, 149, 238, 240
Weston Priory, 64
Witt, Franz Xaver, 34
Wittgenstein, Ludwig, 170n13, 178n6, 208
Worship (hymnal), 77
Worst, John, 288–89n27

Zamenhof, Lazar Ludwik, 258
Zauner, Franz Bischof, 30n8
Zizioulas, John D., 167n6, 292n30
Zotto, Gastone, 302n10
Zwingli, 119

www.ingramcontent.com/pod-product-compliance
Lightning Source LLC
Chambersburg PA
CBHW051933290426
44110CB00015B/1962